THORSTEIN VEBLEN:
A CRITICAL REAPPRAISAL

THORSTEIN VEBLEN:
A CRITICAL REAPPRAISAL

Lectures and Essays Commemorating the Hundredth Anniversary of Veblen's Birth

Edited by

DOUGLAS F. DOWD

Cornell University

GREENWOOD PRESS, PUBLISHERS
WESTPORT, CONNECTICUT

HB
119
V4
D66
1977

Library of Congress Cataloging in Publication Data

Dowd, Douglas Fitzgerald, 1919-   ed.
  Thorstein Veblen, a critical reappraisal.

  Reprint of the ed. published by Cornell University
Press, Ithaca, N.Y.
  Include bibliographical references.
  CONTENTS: Dowd, D. F. Preface.--Dorfman, J. The
source and impact of Veblen's thought.--Hamilton, W.
Veblen, then and now.--Ayres, C. E. Veblen's theory of
instincts reconsidered. [etc.]
  1. Veblen, Thorstein, 1857-1929--Addresses, essays,
lectures. 2. Social sciences--Addresses, essays,
lectures.
[HB119.V4D66 1977]   330'.092'4   77-9623
ISBN 0-8371-9714-7

© 1958 by Cornell University

Originally published in 1958 by Cornell University Press, Ithaca, New York

Reprinted with the permission of Cornell University Press

Reprinted in 1977 by Greenwood Press, Inc.

Library of Congress catalog card number   77-9623

ISBN 0-8371-9714-7

Printed in the United States of America

Dedicated to Professor Robert A. Brady, who has helped to perpetuate the approach and the spirit of Veblen

Quotations from all Veblen's works under its imprint are used by permission of the Viking Press; excerpts from *The Theory of Business Enterprise,* by permission of Charles Scribner's Sons; quotations from J. M. Keynes's *General Theory of Employment, Interest and Money,* by permission of Harcourt, Brace & Co.; from Hans Otto Storm's *Made in U.S.A.,* by permission of Longmans, Green & Co.; from Alfred Marshall's *Principles of Economics,* by permission of Macmillan & Co., Ltd., and The Macmillan Co.; and from an editorial in *Life,* by permission of Time, Inc.

Preface

THERE can be little doubt that Thorstein Veblen was and remains the most eminent and seminal thinker in the area of social analysis yet to emerge in America. Strangely, however, those knowingly influenced by him today are very few in number, and his writings are studied by a small and shrinking number of students. The explanation for this paradox is perhaps to be found in two of the major characteristics of Veblen's thought. First, Veblen's views were distinctly unorthodox, often radical, and always uncompromising. Second, although Veblen was always systematic in his own work, he constructed no "system"; indeed, indications are abundant that Veblen opposed "systems of thought," as such—for better or for worse.

Veblen's greatest vogue was in the twenties and thirties, especially the latter. This stemmed largely from the appeal which his unconventional and critical ideas held for people living through those turbulent and ultimately desperate years. The lack of a clear system—some would say the lack of clarity—in Veblen allowed his followers in that period to move off in quite different directions, from the grandiose reforms of the Technocrats to the narrow statistical investigations of the National Bureau of Economic Research—ultimately to yield a spectrum of "Veblenians" comprising the loosest kind of crackpots at one end and the most circumspect of pure researchers at the other.

Just as Marx eschewed "Marxism," one may be confident that Veblen would have eschewed what has passed for "Veblenism," perhaps with greater reason. For the greatest contributions of Veblen—as of Marx—lie not in the answers he gained, but in the questions he posed,

Preface

and in the approach which he utilized to gain his answers—answers often correct, often incorrect, often equivocal, but almost always standing in sharp contrast with those of his contemporaries.

Perhaps the most disappointing aspects of contemporary social studies are those which show the reverse of the two characteristics of Veblen cited above: first, a strong tendency is apparent to accept uncritically the basic institutions of society, and, second, what appears to be an undue zeal for system, or precision, leads investigations into ever-narrowing paths of compartmentalization. These paths often lead to relatively precise "answers." But the validity of such answers rests upon a myriad of assumptions that wall off important areas of relevant reality, which is to say that social analysis frequently gives way to exercises in logic.

With matters such as these in mind the Department of Economics at Cornell University, recalling that 1957 was the hundredth anniversary of Veblen's birth and that he had entered the field of economics professionally at Cornell in 1891, felt that this would be an appropriate occasion to take another look at Veblen. There was not the intent, nor has there been the result, of disinterring Veblen in a fog of uncritical praise. There is, rather, the hope that the efforts contained in this volume will lead others to look once more, or to look for the first time, at those of Veblen's writings which are relevant to their "fields" of research and teaching, perhaps thereby to gain in depth, breadth, or curiosity.

Veblen's last book was published in 1923. In the thirty-five years which have passed, the social studies have made significant strides forward in technique and content. But they have also lost much in those years in perspective and approach. Veblen would be a better social analyst today than he was in his own years were he able to utilize the accumulation of knowledge and the advances of technique —if one can imagine the existence of a Veblen in these days. And, one can argue, contemporary social scientists would be the better for having made a serious study of Veblen. Veblen had many defects; these may in large part be offset by the virtues of contemporary social science. Contemporary social science has many defects; these may in large part be offset by the virtues of Veblen. Or such is the rationale of this volume.

In November, 1957, the Department of Economics at Cornell spon-

Preface

sored a series of eight lectures on various aspects of Veblen's thought. These lectures are contained in this volume as Articles 2, 3, 4, 8, 12, 13, 15, and 16; they were delivered by Messrs. Hamilton, Ayres, Kaplan, Hill, Fishman, Morrison, and Goodrich and myself. As that program was being arranged, Morris Copeland, a member of the Department of Economics at Cornell and then President of the American Economic Association, organized a round-table discussion on Veblen for the 1957 annual meeting of the Association. Three papers were given, which had also been written for inclusion in this volume. They are contained here as Articles 1, 9, and 10, written by Messrs. Dorfman, Gruchy, and Sweezy, and are reprinted by arrangement with the American Economic Association.

Since the major purpose of the commemorative lectures and essays is to stimulate interest in Veblen, it was thought appropriate to include a bibliography of his writings. Because Joseph Dorfman's *Thorstein Veblen and His America* (New York: The Viking Press, 1934) contains the definitive bibliography of Veblen's writings, permission was asked, and was kindly granted by the author and the Viking Press, to use Professor Dorfman's bibliography with a few additions.

I should like to express my thanks to those at Cornell University who helped to finance the lecture series delivered there: the Social Science Research Center, the College of Arts and Sciences, the Committee on Lectures and Drama, and the Administrative Offices. I should also like to thank Elaine Adams of the News Bureau of Cornell, who helped in many ways.

DOUGLAS F. DOWD

Ithaca, New York
August, 1958

Contents

Preface   *Douglas F. Dowd*   vii

1. The Source and Impact of Veblen's Thought
             Joseph Dorfman   1

2. Veblen—Then and Now   *Walton Hamilton*   13

3. Veblen's Theory of Instincts Reconsidered   *C. E. Ayres*   25

4. Idle Curiosity   *Norman Kaplan*   39

5. On the Scope and Method of Economics   *Morris A. Copeland*   57

6. Veblen's Critique of the Orthodox Economic Tradition
             Lawrence Nabers   77

7. The Cycle Theories of Veblen and Keynes Today
             Melvin D. Brockie   113

8. Veblen and Marx   *Forest G. Hill*   129

9. Veblen's Theory of Economic Growth   *Allan G. Gruchy*   151

Contents

10. Veblen on American Capitalism — Paul M. Sweezy 177

11. The Place of Corporation Finance in Veblen's Economics — Joel B. Dirlam 199

12. Veblen, Hoxie, and American Labor — Leslie Fishman 221

13. The Ideology of the Engineers — Philip Morrison 237

14. Veblen's View of Cultural Evolution — Myron W. Watkins 249

15. The Case of the New Countries — Carter Goodrich 265

16. Technology and Social Change: Japan and the Soviet Union — Douglas F. Dowd 283

17. Veblen's Macroinstitutionalism — G. W. Zinke 303

Bibliography of Veblen's Writings — Joseph Dorfman 319

Contributors 327

THORSTEIN VEBLEN:
A CRITICAL REAPPRAISAL

[JOSEPH DORFMAN]

1

The Source and Impact of Veblen's Thought

THE celebration of the one-hundredth anniversary of Veblen's birth by such organizations as the American Economic Association and Cornell University may be taken as recognition of his impact on the growth of economic thought. That his work continues to be a source of considerable controversy is indicative of its vitality. Some men effectively catch the drift of development and have a vision of things to come. Such men become active forces in that very development, and their names become landmarks and turning points. Time alone is the final judge of a candidate's right to inclusion in this select list. For Veblen time has rendered its verdict.

Veblen's story is complicated by his historical setting, his personality, and his style of writing. Perhaps as the biographer of Veblen, I have an advantage, slight though it may be, in the task of clarifying the picture of the man and his role. It is almost a quarter of a century since I sent *Thorstein Veblen and His America* into the world. Since then, additional information on his career and background has become available, and many things have happened in the world of affairs and the world of economic science. These developments should provide the opportunity for a more mature understanding of this enigmatic figure. It is, therefore, in the light of what I like to think of as a richer experience, but which may well be excessive boldness, that I attempt an assessment of the source and impact of Veblen.

Joseph Dorfman

In Veblen we have at least two men. There is the economist, and there is the artist, a most unusual combination. Generally the two do not mix. In the history of Anglo-American economics, which actually forms one mighty stream, the only other case that comes to mind is that of David Hume.

Let me take up Veblen the artist first. Veblen is a person interested in writing and communication. Of his style the prominent novelist, Hans Storm, wrote that it was

faintly suggestive of the great geographers in its impressive unornateness and stolidity in front of new discoveries, but refined and yet again refined and pared until it lay hard against the bare rock and resisted by virtue of the hardness of the rock itself.... [Veblen] brought into economic writing the rules of good poetics ... in which every word is understood not only in its immediately purposeful meaning, but with all its nimba of picturesqueness, background, and suggestion.[1]

As a writer, too, he is full of whimsy and humor. He loves to tease, to exaggerate, to present fantastic and poetic images, to utilize symbolism and allegory, and to mobilize folklore. He will even use archaic words and phrases to fit the mood of an archaic economic and social order. As he unfolds various aspects of western civilization, he is a throwback to the saga-tellers of his Norwegian forebears and the writers of epic poems with their tales of intermingled tragedy and comedy. The anthropologist and archeologist in him, fed by his northern pride and heritage, provided him with an almost inexhaustible arsenal of examples, illustrations, and "models."

As he spins tales, so he spins webs that entrap the reader into the recognition of the seriousness of phenomena that he may have taken for granted. Veblen merely picked his Don Quixotes from the realm of economics. Behind the humor and the dead pan there is often a stark tale that is reminiscent of the privileged court jester. Veblen's shafts respect no class or group. There are no exceptions, not even himself. With his artistic temperament went the peccadillos that are conventionally associated with it.

Having been reared in one culture and having matured in another, Veblen had a heightened instinct of curiosity. That curiosity received, in the course of his academic training in the seventies and the eighties, the benefit of the discipline and inspiration that seminal minds and

[1] From review in manuscript in the possession of the writer.

The Source of Veblen's Thought

provocative teachers give to promising youth, thereby enabling them to go beyond and transform the established positions, to lift them to a higher plane, as it were. For Veblen was indeed fortunate.

At sturdy Carleton College he studied under the profound philosophic economist, John Bates Clark, who on the one hand was developing his comprehensive marginalist economics beginning with his own version of marginal utility and on the other hand was formulating his creed of Christian Socialism. Clark soon saw the promise of Veblen and encouraged him to go on to graduate work at Johns Hopkins with philosophy as his major and economics as his minor.

His stay at Johns Hopkins was brief but rewarding. He had the advantage of studying logic with Charles S. Peirce, the founder of pragmatism. He was impressed with the lectures of George S. Morris, the teacher of John Dewey and one of the advance guard of the trained Hegelians from the German universities. There was on the social science staff at Johns Hopkins his contemporary, Richard T. Ely, the *enfant terrible* of economics, who was already impressed with Veblen. Veblen established lifelong friendships with fellow students, for example, that future noted American historian, J. Franklin Jameson.

Veblen then went on to Yale, where he had the benefit of the William Graham Sumner of the *Folkways* and the gruff philosopher, Noah Porter, who was making a last stand on behalf of the traditional common-sense philosophy, as it was called, against the onrush of Spencerian evolution and the Kantian and Hegelian idealist systems.

Thus at the very beginning of his career Veblen stood in the thick of the battle of conflicting philosophic systems. But fortunately for us, on his return to academic halls at Cornell in 1891 he left philosophy for economics, although he never lost his original interest.

As an economist his relation to his times is doubly significant, for he played a dual role. He was a theorist, and a catalyst of reform. He came upon the scene between two ages of social and intellectual ferment. As in the realm of affairs, so in the realm of knowledge, there are great tides. Periods of reform and reconstruction rise to great crests; then come troughs marked by consolidation of gains, conservatism, and sometimes reaction. The last great crest of the seventies and eighties was marked by the triumph of the doctrine of evolution in science and a world-wide movement of political and social reform. In economics it was epitomized by the wave of interest in the German historical school. In its native land this movement had sought to broaden economic analysis beyond the narrow foundation of the older classical school of economics, and to that end it had attempted to develop such powerful instruments of research as statistics and history, including comparative economic development. It also sought to give greater scope to the ethical nature of man than the dominant vulgarizers of the classical economics would permit.

In the realm of policy it sought to meet the wave of discontent, and the threat of socialism, by a variety of reformist devices. These included the appeal to the churches to take an active part in solving such critical social questions as the relation between employers and employees, the appeal to government for easing the restrictions on trade unions, and the support of national social security legislation such as workmen's compensation, old age, and sickness insurance. It included also a concern with the problems of conserving natural resources and regulating "natural monopolies." On the one side the movement seemed to provide the beginning of a richer synthesis for expanding knowledge, and on the other side a basis for policies that would check the damage of excessive individualism without embracing the socialism of Karl Marx.

To the younger generation of reforming American economists, encouraged by such eminent elders as General Francis A. Walker and Carroll D. Wright, this German historical movement, flanked as it was by a similar movement in Great Britain, seemed to offer the promise of adaptation to the needs of the developing American economy. As such it provided a basis for the "new economics." This included the revised classical tradition, which embraced the doctrine of marginal utility. In accordance with their Anglo-American heritage, the exponents thought that economic reform could be achieved largely by voluntary organizations and by state and local units more than by the national authority. "Planning" was city planning, and "regulation" was largely that of railroads and other "natural monopolies" by state commissions.

After the turn of the century came stabilization, security, and consolidation, a frowning on innovation and the deprecation of further reforms. The turning away from "social inventions" had its counterpart in the lack of enthusiasm for any kind of innovation in economic analysis. Thus, for example, the original leader of the movement of

The Source of Veblen's Thought

mathematical economics, Simon Newcomb, voiced doubts of the usefulness of further work in this area, and he expressed the hope that economists would turn their energies to educating the public in the simpler "abstractions," as he called them, of the Ricardian economics of an earlier age. Economics had only just begun to have autonomy as an important area in its own right rather than as a limited, narrow topic in the course in moral philosophy. In such heated political struggles as that over "free silver" there was not a little feeling that moderation in matters of policy was essential to protect the infant profession. Narrow practical and intellectual ends became dominant, or so it seemed.

Of the older generation of leaders of the movement for reconstruction, some went into administrative work, others specialized in less controversial subjects such as public finance, and still others devoted themselves to the more abstract problems of the rationale of a static state. But even these protected themselves against the charge of lack of immediate, practical reference by claiming that their analysis tested the validity of the existing economic system's right to survival. Social innovation was considered outside the realm of science.

But because liberal reform found hard sledding, there appeared to be a greater need for a basic revaluation and reorientation. For this the special qualities and abilities of Veblen seemed particularly valuable. He was well equipped to survive intellectually in an age where basic thinking appeared to be at a discount. He just escaped being an immigrant. In effect he was an "outsider" and therefore not easily engulfed in the passing mood. He had a special feeling for languages and old-world, particularly northern, sagas and cultures. His extraordinary linguistic equipment opened to him developments and literature in a variety of areas and lands. His cosmopolitan scholar's pervasive sense of history, along with his knowledge of anthropology, psychology, and the biological sciences, gave him perspective. Having received his doctorate in philosophy, he had special equipment for theoretical discussion and the relation of economics to other fields of knowledge. He had the comprehensive reach of the student of culture, the precision so essential for systematic thinking, and that rugged consistency, courage, and independence that refuse to bend to the expediences of changing winds and fashions.

These qualities distinguished him at the outset. With his strong

Joseph Dorfman

sense for the fundamental, he fixed attention on central economic institutions of his time, and indeed of our own time—for example, the corporation and the technological process. Veblen implicitly recognized that the corporation is a mighty instrument for organizing production and promoting efficiency. But he regarded it as something much more than a mere embodiment of external mechanical forces. Rather it was a complex human organism that lent itself to manipulation by passions and spirits that ran counter to the objective of its function in the economy. More fundamental still it gave play to the intrigues and rivalry of inner groups whose habit of thinking in terms of money as an abstract aim overlay their functions in the institution. This habit at times ran counter also to the needs of the community, when it bred a reduction of output and employment to maintain solvency or increase profits. As the corporate form gains increasing sway over the economic life of the community, the consequences, if left uncontrolled, become all the more serious.

Veblen's view of technology, like his view of the corporation, was intimately related to his conception of human nature. Man to Veblen was a natural force acting upon all other forces of nature. Man was distinguishable by his special characteristics of imagination, playfulness, economic effort, and tasteful production. To a large extent science and the machine are embodiments of these attributes. But there is an aspect of machine technology which leads to purely reflexive and habitual activity, and sometimes machine technology has been abused to produce ugly things. This explains Veblen's simultaneous emphasis on and admiration of technology as well as his occasional concern over its effects. The techniques and institutions that man creates have a way of turning around, creating a life all their own and threatening to become his masters and gods. Veblen saw constantly re-enacted in history a dramatic saga between man's material interests and the institutions he creates to give them expression.

Veblen's views of technology, human nature and corporations, and money and economy do not add up to a closed structure of thought in the typical nineteenth-century sense. Such systems begin with an overwhelming major premise and ineluctably drive, fall the chips where they may, toward a grand, simplified, logical conclusion, as the stationary state of a David Ricardo, the positive religion of an August Comte, the classless society of a Karl Marx, and the idealized order

The Source of Veblen's Thought

of free contract of a Herbert Spencer, where even a policeman would not be needed. Veblen is less doctrinaire and less dogmatic. Where the authors of the great closed systems seek to dominate and organize, Veblen suggests, tempts, pleads, and even hypnotizes. In his method he is more evolutionary, more sensitive to psychological forces, more aware of the relations between the social sciences, and more cognizant of surprising changes in the configuration of forces. He combines forces and elements often thought of as disparate or irrelevant to each other. This is the reason why he occasionally surprised and even shocked his reader or fellow economist. His approach makes him at home with the spirit of the twentieth century and projected his influence forward.

Although bereft of the attractions of the great system-makers and the magic of the great programmatic reformers, his influence has been wide, pervasive, and enduring. Vital and original minds were drawn toward him from the beginning.

There were first of all his own students. Here as elsewhere I can only refer to a few. Veblen moved Herbert J. Davenport to cleanse of apologetics the main tradition of economics with his critical volume, *Value and Distribution,* and then his general treatise, *The Economics of Enterprise,* which still stands as a classic of modern price analysis. There was Robert F. Hoxie, perhaps the finest analytical mind the United States produced in the field of labor, who developed a functional analysis of types of unions with special emphasis on what he called business unionism. There was Ezekiel H. Downey, a pioneer in the first great step of social security legislation, namely, workmen's compensation laws. In his classic defense of such legislation, *History of Work Accident Indemnity in Iowa,* he explained that, since the human organism was imperfectly adapted to a mechanical environment, work injuries are attributable to inherent hazards of industry and should be met by industry.

There was Wesley C. Mitchell, who found in Veblen's work not only inspiration for pioneering studies on business cycles and the money economy but also specific helpful theories, such as in his business cycle theory the important relationships in Veblen's emphasis on the capitalization process. As Mitchell wrote in a private letter in 1910, while working on his monumental *Business Cycles:* "The theory propounded [on the breeding of crises] is fairly close to

Joseph Dorfman

Veblen's on the most important point—a decline in prospective net earnings leads to a shrinkage of business credit and thus brings on a liquidation of outstanding accounts." Furthermore, in Veblen's emphasis on "behavior" and men's actions, rather than on their introspective rationalizations, lay much of the stimulus that re-enforced Mitchell's bent for systematic quantitative analysis and drove him on to making such work a permanent basic feature of economic theory.

There was Walter W. Stewart, who in modern central banking made effective use of Veblen's distinction between industry and business. In his diagnosis of Britain's loss of competitive position in the 1930's, he ascribed the larger and more permanent part of the difficulties to the lag in technological advance and accumulated industrial shortcomings rather than to the current financial maladjustments. In this country Stewart, like Mitchell, was influenced by Veblen to use quantitative data, both financial and industrial, to test from time to time the performance and adequacy of our banking institutions. Finally, let me just mention DR Scott, author of *The Cultural Significance of Accounts*, as further evidence of the stimulus and influence of Veblen on his students.

Let us now turn to his influence on his contemporaries. Perhaps the best external evidence of the wide recognition of Veblen among the most distinguished economists of the day was the petition in 1925, with nearly 225 signatures requesting the nominating committee of the American Economic Association to select Veblen as president. Among the signers were ten future presidents of the association, Morris A. Copeland, Paul H. Douglas, Edwin F. Gay, Alvin H. Hansen, Frank H. Knight, Frederick C. Mills, E. G. Nourse, Sumner H. Slichter, Jacob Viner, and A. B. Wolfe.

The constant references in economic studies to *The Theory of Business Enterprise* at any event belie the misgivings that Veblen originally had about publishing the book, misgivings chiefly, he said, "that it would pass unnoticed by the gild of economists to which it is addressed."

More revealing of his influence was the seepage of his ideas into a wide variety of original enterprises in economics. There was his impact on Carleton Parker, who pioneered in focusing the attention of economists and management on the need in the study of industrial relations to understand the psychological forces involved. There was

The Source of Veblen's Thought

Veblen's impact on John R. Commons' work, especially *Legal Foundations of Capitalism* and *Institutional Economics*, not only through Commons' use of Veblen's distinction between business and industry, but more specifically through Commons' development of such concepts as the "going concern" and "intangible property" as distinct from "tangible property." As an admirer of both, A. B. Wolfe stated: "Commons arrived at substantially the same, though greatly amplified conclusions as to the role played by intangible assets." Veblen was stimulating also to the son, John Maurice Clark, of his old Carleton teacher, as the younger man sought to work out a positive position vis-à-vis Veblen's and Davenport's criticisms of John Bates Clark, which centered on social productivity versus private acquisition. Veblen had an influence on such business-cycle theorists as Alvin H. Hansen which dates back to the days when Hansen was working on his doctoral dissertation, *Cycles of Prosperity and Depression—in the United States, Great Britain and Germany*, and runs through his later productions in Keynesian economics.

In the field of consumption patterns, of course, Veblen's attraction has been enormous, especially evident in such stimulating studies as those of Hazel Kyrk, Theresa S. McMahon, and Jessica B. Pexiotto.

Veblen's "pecuniary emulation" and "conspicuous consumption," especially when given a less colorful name, such as the "demonstration effect"—the increase in consumption expenditures through contact with superior goods—helped to bring about a revision of the conventional demand theory, including a special aspect of this theory, the "consumption function," as analyzed, for example, by James S. Duesenberry, in *Income, Saving and the Theory of Consumer Behavior*. Falling into the same category and given increasing attention especially by those interested in geometric presentation was the case that has acquired his name, the "Veblen case." This has been well described by Sidney Weintraub in *Price Theory* as consisting of goods that "appeal to the snob as a vehicle for 'conspicuous consumption' . . . only when the price goes sufficiently high to prevent these items from being widely bought."

In the areas of the regulation of corporations and security markets Veblen's works have had a practical effect. Witness the popularity of *The Modern Corporation and Private Property*, by A. A. Berle, Jr., and Gardiner C. Means, and of a number of other provocative works dealing with the "managerial revolution" and the corporation, and with the "organizational man" as exemplifying a way of life. Incidentally, Justice Louis D. Brandeis cited Veblen in a famous minority opinion against the encroachment of the great corporations (*Lee v. Liggett Co.*).

In economic history there immediately comes to mind Harold A. Innis, the one Canadian economist who has been president of the American Economic Association. He noted as early as 1929 that Veblen was the "first to attempt a general stock taking of general tendencies in a dynamic society saddled with machine industry just as Adam Smith was the first to present a general stock taking before machine industry came in." Veblen's story in 1915 of how aristocratic, imperial Germany exploited the developments of the machine technology turned out to be so prophetic of the rise and fall of Nazi Germany that a new edition of *Imperial Germany and the Industrial Revolution* was called for. Currently economic historians have suggested its applicability to the Soviet Union.

In recent years *An Inquiry into the Nature of Peace and the Terms of Its Perpetuation,* along with *Imperial Germany,* has come to the fore as among the few books of the World War I era that have endured. Here Veblen's technique has its fullest scope. He takes up in its widest background and with a grand perspective of economic and international relations the greatest of all problems and makes his contribution toward a reconstruction of the world on a more peaceful basis.

Of his predictions and prophecies, which have so often been accurate, I shall refer to only one. This is a prediction that has not been generally noticed. In the closing page of *The Theory of Business Enterprise,* he observed that the "*full* dominion of business enterprise was necessarily a transitory dominion" (italics mine). That dominion is now less complete than ever.

Veblen's early vogue began in the realm of literature through the reception accorded his one really popular book, *The Theory of the Leisure Class.* Although originally, as Veblen put it, "opinion seems to be divided as to whether I am a knave or a fool," the book had the good fortune to be enthusiastically reviewed as a work of genius by the dean of American letters, William Dean Howells. In portraying

The Source of Veblen's Thought

the effect of pecuniary standards on culture, Veblen dissected men's most cherished values in their current form and showed that they were curiously wrought-out products of a historical process stamped with the dollar sign. The full weight of this was caught by his readers only in later years, especially in times of depression and war. Today the book is also increasingly appreciated for the guidance it offers in raising the economic level of underdeveloped countries and above all in strengthening the national defense. Again on December 2, 1957, the New York *Times* editorial page reminded the country that Veblen long ago called attention to the "problems which arise because of men's slowness to adjust their cultural attitudes to the rapid changes imposed by scientific and technological advance."

Certainly no economist of his day or ours has commanded the respect of so many leaders in so many other disciplines: in literature and the fine arts, philosophy, psychology, sociology, political science, anthropology, history, and even the biological and physical sciences.

Veblen is a "philosophical radical," in a twentieth-century American setting. Unlike his British counterparts he was free from Benthamite psychology, was not a system-builder, and was without a positive political program. Yet his indirect influence upon men active in public affairs was very considerable particularly following the great depression, when many of our economic institutions became subject to criticism and revision. Veblen had made it abundantly clear that "prosperity" of business enterprises was not necessarily co-incidental with the welfare of the community at large. During this period some of Veblen's ideas, available for decades, fell at last on fertile soil and took root. His regret might have been that so many of them in application led to a further aggrandizement of the state. So while it may be impossible to point to a single piece of legislation that he would have proposed, there can be no doubt that men who had never read his books came unknowingly under the influence of his thought. No one can say exactly when or how Veblen's ideas, once widely regarded as radical and violently rejected by most of one generation, gradually became a part of our accepted common stock of ideas. We do know, however, that historically such slow and pervasive infiltration is characteristic of an intellectual forerunner.

The cultural role of Veblen is that of all creative artists as described

Joseph Dorfman

by the sociologist, Charles H. Cooley: "The 'significance' of an artist means I suppose, his contribution to a culture of which his work is a part, so that to understand it you must understand *him*."

This was Veblen. Here is a man who was often inchoate, obscure, tangential, unintelligible, and one-sided. He made his generous share of mistakes. Ultimately his value lies in his role as an emancipator of the human mind. He tears down the walls of the institutions, prejudices, and fond illusions that imprison the human spirit. He sharpened the use of reason and presented it as a tool to those who would penetrate to the secrets of society. He transcended the function of the economist, but he also fulfilled it. He marked an epoch in the cumulative growth of the science and the development of western culture.

[WALTON HAMILTON]

2

Veblen—Then and Now

AT the centennial of his birth the career of Thorstein Veblen presents a paradox. The youngster, freshly dedicated to intellectual adventure, will tell you that he has made soundings in Veblen's books and has found no novelty therein. The oldster, a hardened traveler along the paths of inquiry, will retort that Veblen brought freshness and excitement into the whole domain of the social studies. Fortunately, there is no need to choose between these different, but not conflicting, views, for both of them are right. It is one thing to meet the course of events head on and another to look back over one's shoulder at what is established.

If one is tempted to deny to Veblen the role of maverick, he has only to look at the dates of Veblen's several books and to take account of the orthodox and ponderous tomes in the field of humanities then appearing. If one is inclined to extract articles of faith from the printed word, a short excursion into the literature of today will be enough to demonstrate the need for modification of such a creed. As book after book has made its way into the developing stream of thought, the marks of personal identity have little by little faded from Veblen's distinctive contribution, but his influence is far from spent. If loss of identity is the measure of success, his contribution has in ways alike direct and dubious insinuated itself into our common understanding of the culture within which we live.

Even so, the freshness and challenge of fifty, or forty, or thirty years ago have not departed from Veblen's pages. The distinction between "business" and "industry" has not as yet won full recognition as a tool of economic analysis. The processes of production, whether of coal, nylon, furniture, ships, or waste paper, may be carried on under different schemes of economic arrangements. The practice of organized medicine remains the same whether it is dispensed under the auspices of a solo physician, a corporation, a consumers' co-operative, a university hospital, or a bureaucratic soviet. The place of the dynastic state in international affairs is still much as Veblen sketched it, save that its military instrumentation has become far more awesome and hazardous to the public welfare.

The volume *Imperial Germany and The Industrial Revolution*, published just after World War I, was reprinted with text intact at the end of the thirties. A review of the volume quite accurately began with the statement, "As a commentator upon the Munich Pact Veblen was at a disadvantage, for the event occurred in 1938 and the last touches were put upon his text twenty years earlier." Yet, as the reviewer insists, Veblen's treatise remains the best exposition of that tragic agreement.

Like his contemporaries, Veblen was much concerned with the merits—and especially with the demerits—of rival economic systems, as if there were a choice between them. Yet it was Veblen in his theory of cumulative causation who tempted a number of younger men into voyages of concrete discovery. The result was that the national economy was found to be no simple affair with a uniform look, but a conglomerate of distinct industries not too tidily thrown together. The drama and richness of the patterns—patterns created out of expediencies—had contrived to meet passing circumstances and presented a rich and colorful economy which, although forever changing, was still established. As for an alternative between "isms," whether of the right or of the left, it was then too late to choose. But even when Veblen was dealing with abstractions and imponderables, his lines were too suggestive and irritating not to touch off inquiry.

It is easy to visualize a portrait gallery of Veblen in various stages of his development. There is the undergraduate at Carleton College reading an essay "The Toper," explaining to the professor that he has no desire either to condemn or to condone, and insisting that his purpose is purely "objective." There is the graduate student at Yale engaging in dialectical combat with William Graham Sumner and wangling a doctor's degree in philosophy out of Noah Porter. There

Veblen—Then and Now

is the young intellectual appearing on the Cornell campus in coonskin cap and persuading J. Laurence Laughlin to make him an instructor in economics. There is the trio of J. Laurence Laughlin as head of the Department of Economics *designatus,* Thorstein Veblen as assistant professor of the same, and Robert Franklin Hoxie as graduate student making their way from Cornell to the newly organized University of Chicago. There is the wayward professor abruptly departing from Stanford with the notice tacked on his classroom door, "Professor Veblen will not meet his classes again this semester." There is the vision of Thornstein Veblen and Herbert Davenport walking down Northampton Road in Amherst dressed in suits purchased from a mail-order house—which met the demands neither of fit nor of fashion—engrossed in a discussion of the nature of the universe. And there is the portrait painted almost a decade after his death which hangs today in the Sterling Hall of Graduate Studies at Yale. It presents Veblen in an Oscar Wilde pose, leaning back in his chair with knees and feet aloft and a lighted cigarette in a long holder held nonchalantly in his right hand. It is a touch of irony that the portrait of the author of *The Theory of the Leisure Class* should be hung in an academic building which may best be described as a remnant from the great bull market of the 1920's.

Our concern here is with this ubiquitous individual, who was at once a recluse and a man of the world. It would here serve no purpose to recite or to interpret what he has set down in print. As with other germinal writings, the commentary has long ago outmatched the text. A number of students have come up with different and even contradictory theories extracted from Veblen's books and articles. Some of them, oblivious to the words employed, have discovered within the text things never tucked away there. The difference in text and comment is all the greater because of the manner of the writing. Veblen's idiom was his own—not that of American speech or the English language. At his polysyllabic best he was able to transmute a casual observation into a declaration of eternal verity. In like manner, he could phrase an interrogatory in such dictatorial verbiage as to make the obvious seem obscure. The gulf which often appeared between what he said and what he meant has always been confusing to little-minded folk devoid of a sense of humor.

In affairs Simian it is an axiom that what a man writes and what

Walton Hamilton

another reads may be quite different things. Economists, philosophers, judges are accustomed to presume that those of old whose writings lend sanctions to their own work were men of sense and reason such as themselves. It is easier to read "into" a great book rather than to read "out of" it what one would like to hear. To appraise the contribution of any scholar, one must know the quality of the man, the circumstances which shaped his articles of faith, the climate within which the universe beneath his hat was formed. The youngster can secure these imponderables of appraisal only at second hand; the oldster, exposed to the intellectual currents of the last half century, cannot quite separate what was from what is. Veblen's interest was in a theory that reached far beyond the immediate into the "calculable future." But if his concern was with the enduring, he had to approach his subjects of inquiry in terms of immediate problems. Thumb through any volume on current economic or social problems of forty years ago and note how strange the list is compared with the catastrophic catalogue of today. It may be well, then, to substitute for an appraisal of works now classic a venture into some contemporary phenomena which Veblen or a man of his manner would today find exciting. The occasion allows this to be done only by sample, and a trio of fragments must stand for a full-fledged inquiry. The data, setting, and trouble spots of the several problems may be new, but the themes are of a kind with those in which he delighted, and the near-ultimates —or, if you will, the less-than-immediacies—at which he aimed stand out clearly.

The first of these is the strange case of a sulfa drug. The basic chemical sulfanilamide was first used as a dye, and the letter patent by which exclusive rights were conferred upon its inventor had expired before its therapeutic properties were discovered. It had passed into the public domain and—note the term—any ethical drug house was free to make and vend it. Its price was competitive, and as an article of merchandise it offered little that in the pharmaceutical industry could be looked upon as profits. The way was therefore attractive for experimental work designed to create a product which had the therapeutic properties of sulfanilamide and upon which a patent might be had. A manufacturer succeeded in due course in turning out a variant which in time came to be called sulfathiazole. The plan, however, for a successful trip to the Patent Office was delayed, for news reached this manufacturer that a competitor had succeeded in contriving virtually the same drug. The first of these houses had the better research facilities; the second the better sales organization. It was natural, therefore, that the two should come together and that a single application for a patent be made. But before the agreement could be carried through, two other drug houses came forward, each insisting that a chemist in its employ had made the same "invention." There was nothing to do but to effect a quadrilateral agreement. One of the four was to take out the patent. It was to license the other three. All four were to engage in manufacture and sale, and by the letter patent other producers were to be excluded. Again, Fate intervened, and the agreement which bore the sign of the four had to be torn up, for five other concerns appeared, each protesting that within its establishment the first, only, and true inventor was to be found. In the end, it was agreed between the nine that only a single application for a patent was to be made, thus saving the Patent Office from trouble and confusion in finding the true inventor. The judgment as to which concern was to apply for the patent was left, not to the research chemists, but to the attorneys. There was no intent on the part of the allies to invest the company which was chosen to have and hold the patent with any power to collect tribute from the other eight. But for the sake of appearances it was decided that a small royalty was to be paid. As against its holder, any one of the other eight could have gone into court and questioned the validity of the patent. In the circumstances priority would have been almost impossible to establish, even if the court had held that there was an invention. No one of the eight interposed such a challenge, for such an act would have the effect of substituting a competitive for a monopoly price. Thus the letter patent the lawful issue of which is limited to "the promotion of science and the useful arts" was diverted from its constitutional purpose and converted into a sanction by means of which nine ethical drug houses might employ a "miracle drug" to exact toll from the public.

A second of these soundings is the so-called "squeeze play." Its presence marks a trouble spot found here and there throughout the whole economy. In general terms it appears in the power possessed by a major company in an industry to favor its own affiliate and to discriminate against the competing independent. An illustration is the

Walton Hamilton

situation prevailing in the aluminum industry before its tidy and tight structure was disturbed by judicial proceeding. The Aluminum Corporation of America was engaged not only in the processing of aluminum plate, but also in the manufacture of a long list of aluminum products. Independents were engaged in the manufacture of similar products but had to purchase their aluminum plate from the strategic corporation. Alcoa was then at once a competitor of the independents and to them a necessary source of supply.

A kindred situation exists in the provision of features for newspapers. To the newspaper the magic word is "circulation." Circulation is not a simple thing; it is an aggregate of a host of minority groups, each won and held by a distinctive lure. Thus, the newspaper breaks down into an array of pages, columns, features, what not—each put there to attract a special group. This cafeteria-in-print presents separate appeals in its news columns, its editorials, its commentaries, its sports section, its fashions, its women's pages, its comic strips, and the like. Only three or four newspapers can afford to create features of their own; the same feature may appear in newspapers in many cities scattered across the country. From this dual fact there has emerged the syndicate whose function it is to produce for newspaper use a varied miscellany of features. Among such syndicates, that of King Features stands out. It was originally organized as a device to provide temptation to read the newspapers of the Hearst chain. But very early it adopted the policy of furnishing features to newspapers in cities where there was no Hearst organ. Under enterprising and imaginative management the business prospered; the number of features was enlarged and the list of customers lengthened. Whereas a couple of years after its establishment 90 per cent of its product went to the Hearst newspapers, at present not more than 10 per cent is so used. The outside business is thus very profitable, and the circulation zones of different newspapers overlap. So it has come about that the independent newspaper in many a city is in competition with the Hearst newspaper, and yet King Features, a Hearst subsidiary, is their source of supply. Accordingly, like Alcoa, it has the power to impose a squeeze play on the independent. A little while ago King Features moved to withdraw six comic strips from a Newark, New Jersey, newspaper and was met with court action. The Newark paper asserted that over the years it had been a major factor in building up

Veblen—Then and Now

the popularity of the comic strips in question and that if these comic strips were withdrawn the newspaper's circulation would be badly hit. In this instance the judicial proceeding and the importance of the non-Hearst clients combined to cause King Features to see the matter in another light. The protection of the circulation of a newspaper across the Hudson, however, was of less importance than the 90 per cent of its business done outside the Hearst empire.

Another illustration, too familiar to demand more than a word, is presented by the motion picture industry. The integrated major companies, engaged alike in production, distribution, and exhibition, hold the strategic heights. Their integration rests upon sound commercial considerations. Paramount, at first only a producer, drove into distribution and exhibition to make certain of outlets for its product. RKO, once a series of vaudeville houses, went into production to secure to itself an adequate source of supply. Kindred moves in the creation of other majors helped to establish the present industrial pattern. In this course of development it came about that the integrated companies either had acquired or established exhibition houses of their own. Thus, the relationship of the independent to the major came to be of a dual character. To the independent the major was a necessary source of supply. Yet through an affiliated or captive house it was a competitor. The major not only possessed the power but was under an incentive to give preference in first-run features to its own subsidiary and to dictate terms and conditions under which desirable pictures were leased that placed the independent at a competitive disadvantage. A moment's thought will show that in a situation like this competitive bidding for first runs will not do. The captive house can always outbid the independent, since it is money for the major out of one pocket and into another. Here, divestment—drastic as it is—appears to be the only remedy that will probe to the heart of the malady. The examples given can be multiplied. If independents are to have a fair field, a taboo must be placed upon the squeeze play. It is hard to see how this can be done so long as the power to impose it remains intact.

A third, and even more exciting, subject worthy of a Veblenian inquiry is the corporate imperium. The manner of its rise, the devices employed in its defense, and the strategy of its enlargement invite an attack marked by the perspective, penetrating analysis, and ob-

Walton Hamilton

jectivity which Veblen brought to his work. Here a single example will suggest a score of others of like importance and will reveal the color, excitement, and provocation of dynamic industry. About the turn of the century the American Can Company was organized. The day after it secured its charter it acquired by contract a large number of plants engaged in the manufacture of sanitary or packers' cans. Within a year it had extended its dominion to more than one hundred and twenty-five factories. In the several contracts each of these companies pledged itself not to engage in this business again for a period of fifteen years within a territory whose focus was Chicago and whose radius was three thousand miles. Edwin Norton, the organizer of the company, was a signer of one of these contracts; yet some three years later he organized a number of the remaining independents into the Continental Can Company. There is no evidence that American Can intended to assume the role of Providence and to determine what canners of fruits should prosper or decline, what companies making use of its product were to survive, and what were to fail in the competitive struggle. Instead, the crux of its interest was its own survival and growth. To this end it was confronted with three distinct and interlocking problems. The one was to keep and enlarge the markets already held by the several companies which had been merged to form the corporate empire. The second was to exclude newcomers from the business of manufacturing tin cans. The third was to prevent its large customers from setting up manufacturing plants of their own.

A single volume of the Federal Supplement, No. 87, contains the decisions of three District Courts in cases in which American Can was the defendant. In *United States* v. *American Can* a suit was brought against the company under the Sherman Act in the Northern District Court of California. In *Russellville Canning* v. *American Can* a suit under the Robinson-Patman Act was brought in the Western District of Arkansas. In the case which bears the unbelievable name of *Bruce's Juices* v. *American Can* a similar suit was brought in the Southern District of Florida. In the cases instituted by Russellville and Bruce's Juices the complaints alleged a number of practices by American Can which discriminated in favor of its large, and against its small, customers. The list of these included a scheme for quantity discount, the use of phantom freight and freight absorption, and the provision

Veblen—Then and Now

of runways and other services. The scheme of quantity discounts revealed a difference of as much as 5 per cent in the prices made to the big canning companies and to Russellville and Bruce. The two courts found a number of other practices by which preference was shown to large customers. In the case brought by the United States the judge pointed out that the discriminatory practices, themselves unlawful under the Robinson-Patnam Act, were the instruments through which newcomers were kept out of the industry and the Sherman Act was flouted. The price of packers' cans amounts to from one-fourth to one-third of the price of the finished product, so here, even though the intent was only empire building, there had developed a power in American Can to decree life or death for its customers. The court decrees have had their impact upon trade practices. A couple of large canners are putting up their own can factories and both Continental and American are buying companies that produce paper and glass containers. The strategy, tactics, and devices by which the corporate imperium is established, defended, and enlarged are alike numerous and varied. The subject demands a grand inquiry—perhaps a series of them.

It is impossible to extract from Veblen's pages articles of faith which belong to eternity. In spite of the rhetoric employed, he was among the least dogmatic of scholars. His absolute was often an it-seems-to-me, or even a mere question. Because of this quality he has at once many and no disciples. There was in the 1920's a cult which was content to accept, to murmur, and to pass along the word of the master. That cult has long ago disappeared. The real Veblenians are persons who have given themselves to enterprises which Veblen himself could never have completed, and yet who have wrought as they have because Veblen had preceded them. Veblen was able to note and to comment upon the lack of rhythm in commercial activity, but it fell to Wesley Mitchell, taking this cue, to do the classic work on Business Cycles. Veblen could never have constructed an index number of production, but his shift of emphasis from the pecuniary to the things for which numbers stand gave Walter Stewart his impetus to make the pioneer venture, and Stewart's work—invaluable to an appraisal of the changing standing of life—has now become an institution. Veblen could never have immersed himself in the realities of trade unionism, but he opened vistas to Robert Hoxie,

Walton Hamilton
whose courage, patience, analytical skill, and superb imagination have resulted in the basic studies in this field. Charles Wright Mills has exhibited a zest for fact, even in quantitative form, which Veblen never possessed and differs from the older man in his methods of inquiry and objective. Yet there can be no denial that the power elite stands in apostolic succession to the leisure class. Among those who are called Veblenians, Clarence Ayres stands almost alone as an avowed theorist. He is as intent upon the main stream as was Veblen himself, yet his theory of social progress is a creative essay far removed from the theory of business enterprise. In a very different realm the Arcadian adventures of Stephen Leacock reveal alike in theme and detail the influence of his former teacher.

To many of the oldsters Veblen now appears as an emancipator. He came to his constructive task in an academic world of severities. Iron laws had not yet been banished; rigidity in statement barred personal or individual expression, and the building of systems left little opportunity for the creative urge. It was Veblen more than any other scholar who caused youngsters to dispute what was said in the good books and to take trails which the proprieties forbade them to follow. His essay on the place of science in modern civilization provided a challenge through the whole realm of the humanistic studies. It helped persons intent upon finding out to understand that even the most abstract of inquiries was set within the context of a culture. It proclaimed the elementary truth that you know about anything only in terms of the questions which have been asked, and that if the culture had permitted other questions other knowledge would be available. It shifted emphasis from the subject in the abstract to the question of the uses to which the answers were to be put. Here a single illustration will tell more than a dozen pages of polemics.

On a certain occasion an examination for the doctorate was being given at Yale University, and the department in question invited a member of the faculty of the law school to be present. The topic, engaging attention for three hours of torture, was the nature of the state. It began with questions about the Code of Hammurabi, moved graciously through the period of Greece and Rome, floundered a bit amid the trails of the Middle Ages, pitted Church against State in dialectical combat, and came to rest with the writings of Bluntschli

Veblen—Then and Now

in the nineteenth century. At last the chairman stated, "Our time has passed and we have given no opportunity to our colleague from the law school. Suppose we prolong the examination and allow him a quarter of an hour." The colleague from the law school answered, "I thank you for the courtesy, but a single minute is all that I require. I once put the question of the nature of the state to perhaps the most distinguished alumnus of the Yale School of Graduate Studies. Mr. Candidate, will you please tell me (a) what his name was, and (b) what was his answer?" The colleague from the law school had to answer for the candidate, "His name was Thorstein Veblen; and his answer was, 'Why in the hell do you want to know?'"

The great contribution of Veblen was that he made the generation of scholars following him sensitive to the question of "Why do you want to know?"

[C. E. AYRES]

3

Veblen's Theory of Instincts Reconsidered

THORSTEIN Veblen was a social theorist of the first rank, and by far his most important contribution was his theory of instincts. I make this claim notwithstanding the fact that the very notion of instincts is now scientifically obsolete. It is on this account, of course, that a whole generation of hostile critics have focused their ridicule of Veblen upon this, seemingly his most vulnerable point. But in doing so they have only demonstrated their own lack of understanding not just of Veblen but of human behavior. For even after we have rid ourselves of the false simplicity of "inborn," or genetically determined, behavior patterns, the fact remains that human behavior differs very substantially from that of any other creature and that such differences must have their taproots somewhere.

As we all now agree, human behavior is cultural. We owe the concept of culture, and the cultural conception of human behavior, in large measure to the anthropologists, from whom it has spread with varying degrees of tardiness to the practitioners of other social disciplines. Generally speaking, economists have been the slowest to assimilate this conception, but Veblen cannot be included in this general reproach. On the contrary, when his name first began appearing in the economic journals, he was virtually unique among economists for his acquaintance with anthropological literature and his assimilation of such anthropological conceptions as that of culture. Indeed,

C. E. Ayres

it was precisely on this ground that Veblen charged classical political economy with being "pre-Darwinian." The classical conception of the economy was pre-Darwinian, he held, because it assumed "human nature" to be "given," virtually by special creation, whereas the essence of Darwinian evolution is the denial that there is any such thing as "the original nature of man" and the presumption that all human proclivities, propensities, and wants, however fully "internalized" they have become and however natural-seeming they may therefore be, have in fact been formed through a culturally developmental process.

What is the nature of this process? What major forces are at work in it, and from what underlying causes do these forces flow? It was in response to the challenge of such questions that Veblen formulated his theory of instincts. The focal point of that theory and of Veblen's whole conception of economy and society is the antithesis between workmanship and "exploit." I put the word "exploit" in quotation marks not only because Veblen used it but also because it is deplorably inadequate. Veblen himself clearly realized this, as witness the string of alternatives to which he resorted. "Workmanship" speaks for itself. In using this word Veblen made unmistakable reference to the tool-using activities of mankind, those which bring into play the arts and crafts—all the arts and crafts from the finest to the meanest and from the "industrial employments" of primeval man to the "machine process" itself. There is no ambiguity here. But what Veblen sometimes characterized as exploit he also on some occasions characterized as "sportsmanship" and on others as "ceremonialism."

This antithesis was the axis about which all of Veblen's thinking turned. Thus his analysis of the modern economy centers on the distinction between "industrial employments" and "pecuniary employments." Indeed it was his profound conviction that the contrast between making things and making money, which hostile critics have often brushed aside as both obvious and inconsequential, is a contemporary manifestation of a contrast that runs through all organized society and the entire gamut of cultures, from the most primitive to the most sophisticated. As he saw it, throughout the ages mankind has carried on two sets of activities. One of these consists of a congeries of acts of skill supplemented by matter-of-fact knowledge. The other consists of the supposed manipulation of supernatural forces by mystic rites and incantations, conducted in an atmosphere of make-

Veblen's Theory of Instincts

believe and sustained by systems of taboo and prescription, to the observance of which communities are emotionally conditioned, with the consequence of establishing and maintaining artificial distinctions of "ceremonial adequacy" and "ritual uncleanness" by virtue of which communities are divided into superior and inferior ranks and the several ranks are kept in order. In short, man is distinguished from all other creatures both by his amazing skill in manipulating physical objects and by an equally amazing capacity for self-deception and mutual exploitation.

As I scarcely need to say, Veblen was not alone in noticing this contrast. On the contrary, recognition of it runs through all the literature of anthropology, and necessarily so, since the raw facts are obvious. What distinguishes Veblen's insight is his recognition of the significance of the obvious. In particular, even the crudest skills and coarsest tools of primeval man, viewed in the perspective of zoological evolution, represent an almost unimaginable advance over the way of life of even man's closest animal relatives, just as human speech contrasts with the grunts and cries of animals. These arts, achievement of which differentiates man from all other animals, run in a continuous unbroken thread through all human cultures and merit recognition as one of the two characteristic manifestations of human intelligence.

In crediting Veblen, as I do, with unique insight I do not mean to belittle the genius of other pioneers. Two circumstances, I think, explain the failure of anthropologists and social theorists generally to see the significance of what may be justly called the Veblenian antithesis. One is the challenge of myth and magic, and the other is the apparent self-evidence of tools and skills. It required great perspicacity on the part of the pioneers of modern social science to see any sort of rhyme or reason in "the beastly practices of savages" and still more to recognize the same propensities in our own tribal traditions and value systems. This is the task that even in our own day still absorbs most of the energies of anthropologists and sociologists. In the meantime, the manipulation of common tools is so much of a commonplace to all of us that instead of marveling at the prodigious technical achievements of primeval man we are more likely to wonder that it should have taken our ancestors so long to discover that clay can be molded into pots and fibers woven into fabrics.

C. E. Ayres

At this point perhaps I may be pardoned a brief digression. Hostile critics have often attributed the detachment with which Veblen scanned the machinations of financiers to the fact that he was an immigrant farm boy who never really learned to find his way among the complexities of American business. But in doing so, the critics have missed a bet. Whatever Veblen was not, he was adept with common tools. He was a charter member of the do-it-yourself club, and I think it not at all unlikely that his respect for even the simplest skills may have contributed greatly to his appreciation of the vast significance of workmanship.

At all events there can be no question that Veblen's notion of instinct was prompted by his awareness of the all-encompassing significance of the antithesis of workmanship and ceremonialism. How did this amazing polarization of human behavior come about? On the one hand, why has man persisted through the ages in cherishing beliefs and practices that work so plainly at cross purposes with his material activities? And on the other hand, how has he been able so continuously to maintain and enlarge those material activities in the face of stultifying taboos and institutionalized conspiracies in restraint of trade?

Veblen's answer was instinct, and at the time he wrote that was a sensible answer. At all events it seemed so to the scholars and scientists of that day. It was in the spirit of those times that F. H. Bradley defined philosophy, in words strangely analogous to the Veblenian antithesis, as "the finding of bad reasons for things we believe by instinct; but the finding of the reasons is no less an instinct." From William James to William McDougall, in Veblen's time the academic woods were full of instincts.

Furthermore, Veblen's answer was more sensible than most by reason of his vagueness. Veblen's vagueness is notorious. He was vague not only as to what an instinct is but also as to what the human instincts are. He sometimes spoke of "the parental bent" as though it were an instinct, as he also did of "idle curiosity"; and the same is true of ostentation and brutality. Indeed, vagueness as persistent and systematic as Veblen's could only have been intentional; and if we assume intent, Veblen's meaning is clear. Clearly when he spoke of instincts, he had in mind culturally significant patterns of behavior which have persisted from the earliest known cultures to the present. Moreover, it is equally clear that both "idle curiosity" and "the parental bent" are aspects or manifestations of the master pattern he called workmanship, just as the predilections for coercion and exploitation are always to the same effect as predilections for ostentation and make-believe, while these are to the same effect as ceremonialism and conjury. In short, as Veblen conceived instinct, there are only two sets of instinctive proclivities, and these constitute the obverse and reverse of all cultures.

Thus Veblen's concept of instinct is indissociable from the antithesis which was the major premise of all his thinking; and in dismissing that concept Veblen's critics have likewise jettisoned the most important social insight of modern times. Moreover, they have done so quite unnecessarily. In effect they have assumed that since the notion of instinct is fallacious therefore whatever anybody has conceived to be instinctive is likewise fallacious. But it is at least conceivable that the Veblenian antithesis is valid, and that Veblen was in error only in attributing these contrasting and mutually stultifying aspects of human behavior to instinct. If we make that assumption, we are then in a position to inquire whether any alternative explanation of this great anomaly of human behavior can now be offered.

More than half a century has passed since Veblen formulated his theory of the instincts of workmanship and sportsmanship and of the way they work at cross purposes in all human affairs. It is now quite conclusively established that no such complex behavior patterns are in any literal sense "inborn." We now know that such patterns are wholly cultural. Hence the problem of their origin is indissociable from the problem of the origins of culture. We know also that Veblen was wrong in supposing, as he seems to have done, that workmanship prevailed from the beginning, so to speak,.and that sportsmanship, or ceremonialism, developed only when a supposedly idyllic "savage" state was supplanted by "barbarism." Archeological evidence is conclusive that ceremonial burial, for example, goes as far back as any human remains. Speaking specifically of "conspicuous waste," Melville Herskovits has remarked, in his *Economic Anthropology*, "As a matter of fact, it seems likely that Veblen, in coining this phrase and in indicating its dynamic and institutional implications, hit upon one of those principles which, in generalized form, are applicable to human societies everywhere." Since all authorities are agreed that evidence of the use of tools, including fire, is decisive in the identification of human remains, the Veblenian antithesis would seem to be somehow inherent in the very nature of culture. The question is, How?

At this point we might do well to draw upon the results of an inquiry which had scarcely more than begun in Veblen's pioneering years. It is well established now that culture itself is an outgrowth, or manifestation, of the symbolic process. All authorities agree that the origin of language must have coincided with the origin of culture. Neither is conceivable except in terms of the symbolic process.

Since the power of association is basic to the symbolic process, the origin of culture presupposes the evolutionary character of the human species, and especially of the human brain. The species most closely related to man seem, so to speak, to be just on the point of achieving speech and of using tools. They can be taught to associate signals, such as the ringing of a bell or a word of command, with arbitrarily related activities; but they do not have the power to initiate such signals, as man does. In this sense the cultural activities of man are all conditioned by the organism. But it is now generally agreed that in raising the limits of human activities the organism does not prescribe any patterns. Every human infant's capacity for speech is conditioned by his genetic inheritance. But also and no less important it is conditioned by the existence of a language which he may learn to speak and use.

How language and the other elements of culture came into existence in the first place we do not know and perhaps never will know. But it does seem clear that the power of speech and the use of tools condition each other and that both likewise condition and are conditioned by patterns of interpersonal relationships. That is, the skillful use of tools is prodigiously enhanced by communication, which is itself an interpersonal relationship; while at the same time the effort to use tools is a powerful stimulus to communication and to interpersonal organization. Thus the presumption is very strong that these three cultural activities developed together—if, indeed, they are three and not one. For we have only to view them in such a light to see that all three are manifestations of what Veblen called the instinct of workmanship. Each is essential to what is sometimes called operational efficiency.

Two points need emphasis here. One is the operational function of

Veblen's Theory of Instincts

symbols. When the word symbol is mentioned, most people think first of sacred symbols, since it is these that most vividly exemplify the mysterious potency of symbols. That, I think, is why even in recent years investigation into the nature of symbols has been most particularly concerned with occult symbols and the strange behavior in which they play a vital part. Hence, although no student of symbols has ever denied it, we tend to disregard the fact that most symbols are secular, nonoccult, and operational, like the symbols mathematicians use. All words are symbols, and most of them are for the most part operational, like the names of streets, which may honor departed heroes but for the most part serve as instruments by use of which we find our way about.

The second point that needs to be emphasized is the operational character of interpersonal relationships, or perhaps I should say the interpersonal character of operational relationships. Much the same thing is true here. Because it is power relationships—the strange and bewilderingly various means by which human beings maintain a hold on each other—that most intrigue the imagination and seem to challenge explanation, we have focused our attention on that sort of relationship to such a degree as to produce the impression all relations between persons are inherently occult, or morbid, or both. But such is clearly not the case. Most interpersonal relationships are for the most part operational. Notwithstanding the war between the sexes and the maneuvering for advantage which may color the relations of husbands and wives, most of their interpersonal relationships are exemplified by such questions as, "When will you be home for dinner?" or "Where did you put my reading glasses?"

I do not mean to suggest that in the development of culture operational efficiency preceded make-believe and conjury, though I have an idea that some such reasoning as this may have contributed to Veblen's conception of "the savage state." For if it is true that communication, tool-using, and organization mutually condition each other, it is no less true that the operational efficiency of even the most primitive human activity is well-nigh miraculous. To us the fumbling efforts of Dawn man to use sticks and stones and fire seem almost inconceivably crude. But to Dawn man himself the potency of his devices must have seemed even more astonishing than nuclear fission now seems to the least educated.

C. E. Ayres

In this connection we must also remember that the evolutionary make-up of our species includes a glandular system of extraordinary delicacy. We are a highly emotional species; and although this circumstance does not spell out any activity patterns, just as the human brain does not, nevertheless it does mean that we are highly susceptible to astonishment, awe, horror, and intimidation. Thus although we do not know what were the first words that were uttered by Dawn man or who the creatures were who uttered them, we can assert with a high degree of confidence that the effect on themselves of their utterances must have been "electrifying." Or perhaps I should say "verbalizing," since the creatures in question could scarcely have used metaphors that employed the mysteries of electricity.

The point I am trying to suggest is that man himself is the supreme mystery—that the symbolic process itself, man's power of symbolic organization, is the root-source of all mystery-making. All occultism is the imagined projection of operational symbolism. All magic is the imagined extrapolation of operational efficiency. If shouting his name will summon a person—an operation of astonishing efficiency for which the entire natural universe affords no parallel—then why should not shouting *his* name summon a demon? How true it is that in the beginning was the word, and the word was God! The natural and the supernatural are obverse and reverse of the symbolic process from which all culture flows.

Certainly this presumption trues with all that we know of primitive behavior. It is the universal testimony of anthropological observers that primitive peoples credit sticks and stones of proved efficiency with occult power, and that they likewise credit words, and especially names, with having occult power over the things and persons named. The suggestion is very strong that belief in occult forces and mystic powers goes back "to the very beginning"—that is, as far back as language and tool-using go—and that such beliefs are the converse of the operational use of tools and language.

This supposition also coincides with another conclusion to which anthropological investigation has seemed to lead. In earlier years anthropologists used to debate whether myths originated first and set the stage for the practice of magic, or whether the attempt to influence the course of events by magic led to the proliferation of myths. But this argument now seems to have been resolved by the recognition

Veblen's Theory of Instincts

that magic is as old as myth, and vice versa, and that the two are indeed aspects of a single pattern. Another aspect of the same pattern is the mystic potency (or mana) with which certain individuals and social classes are supposed to be endowed. It is now well recognized that ceremonies of initiation by which such "ceremonial adequacy," as Veblen called it, is achieved are the prototype of all mystic rites, that the supernatural transformations so achieved are the prototype of all magic, and that the rankings so effected are the prototype of all social hierarchies. In short, all mystic rites and ceremonial practices, all forms of magic, conjury, and incantation, all supernatural beliefs, and all systems of arbitrary social discrimination—caste systems, sex discriminations, *et hoc genus omne*—are interrelated and mutually conditioned and conditioning.

All this is of course what Veblen called "ceremonialism" and attributed to the "instinct of sportsmanship" or of "exploit." As a mode of behavior or aspect of culture, it is certainly not instinctive. But if twentieth-century scholarship is on the right path at all, Veblen likewise would seem to have been on the right path. For if these two aspects of culture arose together and are obverse and reverse of the symbolic process, as our present knowledge strongly suggests, then Veblen was right in representing workmanship and ceremonialism as constants that go back to the very origins of man himself and have persisted through all cultures.

Moreover, there is another particular in which such a reading of the evidence bears out the insight of this great pioneer. As Veblen conceived them, workmanship and sportsmanship are at cross purposes with one another. Each interferes with, checks, or as Veblen often said, "contaminates" the other. That is why I have referred to them as antithetical. As Veblen interpreted the record, all human cultures have been the scenes of struggles between conflicting forces the outcome of which is far from certain. Indeed, no words of his have been more often quoted than the sentence in *The Instinct of Workmanship* in which he says: "History records more frequent and more spectacular instances of the triumph of imbecile institutions over life and culture than of peoples who have by force of instinctive insight saved themselves alive out of a desperately precarious institutional situation, such, for instance, as now faces the peoples of Christendom."

This sentence provides also a striking example of the inadequacy

C. E. Ayres

of the notion of instinct. Seemingly the case is one of "instinctive insight" versus something else. But it is the essence of Veblen's theory that "imbecile institutions" are so by virtue of being manifestations of the instinct of sportsmanship, with its overtones of exploit, violence, make-believe, and ceremonialism generally. Moreover, if Veblen's conception of instinct is valid, these matters—being instinctive themselves—are just as much a part of "life and culture" as workmanship.

It is verbal confusion such as this that has led many critics to dismiss Veblen's whole analysis as a fantastic hodgepodge. But I repeat: in doing so they have thrown out the baby with the bath water. It is of course true that one instinct is just as valid as another. If the term "instinct" means anything at all, it must refer to species characteristics which have been developed in the course of the evolutionary struggle for existence, each of which has the same significance as any other. This is not how Veblen conceived workmanship and "imbecile institutions." But if these contrasting aspects of culture be identified as obverse and reverse of the symbolic process, it is then clear why and how each has always been a drag upon the other. For so conceived, each is a travesty of the other. Supernatural beliefs are a travesty of matter-of-fact knowledge; but material fact is no less a travesty of "the higher truths." Ceremonial observances are an impediment to workmanlike efficiency; but common labor is an affront to devout observances.

The study of this conflict was Veblen's life work. His first book was an effort to show that from the point of view of workmanship the all-pervasive way of life which he identified with "the leisure class" spells waste. *The Theory of Business Enterprise* is a study of the polarization of the modern economy by "industrial employments" and "pecuniary employments." Then comes the exposition of how through the ages "the instinct of workmanship" is contaminated by "imbecile institutions." This is followed by the interpretation of the industrialization of "Imperial Germany" and Japan in terms of the "borrowing" of advanced industrial technology by still feudalistic societies, and this by the interpretation of peace as by nature workmanlike and the attribution of war to the spiritual necessities of the leisure class. So also "the higher learning" is the scene of a continuous struggle between scholars and "captains of erudition"; the "vested interests" have the "usufruct" of "the state of the industrial arts"; and the engineers dream

Veblen's Theory of Instincts

of supplanting the price system. In the end, the case of America is represented still as desperately precarious, since it is that of a great industrial system beset by imbecile institutions, notably "absentee ownership."

The most important defect of the instinct theory is the failure to provide any criterion for a comparative judgment of the value to mankind of workmanship and sportsmanship. As instrumentalities of evolutionary survival, all instincts must be presumed either equally valuable or equally indifferent, according to the value that is imputed to evolutionary survival. Veblen seems to have been keenly aware of the moral indifference of the evolutionary process; he declared over and over again, throughout all his writings, that no moral judgment was being passed and even that none was within the competence of scientific analysis such as he was undertaking. Nevertheless his bias showed on every page. Indeed, it was so strong that it is bound to show in even the briefest review of his work, such as I have just attempted. His famous irony was almost altogether a product of the contrast between his burning contempt of leisure-class posturings and businesslike prevarications and his bland assurances that no moral judgment was being passed and that, if the subject of his analysis seemed to be a stinking mess, it was being so described with no thought of moral disapproval but only because it was in fact a stinking mess.

In this regard, as in many others, Veblen's "instinct" served far better than his instincts. For if these aspects of human behavior are indeed the obverse and reverse of the symbolic process, then the moral significance of their antithesis is unmistakable. Even though it be assumed that they originated together, one is unmistakably genuine and the other no less unmistakably counterfeit.

Moral judgments are judgments of causal relationships. We judge things good or bad, and we judge acts right or wrong, in terms of the fashion in which they affect the rest of our lives and the lives of others. Such judgments may be based on fact, or on fancy. Thus, for example, the judgment that the seeds of the wheat plant are edible and strength-building and therefore good is based on fact, and so is the judgment that rain makes the wheat grow. But the judgment that rain may be prevented by a violation of tribal taboos, or may be induced by performance of sacred rites, is based on fancy. Judgments that it is right to perform rain dances and wrong to violate taboos have no basis

C. E. Ayres

whatever save the traditional beliefs of the people among whom such traditions prevail.

In recent decades students of the behavioral sciences have greatly exaggerated the moral role of fancy to the extent of virtually denying any moral significance to fact. They have done so in part because of our common disposition to take the factual aspect of behavior for granted. As I have already noted, tools, and skills, and operational procedures generally, seem now to pose no mystery, whereas fancy does. The amazing proliferation of fancy, the fantastic variety of its multiform manifestations throughout all the cultures of mankind, the prodigious hold it maintains upon all peoples, and its persistence generation after generation and age after age—these circumstances in ever greater part have focused the attention of scholars upon taboos and superstitions and mystic rites to the almost total neglect of the basic facts of life by which, notwithstanding their fancies, all peoples live.

Nevertheless the facts remain. In the opening paragraphs of *The Quest for Certainty* (his Gifford Lectures) John Dewey pointed out that through the ages man has had two ways of dealing with the uncertainties of life, by doing something about the particular uncertainties in question and by imagining them to be unreal. The former has been prodigiously successful, as witness all the vital statistics. But the latter, being immune to statistical evidence—now as always—still persists and still dazzles us with the *ignis fatuus* of an imaginary perfection. In short, like Veblen, Dewey faced the issue which the present generation is so loath to face, that facts are facts and that by whatever anthropological name they may be known fancies are fancies still.

Throughout his writings Veblen identified workmanship, technology, science, the arts and crafts, as "the life process" of mankind. He did so in that celebrated sentence which I have quoted from *The Instinct of Workmanship*. His antithesis of workmanship and sportsmanship is the antithesis of reality and illusion. In attributing this antithesis to instinct he was of course in error. But in his recognition that such an antithesis does pervade all cultures, he was profoundly right and was one of the great pioneers of modern times.

For, as we are now beginning to learn, our own thinking is, as he would say, contaminated by illusions which everywhere stand in the

Veblen's Theory of Instincts

way of a fuller realization of our scientific and industrial potentials. Those of us who are over fifty remember the days when eminent and competent scholars were declaring that it would be impossible for the Nazis to wage any large-scale war, since they had no gold reserves. Fortunately we are beginning to recover from such fancies. Only a few years ago the London *Economist* remarked editorially that we have now learned that whatever is physically possible is also financially possible. With every passing year we are seeing more and more clearly that what counts is the volume of physical production, the level of employment, the gross national product. Everything else is incidental; or if it is not, it is sugar in the gasoline and sand in the bearings. What a triumph for Veblen's "theory of business enterprise"! [*]

We also realize more clearly today than ever before that our quest for certainty is far from finished. We stand on the threshold of scientific and industrial triumphs such as might bring comfort and security to all mankind. Sources of energy—the basic limiting factor of all life—are being found which might be virtually limitless. But they might also be totally destructive, if what Veblen called "the instinct of sportsmanship" should yet prevail. More than at any previous moment in the history of mankind—more even than when Veblen wrote these words—we now find ourselves in "a desperately precarious situation," one which may yet provide the most spectacular instance in all history "of the triumph of imbecile institutions" over life and work.

[*] See the essay by G. W. Zinke in this volume for an extended qualitative demurrer to this position.—EDITOR

[NORMAN KAPLAN]

4

Idle Curiosity

MY own curiosity about idle curiosity is, I confess, idle. Nevertheless, I have found it instructive that Veblen's first discussions of this phenomenon appeared in the very early volumes of the first journal of sociology in the United States.[1] This is important only insofar as it helps to restrict the present discussion to some of the areas where a sociologist may be most comfortable and perhaps even be able to offer a few new remarks based on some of the works in his field that have appeared since Veblen wrote.

Although the notion of idle curiosity played a central role in much of Veblen's work (together with the instinct of workmanship, it has come to be considered among his important contributions), I would like to concentrate my attention on the relationship between this notion of idle curiosity and the development of science. Characteristically Veblen viewed idle curiosity not merely as a psychological attribute; he was also concerned with the social conditions in which idle curiosity might or might not flourish. After some introductory remarks concerning this relationship as Veblen saw it, I would like to consider the following questions: What was Veblen's conception of idle curiosity, and how is this related to creativeness? What is the relationship between the universities and their research activities and Veblen's notion of idle curiosity, and what has happened since Veblen's time?

[1] T. Veblen, "The Place of Science in Modern Civilisation," *American Journal of Sociology*, XI (March 1906), 585–609.

Norman Kaplan

I. IDLE CURIOSITY AND SCIENCE

In considering the development of science and knowledge at the beginning of this century, Veblen was perhaps among the first social scientists to consider systematically the relationships between science and society. Although there are a number of surface similarities between Veblen's analysis and that of Marx, and although Marx is unquestionably one of the intellectual godfathers of what is today known as the sociology of knowledge or the study of the social determinants of knowledge, there can be little doubt that Veblen's contribution represents a substantial advance over that of Marx. For while Marx tended to emphasize the relationship of the ideological elements of man's thought to the system of production in a society, Veblen viewed the whole sweep of man's knowledge from "pure" ideology to "pure" science as inextricably related not only to the system of production (which is also given a crucial role in Veblen's analysis) but also more broadly to other elements in the society and culture.

To the cultural system that exists at any given time Veblen relates the way in which people think (in the sense of the kinds of concepts and conceptual schemes with which the world is viewed), what they are likely to think about (in the sense of the kinds of problems deemed significant or legitimate), and the canons of validity for the acceptance of different kinds of knowledge. Such a relationship also holds for the uses to which the products of man's thought are put. But this, in Veblen's view, is still not sufficient to explain man's quest for knowledge through history—in different ways and for differing kinds of knowledge and with differing ends in mind at various times in history. At this gap in the analysis Veblen turns away from social and cultural conditions and posits the existence of idle curiosity. He notes: "Men instinctively seek knowledge, and value it. The fact of this proclivity is well summed up in saying that men are by native gift actuated with an idle curiosity." [2]

Man has always possessed idle curiosity in greater or lesser quantities, and this propensity has flourished or waned but has always been shaped or affected by the given cultural conditions including the state of knowledge. Thus he says:

[2] T. Veblen, *The Higher Learning in America* (New York: Huebsch, 1918), p. 5.

Idle Curiosity

In what manner and with what effect the idle curiosity of mankind first began to tame the facts thrown in its way, far back in the night of time, and to break them in under a scheme of habitual interpretation; what may have been the earliest norms of systematic knowledge, such as would serve the curiosity of the earliest generations of men in a way analogous to the service rendered the curiosity of later generations by scientific inquiry—all that is, of course, a matter of long-range conjecture, more or less wild, which cannot be gone into here.[3]

But whereas idle curiosity furnished much of the initial propelling power in man's quest for knowledge during much of our previous history, various other personal motivations, aided by specific cultural conditions, served as the continuing forces in this quest. Veblen is suggesting that idle curiosity has always played a central role in man's search for knowledge but that it has frequently been turned to ends other than "pure" knowledge—whether these be the ends of religious power or political power or practical utility. What distinguishes the modern scientific era, however, is the fact that idle curiosity has now become the dominant norm of the seekers of knowledge.[4]

I take it, then, as a "given" that idle curiosity is a dominant norm of science specifically, that it is possible to distinguish a cultural milieu or climate in which it can be said that science flourishes, and that there are other cultural milieus in which science does not flourish but withers. Whether Veblen had a sufficiently good basis for positing idle curiosity as a dominant norm of science will also not be questioned in detail in the present paper. The norms and values of a society necessary for the growth of science, as well as the internal values of science in relation to society, raise a number of basic questions and problems which cannot be dealt with adequately in the context of the present paper.

With this as a backdrop then, we can now turn our attention to the first of the questions we have raised—namely, what is Veblen's notion of idle curiosity?

[3] T. Veblen, "The Evolution of the Scientific Point of View," in *The Place of Science in Modern Civilisation, and Other Essays* (New York: Huebsch, 1919), p. 40.

[4] T. Veblen, "The Place of Science in Modern Civilisation," in *The Place of Science in Modern Civilisation, and Other Essays*. Cf. p. 19.

Norman Kaplan

II. THE NOTION OF "IDLE CURIOSITY"

At first glance, putting the word "idle" together with "curiosity" seems contradictory. Curiosity implies an active, agile mind wondering about ideas, things, or people. If you are curious about something, there is a strong presumption that you will follow your curiosity— you will think about the problem, you will study it, you will try out your ideas. Above all, curiosity carries the strong implication of work, of action—the very opposite of idleness obviously. On the other hand, is it not possible to conceive of some inquisitive souls who, while desiring to know, are so lazy and indolent that they find themselves unable or unwilling to take any action—especially the hardest and most demanding one of simply thinking about the problem? They are content to wonder about things, and they are content to do no more. We might feel that such persons could not be really curious, but, as we would not be inclined to split hairs, we would admit the possibility of their existence. But is this the posture of a scientist? Can this be the kind of norm Veblen would have us believe lies at the heart of scientific inquiry?

Clearly such an attitude makes little sense, and, although Veblen has been accused of many vices, this is surely not one of them. Veblen has attached a very special meaning to the word "idle." It refers, in the first place, to disinterestedness, an absence of an "ulterior end," especially in terms of concern for the uses to which the product of curiosity, namely, knowledge, will be put—whether it might result in technological improvements or not.[5] The word "idle" has also an element of play and the dramatic associated with it as part of the positive motivation attached to the idleness of the curiosity. Throughout his essay on "The Place of Science in Modern Civilization" Veblen refers again and again to these notions of play and drama.[6] This is perhaps a factor in David Riesman's definition of idle curiosity as "the spirit of playful inquiry, unrelated to any immediate pragmatic need or gain."[7]

[5] *Ibid.* Cf. pp. 17, 19, 25, and 28.

[6] For example, when he suggests that "this idle curiosity is, perhaps, closely related to the aptitude for play" (p. 7) or when he suggests that with idle curiosity the interpretation of facts takes on a "dramatic form" (p. 7). There are other examples on pp. 8, 9, 16, 26.

[7] *Thorstein Veblen: A Critical Interpretation* (New York: Scribner, 1953), p. 42.

Idle Curiosity

But playful inquiry does not quite convey the significance of what Veblen had in mind. There seems to be a very strong, though still somewhat implicit, link to creativity in basic or pure research as these terms are used today. The disinterested inquiry, where the only goal which is considered legitimate is that of "knowledge for its own sake" leading to the dramatic break-through—this is the stuff on which creative minds in basic research thrive.

One may speculate, quite idly I am afraid, about why Veblen should have put these two unlikely words together as one of his central concepts. There may even be a germ of truth in Riesman's essentially psychological interpretation of Veblen, the man:

> I might go further and suggest that one of Veblen's greatest concepts, that of "idle curiosity" . . . might be thought of as defense against the all-too-practical, all-too-grown-up people who wondered, both on the farm and later, where Veblen's "lazy" and speculative mind would lead him.[8]

Whatever the childhood experiences and the original reasons, and whether or not Veblen was trying to justify himself and his own activities, the fact remains that he was one of the first among the contemporary social scientists to point up the importance of disinterested seeking after knowledge as a condition for scientific inquiry.

Actually he does more than this for he looks at idle curiosity on at least two different levels—as an attribute of individuals and as an attribute of the culture in the form of a cultural value and a scientific norm. Whether or not one wishes to argue with Veblen about his use of the term "instinct" (and I think such arguments essentially fruitless), there can be little question that Veblen saw these propensities as being heavily influenced by the culture and society in which the individual lived.

What Veblen does is to lift his discussion (and our attention) from a more or less sterile consideration of curiosity or workmanship as purely instinctive to the question of the social and cultural conditions in which these characteristics thrive or fail to thrive. Idle curiosity is an attribute of individuals, and one may perhaps properly speak of one individual possessing "more" idle curiosity than another individual. But more importantly, one can, and indeed one must, also speak of the social and cultural characteristics of this attribute if one wants to

[8] *Ibid.*

Norman Kaplan

understand the operation and the effects of idle curiosity. Although it may be assumed that few cultures throughout history have attached the "usual" meanings of idle when this is combined with the notion of curiosity (meanings such as slothful, unemployed, doing nothing, baseless or groundless, and so on), there can be no question that the directions or the ends of idle curiosity—what people are curious about as well as the intellectual and conceptual approaches, in other words, how people exercise their curiosity—have varied with different cultural definitions. Moreover, who was likely to be idly curious and where it was considered legitimate to be so have varied with the type of social structure, the state of education, and the stratification system and structure of society generally. In our own society, as will be noted in detail later, the university was one of the few places or social contexts in which Veblen felt that the exercise of idle curiosity was, or should be, a legitimate activity.

Before considering the functioning of idle curiosity in the university, a few questions still merit our attention. These are, firstly, the relationship of idle curiosity to pure or basic research and, secondly, the relationship of idle curiosity to applied research and to Veblen's own instinct of workmanship on the one hand and to his critique of waste and idleness in the industrial system on the other.

It is perhaps an example of one of many such delicious ironies, which Veblen did not live to relish, that idle curiosity should have become a byword among both scientists and nonscientists as a desirable, reputable, and indeed essential norm of science. In his writings one senses the Veblenian voice crying in the wilderness that this is an important notion and to lose sight of it is to lose sight of science. Yet only within the last decade or so are basic research and the motivation behind it coming to be accepted by large segments of American society. Just eleven days after the launching of Sputnik I the National Science Foundation presented a report to the President of the United States entitled "Basic Research—A National Resource" in which it was noted that basic research is still underemphasized in this country.

There has been a good deal of controversy and disagreement on the distinctions between basic or pure research on the one hand and applied or developmental research on the other. Many observers have felt that the distinction was a difficult one to draw, especially in prac-

Idle Curiosity

tice, precisely because one of the most important distinguishing criteria was the motivation of the scientist. In the third annual report of the National Science Foundation, for example, it was noted that

a worker in basic science research is motivated by a *driving curiosity* about the unknown. When his explorations yield new knowledge, he experiences the satisfaction of those who first attain the summit of a mountain. . . . Discovery of truth and understanding of nature are his objectives.[9]

Or as a committee of higher educators put it:

The distinction between basic, or fundamental, and applied research is, in many instances, a difficult one. Stated in broad terms, however, basic research is uncommitted research, *prompted by disinterested curiosity,* and aimed primarily at the extension of the boundaries of knowledge.[10]

Thus for the man who in his own lifetime felt that he exerted so little influence on the affairs and thinking of men, we can conclude that here again Veblen is coming into his own. From a wide variety of sources one finds ample evidence of the acceptance of Veblen's basic contention that an important part of the search for knowledge is motivated by disinterested curiosity—and this seems to be accepted today by not only the small group of scientists engaged in this activity but to some extent even by the lay public as well.

The other question raised concerning the relationship of idle curiosity to workmanship and wastefulness is more difficult to follow through in Veblen. The instinct of workmanship, Veblen says,

occupies the interest with practical expedients, ways and means, devices and contrivances of efficiency and economy, proficiency, creative work and technological mastery of facts. Much of the functional content of the instinct of workmanship is a proclivity for taking pains.[11]

Workmanship influences the exercise of idle curiosity in two ways primarily. In the first instance knowledge gained through idle curiosity, where there was originally no thought of its usefulness, may now be

[9] National Science Foundation, *Third Annual Report* (Washington: U.S.G.P.O., 1953), p. 38 (italics mine).

[10] *Sponsored Reseach Policy of Colleges and Universities* (Washington: American Council on Education, 1954), p. 42. (italics mine).

[11] T. Veblen, *The Instinct of Workmanship* (New York: Macmillan, 1914), p 3.

turned to practical use through the mechanism of the instinct of workmanship. This has been a particularly strong characteristic of American science, especially in the years before and during the Second World War, an emphasis on using the basic research of the scientists of other nations with little respect for, or encouragement of, basic research in the United States.[12] But if I read Veblen correctly, he considers the more pertinent aspect of the interrelation the fact that the instinct of workmanship "affords the norms, or the scheme of criteria and canons of verity, according to which the ascertained facts will be construed and connected up in a body of systematic knowledge." [13]

We may detect a certain ambivalence in Veblen's attitude here. To gain new knowledge and understanding, man's curiosity must be untrammelled by practical objectives and by the limited horizons of pecuniary or other such influences. But given Veblen's antipathy for waste (an antipathy which he carries over even to duplication of research, an area where one may seriously question the legitimacy of the concept of duplication), one has a slight uneasiness in viewing an anarchic, wasteful flow of idle curiosity.

Idle curiosity is a necessary norm for the conduct of science, but it operates with a proclivity for workmanship. On one level the propensity for workmanship helps to assure the ultimate applications of the fruits of basic research motivated by idle curiosity. To the extent that this does happen and the applied technology is affected it will, in turn, result in new norms for workmanship which will mean new ways of looking at and interpreting the results of basic research. If the results of basic reasearch are not ultimately applied, it would seem to follow that eventually idle curiosity would be adversely affected. But it is the essence of idle curiosity that no thought be given to ultimate usefulness, practical value, and like considerations. Since Veblen is against waste in all forms and since such proliferation and possible duplication did appear to be considered by him as wasteful, what then keeps idle curiosity from becoming too "idle"? Or is Veblen really advocating a free, almost anarchistic kind of idle curiosity guiding the search for new knowledge in the sciences?

[12] See, for example, Vannevar Bush, *Science: The Endless Frontier* (Washington: U.S.G.P.O., 1945), as well as a number of other warnings about the sad state of basic research in the United States at the close of the Second World War.
[13] *The Higher Learning*, p. 5.

Idle Curiosity

I am afraid that Veblen does not provide a clear-cut answer. It is difficult to believe that Veblen would have sided with the "free enterprisers" among the British scientists who claimed, for example:

> It is the very essence of true science that its basic principles are not affected by the needs of humanity. Those basic principles are the free search for demonstrable truth and the formulation of generalizations covering the discoveries made. The needs of humanity do not change them.[14]

This position of John R. Baker and Michael Polanyi was in marked opposition to that taken by J. D. Bernal, J. G. Crowther, and others, who were more inclined to speak of "the social function of science." And yet, we cannot be sure where Veblen would have stood if he had followed through the implications of his own conflicting positions.

One possible solution to this dilemma may be suggested here. It appears that Veblen failed to take into account sufficiently the internal state and development of science as one of the key factors which serve to define problems as relevant and thus as legitimate areas for the exercise of idle curiosity. This limits the application of idle curiosity to those problems that are considered scientifically relevant. The second factor—namely, the external socio-culture elements which help to channel the idle curiosity of scientists into problems considered relevant at a given time in a given society—is intimately related to the first and, although emphasized by Veblen in other contexts, was not sufficiently tied in to idle curiosity. The cultural elements need not be pecuniary considerations or practicality; they might be considerations of the needs of humanity. It may be suggested that these two factors taken together exert a strong restrictive influence on otherwise free and idle curiosity. Another possibility which cannot be discounted entirely is that Veblen may have been thinking of the rare break-throughs made by the handful of scientific greats who seemed to have cut through the restrictions imposed on most other men by the science and the society.

In any case, we have succeeded in pointing to more questions than answers in our preliminary review of the concept of idle curiosity and its relationship to pure and applied research in science. Having explored some of these links, we may now proceed to examine its central role in Veblen's controversial, though highly significant, work on

[14] John R. Baker, *Science and the Planned State* (New York: Macmillan, 1945), p. 63.

Norman Kaplan

higher learning in the universities. Specifically, we turn to the other major questions posed at the outset: "What is the relationship between the universities and their research activities and Veblen's notion of idle curiosity, and what has happened since Veblen's time?"

III. IDLE CURIOSITY, BASIC RESEARCH, AND THE UNIVERSITIES

First published in 1918 after many delays, but first written in 1904, Veblen's *The Higher Learning in America* is the basic reference for many of the observations to be made on the interrelations of idle curiosity in the university. In this work he begins with general comments on systems of knowledge, moves on to the place of knowledge in different societies at different times, and then to its institutionalization in the universities and to the state of these places of higher learning.

At the outset Veblen contends that "in point of its genesis and growth any system of knowledge may confidently be run back, in the main, to the initiative and bias afforded by two certain impulsive traits of human nature: an Idle Curiosity, and the Instinct of Workmanship." [15] Then very quickly he sketches the historical developments that have led to changes in the systems of knowledge and to their acceptance in society to the point where modern civilization has become, as he sees it, a "culture of the intellectual powers." Most other historians have not sounded as confident about the place of knowledge and science in our civilization as did Veblen. It is difficult to see, for example, the basis for such statements as the following:

This esoteric knowledge of matter-of-fact has come to be accepted as something worthwhile in its own right, a self-legitimating end of endeavor in itself, apart from any bearing it may have on the glory of God or the good of man. . . . [In the past] a quest of knowledge has overtly been rated as meritorious, or even blameless, only in so far as it has appeared to serve the ends of one or another of the practical interests that have from time to time occupied men's attention. But latterly, during the past few generations, this learning has so far become an avowed "end in itself" that "the increase and diffusion of knowledge among men" is now freely rated as the most humane and meritorious work to be taken care of by any enlightened community or any public-spirited friend of civilization.[16]

[15] *Op. cit.*, p. 5.   [16] *Ibid.*, pp. 9–10.

Idle Curiosity

But whether or not learning as such was so highly valued at the turn of the century in actual fact, and assuming this is not a tongue-in-cheek observation, Veblen leaves little room for comfort in his predictions about the continuing pre-eminence of intellectual enterprise in western civilizations. It may be merely a transient episode, he notes, and intellectual matters may soon be relegated to a secondary place— as an instrumentality in the service of "vain-glorious patriotism, or dynastic politics, or the breeding of a commercial aristocracy." It appears to him that "the aspirations of the American community appear to be divided—between patriotism in the service of the captains of war, and commerce in the service of the captains of finance." Even so, Veblen feels that the spokesmen of these captains are still careful "to declare a perfunctory faith in . . . disinterested intellectual achievement."[17]

These observations are important because they serve as further evidence of the strength and general character of Veblen's analyses. He is not content merely to plunge into a discussion of the state of the higher learning in the university—the main problem he set for himself in this work. Rather Veblen is careful to delineate the historical and contemporary social context in which the pursuit of knowledge exists as a value in society, and in addition he describes the social organization of the university. Thus he reminds us that both the pursuit of knowledge and the university have specific sociocultural roots and have shaped and been shaped by the society and its values in particular ways. He asserts that "the university is the only accepted institution of the modern culture on which the quest of knowledge unquestionably devolves"[18] and then immediately moves toward linking higher learning and the university.

This is not as easy or as obvious as it would first appear. Higher learning for Veblen is not necessarily "instruction in any study," as the founder of one American university once put it. It is the disinterested pursuit of knowledge—both scientific and scholarly—and this restriction has immediate consequences for the kinds of institutions Veblen can and must examine. He rules out of consideration, for example, professional schools and professional training, undergraduate instruction and colleges, schools of education, in fact, all schools, no matter how high the level of instruction, in which the

[17] *Ibid.*, p. 12.   [18] *Ibid.*, p. 15.

goal is something other than the pursuit of knowledge for its own sake. "Training for other purposes," he says, "is necessarily of a different kind and is best done elsewhere; and it does not become university work by calling it so and imposing its burden on the men and equipment whose only concern should be the higher learning."[19]

It is perhaps worth quoting Veblen at some length to get the flavor of his argument against those who would make the university something else. He says:

It is true that, by historical accident, the university at large has grown out of professional training-schools,—primarily schools for training in theology, secondarily in law and medicine. It is also true, in like wise and in like degree, that modern science and scholarship have grown out of the technology of handicraft and the theological philosophy of the schoolmen. But just as it would be a bootless enterprise to cut modern science back into handicraft technology, so would it be a gratuitous imbecility to prune back the modern university to that inchoate phase of its life-history and make it again a corporation for the training of theologians, jurists and doctors of medicine. The historical argument does not enjoin a return to the beginning of things, but rather an intelligent appreciation of what things are coming to.[20]

We can now turn to the connection between the higher learning and the university as Veblen saw it at the beginning of this century. And just as in Veblen's time, it is well to consider the function and activities of the university. "The conservation and advancement of the higher learning" Veblen notes,

involves two lines of work, distinct but closely bound together: (a) scientific and scholarly inquiry, and (b) the instruction of students. The former of these is primary and indispensable. It is this work of intellectual enterprise that gives its character to the university and marks it off from the lower schools. The work of teaching properly belongs in the university only because and in so far as it incites and facilitates the university man's work of inquiry.[21]

This kind of statement of principles still rings true and still needs reiteration today.

What we have been describing is Veblen's conception of the ideal situation. This is what higher education should have as its goals—

[19] *Ibid.*, p. 17.   [20] *Ibid.*, p. 33.   [21] *Ibid.*, pp. 16–17.

Idle Curiosity

this is what the higher learning should be like. Not only should it be, but also it could be so. With idle curiosity as a dominant norm of scientific and scholarly inquiry and with the state of development of the sciences now linked to a growing technology, both the internal factors as well as the external factors in technology and society seemed to Veblen to be auspicious for a tremendous spurt in the development of science. One need hardly comment from the benefit of the hindsight of our present perspective how right he was with respect to both the United States and Russia. But one important ingredient was still lacking; despite the lip service to this general set of values, Veblen felt that the specific institutional mechanisms necessary to make the growth of science a reality in the United States were not shaping up properly. In particular the universities, which all agreed should provide the locale and the mechanisms, were being bent to other purposes. And by implication it would follow (though Veblen himself did not stress this) that the development of science would suffer.

What has been the role of the university both as context and as a set of institutional mechanisms for the encouragement of basic scientific research? For Veblen the major deficiencies lay in the possible contamination of the universities by the Captains of Finance and the Captains of Erudition plus the historical fact that the graduate schools were in a subordinate position to the undergraduate colleges. The Captains of Finance exercised control through the governing boards in their role as trustees. Veblen saw them as trying to subvert the purposes of the university (while paying lip service to the ideals) by incorporating pecuniary norms, by emphasis on accounting and real estate, and even by indirect thought control, especially among the social scientists. Though they were said to support idle curiosity, Veblen did not feel they understood the major purposes of a university. The Captains of Erudition, otherwise known as the presidents, chancellors, or rectors, not only supported the Captains of Finance in theory; they also carried out the policies designed to de-emphasize the proper functions of the university. In the undergraduate schools with their superior relationship to the graduate schools, with their emphasis on sports and Greek-letter societies, and their concern for student comportment Veblen saw grave threats to the ability of the universities to carry out their proper functions in the pursuit of learning actuated by idle curiosity.

Norman Kaplan

In fact he concluded that "anything like an effectual university—a seminary of the higher learning, as distinct from an assemblage of vocational schools—is not a practicable proposition in America under current conditions."[22] As if to nail down this conclusion, and to show that he was not just being bitter about such institutions as Chicago and Stanford, Veblen comments on a new development, almost at the very end of his analysis—the rise of independent research centers. Again his words sound strangely prophetic, and it is worth quoting him:

So it is that, with a sanguine hope born of academic defeat, there have latterly been founded certain large establishments, of the nature of retreats or shelters for the prosecution of scientific and scholarly inquiry in some sort of academic quarantine, detached from all academic affiliation and renouncing all share in the work of instruction. . . . They are assuming to take over the advance in science scholarship, which has by tradition belonged under the tutelage of the academic community. This move looks like a desperate surrender of the university ideal. The reason for it appears to be the proven inability of the schools, under competitive management, to take care of the pursuit of knowledge.[23]

There can be little doubt that these independent research institutes have become an even more important factor in the total research picture than when Veblen first wrote of them, and especially since 1940. Interestingly enough many of these institutes are now administered by universities and may even occupy space adjacent to a university, but are not really of the university in the sense that their personnel do not normally teach, are not considered part of the faculty, and usually do not have academic tenure. Recent estimates of the federal monies expended for research showed that over 60 per cent of the funds going to the universities went to such research centers administered by colleges and universities. Only a quarter of these funds was devoted to something that could be labeled as basic research. In contrast, the universities proper devoted almost two-thirds of their available funds to basic research.[24] The contrast may appear gratifying, but one could also ask, why only two-thirds devoted to basic-research effort? And why the need for the separate research institutes?

[22] *Ibid.*, p. 263.　　[23] *Ibid.*, p. 272.
[24] National Science Foundation, *Basic Research: A National Resource* (Washington: U.S.G.P.O., Oct. 15, 1957), pp. 31, 36.

Idle Curiosity

Much of the answer, strangely enough, can be found in Veblen. Looking only at basic research, there is little disagreement that the academic environment is a necessary condition for its successful execution. Everyone, whether he be in industry, government, or university, attests to this. However, there is widespread disagreement as to where this academic atmosphere can be found or achieved. It is by no means taken for granted that the obvious place to find an academic atmosphere is in *academia*—in a university proper.

Without having read Veblen necessarily, and from quite different premises, many observers would not look in the most obvious place because the pursuit of knowledge—whether disinterested or not, whether motivated by idle curiosity or not—is not the foremost goal of many institutions of higher learning. The critics are nct, by and large, talking of the over eight hundred institutions—junior colleges, teachers colleges, and so on—which do not even make pretences in this direction. Mostly they are thinking of the less than two hundred universities and colleges in the country where some kind of research is undertaken. And even when a finer breakdown is made and attention is focused on the top ten or twenty-five universities in the country, many of the same shortcomings will be noted. Where teaching loads, especially with undergraduate classes, counseling of undergraduates, committees, and the like take much time, the scientist will have less time for independent research. Where he is poorly paid and must seek supplementary sources of income by consulting or by writing texts, where his time is not considered valuable, it will be difficult to find the right academic atmosphere for the pursuit of knowledge. As a recent Harvard University report put it with respect to such a fairly trivial consideration as secretarial time: "It is inefficient for the university to pay good salaries to its faculty and then use this high priced time for work which could be done by lower paid personnel." [25] And as another observer put it, if this is true at one of the richest universities in the country and one which does seem to pay its faculty more generously than most, then *a fortiori*, it must be a serious problem in all the other less fortunate universities.[26] This same observer has been

---

[25] Harvard Faculty Committee, *The Behavioral Sciences at Harvard* (Harvard, June 1954), p. 276.

[26] Charles V. Kidd, *American Universities and Federal Research Funds* (Unpublished Ph.D. thesis, Harvard University, May 1957, 2 vols.), I, 270.

led to the conclusion, shared by many connected with research in this country, concerning the best research environments:

The environment is certainly more favorable for research in some governmental, industrial, and foundation laboratories than in most universities. . . . Organizations providing this degree of freedom [to choose and pursue their own work], no matter whether they are financed by endowment, government, or industry, are in every sense as natural a home of basic research as universities.[27]

In other words, the Captains of Research (if I may coin a new term) have taken part of Veblen's dictum quite seriously. They are earnestly, for the most part, trying to provide exactly the kind of academic environment Veblen suggested was necessary for the conduct of basic research; but they are trying to provide this environment outside the basic structure of the university. Research is now big business and big defense, but it is also an index of the adequacy of our social and economic system and our way of life, especially since we have proclaimed for such a long time that only in our kind of free society could science and the good things in life come to be. And the proper atmosphere for scientific work is now serious business. Over half of the funds expended on basic research in 1953–1954 were used by researchers not in the universities and not even attached to them administratively. Fully 39 per cent of all the funds supporting basic research was expended in industrial laboratories.[28]

But though this is a tragic picture of the pursuit of new knowledge in the universities, it is only part of the picture. For Veblen laid great emphasis on still another feature of the university which cannot be found outside of it, namely, its students. He said:

Only in the most exceptional, not to say erratic, cases will good, consistent, sane and alert scientific work be carried forward through a course of years by any scientist without students, without loss or blunting of that intellectual initiative that makes the creative scientist. The work that can be done well in the absence of that stimulus and safeguarding that comes of the give and take between teacher and student is commonly . . . mechanically systematized task-work.[29]

[27] *Ibid.*, p. 249.   [28] *Basic Research: A National Resource*, p. 30, Table 2.
[29] *The Higher Learning*, p. 273.

Idle Curiosity

Basic research, or the uncommitted pursuit of new knowledge actuated at least in part, if you will, by idle curiosity, is now becoming a recognized concern of our whole society. A new look is being taken at the now-recognized inadequacies, not only of colleges and universities, but of our whole educational structure. Undoubtedly there will be some reappraisals of the conditions and climate necessary for the conduct of research in the universities. I would like to suggest that Veblen has furnished us with a useful point of departure for such studies.

[MORRIS A. COPELAND]

5

On the Scope and Method

of Economics

ONE of Thorstein Veblen's main, though not yet fully recognized, contributions to economics relates to the scope of the subject and the methods that should be employed in investigating it.

That this should be so is hardly surprising when we consider his special qualifications for such a contribution. Probably there was no contemporary economist who could match his familiarity with the then current developments in both biological and physical science and with the previous history of science. Moreover, along with his peculiarly wide background in science he had an extraordinary ability to understand sympathetically *Weltanschauungen* which differed widely from his own and from each other, e.g., those of Quesnay, Hume, and Marx.

The general nature of Veblen's contribution in the area of economic methodology is indicated by the title of his famous paper, "Why Is Not Economics an Evolutionary Science?"[1] He thought economics should be investigated in a manner that deserves the characterization, "modern scientific method," that it should be treated as a branch of natural science. He thought that, since the natural science approach to the study of the structure and functioning of living organisms had

[1] Reprinted in T. Veblen, *The Place of Science in Modern Civilisation* (New York, 1919), pp. 56–81.

Morris A. Copeland

come to be predominantly evolutionary or genetic and since economics is concerned with the functioning of one kind of living organism, man, scientific method in economics ought to mean an evolutionary or genetic approach. And as a result his conception of the scope of the subject was somewhat different from that of most of his contemporaries and indeed somewhat different from that of a good many economists today.

It will be convenient to consider what Veblen's proposal that economics should be an evolutionary science involves under the following headings: (1) his conception of evolution, (2) the historical relativity of economic truths, (3) the need for a sense of cultural perspective, (4) explanation, causation, and genetic process, (5) public policy, and (6) the scope of economics.

1. HIS CONCEPTION OF EVOLUTION

The conception of evolution Veblen had in mind when he proposed that economics ought to be approached as an evolutionary science was post-Darwinian rather than Hegelian or Bergsonian. This meant he had a post-Darwinian idea of the place of economics in the family tree of science, an idea of the place on which there is today widespread tacit agreement, even though this place carries implications that a good many economists would not accept. As I understand him, he thought of economics as a branch of that part of zoology concerned with man, a branch of functional anthropology. If one accepts the hypothesis that the *genus homo* like other *animal genera* is to be understood as having resulted from a process of natural evolution, this view of the scientific study of man seems an inescapable logical corollary. Of course it involves recognizing that in the case of the functional study of man three broad branches have become differentiated: physiology, which deals with the functioning of human bodily organs, tissues, and so on; psychology, which deals with the behavior of the individual human organism as a whole; and social science which deals with human group behavior.[2] If one takes a natural evolutionary

---

[2] The study of group behavior is indisputably a part of the job of the biologist in the case of other animals that have developed elaborate forms of group behavior, e.g., hymenoptera. I have discussed something of what it means to treat economics as a natural science in "Economic Theory and the Natural Science Point of View," *American Economic Review,* March 1931. Comparable questions for

Scope and Method of Economics

viewpoint and regards economics as a social science, he implicitly makes economics a subbranch of the branch of zoology concerned with the human animal.[3]

If economics is a branch of zoology, it seems reasonable that economists should look more to biologists than to physicists for methodological guidance. Certainly Veblen did. In much of his work he was concerned with the process of social evolution, and he conceived this process as very much like the process of evolution of species. Indeed he makes the analogy explicit when he speaks of "a post-Darwinian, causal theory of the origin and growth of species in institutions" [4] and of natural selection as applying to the process by which changes in conventions and habits of thought come about.[5]

Veblen's concept of social evolution surely merits high praise. And there are other aspects of this concept besides the analogy to the evolution of species to which it will be convenient to give attention at a later point. Also there are other applications of the methodology of biology to economics that it will be best to deal with later.

At the moment we may note that for Veblen looking more to biologists for methodological guidance meant looking less to physicists. For example, he seems to have had little or no use for the concept of equilibrium, which had been borrowed from mechanics. I concur in his strictures on the use of this concept in a normative sense and in his objection to the static implications that its usual sense entails. This does not rule the concept out of economics entirely, but it does rule out most of the use that has been made of it.[6]

---

psychology are dealt with in my paper, "Psychology and the Natural Science Point of View," *Psychological Review*, Nov. 1930.

Such a view of the anthropological studies seems a logically inescapable corollary of the hypothesis of natural evolution; but of course this corollary is not psychologically inescapable. Where the will to believe or disbelieve is strong, plausible rationalizations seem always to be forthcoming, and the idea that man is something more than a mere animal is a persistent one.

[3] Veblen does not seem to have said explicitly that he thought of economics in this way as a branch of natural science. I believe he took it to be a matter of course that such a view followed from the hypothesis of natural evolution. It happens that on the only occasion on which I met Veblen we discussed psychology and he made it clear that he thought the hypothesis of natural evolution required regarding psychology as a branch of natural science.

[4] *Place of Science*, p. 265.   [5] *Place of Science*, p. 149.

[6] See, for example, *Place of Science*, pp. 189 ff., for his comments on the concept of equilibrium. In one interpretation of Keynes's *General Theory* the con-

Morris A. Copeland

One other point suggested by the proposition that economics is a branch of zoology seems appropriate here, a comment on a curious out-of-place survival of an earlier conception of the family tree of knowledge. A century and more ago the division of academic labor was not between individual psychology and social science but between mental and moral philosophy. Mental philosophy was concerned with man as a passive, observing, and understanding being whose experiences were organized by association one with another; that is, it was concerned with the processes of perception, memory, and imagination. Moral philosophy was the study of man as a moral agent or active, decision-making being. Individual choice was then a part of the subject matter of moral philosophy, and the Benthamite school of moral philosophy provided a theory of individual choice that came to be widely accepted. But today individual choice is undeniably part of the subject matter of psychology. At the same time many economic texts written during the past decade, like their predecessors, offer as an "explanation" of consumer demand a purportedly general theory of individual choice that is obviously a refinement of Bentham's felicific calculus. It goes without saying that as a general theory it has no standing whatever among modern psychologists. Logically the economists who adhere to it should feel embarassed, but somehow they do not seem to.

2. THE HISTORICAL RELATIVITY OF ECONOMIC TRUTHS

Perhaps the most important and most far-reaching implication of the view that economics should be approached as an evolutionary science is the implication of the historical relativity of economic truths, the implication that the only economic propositions that can be said to be scientifically valid are historical truths. Every economic generalization that has scientific validity must be limited in its applicability to a specific historical period or to specific historical periods and to a specific culture or to specific cultures; i.e., it must refer to a particular society or societies.

---

cept of equilibrium there used is an illustration of a use that is neither normative nor static. Since many economists have insisted on a static interpretation of the *General Theory*, I may say I mean the interpretation Paul Samuelson gave it in his 1939 "Interactions" article. See *Readings in Business Cycle Theory* (Philadelphia, 1944), pp. 261 ff., where this article is reprinted.

Scope and Method of Economics

But this implication has a corollary relating to the nature of propositions that have scientific validity. Those who agree with Veblen in regard to the historical relativity of economics agree also that any scientifically valid descriptive economic generalization must be empirically definite. This means there should be facts relating to the communities or societies to which the generalization refers that support it and facts relating to other communities—possibly in some cases to nonhuman primate communities—that make the generalization inapplicable to them.

No doubt there are still a good many economists who are not prepared in such a thoroughgoing sense to give up the idea of economics as a deductive science conceived in the image of Euclid, and who would like to think of "the law of diminishing returns" or the proposition that the first derivative of an indifference curve is negative, the second positive, as a universal, timeless truth. But these economists will probably have to concede that neither the so-called law nor the indifference curve proposition is empirically definite in the sense just proposed. And it may be added that, when economics is conceived as a social science concerned with the group behavior of human beings, neither proposition is a proposition in economics. There are various senses for diminishing returns. In the sense in which universal validity can plausibly be claimed for this "law" it would appear to be a proposition in physical science. But I am not aware that any physical scientist has claimed it to be a physical law. As for the indifference map proposition I have just pointed out that it belongs to the field of psychology.

If the idea of the historical relativity of economic truths has not yet come to be generally accepted, I think it is reasonable to suppose that it is in process of becoming so.

3. THE NEED FOR A SENSE OF CULTURAL PERSPECTIVE

Another important implication of Veblen's contention that economics ought to be an evolutionary science is that an economist should have a sense of cultural perspective. This means that he should recognize that the scheme of values characterizing the cultural situation in which he happens to find himself has been preceded by other quite different and equally valid schemes of values and that there is reason to expect that it will be succeeded by still other equally valid schemes of values, and also that there are other equally valid schemes in other present-day cultures.

Veblen felt that many of his contemporaries lacked such a cultural perspective, that they treated economics not as an evolutionary science but as what he called "bourgeois homiletics." Thus he charged both J. B. Clark and G. Schmoller with a lack of perspective, because each of them naïvely accepted the righteousness or naturalness of the cultural situation prevailing at the time in his native land.

On the positive side the sense of cultural perspective would require adequate recognition of institutional facts in any explanation of the way an economy operates. For example, the distribution of income among factors of production cannot be adequately understood merely in terms of the hypostatized properties of a production function. "The productivity of labor, or of any conceivable factor in industry, is an imputed productivity—imputed on grounds of convention afforded by institutions that have grown up in the course of technological development." [7]

Again the sense of cultural perspective would rule out "the 'conjectural history' that plays so large a part in the classical treatment of economic institutions," e.g., the still prevalent account of the origin of trade that assumes it developed out of a putative barter stage anachronistically assumed to have the scheme of values characteristic of a society in which internal trade has already come to be a pervasive fact.[8] Veblen did not attempt a rounded scientific historical account of the origin of trade, but he did give us an indicative suggestion as to how trade might have arisen out of a prior cultural situation in which the scheme of values was definitely not of a bourgeois character. He suggested a predatory stage of culture in which the accumulation of booty was the basis of award of the highest popular esteem, and a process of evolution from this stage into one in which pecuniary employments became the means of entry into the leisure class.[9] My present concern is not to affirm the historical accuracy of

[7] T. Veblen, *The Instinct of Workmanship* (New York, 1914), p. 146.

[8] *Place of Science*, pp. 65–66. Another illustration of "conjectural history" that is still widely accepted is Adam Smith's account of the origin of money. Cf. the author's *A Study of Moneyflows in the United States* (New York, 1952), pp. 215–216.

[9] T. Veblen, *The Theory of the Leisure Class* (New York, 1899), chs. ii, ix.

Scope and Method of Economics

this hypothesis—presumably a rounded scientific historical account would have to be a good deal more specific about places and about approximate dates than Veblen was. My present point is only that such an historical account of the genesis of the institution of trade would have to trace a process of evolution from a nontrade cultural scheme of values to the kind of scheme we have in cultures in which trade is a pervasive fact, and that Veblen's hypothesis involves a process of evolution of this sort.

4. EXPLANATION, CAUSATION, AND GENETIC PROCESS

In tracing the development of the higher learning Veblen identifies three ways in which men have sought to account for the facts of the world in which they lived. In the Middle Ages the scholastics, construing the facts on the assumption of a superpersonal, overruling authority conceived in the image of man, felt that to explain anything one must find a sufficient reason for it. On this view a law of nature is a divine decree and explaining it means adequately demonstrating the reason for it. But presently, under the cultural impact of the handicraft technology, men came to think not in terms of authoritative divine decrees, but in terms of the workmanship of Nature as a consummately skillful master craftsman.[10] Hence men came to seek an understanding of any fact of nature in terms of the efficient cause of it rather than the sufficient reason for it, in terms of an effect as a product and its cause as the event or action that produced it. More recently, under the influence of the machine technology, Veblen held that an "unteleological, mechanistic conception" of "a genetic process of cumulative change" had come to replace the more anthropomorphic concept of efficient cause.[11]

Veblen emphasized that the more archaic ways of thinking tended

---

[10] See, for example, *Instinct of Workmanship*, pp. 258 ff., 292, and *Place of Science*, pp. 11 ff.

[11] *Instinct of Workmanship*, pp. 326–327. But Veblen insisted that science still retained a definite amount of anthropomorphism. In particular he cited the bias against the idea of "action at a distance." See his famous comment that "Only the 'occult' and 'Christian' 'Sciences' . . . take recourse to 'absent treatment'" (*Place of Science*, p. 36). [For an extended discussion of this question, see Article 13 below by Philip Morrison.—EDITOR]

to survive longer in those branches of learning that were less closely involved with modern technology and in economics in particular. Thus the wide-spread insistence—then and even now—on explaining consumer demand and saving and labor supply in terms of the rational behavior of individuals, each maximizing his own utility, is an insistence that the only satisfactory way to account for human conduct is to find a sufficient reason for it.[12] Anyone who has much appreciation of the nature of present-day physical and biological science would want a much more modern approach. And among other things such an approach would surely concern itself with the cumulative process by which individuals' tastes have come to be what they are instead of merely taking these tastes as givens, as modern versions of the felicific calculus do.

Veblen made it clear that a scientific theory of consumer behavior would deal with tastes genetically. Indeed he offered a genetic hypothesis for the development of pecuniary canons of taste and for the irksomeness of humilific labor. Since our present concern is methodological, we need not attempt to pass on its empirical validity: we need only note its general nature. It is historical in that it traces an evolutionary process through time and within various geographical areas, even if the times and places are not very precisely specified. And the tracing runs in terms of a process of cumulative change and of a natural selection through the impacts of value standards and habits of thought on one another. Further, the genetic process it traces is a phylogenetic—not an ontogenetic—process; it is a process of change in the scheme of values prevalent in a community, not a change in the scheme of values of an individual human being. It is concerned with the kinds of choices consumers in a late Victorian community were making. It provides a theory or at least part of a theory of the market preference behavior of such a group (i.e., of the community). But this theory does not consist of an analysis of group demand into the demands of the individuals that compose it; it is a sociogenetic theory.

[12] *Place of Science*, pp. 235–237. His comment is on marginal utility theory, but of course it applies equally to indifference analysis. It may be added that this kind of explanation of individual choices lacks empirical definiteness in a sense slightly different from that proposed above. It is a theory that fits the way people have behaved after the fact, but it fits any hypothetical past behavior that did not actually take place equally well.

Scope and Method of Economics

In all these respects what Veblen proposes is surely an account of the kind economists ought to aim to give for the scheme of values in say the present-day United States that finds expression in household budget behavior; i.e., it is an account that conforms to the canons of modern science. But of course it is only a partial account, for instead of tracing the development of the standard of living it traces only the impacts of the institution of the leisure class on this standard.[13] Nonetheless, for our methodological purpose it is very instructive.

According to the neoclassical tradition consumer demand, saving, and labor supply are explained in terms of the rational, utility-maximizing behavior of individual consumers, savers, and laborers; business demands and supplies, in terms of the rational profit-maximizing behavior of individual entrepreneurs. Insisting on a profit-maximizing explanation, like insisting on a utility-maximizing explanation, means insisting on a sufficient reason approach. So also does writing a treatise on theory that says little or nothing about government demand and taxation (as several intermediate theory texts still do) because no comparable rationalization seems to fit the conduct of the affairs of government.

Veblen did not say explicitly that it becomes part of the job of economists, when they undertake to treat economics as an evolutionary science, to provide a genetic account of the development of government functions and expenditure requirements and of the tax structure. But certainly it is. As for business behavior, Veblen did not rule out profit-maximization.[14] But he did seek to provide a genetic account of the development of business enterprise as an institution, and he concerned himself with other aspects of business management beside profit-maximizing, e.g., with what he regarded as the increasingly remote contact of the businessman with the industrial and technological facts of his business.[15] But in addition to those aspects of business management he dealt with there are many that seem to call for a genetic approach rather than a rationalization in terms of

---

[13] Veblen did something also toward tracing the impacts of the machine technology on the standard of living. See T. Veblen, *The Theory of Business Enterprise* (New York, 1904), pp. 324 ff., 356 ff.; also *Instinct of Workmanship*, pp. 312 ff., where he points out that "Invention is the mother of necessity."

[14] "The business man's object is to get the largest aggregate gain from his business" (*Theory of Business Enterprise*, p. 93).

[15] *Instinct of Workmanship*, pp. 222 ff.

Morris A. Copeland

the maximizing of profits, e.g., the dividend policy of corporations (to which admittedly this type of rationalization does not apply). Also a genetic approach would seem to be needed to understand how the present mores of the accounting profession that define business profit and cost have come to be what they are.[16]

Veblen devoted a good deal of his attention to the evolution of the state of the industrial arts—a state which economists had not infrequently taken as given. In this connection he noted that, while currently most decisions to introduce technological changes are business decisions, this has by no means always been the case. Also he noted that, while currently there is a good deal of interest in inventing technological improvements, this was distinctly not so in what he termed savage cultures. But undoubtedly much the most significant feature of his account of the evolution of technology was his hypothesis of the merits of cultural borrowing.[17] Since this hypothesis is considered somewhat extensively elsewhere in this volume it may suffice here simply to mention it by way of underscoring the proposition that Veblen's accounts of sociogenetic processes are never mere historical narratives. He always endeavored to include an hypothesis or hypotheses in his account of such a process.

If one were to judge Veblen's account of the evolution of the leisure class or of technology in terms of the number of pages concerned with such matters one would doubtless be constrained to conclude that in both cases he leaned heavily on an hypothesis that involves differences in the hereditary complements of the psychological traits of different races and, in particular, differences in the vigor of such traits as the instincts of workmanship and of pugnacity. But this does not appear to be the case, and fortunately not, for interpretations of cultural evolution that run in these terms have not stood up well under the criticisms to which they have been subjected. Curiously, despite all that Veblen has to say about instincts and hereditary biases and propensities, his sociogenetic accounts do not seem to need them. In general they would apparently not suffer significantly if all refer-

[16] Veblen touches on this matter only incidentally, e.g., *Theory of Business Enterprise*, p. 155.

[17] See, for example, T. Veblen, *Imperial Germany and the Industrial Revolution* (New York, 1915), pp. 241 ff. [For extended discussions of this point see Articles 14, 15, and 16 below by Myron W. Watkins, Carter Goodrich, and Douglas F. Dowd.—EDITOR]

Scope and Method of Economics

ences to dolichocephalic blonds and brachycephalic brunettes were to be deleted. Essentially his sociogenetic accounts are stated in terms of a process of natural selection among institutions and other culture traits that results from the impacts of these culture traits on one another.

Veblen thought of the machine industry as undermining and requiring the rejection of the somewhat anthropomorphic concept of efficient cause, and of the concept of a genetic process of cumulative change as being the principal replacement for it. This view seems to have biased, indeed to have narrowed, the scope of his economic inquiries. A very large part of his work is concerned with such processes, with cultural evolution and with his theory of modern welfare which runs in these terms.[18] Also, as I understand him, he ruled out of his inquiries as not in accord with his conception of a scientific approach —i.e., not amenable to a genetic approach—much of the field now known as microeconomics.

For Veblen the prime example of a genetic process of cumulative change apparently was the evolution of the species of living organisms, although he doubtless had in mind other examples as well, particularly the ontogenies of various species of plants and animals and the genetic processes with which astrophysics is concerned. Now the obvious analogue of the phylogenetic process of the evolution of species in the field of social science is cultural evolution, and Veblen thought economists should be extensively concerned with this analogue. When it comes to dealing with things like the family system that change slowly, this means taking a very long-run view, a view that deals in eras that last for centuries. Hence a good deal of the time Veblen was concerned with periods such as the era of handicraft. It is true he did not confine himself to this very long-run view. But his genetic process concept meant a bias also in the type of shorter-run inquiries he undertook. The concept fits topics like the cultural incidence of the machine industry. He thought of the prevalence of mechanical processes as affecting everyone's ways of thinking and so leading to broad institutional changes. But he thought also that for some classes of the population the influence was particularly strong—for manual workers, engineers, and physical scientists. This extra-strong influence was a part of his hypothesis regarding the

[18] *Theory of Business Enterprise*, ch. vii.

development of trade unions,[19] also of his hypothesis regarding the growth of the kind of social unrest that includes agitation for revolutionary social reform.[20]

Again Veblen's concept of a genetic process of cumulative change fits the business cycle. Indeed one of his most ingenious contributions was conceiving the business cycle as just such a process, or rather as a concatenation of such processes, with prosperity tending to improve for a time but presently generating a crisis, a crisis resolving itself into depression, and depression tending to perpetuate itself until some outside influence converts it into prosperity.[21]

Veblen's analysis of the business cycle is about the only portion of his work that deals at all extensively with a topic economists in the neoclassical tradition would currently regard as a part of economic theory.

In general it is surely unfair to assume that any recent economist's notion of the scope of the subject is no broader than the parts of the field he has himself cultivated. And certainly Veblen never pretended to a balanced coverage of economics. Nonetheless, I think some significance attaches to the fact that he neglected so much of what is commonly regarded as the field of economic theory. I think his neglect helps to support the view that he would rule out most of microeconomics as unscientific. I believe time will prove him right in ruling out the search for sufficient reasons, though wrong in ruling out practically all the rest of microeconomics too, if this is what he meant.

But his view of the scope of economics must have been somewhat broader than the area covered by his own writings. It is significant that in discussing the cultural influence of the machine industry Veblen emphasized that, partly because of this influence, partly because of the influence of the price system, "modern science at large takes to the use of statistical methods." [22] It is true that he did not urge explicitly that economics should be a statistical as well as an evolutionary science. But he seems to have exerted a real push in this direction. Several of those who drew most heavily on Veblen for inspiration have certainly emphasized the statistical approach, notably Wesley Mitchell and Walter Stewart.

[19] *Theory of Business Enterprise*, pp. 327 ff.   [20] *Idem*, pp. 336 ff.
[21] *Idem*, ch. vii. Veblen was something of a secular stagnationist.
[22] *Instinct of Workmanship*, p. 322.

Scope and Method of Economics

Perhaps it should be suggested at this point that if Veblen had given more explicit attention to the potential significance of statistics for economics he would almost certainly have had to broaden his concept of modern scientific method so as to include more than his genetic processes of cumulative change under the heading of scientific hypotheses.

5. PUBLIC POLICY

Veblen seems to have held, like many economists who were less disposed than he to deviate from the classical tradition, that policy judgments have no place in a scientific inquiry.[23] Like them, too, he was conspicuously unsuccessful in excluding such judgments from his economic inquiries.

One can gather the general outline of the kind of broad economic policy he was disposed to approve from *The Engineers and the Price System*.[24] This policy would entail avoiding "virtually all unemployment of serviceable equipment and manpower on the one hand, and all local and seasonal scarcity on the other." It would mean eliminating all sorts of wasteful and obstructive practices inherent "in the businesslike control of industry" (competitive sales effort is cited by way of illustration). And it would involve the abolition of absentee ownership, i.e., the abolition of intangible properties and of business proprietorship net worths as sources of individual income and as a basis for the "businesslike control of industry." But our present interest is not primarily in these particular policy propositions. Primarily it is that one does not have to probe far to find policy implications in Veblen's writings.

Public policy implications enter them at other points, too, and in ways that are quite significant parts of Veblen's methodological contribution. Much of his examination of the American economy of his day consists of analyses of various forms of business activities that are concerned with "making money" but that contribute somewhat un-

[23] *Place of Science*, pp. 19–20. But see my comment on the place of normative judgments in biological (including anthropological) science in the *American Economic Review*, March 1931, pp. 68–69.
[24] (New York, 1921). See ch. vi, "A Memorandum on a Practicable Soviet of Technicians," especially pp. 144, 152–154, 156–160.

certainly to "making goods,"[25] and may even obstruct the processes of production. Several of these analyses are interesting anticipations of later developments.

One such analysis dealt with business price policy. He made it clear that he thought this is in general a kind of monopoly policy and that the usual situation is one "where the monopoly is less strict, where there are competitors."[26] His theory of monopolistic competition included an examination of selling cost as different from production cost and as largely competitive in nature.[27]

Several of Veblen's analyses that involve public policy implications had to do with what has come to be known as corporation finance.[28] In fact, they constitute one of the earliest attempts to deal analytically with this subject. Possibly his pioneering work in this area would have been more generally recognized had it not been for the fact that he emphasized financial operations and practices that involved making a good deal of money without contributing much to making goods, whereas the conventional treatment of corporation finance has tended to play down these aspects of the subject.

Although an analysis of a situation in which someone can make money without a significant positive contribution to production carries an inescapable public policy implication, Veblen seems to have thought that it was quite proper to include such analyses in an economic inquiry. Presumably he thought so because such analyses seem capable of being carried out on an objective basis. Possibly Veblen did not always succeed in maintaining his objectivity when he made them. But I think he was right about the possibility of making them objectively, and right in regarding them as an important part of the economist's job.

Another type of economic analysis involving policy implications in which Veblen was something of a pioneer has to do with the legal system and the contrast betwen the *de jure* freedom of the individual worker to contract for employment and the *de facto* coercion imposed by the limited alternatives open to him.[29] An interesting feature of

[25] The distinction between making goods and making money is Veblen's, but the language is Wesley Mitchell's.
[26] *Theory of Business Enterprise*, p. 54.   [27] *Idem*, pp. 55 ff.
[28] Especially *idem*, pp. 35 ff., 89 ff., and ch. v. [See Article 11 below by Joel Dirlam.—EDITOR]
[29] *Theory of Business Enterprise*, pp. 277 ff.

Scope and Method of Economics

Veblen's analysis of this contrast is the suggestion that the *de facto* situation had, up to the time of his writing, made more impression on juries than on the higher courts.

Still another way in which policy considerations entered into Veblen's investigations is illustrated by his *An Inquiry into the Nature of Peace and the Terms of Its Perpetuation*. In this inquiry he followed somewhat the procedure advocated by the elder Keynes.[30] That is, he started (despite his assumption of an instinct of pugnacity) with the policy premise that social conflicts—class conflicts as well as international conflicts—ought, if possible, to be avoided. Given this premise, the question of the prospects for peace and of the means of attaining it can be investigated objectively, or, as J. N. Keynes put it, as a part of political economy in the sense of a positive science. Much of Veblen's inquiry is concerned with the genetic processes leading to the development of great powers, both those powers that are "bent in effect on a disturbance of the peace" and those powers that "will fight on provocation"; most of the rest of the inquiry with speculation about possible and probable further developments on the basis of the then-current characteristics of these powers.

This method of separating "scientific" economic inquiry from ethical "nonscientific" inquiry involves a kind of dilemma. On the one hand, the separation may be effected through a genuine division of academic labor; i.e., the two inquiries may be conducted by different persons. In this case the economist becomes a kind of academic helot. On the other hand, the separation may be accomplished by a selection of the premise which defines the field of inquiry that is made by the economist himself. In this case, if he selects a policy premise to which many economists subscribe—say, avoiding wars or minimizing general unemployment—a significant enlargement of the policy inquiries that fall within the scope of economics may result, and the separation becomes mainly a matter of a clear labeling of the policy premise. Veblen took the second horn of this dilemma.

[30] T. Veblen, *An Inquiry into the Nature of Peace and the Terms of Its Perpetuation* (New York, 1917); J. N. Keynes, *Scope and Method of Political Economy* (London, 1890), ch. ii, secs. 4, 5, and Note B.

Morris A. Copeland

6. THE SCOPE OF ECONOMICS

Veblen did not say just what he thought the scope of economics should be. His concern with questions of the cultural incidence of economic institutions like the machine industry and the leisure class gave him a grand disregard of boundaries within the field of social science. Thus we find him discussing recent changes in a wide variety of our culture traits including religion, art, higher education, patriotism, gambling institutions, athletic events, styles in dress, the status of woman, and so on. No doubt the case for encouraging inquiries that cut across conventional subject-matter dividing lines in the way Veblen did is a strong one. And it may well be that we have developed a division of academic labor in the social sciences that is too minute. But some division of this field, even some division within the field of economics, clearly seems advisable.

It would, I take it, be quite consistent with Veblen's view to think of economics as marked off from the other social sciences that devote much of their attention to so-called industrialized societies on the basis of the institutions which are the economist's primary concern. Presumably he is primarily concerned with economic institutions such as technology, the division of labor, the price system, trade, money, the income and money circuit, the wage system, and property. Presumably, too, if the scope of economics is defined in this fashion, there will be primitive societies in which economic and other institutions are not clearly differentiated, societies that are mainly subjects of study for the general anthropologist and that the economist *as* economist will not deal with very extensively.

On Veblen's view, then, economists should concern themselves with economic institutions and closely related culture traits, probably with all important economic institutions and traits to be found anywhere in the world today apart from the relatively few remaining communities that have had little contact with modern industrialism. A major item in the task of economists should be to seek to understand each such institution or trait in terms of the genetic process of cumulative change by which it has come to be what it is. No doubt, too, economists should interest themselves in comparisons between similar institutions and similar institutional developments in different societies.

Scope and Method of Economics

Again on Veblen's view economists should engage in analyses involving various public policy questions—should concern themselves with the ways in which the pecuniary incentives in an economy encourage activities deemed not to be in the public interest, with the legal institutions which are supposed to provide just relations between individuals and the extent to which in fact they do so, with policy objectives on which there is something like a consensus and with the means by which they might be carried out as well as the prospects that these means may be forthcoming.

But there are other types of inquiry which economists should undertake, too. Some of these Veblen seems to have felt were merely descriptive and so not sufficiently theoretical to be called scientific: mere descriptions of things as they are, mere correlations between variables that seem to move together, mere narratives of the steps by which things have come to be what they are, mere statistical measurements of economic magnitudes, mere statistical economic time series. Other inquiries economists should engage in have to do with the way an economy operates or the way particular institutions or organizations in it operate. As I have noted, Veblen considered and made an important contribution to the theory of business cycles. But there are many other operational questions that should be investigated; presumably he would have included some, but not all, of these. It is not clear, for example, that he would have thought much attention should be paid to the way noncumulative changes in the supply and demand conditions in an industry influence the industry's prices and the income originating in it. Certainly studying such influences is an important part of the economist's job. Still other inquiries that are parts of that job relate to public policy questions. Thus one can study the genesis of public policies as well as of institutional structures. And while technically most of the other subjects economists should be concerned with that involve public policy questions could be considered as special cases of the types of inquiries noted above, there are a substantial number that these do not obviously suggest, e.g., public policy questions relating to taxation, to utility rates, to collective bargaining in the labor market, to international aid, to social security, to farm prices, to mergers.

If the push that Veblen gave to economics was not a particularly well-balanced push, it was nonetheless a signally important push for-

Morris A. Copeland

ward. And there is good reason to think that, along with the recently widened knowledge of quite different present-day economic systems, we are getting a wider cultural perspective that will give a strong reinforcement to that push. It may well turn out that much the most important and most lasting of Veblen's contributions to economics is the proposition that economics ought to become an evolutionary science in fullest sense of what he intended by these words.

A POSTSCRIPT ON VEBLEN'S AUDIENCE

The primary corollary of the proposition that economics should be an evolutionary science is that the applicability of all economic theories should be restricted in respect to time and place. The applicability of Veblen's *Theory of the Leisure Class* is so restricted. One who reads it today is apt to think of changes in the forms of conspicuous leisure that have become prominent since he propounded it.

One of these is ideological. A person who is very securely a member of the leisure class and who in his pursuit of the higher learning has encountered heterodox socioeconomic philosophies may embrace leftist, even subversive ideas. It is not suggested that he is likely to do so with the intent of demonstrating the security of his leisure-class status, only that his doing so does have this effect. And since it does, embracing such ideas is clearly a form of conspicuous leisure. Apparently it is a form that has become prominent since 1899.

Most of Veblen's earlier articles appeared in the *Journal of Political Economy,* the *Quarterly Journal of Economics,* and the *American Journal of Sociology;* most of his later articles in the *New Republic,* the *Dial,* and the *Freeman.* There was a significant change between Veblen's earlier works and his works in the twenties in respect to the audience to which he addressed himself. His earlier works were addressed to his fellow professional economists and to other social scientists. His later works were of a more popular nature; some of them seem to have been written mainly for a group of members of the vicarious leisure class that had come to be among his most ardent admirers in the twenties, a group of lady lecture goers who had an amateur interest in social reform.

No doubt this group of admirers found Veblen's somewhat leftish social philosophy intriguing; embracing it was for them a form of

Scope and Method of Economics

conspicuous leisure. No doubt, too, they were attracted by his extensive vocabulary and the niceties of his diction; only one with sufficient leisure to be somewhat steeped in the higher learning could appreciate Veblenese.

But Veblen's theory of the cultural incidence of the machine industry assumed that radical social philosophies would appeal chiefly to manual workers, engineers, and physical scientists. No doubt he was right in thinking that the practice of a pecuniary employment inculcated a firm belief in the existing order. But there is no reason to think the inculcation extended to other members of the family; although not directly exposed to the machine industry, they might absorb some of its influence. Hence a wife or daughter—sometimes even a son—might find embracing pinkish ideas an enticing way to perform her—or his—vicarious leisure.

But the shift in the audience to which Veblen addressed himself surely indicates too that economists in the twenties were less interested in what he had to say than economists a quarter-century earlier had been. His earlier appeal was to colleagues many of whom had studied in Germany and had thereby gained something in the way of cultural perspective. The decline in interest in Veblen's ideas during the later years of his life is, I think, attributable at least in part to a temporary decline in cultural perspective due to the comparative lack of contacts of American economists outside the English-speaking world, a situation from which we have only recently begun to recover.

[LAWRENCE NABERS]

6

Veblen's Critique of the Orthodox Economic Tradition

VEBLEN appeared in a number of roles with more or less success: historian, ethnologist, sociologist, political scientist, philosopher, professional cynic, seer, and social reformer, the last in spite of numerous disclaimers. But he was pre-eminently an economist by training and inclination, as the biographical details make clear. A large share of his work, which for purposes of academic administration is catalogued under other headings, Veblen regarded as an integral part of his economic analysis. These classificatory subtleties, he felt, are a largely useless and generally misleading heritage of the past. In speaking of the last and most complete statement of his economic thought, Veblen indicates that "it makes little use of the received theories of Political Economy; not as departing from the received theories or discrediting them, but because the inquiry is concerned chiefly with economic forces and phenomena which are of later date than the received doctrines."[1] His attitude by this time was one of unconcern with and disregard for conventional analysis.

This unconcern with conventional economic categories had its origin

---

[1] T. Veblen, *Absentee Ownership and Business Enterprise in Recent Times* (New York: Viking, 1954), pref. The references to Veblen's writing are only to representative passages. He was enormously repetitive and more than occasionally contradictory. One of Veblen's favorite authorities in the later work was the earlier Veblen.

in a general philosophical position, as we shall presently see. But more important it sprang from a critical analysis of "received doctrine" during the formative period of his own work. Regardless of the central topic under discussion, he sooner or later asks the question: "What are the implications of this for the accepted body of economic analysis?" It is possible, therefore, without too much distortion to reconstruct Veblen's version of the orthodox economic analysis of his day and his alternatives to that analysis.

Veblen's critique was developed during the period when the formal, if not greatly substantive, changes in economic doctrine after the deceptively named "marginalist revolution" were being integrated into economic thought. The decline of the classical modes of analysis following John Stuart Mill had occurred for two principal reasons: first, the labor theory of value was inadequate in providing a consistent basis for the problems of pricing, allocation, and efficiency, which were becoming increasingly important once the end of the period of rapid economic growth was in sight; and second, the radical implications of a theory of distribution based on the labor theory of value were clear by this time even to those who had not read Marx.

The new orthodoxy [2] accepted in large measure the existing state of affairs; nor did any significantly new policies or attitudes toward business, the state, the position of individuals in the economy, or the apodictic certainty of progress emerge. Its innovations were the development of a theory of distribution, which for a while seemed to give more logical support to the existing status than was possible before, and a method of demonstrating that under certain circumstances, which were in large measure thought to obtain in the real world, the economy would operate with the greatest attainable efficiency.

Veblen saw with clarity the continuity of the body of received doctrine with the past. His central thesis is that though it may have had some operational significance (in his own term, serviceability) in the eighteenth and early nineteenth centuries, economic conditions had changed so radically that it had little meaning by his time. That

---

[2] The term neoclassical is generally used. Both terms will, however, be used here interchangeably, although the "neo" should be underemphasized, for the changes, as mentioned, are largely formal or, to err on the side of caution, were largely formal in the period of the development of Veblen's critique.

Critique of Orthodox Economics

is to say, orthodox economics was not serviceable either as an explanation of the operation of the economic mechanism or as a guide for policies conducive to the welfare of the population. Its function, he felt, was to provide a rationale for current business practices, even though those practices were seldom of the kind contemplated by the prevailing economic doctrines.

The purpose of this essay, then, is to examine Veblen's reconstruction of orthodox economic analysis and to set forth his alternatives. If we take the corpus of contemporary economic analysis in its entirety, it would be possible to find largely consistent positions on the major theoretical and practical issues. But most of the issues can be grouped around the analysis of value, distribution, and price-allocation. We shall confine ourselves to these problems.

I

Veblen remarks that "Adam Smith was a creature of his own time, and what he has to say applies to the state of things *as he saw them*." [3] The remark is universally true of all economists, or for that matter of everyone who must look outside himself for some part of the "stimulus to action." Without becoming entangled in the problems of *Wissensoziologie*, let us say that individuals see different things in the same ostensible fact situation. Those differences, Veblen argues, can be explained in terms of the intellectual and cultural heritage of the observers. In the social sciences this heritage leads most honest workers to come up with traditional answers "due to the fact that their intellectual horizon is bounded by the same limits of commonplace insight and preconceptions as are the prevailing opinions of the conservative middle class." [4] In other words, the limitations lead to seeing some facts and not others, and those facts seen are interpreted or given meaning in a context acquired independently of the facts. It is not necessary to argue that Veblen somehow escaped, that he was the aloof, freely poised intellect. His vision was simply different, and we may use his own test for the adequacy of the vision, its service-

[3] T. Veblen, *The Vested Interests and the Common Man* (New York: Viking, 1946), p. 27 (italics mine).

[4] T. Veblen, *The Higher Learning in America* (Stanford, Calif.: Academic Reprints, 1954), p. 186.

ability. It is to these visions of what Josiah Royce has called "the world of the outside order" that we must turn in understanding the source of the differences between Veblen and the orthodox tradition.

The dominant attitude toward the individual was developed during the formative period of modern capitalism. The intellectual origins of these ideas are to be found in the Protestant Reformation and were incorporated into economic thought through the work of the Philosophical Radicals. Their program was based on Utilitarianism and its applications to psychology and logic, plus a program for reform emphasizing free trade, legal changes strengthening property and individual rights, decreased individual supervision by the state in both personal and economic matters, and in general the program of *laissez faire*.[5] The corpus of orthodox economic thought had not by Veblen's time progressed far from the Philosophical Radicals either in terms of policy or philosophy.

Talcott Parsons has characterized the philosophical system of utilitarianism as involving the fourfold tenets of empiricism, atomism, rationality, and the randomness of ends.[6] The last three are important for our purposes. Each individual is conceived of as an independent atom pursuing in a rational fashion ends which have meaning only in terms of himself. There is a presumed lack of necessary uniformity in the distribution of those ends. The rules of rational behavior are given by Bentham's hedonistic calculus. This approach in its purest Benthamite trappings was taken without qualification as late as the last quarter of the nineteenth century. W. Stanley Jevons, after stating that his own theory "is entirely based on a calculus of pleasure and pain," continued to define that calculus, quoting Bentham, in terms of its intensity, duration, certainty, propinquity, fecundity, and so on.[7] Few of Jevons' contemporaries were so unqualified in their use of the language of utilitarianism, but the attitude remained the same, for ultimately the most consistent justification of individualistic *laissez faire* rests on such grounds.

In the economic theory of the nineteenth century the exchange problem took logical priority over production. That is, individuals

[5] Elie Halévy, *The Growth of Philosophical Radicalism*, trans. Mary Morris (London: Faber and Faber, 1934), ch. i.
[6] *The Structure of Social Action* (Glencoe, Ill.: Free Press, 1949), pp. 58 ff.
[7] *The Theory of Political Economy* (4th ed.; London: Macmillan, 1911), pp. 23 ff.

Critique of Orthodox Economics

were thought to be engaged in the production of services or commodities involving physical pain-costs up to the point where the last unit of pain-cost was equal to the pleasure-return from exchange. These pleasures and pains were evaluated in terms of the hedonistic calculus.

Since all this was very abstract, it required empirical content. The pain of the last unit of labor was equated to the pleasure equivalent of the wage, thus securing the maximum net pleasure-return; this principle served as the point of departure for the discussion of wages and the labor market. Businessmen were thought of as incurring costs (not suffering pains except in the sense of foregoing pleasures) in acquiring or producing commodities for sale up to the point where the last unit of foregone-pleasure-cost is equated to pleasure-returns, thus securing the maximum net returns. After much theoretical investigation the theory of cost and production and, in time, a theory of distribution was derived from this principle. Throughout it was assumed that individuals continue to act in a rational fashion, that is, in a manner resulting in the greatest amount of pleasure (net wage or profit).

The strategic individual in the process was the businessman—in this matter alone Veblen would not have disagreed.[8] The facts of business enterprise made this inevitably so, and the neoclassical theorists were willing in large measure to accept it as given without inquiring too far into the reasons. The attitude generally expressed is that the businessman is no different in the rationale of self-seeking than anyone else. He is differentiated from other individuals simply because of his greater skill and ability in the complex calculations involving maximum pleasure-profit positions. These calculations lead simply to a recognition of the maximization conditions already inherent in the data. Alfred Marshall, Veblen's great orthodox contemporary, has put the matter thus:

> There is no breach of continuity as we ascend from the unskilled labourer to the skilled, thence to the foreman to the head of a department, to the general manager of a large business paid partly by a share of the profits, to the junior partner, and lastly to the head partner of a large private business: and in a joint-stock company there is even somewhat of an anti-climax when we pass from the directors to the ordinary shareholders, who undertake the

[8] T. Veblen, *The Theory of Business Enterprise* (New York: Scribner, 1904), p. 4.

chief ultimate risks of the business. Nevertheless business undertakers are to a certain extent a class apart.

For while it is through their conscious agency that the principle of substitution chiefly works in balancing one factor of production against another; with regard to them it has no other agency than the indirect influence of their own competition.[9]

The businessman was conceived of as the organizer of the industrial process, as the investor and innovator, whose constant concern was with the rational process of profit-pleasure maximization. The firm was an extension of the businessman. Like him it was an independent, self-sustaining unit producing commodities the same as those produced by a large number of other firms, each completely independent just as every other individual in the utilitarian universe. The relationship among those independent atoms (individuals and firms) was designated with considerable looseness as competitive. "A man competes freely when he is pursuing a course, which without entering into any combination with others he has deliberately selected as that which is likely to be of greatest material advantage to himself."[10] Under these rules it becomes possible to demonstrate with fairly rigorous logic, given large numbers of individuals and firms and the homogeneous product implied by the atomistic preconceptions, that everyone will obtain the greatest possible amount of net utility or profit. The belief in the attainment of the greatest possible benefit for all by the simple and obvious system of natural liberty was lifted from the realm of faith and enshrined with due qualifications as a scientific *quod erat demonstrandum*. This vision of a competitive economy is used in a number of different ways by the neoclassical economists: First, competition was held to be the normal case, that is, the one most frequently encountered in the real world; departures were treated as temporary aberrations. Second, since competition was the normative case, departures were socially undesirable and should be dealt with by legal or legislative means. Third, competition defined

[9] Alfred Marshall, *Principles of Economics* (8th ed.; London: Macmillan, 1946), p. 663. It is perhaps unfair to refer to Marshall in the context of the stereotype of neoclassical economics being developed. He was, as is well known, cautious and not at all given to the unqualified simplifications typical of the orthodox epigoni. However, the passage is typical.

[10] Alfred Marshall, *Economics of Industry* (2nd ed.; London: Macmillan, 1881), p. vi.

Critique of Orthodox Economics

the general direction in which the economy tended as an historical generalization.[11] With whatever particular qualification necessary in the case of an individual writer, this characterization of the operation of the economy would probably have been accepted as fair by the orthodox economists of Veblen's time. In any event this is the vision of the world attributed to them by Veblen.

Veblen would have none of the orthodox view except their attitude toward the strategic importance of the businessman (but with a different emphasis). Their treatment of the individual and his behavior evoked some of Veblen's finest satire. The view of man as a "lightning calculator of pleasures and pains, who oscillates like a homogeneous globule of desire of happiness under the impulse of stimuli that shift him about the area but leave him intact"[12] was far from what Veblen held to be the case; nor could a society survive in which decisions were so made, for in the lack of development of patterns of "conventional relations . . . it is not conceivable that the institutional fabric would last over night."[13]

For our purposes it is unnecessary to reconstruct in any detail the complex social psychology that Veblen developed with varying emphasis throughout his writings. Briefly, man may be taken as a cultural phenomenon. All he knows, his patterns of life and belief, are aspects of his cultural heritage. "Each move . . . is necessarily made by individuals immersed in the community and exposed to the discipline of group life as it runs in the community, since all life is necessarily group life. The phenomena of human life occur only in this form."[14] But Veblen was no cultural determinist in the strict sense. The individual was an active, creative element in his environment. "He is in an eminent sense an intelligent agent. By selective necessity he is endowed with a proclivity for purposeful action."[15] The source of the purposeful action is to be found in Veblen's well-known "instinctual" theory. Veblen makes use of four instincts: idle curiosity, the parental

---

[11] Cf. Joseph A. Schumpeter, *History of Economic Analysis* (New York: Oxford University Press, 1954), pp. 927 ff.

[12] T. Veblen, *The Place of Science in Modern Civilization* (New York: Viking, 1942), p. 73.

[13] *Ibid.*, p. 251.

[14] T. Veblen, *The Instinct of Workmanship and the State of the Industrial Arts* (New York: Viking, 1946), pp. 103–104.

[15] T. Veblen, *Essays in Our Changing Order* (New York: Viking, 1945), p. 80.

bent, the instinct of workmanship and the predatory bent.¹⁶ The purposes of instinctual behavior are formed, limited, or retarded by the institutional environment. Veblen at times sets the traditional patterns of "use and wont" against the instinctual drives. He speaks of the instincts as being "overborne by cumulative habituations to the rule of the self-regarding proclivities that triumphed in the culture of predation, and whose dominion has subsequently suffered some impairment in the later substitution of property rights for tenure by prowess." ¹⁷

These remarks should be sufficient to indicate that there is no point of contact between Veblen's approach and that of the orthodox tradition. To oppose the notion that labor, or foregone pleasure, is painful with motive power given by the desire to avoid pain, Veblen takes individual behavior as determined by the working out of instinctual drives in a particular cultural context; nor can any utilitarian counterpart be found for idle curiosity, which in conjunction with the instinct of workmanship is responsible for social progress in Veblen's analysis. It would be a mistake to view Veblen's attitude toward the individual simply as a response to the neoclassical formulation. His view of human nature is the rationale for his exploration of the institutional environment in which the instinctual proclivities assume significance. If the economic man of the orthodox tradition is a valid point of departure, then these investigations become pointless.

The same considerations apply in Veblen's view of the businessman and his environment. He sees a different business world than did his orthodox contemporaries. The prevailing attitude was that the economy was composed of a large number of small firms purchasing factors in a competitive factor market and accepting the prevailing prices in their product markets. The premium was on achieving profits through better management and by innovation that would permit an increased margin at given prices. The profits are short-run because any advantage will be copied by competitors. Thus the full advantages will accrue

---

[16] Too much has been made of Veblen's use of the term, instinct. It is enough, as he says, to take the expression "to signify a concurrence of several instinctive aptitudes, each of which might or might not prove simple or irreducible when subjected to psychological or physiological analysis" (*Instinct of Workmanship*, p. 27).

[17] *Ibid.*, p. 182.

Critique of Orthodox Economics

to the consumer in the form of a greater quantity of the product at a lower price.

Veblen's economic world was completely different from this. His world was that of the *United States Industrial Commission Reports*—the story of business intrigue and high finance put together in thirteen massive volumes by a joint committee at the turn of the century. It tells the unpleasant tale of the sugar trust, the whisky combination, the steel combination, the oil pools, the railway pools, and the rest. The characteristic results of the Industrial Revolution were the giant corporation and the trust movement as a device for ending the destructive power struggle among the corporate giants. In manufacturing alone the number of wage earners increased from 1,311,246 in 1860 to 6,615,046 by 1910, bringing about a complete social transformation.[18] As Beard points out, the "great pecuniary accumulations were thenceforth made largely in business enterprise—including the work of the enterpreneur, financier, speculator, and manipulator under that general term. Inevitably the most energetic and keenest minds were attracted by the dominant mode of money-making."[19] Much confusion has arisen in interpreting Veblen's remarks on business enterprise because of a failure to realize that his unit of analysis is always the giant corporation, not the atomistic firm of the neoclassical economists. His "representative firm" has a large number of stockholders with direct management control; it has been reorganized a number of times and has made extensive use of debenture financing.[20]

The neoclassical version of the businessman's activities as coordinator of the industrial process, like the neoclassical view of the individual, called forth Veblen's typical satire:

[This view] has a great sentimental value and is useful in many ways. There is also a modicum of truth in it as an account of facts. In common with other men, the businessman is moved by ideals of serviceability and an aspiration to make the way of life easier for his fellows. . . . Instances are perhaps not frequent, but they are also not altogether exceptional, where a prosperous captain of industry will go out of his way to heighten the

---

[18] Cf. Charles A. Beard, *Contemporary American History* (New York: Macmillan, 1923), ch. ii, esp. pp. 33 ff.
[19] *Ibid.*, p. 33.
[20] Esp. *Theory of Business Enterprise*, pp. 114 ff., 143 ff.

serviceability of his industry even to a degree that is of doubtful pecuniary expediency for himself. Such aberrations are, of course, not large; and if they are persisted in to any very appreciable extent the result is, of course, disastrous to the enterprise. The enterprise in such a case falls out of the category of business management and falls under the imputation of philanthropy.[21]

The motivation of Veblen's businessman is on the face of it similar to that of Smith's, J. S. Mill's, or Marshall's businessman: pecuniary gain and the accumulation of wealth. For an explanation of this motivation, Veblen appeals to the analysis of behavior in *The Theory of the Leisure Class*. That is, in a society in which pecuniary canons determine social relationships, which in turn involve invidious comparisons of status, the accumulation of wealth is essentially a mark of success. This is another example where much of Veblen's work was concerned with an explanation of a concept which his orthodox contemporaries are willing to postulate.[22] However, the method by which wealth is accumulated or profits are maximized is quite different in Veblen's analysis. If the primary interest of the businessman is pecuniary gain in an environment where the manipulations by large corporations of their markets give the widest range to business discretion, then he will be preoccupied with "an alert redistribution of investments from less to more gainful ventures, and to a strategic control of the conjunctures of business through shrewd investments and coalitions with other businessmen."[23]

The implications of this argument turn on a particular conception of the industrial process. The organization of the economy as a whole is thought of as continually approaching that of one single, integrated, balanced establishment:

It is eminently a system, self-balanced and comprehensive; and it is a system of interlocking mechanical processes, rather than of skilful manipulation. It is mechanical rather than manual. . . . It runs to "quantity production" of specialized and standardized goods and services. . . . This industrial system runs on as an inclusive organization of many and diverse interlocking mechanical processes, interdependent and balanced among themselves in such a way that the due working of any part of it is conditioned on the due working of all the rest.[24]

[21] *Ibid.*, pp. 41, 42n.   [22] *Ibid.*, p. 20.   [23] *Ibid.*, p. 24.
[24] T. Veblen, *The Engineers and the Price System* (New York: Viking, 1947), pp. 52–53.

Critique of Orthodox Economics

Then only fortuitously, according to Veblen, will the ends of pecuniary gain coincide with efficiency requirements of the industrial process. This point is central to an understanding of his theory of distribution and allocation, so we shall return to it later.

It is clear that the "representative firm" of the neoclassical economists as a business unit had no significance in Veblen's view of the economy; nor could it have significance as a productive or industrial unit. Veblen at one point chides Marx for "continuing to speak of industry as an affair of detachable factors and independent segments of work going on in severalty."[25] Neither is Veblen's businessman like his orthodox counterpart. During the period of modern capitalism a series of developments occurred in the status of the representative businessman. Prior to the Industrial Revolution at the end of the eighteenth century, he was the shopkeeper and trader who slowly developed with the tide of technological innovations into the "Captain of Industry" engaged in the direct management and development of the industrial process, albeit for pecuniary gain. As business became more complex and markets larger, the Captain of Industry developed into the Captain of Corporation Finance who resigned his position as the overseer of the industrial process to the technicians and engineers.[26] The principal tasks of the businessman became the maintenance of the credit structure and the returns on invested capital through the manipulation of prices and market conditions.[27] The last stage in the development was the coming of The Captain of Solvency as the representative businessman; the investment banker and his financial interests were constituted into a general staff of financial strategy commanding the country's financial resources,[28] thus assuming the strategic role in business. In this new situation beginning around the turn of the century, the Captains of Corporate Finance became simple Lieutenants of Solvency.[29] We are here far removed from the neoclassical vision of the entrepreneur as the technological innovator and the shrewd manager of affairs engaged in the game of searching out the minimum points of constantly downward shifting cost functions.

[25] *Absentee Ownership*, p. 271n.
[26] *Engineers and the Price System*, ch. ii, *passim*.
[27] *Absentee Ownership*, pp. 110 ff.
[28] *Ibid.*, pp. 338 ff.
[29] *Engineers and the Price System*, pp. 66 f.

Lawrence Nabers

II

The discussion of the conflicting views of Veblen and his orthodox contemporaries has brought us to the point where we must examine certain philosophical and methodological issues which play a major role in Veblen's critique. The movement of events, institutional change, technological development—those aspects of culture that are found in all except the very likely nonexistent static societies—proceed on a different level from thought, belief, and ritual. The result is that systems of law and custom are superimposed on a working order to which they may bear little, if any, relation, having been formulated in terms of an earlier order.[30] This leads to the customary stresses occurring when man's beliefs are inconsistent with the requirements of day-to-day living. The one way in which the cultural stresses arising out of the disparate relation between customs and the underlying matter-of-fact solutions of environmental problems may be lessened is through borrowing the matter-of-fact solutions from some other society without at the same time taking over their ritual and custom. Veblen explained the industrial pre-eminence of imperial Germany in these terms; and in one of his last writings he argues that the economists of the new generation (1920's) have a significant advantage over their predecessors because "the experience which has given its bias to these latter-day economists is of a later date than that to which their predecessors were exposed; it is of the twentieth century, rather than the nineteenth,"[31] and presumably more relevant. The advantages of the latecomer and the borrower are, of course, much the same.

One way in which the body of beliefs is transmitted is through the media of economic doctrines. The formative period of modern economic thought was during the eighteenth century, the important exemplars being the physiocrats and Adam Smith. The generations of economists following Smith took over in large measure the preconceptions implicit in the early classical analysis. Four of these preconceptions, which are closely related, will concern us here: the belief in a natural law or order; the belief in teleological meliorism; the taxonomic interpre-

[30] *Vested Interests*, pp. 7 ff.
[31] *Essays in Our Changing Order*, p. 4. Also cf. the reasons for the superiority of the dolicho blonde group in northern Europe, *Instinct of Workmanship*, pp. 34 ff.

Critique of Orthodox Economics

tation of economic theory; and the attitude towards private property.

It is possible and logically consistent to interpret the physiocratic system as a working out of the law of nature,[32] though this scarcely does the physiocrats justice in Veblen's own terms because of their essential concern with matter-of-fact problems.[33] We may, however, take Veblen's point heuristically. If we interpret the *Tableau* as a model of the natural order, recognizing the fact that it is simultaneously the model of the theoretical economic system of the physiocrats, the preconceptions inherent in the natural law doctrines a fortiori inhere in the economic theory. Economic theory then becomes an exploration of how the natural order works. It also serves as a bench mark for the development of policies directed against deviations from the natural order.[34]

Veblen further identifies the natural law doctrine with a "propensity to the accomplishment of a given end." [35] It is this end that must be defined by economic theory. The same considerations apply to all the disciplines. For example, the purpose of astronomy is to define nature's organization of the heavenly bodies. The issue is simpler here because there is no possibility of interfering with nature's work. But whenever man is involved, there is the possibility of deviation from the natural order. Thus we have a natural law ethics, though man through his selfishness, or more important through his ignorance, may deviate. His goal or purpose, however, is the attainment of the natural, ethical life.

If, then, the economy is conceived of as possessing a natural design, teleological considerations (in the sense of a propensity to reach a particular goal) must be dealt with at two levels: First, all deviations will tend to disappear; it is thus possible to define the direction and meaning of short-run tendencies. Second, the natural organization of the economy is itself directed toward the fulfillment of some long-run end; in this case the end is progress. Economic progress in turn is defined in terms of the increasing accumulation of goods, more specifically the accumulation of capital. "Every increase . . . of capital, therefore, naturally tends to increase . . . the real quantity of

---

[32] *Place of Science*, p. 87.
[33] Cf. Leo Rogin, *The Meaning and Validity of Economic Theory* (New York: Harper, 1956), p. 16. But see *Place of Science*, pp. 86–87.
[34] *Place of Science*, pp. 89–90.   [35] *Ibid.*, p. 92.

industry, the number of productive hands, and consequently the exchangeable value of the annual produce of the land and labour of the country, the real wealth and revenue of its inhabitants." [36] In the physiocratic system, Veblen argues, the teleological preconceptions have reached their highest point. Essentially any belief in a natural order which is inner directed is not far removed from primitive animism which attributed to inanimate objects a direction and force like that of living objects. The animism of the physiocratic natural order, however, is of a high level. It is conceived in a large way, unified and harmonized as a comprehensive order of nature as a whole.[37]

The translation of economic doctrines from France to England brought a change in emphasis. The prevailing impersonal, mechanistic philosophical and social thought in England gave greater weight to the analysis of causal relations proceeding through time with the motive force given by the prior event. This mechanistic, as contrasted to teleological, interpretation was self-sufficient without the natural order assumptions, and Hobbes' reconciliation is extraordinarily obscure. The doctrine of natural law is explicitly abandoned by Locke and, more important for the development of the orthodox tradition, by Bentham. Nevertheless, Veblen argues that animistic (used in this connection in the special sense of end-directed) elements remain important in the "higher synthesis" of political economy. It has, however, become "colorless" and has degenerated "to the tamer levels of normality and causal uniformities." [38] Thus the development of such parts of the theoretical system as the theory of normal price, natural wages, and so on is held by Veblen to reveal the essentially animistic tendencies characteristic of classical thought.[39] Above all, the animistic preconceptions, although they had lost their loftier formulation as the doctrine of the harmony of interests, remained in the preoccupation of economists with the definition of the conditions of economic welfare and the predisposition toward essentially normative models.[40] Reference has already been made to the way in which the concept of competition has been used by the neoclassical economists.

---

[36] Adam Smith, *An Inquiry into the Nature and Causes of the Wealth of Nations* (New York: Modern Library, 1937), p. 321. Also *Place of Science*, pp. 115, 127 ff.
[37] *Place of Science*, p. 32.   [38] *Ibid.*, p. 93.   [39] *Ibid.*, pp. 116 ff.
[40] *Ibid.*, p. 145.

Critique of Orthodox Economics

The teleological mechanism implicit in the orthodox tradition has had, according to Veblen, another important methodological result: it has led economic theory to be constructed in terms of "normal cases" on the one hand and deviations from those normal cases on the other; or to cataloguing results in terms of their *differentia specifica*. Once the *differentiae specificae* are listed, it becomes possible to ignore them and confine attention to the nature of the genus. Veblen's discussion of this point is endlessly repetitive and obscure. His arguments are to be taken in the context of the discussion of the implications of evolution for science and society at the turn of the century. To a generation concerned with the application of the principles of atomic physics to scientific methodology, the discussion has become jejune. Nevertheless, insofar as it comes to an important methodological criticism of his contemporaries, it is relevant for our purposes.

In discussing Irving Fisher's *The Nature of Capital and Income* Veblen points out that the bias inherent in reasoning from normal cases has led to some unacceptable results:

Taxonomy for taxonomy's sake, definition and classification for the sake of definition and classification meets no need of modern science. . . . It is on this head, as regards the serviceability of the taxonomic results that Mr. Fisher's work falls short. *A modern science has to do with the facts as they come to hand,* not with putative phenomena warily led out from a primordial metaphysical postulate, such as the "hedonic principle." [41]

The essence of Veblen's criticism, then, is that all the facts must be considered in the development of explanatory principles—and they must be considered in terms of their changes through time, including qualitative as well as quantitative changes.

More specifically, in speaking of Marshall's great work, Veblen acknowledges the wideness of range and the willingness to include all available factual information; however, Marshall conceives of the economic system as a "self balancing mechanism, not . . . a cumulatively unfolding process or an institutional adaptation to cumulatively unfolding exigencies." [42] A system so conceived clearly derives from the "normal or natural" types, ultimately based on a "colorless" teleology. It further is subject to criticism because the system becomes the

[41] *Essays in Our Changing Order,* pp. 149–150 (italics mine).
[42] *Place of Science,* p. 173.

basis for a taxonomy of events in which it is possible to abstract from facts not fitting neatly into the general framework, particularly facts concerned with quantitative, temporal change.[43]

What do these rather complex methodological and philosophical considerations signify? Current doctrines are circumscribed by the preconceptions inherent in the prevailing beliefs of the time. These beliefs are a heritage of past thought which may not be relevant to the problems of the current age and may involve beliefs which are unscientific in the sense of (a) no longer being serviceable or (b) failing to correspond with the matter-of-fact knowledge of the society. The lack of serviceability of these preconceptions in the case of economic theory is attested by the fact that a large number of details, which would be dealt with if the approach were oriented toward an explanation of development, process, and change, are excluded. Further, taking over philosophical beliefs from an earlier generation, the orthodox economic tradition developed with an almost unrecognized, but built-in, bias toward economic progress. This does not mean that progress has not occurred; Veblen recognized that the rate of economic development has been high and continuous under capitalism. But the inherent bias in economic theory leads to a distortion of analysis, results that have little meaning in terms of current developments, and a natural predilection for the *status quo;* for if progress is inevitable in the current state of things, pressure for change of the institutional arrangements becomes if not dangerous at least mischievous.

The orthodox tradition took as its basic model the stage of economic development characteristic of an earlier period—the entrepreneur-manager, the small firm, competitively organized markets and so on—in conjunction with the bias toward private property current during that period. As Veblen says:

The standard theories of economic science have assumed the rights of property and contract as axiomatic premises . . . and their theories are commonly drawn in such form as would fit the circumstances of the handicraft industry and petty trade. . . . These theories . . . appear tenable on the

[43] Further mention might be made of Veblen's polemics against the static-dynamic dichotomy, which caused its share of confusion among orthodox economists at the turn of the century. But the bearing on the foregoing discussion is obvious. Cf. *ibid.,* pp. 189 ff.

Critique of Orthodox Economics

whole, when taken to apply to the economic situation of that earlier time. . . . It is when these standard theories are sought to be applied to the later situation, which has outgrown the conditions of handicraft, that they appear nugatory or meretricious.[44]

Veblen's extensive discussions of the origins of private property need not detain us here.[45] The accumulation of wealth requisite for the development of the modern market system made inevitable the development of property and contract rights just as it made inevitable that complex of pyschological predispositions which may be loosely designated as the Protestant ethic. These property rights became, as might be expected, an integral part of the natural order. The presumed [46] basis in the orthodox tradition for property is in individual workmanship, which is responsible for the creation of a valuable article. This right of private property vests the owner with the power to sell or dispose of the product of his labor by whatever method he desires. By extension of the principle even natural resources are included as objects amenable to the rules of ownership.[47] We shall return to the analysis of the importance of private property in Veblen's critique of the orthodox tradition, for it becomes crucial in an analysis of the distribution problem.

III

Given the attitude toward the individual, the analysis of the structure and operation of the economy, and the preconceptions underlying traditional thought, we must turn our attention to the unifying principle behind any systematic economic speculation, namely, the theory of value. The essential requirements of any theory of value are (1) its postulates must be consistent with the vision of the data which is held; (2) it must be serviceable in that it facilitates further

---

[44] T. Veblen, *An Inquiry into the Nature of Peace and the Terms of Its Perpetuation* (New York: Viking, 1945), pp. 317–318.

[45] Inter al. cf. *Essays in Our Changing Order*, pp. 32 ff., and *Absentee Ownership*, ch. iii.

[46] Presumed, for Veblen points out that property is a cultural phenomenon. It has its origins in the "invidious distinction between drudgery and exploit" (*Essays in Our Changing Order*, pp. 42, 44). He states characteristically that "the origins of property are to be found in priestly fraud and royal force" (*Instinct of Workmanship*, p. 159).

[47] *Absentee Ownership*, p. 50.

analysis; (3) the results obtained from further analysis must in turn be consistent with observation if the results are of a descriptive nature, or with the rest of the system of thought if the results are of an analytical nature, or with the wider view of the "good society" if the results are normative.

In modern discussions of the value problem so consistently is value taken to refer to relative prices that the ultimate meaning of the term has been lost sight of. The term was borrowed from philosophy, where its meaning, if not its determination, is clear: simply, value stands for worth. The criteria of worth have been variously defined: conduciveness to the greater honor and glory of God, the survival of the race, an increase in pleasure, and so on. In economics the implications of value are the same, but because of the limitation of analysis to "economic goods" the criteria can be defined with less generality.

If society is thought of in terms of congeries of independent (human) atoms, each seeking its own individual end, which is presumed to be inner satisfaction, then all services or commodities conducive to that inner satisfaction have value. As Veblen points out in describing the position of the classical economists, when the determination of legitimate activity is defined by law and custom, "all normal, legitimate economic activities carried on in a well-regulated community serve a materially useful end" [48] and presumably their value will be proportioned to the degree of usefulness to the individual. This conception of value could only have arisen in a society in which the judgments were subjective, individualistic, and, as Veblen suggests, determined by the "self-regarding sentiments of cumulous rivalry." [49] When we contrast the medieval conception of the just return defined vis-à-vis the requirements of equitable, material livelihood for the participants in the economic process, the individualistic nature of the orthodox analysis of value becomes even clearer.[50]

The utilitarian view of the psychology of individuals was taken over by the orthodox economic tradition. The process of valuation, that is, the determination of the worth of a commodity, is judged in terms of the pain experienced in the creation of the commodity (the labor-cost) or the pleasure derived from the attainment, or both as in the full articulated system of analysis following Marshall and his work.

[48] *Place of Science*, p. 287.   [49] *Instinct of Workmanship*, p. 199.
[50] *Ibid.*, p. 233.

Critique of Orthodox Economics

In any event the goal of the individual is to make himself better off. Benefit to the community is irrelevant as far as the individual is concerned. Discussing the traditional approach in another place, Veblen remarks: "Whatever form of expenditure the consumer chooses, or whatever end he seeks in making his choice, has utility to him by virtue of his preference. . . . The question of wastefulness does not arise within the scope of economic theory proper." [51]

The foregoing implies that the economists of the orthodox tradition would be solely concerned with phenomena which could be quantified in a pecuniary sense, or in terms of physical units which are proportioned to pecuniary units. The causal relations in the pecuniary sequences making up economic activity become the center of analysis, subject to the preconceptions imposed by the acceptance of private property and individualistic valuation.[52] Two aspects of the pecuniary sequence constitute the central problems of analysis: distribution and exchange with an implicit analysis of progress and allocation. The purpose of the orthodox theory of value was to facilitate the solution of these two problems. The specific analysis of their solutions will be developed in the following two sections.

Veblen's critique of orthodox value theory proceeds on two levels. First, as we have already indicated, Veblen would have none of the traditional analysis of the behavior of individuals. The process of individual valuation is a purely cultural phenomenon except insofar as a relative constancy of instinctual behavior gives a degree of continuity to valuation over time. Second, accepting distribution and exchange as the central problems for analysis, the point of departure of the orthodox tradition is not serviceable as far as Veblen is concerned.

This lack of serviceability is attributed even more to the failure to take into account the actual operation of the economy than the failure to understand the cultural basis of behavior. If we want to analyze the problems of distribution and exchange in terms of their relation to such considerations as progress and efficiency, then to assume, as is customary in the orthodox analysis, the identity of real magnitudes with pecuniary magnitudes is more than misleading:

But great as may be the due of courtesy to that conception [of hedonism] for the long season of placid content which economic theory has spent be-

[51] T. Veblen, *The Theory of the Leisure Class* (New York: Viking, 1943), p. 98.
[52] *Place of Science*, p. 138.

neath its spreading chestnut tree, yet the fact is not to be overlooked that its scheme of accountancy is not that of the modern business community. The logic of economic life in a modern community runs in terms of pecuniary, not of hedonistic magnitudes.[53]

The pecuniary magnitudes must be seen in the light of business rivalries, a complex credit system, irrationalities in both business and individual behavior rather than the "'refined system of barter' culminating in a net aggregate maximum of pleasurable sensations of consumption"[54] posited by the orthodox tradition:

But since it is in just this unhedonistic, unrationalistic pecuniary traffic that the tissue of business life consists; since it is this peculiar conventionalism of aims and standards that differentiates the life of the modern business community from any conceivable earlier or cruder phase of economic life; since it is in this tissue of pecuniary intercourse and pecuniary concepts, ideals, expedients, and aspirations that the conjunctures of business life arise and run their course of felicity and devastation; since it is here that those institutional changes take place which distinguish one phase or era of the business community's life from any other; since the growth and change of these habitual, conventional elements make the growth and character of any business era or business community; any theory of business which sets these elements aside or explains them away misses the main facts which it has gone out to seek.[55]

Veblen nowhere spells out an explicit alternative value theory to serve as a point of departure for his analysis of distribution and allocation. This has had the result of obscuring the consistency of his observations and has exposed him to the charge of eclecticism, which is not necessarily bad, but which is certainly not as impressive as an integrated performance. However, implicit in Veblen's arguments is a consistent basis of analysis which, it can be argued, constitutes a theory of value. Value simply implies serviceability to the community. The point becomes clearer when we see it in contrast to the orthodox position where value involves serviceability to a single individual. In the latter case the measure of serviceability is in the degree of satisfaction-gain to the individual. For Veblen the proper measure of value is the degree to which a commodity contributes to the ability of the economy seen as an interrelated and inseparable concat-

[53] *Essays in Our Changing Order*, p. 160.   [54] *Place of Science*, p. 250.
[55] *Idem.*

Critique of Orthodox Economics

enation of industrial processes, to produce required goods and services. For the time being, we shall allow the circularity of the argument to stand, namely, the fact that the goods and services are required because they contribute to the ability of the economy to produce.

This definition of value implies that there are two kinds of activities, industrial—those activities necessary to produce required goods and services—and pecuniary or business—those activities which are not strictly necessary.[56] Here again is the dichotomy which we have mentioned before as being essential to an understanding of Veblen's work. This definition of value is strongly normative, for if a service is not of use to the community or if it acts in large measure to interfere with the industrial efficiency of the community, then it would be to the advantage of the community to eliminate it. However, the distinction between the industrial and the pecuniary employments is tied so inseparably to the institutional fabric constituting the modern western capitalist community that little could be done without the complete and total alteration of the economic system. Veblen was not overly sanguine about this possibility.[57]

There are three sources of value judged in terms of serviceability to the community: the state of the industrial arts, the size of the population, and natural resources. "The state of the industrial arts is a joint stock of technological knowledge and practice worked out, accumulated, and carried forward by the industrial population which lives and moves within the sweep of this industrial system."[58] Veblen gives priority to the state of the technological arts, for, he argues, "the growth of the population is governed by the state of the industrial arts in such a way that the numbers of the population cannot exceed the carrying capacity of the industrial arts";[59] further, the state of the arts determines what natural resources will be useful as well as how they will be made use of.[60]

Distribution and exchange are purely pecuniary aspects of the operation of the economic system subject to the rules of private property and free contract, which in the orthodox analysis are taken as the immutable conditions postulated by the analysis.[61] The standards

---

[56] *Ibid.*, pp. 293 ff. [57] *Engineers and the Price System*, chs. iv, v, *passim*.
[58] *Absentee Ownership*, p. 65. [59] *Ibid.*, p. 62. [60] *Ibid.*, p. 63.
[61] *Place of Science*, p. 236.

of valuation of commodities are standards of private gain in terms of price; whereas if industry were conducted in terms of benefit to the community, the price valuations would be meaningless.[62] In speaking of Marx's analysis in terms of the labor theory of value (and it might be added parenthetically that Veblen discusses Marx with less than his customary asperity), he points out that variations of proportions between the exchange ratios of human labor involved in commodities and their prices are attributable to the "strategy of self interest"; and then he says revealingly: "Under a socialist regime, where the labourer would get the full product of his labor, *or where the whole system of ownership, and consequently the system of distribution, would lapse, values would reach a true expression, if any.*" [63]

The circularity in Veblen's statement of the value problem has been mentioned, namely, the definition of value in terms of itself. The circularity of the argument becomes irrelevant when the concept of required goods and services is given empirical content. Much of Veblen's analysis of the economic system was devoted to a description of those aspects of the system which he felt to be not required or in his own term, disserviceable. In general those activities fell into four groups: First, there are those activities characterized by the invidious use of leisure and conspicuous consumption of commodities along with the cultural complexes of behavior which have been developed in furthering the pecuniary canons of taste. Second, there are those activities which result in interfering with the industrial process, involving "certain customary kinds of waste, which are unavoidable so long as industry is managed by businesslike methods and for businesslike ends." They include unemployment of resources or labor whether through design or ignorance, salesmanship, production of spurious goods for business reasons, excess capacity, duplication, and so on.[64] The third group of commodities disserviceable to the community in the sense of not enhancing the community's economic welfare are those "whose value lies in their turning the technological inheritance to the injury of mankind"; [65] that is, the military establishment and the constabulary insofar as the function of the latter is to protect the predatory rights of the leisure class. Finally, there is a group of activities of most probable net detriment such as race tracks, saloons,

[62] *Engineers and the Price System*, p. 147.
[63] *Place of Science*, p. 421 (italics mine).
[64] *Engineers and the Price System*, p. 108.   [65] *Place of Science*, p. 356.

gambling houses, and houses of prostitution. Then typically Veblen suggests:

> Some spokesmen of the "non-Christian tribes" might wish to include churches under the same category, but the consensus of opinion in modern communities inclines to look on churches as serviceable, on the whole; and it may be as well not to attempt to assign them a specific place in the scheme of serviceable and disserviceable use of invested wealth.[66]

The application of Veblen's distinctions between pecuniary and nonpecuniary employments is difficult and must proceed *ad hoc*. If such categories of private property and the maintenance of national integrity are accepted as socially desirable in themselves, the catalogue of serviceability is largely reversed. The analysis, however, does provide a point of departure for a treatment of distribution and allocation which throws a completely different light on these problems than the orthodox tradition.[67]

IV

The problem of the distribution of income was central in economic analysis beginning at least with Ricardo. He posed the economic problem in terms of the distribution of income which would be most conducive to economic progress. Thus, the reason for his attack on the corn laws was their tendency to distort the distribution of income in favor of the landed classes through raising the cost of wage goods, in turn lowering profits. Under these conditions progress would be impossible. This argument required positing an inverse relationship between profits and wages resting ultimately on the notorious wages fund doctrine. It has already been indicated that the inadequacies

---

[66] *Ibid.*, pp. 357–358.

[67] Frank H. Knight among others has objected that any system of analysis which rejects as a point of departure consumer sovereignty has dangerous political implications. Specifically in his review of *The Place of Science, Jour. Pol. Econ.*, XVIII (1920), 518–520, he says: "It goes without saying that there is a great deal in this distinction between real value and trumpery, but we wish to remark that it is a canon very difficult to apply in a democracy" (p. 520). Veblen would have replied: (1) consumer sovereignty is myth derived from an acceptance of the hedonistic calculus; (2) in any event the gains to be made from the application of the canons of serviceability for society as a whole would outweigh any other possible loss; and (3) to the implied question of who is to make the decisions for individuals he would ask, "Who makes them now?"

of the classical analysis of distribution became increasingly obvious during the course of the nineteenth century: there was the strong implication from the labor theory of value that labor, the source of value, was exploited in the economic process through receiving only a proportion of the total product. Explanations running in terms of the productivity of the other factors of production, such as abstinence, co-ordination, and so on, were not fully integrated into formal value theory. Next there were the problems of applying the wages fund doctrine when one of the most important phenomena to be analyzed was increasing productivity. Finally, there was an increasing concern with problems of efficiency, price, and allocation, which could not conveniently be dealt with in terms of the labor theory of value. The stage was thus set for the "marginalist revolution."

The distribution problem was posed until recently in terms of a class structure presumed to be functionally meaningful. The division of society into three groups, workers, capitalists, and landlords, is as old as the beginnings of modern capitalism, when the requirements of trade and industry separated the workers from their tools and established on the basis of the ownership of the means of production the distinction between employers and employees. The origins of the landed classes are in a similar fashion to be found in private property and contract arising with the break-up of the feudal order. In the course of the nineteenth century a fourth factor of production was added to the traditional three. The "undertaker" or entrepreneur as distinct from the capitalist or owner of the means of production began to be distinguished in recognition of an increasingly obvious historical fact. His activity was usually thought of during this period as a special kind of labor, that of co-ordinating or directing the industrial processes.[68] The distribution of income, then, was the division of the social product among these functional economic classes—functional in the sense that each contributed its share to the creation of the product.

In the earlier scheme of analysis the relationship among the income shares was worked out in a somewhat unsatisfactory fashion. Each of the shares was from one point of view considered residual: thus rent was the residual payment between price and the other necessary payments which made up the wages fund. Profits plus interest on

[68] *Place of Science*, pp. 288–289.

Critique of Orthodox Economics

capital invested was the residual of the wages fund after the necessary (subsistence) payments to laborers. And wages were generally looked upon as the residual payment from the wages fund after profit plus interest was taken out; thus the payment could go below the subsistence level for the mass of workers until changes in population adjusted the size of the labor force. Now this analysis is unsatisfactory because it leaves unanswered the question of equity of payment as well as for formal reasons previously mentioned.

The transition to the neoclassical analysis turned on defining economic classes as factors of production. Taking the firm as the central unit of analysis rather than the economic class, it is possible to argue that in the process of maximizing profits each firm will use the factors of production up to the point where the contribution to the product of the firm of the last unit of the factor of production used will be equal to the price which must be paid for that factor of production. Granting the assumption as to the relative smallness of each of the units engaged in this process, the price cannot be affected by any of the participants. For the economy as a whole (by-passing issues raised by variations in factor efficiency) all the factors of production will be rewarded in accordance with their contribution to total output, no more or no less. Thus, changing the point of view, the economic classes receive in the form of income exactly what they contribute to output. The equitable features of this arrangement were thought to be obvious. This was the state of distribution theory as it left the hands of Alfred Marshall and J. B. Clark, and it is to this analysis that Veblen addresses himself.[69]

To begin with, Veblen's conception of the class structure was totally different from the orthodox tradition. In the analysis of class structure he remains consistent to the categories of industrial and nonindustrial employment. In a more extended breakdown, Veblen makes the distinction between the upper, middle, and lower classes, which he identifies respectively with the aristocracy or the predatory classes proper, the business class, and the industrial class. The first two, granting the distinction previously discussed, are nonindustrial.[70] The

---

[69] The argument has been greatly simplified, although greater detail would not affect the conclusions. For a fairly complete discussion cf. George J. Stigler, *Production and Distribution Theories* (New York: Macmillan, 1941), esp. chs. iv, xi, xii.

[70] *Instinct of Workmanship*, p. 184.

rationale for the maintenance of this distinction is private property. It is the ownership of the means of production and natural resources which gives the nonindustrial classes the ultimate power to manipulate industry for the purpose of pecuniary gain. To put the matter somewhat differently, class distinction runs between "those who own more than they personally can use and those who have urgent use for more than they own." [71]

It must be remembered that Veblen's analysis is drawn in terms of large-scale, modern corporate enterprise with a considerable degree of purely financial control where "the pecuniary magnate . . . is superior to the market on which the capitalist-employer depends." [72] In these circumstances the class division may be looked at as "between those who own wealth invested in large holdings and who thereby control the conditions of life for the rest; and those who do not own wealth in sufficiently large holdings, and whose conditions of life are therefore controlled by these others." [73] Another way of putting the proposition is that in an advanced industrial society the division is between the vested interests and the common man, a vested interest being defined characteristically as a "legitimate right to get something for nothing, usually a prescriptive right to an income which is secured by controlling the traffic." [74] The prescriptive right is, of course, a property right. Ancillary to the vested interests are such groups as go to make up the "gentry," the "crown," and the "clergy." [75] The distinction is not hard and fast in Veblen's analysis. There is much movement back and forth between the classes, but "the great distinguishing mark of the common man is that he is helpless within the rules of the game as it is played in the twentieth century under the enlightened principles of the eighteenth century." [76] The common man is with marginal exceptions the industrial class. Thus the problem of distribution for Veblen is the division of the product between these two groups, which cuts across the lines of demarcation drawn in the orthodox tradition.

To return to the neoclassical treatment of the theory of distribution, Veblen points out that the basis for ownership is alleged to be the productive labor of the owners. The institution of property itself

[71] *Absentee Ownership*, p. 9. [72] *Place of Science*, p. 382.
[73] *Vested Interests*, p. 160. [74] *Ibid.*, pp. 161–162. [75] *Idem.*
[76] *Ibid.*, p. 163.

Critique of Orthodox Economics

is traced in the conjectural history of the orthodox tradition to the productive labor of the hunter, the fisher or the herdsman.[77] If it is granted that productive goods and services, which by assumption are owned, are the most important elements in modern economies, and if exchange can only occur via the mechanism of pecuniary transactions, then the society must treat pecuniary transactions as productive and by the application of the principle of exclusion, nonpecuniary transactions as nonproductive.[78] But since the industrial arts yield no determinable income to any one individual, it is impossible to attribute productivity to what Veblen regarded as the most important factor in determining the level of output, namely, the prevailing technology, that is, the state of the arts. "It is the indispensable foundation of all productive industry, of course, but except for certain minute fragments covered by patent rights or trade secrets, this joint stock is no man's individual property." [79] If this joint stock of knowledge belongs to the community at large then the efficiency of any single individual in the industrial process is determined by the state of the arts, which is in turn a function of the level of culture attained by the community; and the imputation of efficiency to any given workman or any other factor of production is impossible.[80]

Thus, given the value categories with which Veblen operates, the neoclassical marginal productivity theory of distribution can have no meaning. For while the entrepreneur, for example, may be productive in the sense of increasing the pecuniary return of the firm, his activities according to Veblen should be interpreted in terms of the interruption of the industrial process, which implies, if anything, negative value productivity. In the same wise, wages paid to salesmen, buyers, accountants, and the like may only be imputed from pecuniary, not industrial, productivity. Even individuals engaged directly in the productive process are working in accordance with the instructions given by business management; so their tasks are limited by the restriction of output or the production of commodities which are less

[77] *Essays in Our Changing Order*, pp. 32–33.
[78] *Instinct of Workmanship*, pp. 208–209.
[79] *Engineers and the Price System*, pp. 27–28.
[80] *Instinct of Workmanship*, pp. 144–145. The consideration applies with somewhat less force to the problems of short-run production where it is possible to impute the degree of productivity from engineering data. But Veblen is arguing specifically in the context of distribution theory.

serviceable to the community than they might have been. Therefore their wages cannot be imputed from the utility of the product to the community:

It might, therefore, be feasible to set up a theory to the effect that wages are competitively proportioned to the vendibility of the product; but there is no cogent ground for saying that the wages in any department of industry, under a business regime, are proportioned to the utility which the output has to any one else than the employer who sells it. When it is further taken into account that the vendibility of the product in very many lines of production depends chiefly on the wastefulness of the goods . . . the divergence between the usefulness of the work and the wages paid for it seems wide enough to throw the whole question of an equivalence between work and pay out of theoretical consideration.[81]

Veblen's objections to the neoclassical analysis of distribution has proceeded on three grounds: First, the view of the class structure is inadequate when the facts of the modern productive processes are considered. Second, the identification of pecuniary with industrial returns is incorrect. It was developed because the acceptance of private property as an aspect of the natural order made it inevitable that the analysis should run in terms of pecuniary magnitudes. And finally, it would be impossible to impute a return to the state of the arts, which from the social point of view is the most important determinant of productivity.

Granting the existing institutional structure the neoclassical analysis did not according to Veblen provide us with an explanation of the phenomenon of distribution. Where is such an explanation properly to be found? Veblen begins with the category of capital seen as an aspect of ownership: "The state of the industrial arts continues, of course, to be held jointly in and by the community at large; but equitable title to its usufruct has, in effect passed to the owners of the indispensable material means of production." [82] In other words, through the ownership of the means of production, the vested interests are able to secure in the form of a proprietal income the pecuniary returns of business activity, such returns giving them their claim on the real product of the economy.

These usufructs on the product of the technology take the form of capital. Capital in the orthodox discussions has been variously treated.

[81] *Theory of Business Enterprise*, pp. 62–63n.   [82] *Vested Interests*, p. 60.

Critique of Orthodox Economics

It usually has reference to physical quantity whether fund or flow, though the definition of the immediate uses of capital have varied extensively. Veblen treats capital as a purely pecuniary magnitude. Its value is defined as the capitalized earning power of the firm as the basic unit of valuation. The same arguments apply, *mutatis mutandis*, to land. It is clear, then, why the returns to capital cannot be imputed either from the cost of the capital or from its productivity (in a real rather than a pecuniary sense). The returns to the firm are the result of peculiarly business activities, and as such the value of capital may reflect the differential advantages to the firm which appear in the corporate accounts as good will or as asset values inflated through revaluation. Even if this were not true, it still remains that the state of the arts, or the common fund of industrial knowledge, cannot be sliced up into so many units each of which contributes some fraction of the total productivity.[83]

In an interesting application of the argument Veblen remarks on the ability of nations to make rapid recoveries from the destruction of war. Economic historians, he suggests, have been persistently surprised at this ability especially after an extensive destruction of capital values; but their surprise is due to their apprehension of capital in terms of standard economic theory where real value is identified with pecuniary assessment. If the state of the industrial arts is properly conceived of as a system of habits of thought and knowledge which would have suffered slight damage, the phenomenon would come as a lesser surprise.[84]

Granted the predominance of absentee ownership in Veblen's vision of the economy, the share of income received by the ownership group is determined by usufructs in the form of equities and claims on the industrial process. The income so derived is capitalized to determine the value of the claims for exchange purposes. It might be added that Veblen's analysis of cyclical fluctuations as an example of the wastes of the operation of the business system takes its point of departure from the capitalization process which in its detailed working out becomes a credit phenomenon. But the orthodox tradition could not, because of its identification of the industrial with pecuniary activities,

---

[83] See the extended discussion in *Theory of Business Enterprise*, ch. vi, *passim*.
[84] T. Veblen, *Imperial Germany and the Industrial Revolution* (New York: Viking, 1939), pp. 263–264.

develop a theory of the cycle articulated with its general theory of value and distribution. Of necessity, monetary theory and cycle theory developed as special theories.

As far as the determination of return to the industrial classes is concerned, Veblen takes the position that the amount must be determined *ad hoc,* for in the last analysis the relationship between employer, or manager as a lieutenant of the vested interests, and the workers is one of bargaining:

> The two parties to the quarrel—for it is after all a quarrel—have learned to know what to count on. And the bargaining between them therefore settles down without much circumlocution into a competitive use of unemployment, privation, restriction of work and output, strikes, shutdowns and lockouts, espionage, pickets, and similar manoeuvers of mutual derangement with a large recourse to menacing language and threats of mutual sabotage.[85]

In other words, the determination of the return to the industrial class is a matter of the determination of the market price of the product, labor, given the businesslike methods of market relationships. But this brings us to the next section where we shall compare specifically Veblen's analysis of the operation of the market mechanism with that of the neoclassical economists.

V

In the course of the development of Veblen's economic thought an important change in emphasis occurred. Prior to *The Instinct of Workmanship* (1914) the emphasis is on the question of the distribution of wealth and the effects on society of the concentration of the claims on wealth in the hands of a leisure class of absentee owners. It is, of course, impossible to separate the analysis of distribution from that of allocation even in Veblen's treatment, for the way in which the vested interests extract their income from the industrial process determines the organization of industry and commerce subject only to the inherent logic of mechanical organization, which could be distorted through a considerable range. With *Imperial Germany* (1915) and especially with extensive passages in the chapter "Peace and the Price System" in *The Nature of Peace* (1917) the emphasis is increas-

[85] *Absentee Ownership,* p. 406.

Critique of Orthodox Economics

ingly on efficiency, organization, and such problems. *The Engineers and the Price System* (1921) completes the shift. No change is involved in any of Veblen's analytical categories; it is simply a change in emphasis. Thus in *The Theory of Business Enterprise* the point of departure is the nature of capital and its relation to credit, which we have treated as a distributive category. The value of capital is enhanced through the interruption of the industrial process, but the strategic element is the class structure. In the later work the analysis settles on the industrial process itself with the distributive results in the background.

Several possible reasons for the shift in emphasis are to be found: First, after the turn of the century there were a number of changes in the complexion of industrial organization, which increasingly took up Veblen's attention: the beginnings of rationalization, the development of new power sources, and the growth of industrial chemistry.

When the growth of industrial chemistry and electricity set in there also set in by insensible degrees, a new era in the articulation of industrial processes. . . . The number and interplay of technological factors engaged in any major operation in industry today are related to the corresponding facts of the middle nineteenth century somewhat as the mathematical cube is related to the square; and the increase and multiplication of these technological factors is going forward incontinently, at a constantly accelerated rate.[86]

The mathematical analogy is to be taken, of course, like the more famous Malthusian relation. But the change in the industrial order, with its increasing demands for management and control by technicians who understand the industrial process, concerned Veblen most immediately for the rest of his life.

Next, the higher level of prosperity for the nation as a whole with the corresponding decline in agrarian discontent lessened the popular emphasis on some of the more malodorous business activities that were personalized in the conduct of the Captains of Industry and Solvency leading to the preoccupation with the sources and uses of their wealth. Finally, in the economic writings of the day the difficulties with the theory of distribution and the fatuous nature of some of the conclusions, particularly those of J. B. Clark, were increasingly realized,

[86] *Ibid.*, p. 271.

and the attention of the profession at large was shifting to a more specific analysis of the price problem. As Joan Robinson has remarked: "Marshall turned the meaning of value into a little question: Why does an egg cost more than a cup of tea? It may be a small question but is a very difficult and complicated one. It takes a lot of time and a lot of algebra to work it out. So it kept Marshall's pupils preoccupied for fifty years." [87] Veblen was conscious of the center of theoretical interest, and his own shift in emphasis was partially in response to the shift in neoclassical analysis.

Joan Robinson might have added that there was a wider purpose than simply to determine the price of a cup of tea, namely, a demonstration of the conditions under which it would have been the best of all possible prices. The problem was solved in terms of the orthodox vision of the economy as discussed in section II. In justice, it should be pointed out, however, that the later theorists began to take this vision as postulate rather than reality, although in many cases the distinction is a fine one. Briefly, with the large number of firms presupposed, those firms must have minimum costs at an output small enough so that no firm may influence the market in which it sells its commodity. The same conditions hold true, *mutatis mutandis*, for purchases of commodities or factors of production. The pressure of newcomers to the market will set prices at minimum cost levels, implying minimum acceptable profits but assuring that industrial establishments will be operating at optimum efficiency. Consumers will then be getting commodities at minimum attainable prices and will be maximizing the satisfaction derivable from those commodities in the manner we have already discussed. Subject to certain qualifications, the importance of which it was generally assumed were not great enough significantly to effect the result, this process would lead to the maximization of the net social return.

Many of the objections of Veblen to this argument have already been discussed. They proceeded on two levels, which are closely related: First, business enterprise cannot in the context of Veblen's statement of the value propositions be said to operate with efficiency; this point is the familiar one. Second, confining our attention to the market relationships only, the orthodox model of market behavior is highly unrealistic. In this connection Veblen anticipates a sub-

[87] *On Re-reading Marx* (Cambridge: Students' Bookshop, 1953), p. 22.

Critique of Orthodox Economics

stantial portion of present-day oligopoly and bilateral bargaining theory. In fact, he holds these models of behavior to be the only significant ones.

To recapitulate Veblen's first set of objections to the orthodox position, the requirements of profit maximization are inconsistent with the efficient operation of an articulated industrial system. "So long as the price system rules, that is to say, so long as industry is managed on investment for a profit, there is no escaping this necessity of adjusting the process of industry to the requirements of remunerative price." [88] In the post–World War I period Veblen began to make use of the ugly word, sabotage. Businessmen were thought of as sabotaging the industrial process through the restriction of supply, the obstruction of traffic, and meretricious publicity with a view to more profitable sales.[89]

The potentialities of effective sabotage can only be fully realized if the firm has some degree of control over the market. Up to the last half of the nineteenth century competition was described by Veblen as relatively free in the sense that markets were increasing faster than the productive capabilities of industry. This led to an emphasis on quantity of output with gains to be made through the spreading of overhead. Prices in this situation could not be varied because of any one firm's increase in output, so the economic order, when not threatened by a cyclical downturn, offered a fair prospect of continued profit at increasing levels of output.[90]

This condition of free competition, which bears some resemblance to the orthodox competitive models, during the last half of the nineteenth century began "dying at the top" in what Veblen called the key industries, that is, those industries on which the rest of the industrial establishment was immediately dependent, such as coal, steel, oil, transportation, and structural work.[91] From the key industries the decline of free competition spread throughout the rest of the economy. The critical point was reached, Veblen argues, when these key industries had been brought under absentee ownership on a scale sufficiently large to furnish a basis of collusive management.[92]

Specifically, the development of improved technology during this

[88] *Nature of Peace*, p. 325.
[89] *Vested Interests*, p. 100.
[90] *Engineers and the Price System*, pp. 35 ff. Also *Absentee Ownership*, pp. 72 ff.
[91] *Absentee Ownership*, p. 77.
[92] *Ibid.*, p. 213.

period permitted firms to produce quantities far beyond the current business needs. The business need is defined as that quantity consistent with profit maximizing. In other words, the strategic firms were operating under conditions of decreasing cost in the area of profit maximizing quantities. But because of their size with respect to the market they were unable to take advantage of the situation, for any increase in output would lower the market price. On the demand side, the available markets had reached their limits or at least were not expanding as rapidly as productive capacity. These conditions led to a substitution of competitive selling in place of the competitive production of goods, for the principal gains were to be made at the expense of other firms without affecting total industry output, which would have resulted in decreases in industry prices. Thus, as Veblen remarks, "the chief expedients in this businesslike competition . . . [were] salesmanship and sabotage. Salesmanship in this connection means little else than prevarication, and sabotage means the businesslike curtailment of output."[93]

The typical market situation was one in which the firms were large with respect to the market, and the recognized interdependence of pricing and production policies led to an increasing use of the devices of salesmanship (Veblen would have included the attributes of what has come to be known as product differentiation or variation under this head) for purposes of increasing market shares. While these structural conditions were developing, the relationship among firms was characterized by cutthroat competition, which raised the threat of significant declines in earning capacity.[94] This situation would not for long be maintained because it directly militated against the position of the "vested interests," who are increasingly responsible for business activities as the financial control begins to dominate in the strategic areas of industry.[95] As a result,

the country's business concerns have entered into consolidations, coalitions, understandings and working arrangements among themselves—syndicates, trusts, pools, combinations, interlocking directorates, gentlemen's agreements, employers' unions—to such an extent as virtually to cover the field of that large scale business that sets the pace and governs the movements of the rest.[96]

[93] *Ibid.*, pp. 78 ff. [94] *Ibid.*, pp. 337 ff. [95] *Ibid.*, pp. 339 ff.
[96] *Engineers and the Price System*, p. 124.

Critique of Orthodox Economics

This does not imply the end of sabotage and salesmanship, for it is still the purpose of business to manipulate consumers and to limit production even though the problems arising out of competitive relations among firms have been settled.

Thus for Veblen the orthodox analysis of the allocative mechanism operating through the market-price mechanism had little meaning. The definition of efficiency vis-à-vis the ability of the system to meet the demands of the individual consumer was inconsistent with Veblen's definition of efficiency vis-à-vis society. It further overlooked the important fact that the individual was manipulated by business through salesmanship to suit the ends of business. The consumer could scarcely be taken as the bench mark for the analysis. Next, technology was such as to make large-scale business inevitable. This led to the development of collusively oligopolistic pricing and marketing practices, for the alternatives were such as to damage the position of the "vested interests." The only way, then, in which the mechanism of allocation could be analyzed was through a careful study of the development of business practices with full recognition of the conflict between industrial and pecuniary ends.

[MELVIN D. BROCKIE]

7

The Cycle Theories of Veblen and Keynes Today

DESPITE the relatively "mild" nature of the recessions of 1948–1949 and 1953–1954 in the United States, a significant portion of lay and professional commentators today (1957) appear to foresee something perhaps more dire in the near, or at least temporally relevant, future. The talk has drifted away from concerns like "rolling readjustment" and "inventory cycles" and is preoccupied more with: (1) a possible "hair curling" depression, (2) "What do you think is going to happen?" or (3) Is another "big one" coming? To be sure, terms such as "big one" and "hair curling" in economics are inexact, but it is reasonably clear what this censor group means in the general context. They are referring, not to the collapse of 1937–1938, but to the disaster of 1929–1933.

I

The answer to these queries may possibly be found in a *rapprochement* of the "overcapitalization" theory of T. B. Veblen [1] and the "trade cycle" analysis of J. M. Keynes.[2] For, heretical as it may sound,

[1] T. Veblen, *The Theory of Business Enterprise* (New York: Scribner, 1904), especially pp. 177–267.
[2] J. M. Keynes, *The General Theory of Employment, Interest and Money* (New York: Harcourt, Brace, 1936), pp. 313–332.

Melvin D. Brockie

Veblen had many things to say which are supplementary to the more recent Keynesian formulation and which are especially relevant today. It is also evident, if one may judge from an examination of the journals of the past two decades, that Veblen's cycle views are either unfamiliar, obscure, or out of favor insofar as economists generally are concerned.[3]

Although neglect of his insights has been a part of the normal order of affairs for Veblen, both while alive and, except for a few brief years in the early nineteen-thirties, ever since, he is nonetheless too important a figure to dismiss from all further controversy in the matter of business cycles or, beyond this, of economic analysis in its more general context. Professor Dorfman has worded the case more strongly; writing an introductory statement in 1939, he concludes:

If the men who count in the social sciences in the United States were asked today who was America's most creative thinker in this field, few would dissent from the choice of Thorstein Veblen. They might not approve his views in general, let alone the details, but they would acknowledge that he showed a far more penetrating insight into the nature and future course of development of the modern business civilization than any of his contemporaries or successors.[4]

---

[3] One noteworthy exception is the discussion of the similarities between the cycle theories of Veblen and Keynes by R. Vining, "Suggestions of Keynes in the Writings of Veblen," *Jour. Pol. Econ.*, XLVII (Oct., 1939), 692–704.

More generally speaking, the definitive biography of Veblen also presents his cycle views, but this was published prior to the appearance of Keynes's *General Theory*. See J. Dorfman, *Thorstein Veblen and His America* (New York: Viking, 1934). For a much briefer, yet trenchant portrait and evaluation of Veblen, see J. M. Clark, "Thorstein Bundy [sic] Veblen," *Amer. Econ. Rev.*, XIX (Dec., 1929), 742–745.

[4] T. Veblen, *Imperial Germany and the Industrial Revolution* (New York: Viking, 1946), p. xi.

Another appraiser declares: "Veblen attempted to forge an integrated system of economic theory along entirely original lines" (K. L. Anderson, "The Unity of Veblen's Theoretical System," *Quart. Jour. Econ.*, XLVII [Aug., 1933], 599). However, K. E. Boulding believes that Veblen's principal ideological impact lies elsewhere, commenting: "The influence of Veblen, ironically enough, has been felt most in a field which he thoroughly despised—the law" ("A New Look at Institutionalism," *Amer. Econ. Rev.*, XLVII [May, 1957], 7).

Veblen and Keynes

II

Veblen introduces his "overcapitalization" theory [5] with four conditions which underlie "the patent fact that crises, depressions, and brisk times are in their first incidence phenomena of business, of prices and capitalization." [6] First, "industry is carried on by means of investment which is made with a view to pecuniary gain (the earnings)." [7] These gains, of course, are calculated as a percentage on total investment and are measured "in terms of money." Second, "the industry to which the business men in this way resort as the ways and means of gain is of the nature of a mechanical process, or it is some employment (as commerce or banking) that is closely bound up with the mechanical industries." [8] Third,

credit, whether under that name or under the name of orders, contracts, accounts, and the like, is inseparable from the management of modern industry in all that concerns the working relations between businesses that are not under one ownership, or between which the relations resting on

---

[5] The essence of the theory is contained in Chapter VII of *The Theory of Business Enterprise*. However, for a more complete presentation Chapters V and VI should also be read. Probably the best two-page summary of the theory is presented by W. C. Mitchell, *Business Cycles* (Berkeley: University of California Press, 1913), pp. 14–15.

[6] *Theory of Business Enterprise*, p. 185.

[7] *Ibid.*, p. 186. To Veblen, this insistence upon pecuniary gain by the "business" sector is an all-powerful drive which, in Schumpeter's opinion, indicates that "Veblen comes the nearest [excluding Marxists] to being an" example of an accredited exponent "of what we may call the depredation theory of entrepreneurial gain" (J. A. Schumpeter, *History of Economic Analysis* [New York: Oxford University Press, 1954], p. 896).

Of course, allusions to Veblen's relation to Marxism are not new, but a carefully worked comparison of the principal tenets of the two is a rarity. For one such gem we are indebted to Professor A. L. Harris, who writes: "The central ideas of Marx are tentatively placed against those of Veblen as follows: 'Dialectical Materialism and Institutional Mutationism'; 'Class Struggle and the Conflict in Occupational Habituations'; 'The Overproduction and the Overcapitalization Theories of Business Cycles'; 'The Theory of Increasing Misery and the Technological Deficit'; 'The Concentration of Capital and Working Class Thriftlessness'; 'The Proletarian Dictatorship and the Soviet of Technicians'; 'The Dialectical and the Genetic Accounts of Capitalism, the Labor Process, Private Property, and the State'" ("Types of Institutionalism," *Jour. Pol. Econ.*, XL [Dec., 1932], 741).

[8] *Theory of Business Enterprise*, p. 187.

separate ownership have not been placed in abeyance by some such expedient as lease, pool, syndicate, trust agreement, and the like.[9]

Fourth, "the conduct of industry by competing business concerns involves an extensive use of loan credit."[10] This loan credit refers primarily to loans or debts involving notes, stocks, bonds, deposits, and the like, while the credit referred to in point three above includes transactions involving deferred payments for the purchase and sale of goods within the broad framework of contract law and its relation to future performance.

"An era of prosperity is an era of rising prices,"[11] says Veblen. Prices may rise above the prevailing level in a particular industry or group of industries because of some specific factor (e.g., purchase of supplies required by the Spanish-American War). The rise of prices becomes so general as to be considered a "habitual fact." Businessmen launch new investments, current demand is thereby increased, and anticipation of further advances in demand stimulates businessmen and prices throughout the economy. Veblen thus emphasizes the psychological phenomena of "habits of buoyancy" and "speculative recklessness" that are abroad in such circumstances.

As prices rise, profit margins in the industries "nearer the seat of [initial] disturbance" increase markedly inasmuch as production costs lag, (1) because costs of supplies drawn from the more "remote" lines of industry rise slowly due to lags and dampening influences, and (2) because wages lag. Higher current profits, and optimistic expectations of still larger profits, lead to higher capitalizations of business units. As market capitalization increases, a larger loan collateral base is thereby created upon which further extensions of credit are made. These loans in turn tend to promote further price increases and the process runs on as long as the selling price of the output maintains a differential advantage over the expenses of production.

Ultimately, however, even though farm prices (and hence raw material prices) may not increase and a cheapening of the processes of production might occur, the total "expenses of production . . . overtake or nearly overtake the prospective selling price of the output."[12] As profit margins decrease, the inflated capitalizations of the preceding era seem excessive, not only in current terms, but in view

[9] *Ibid.*, pp. 188–189. [10] *Ibid.*, p. 189. [11] *Ibid.*, pp. 198 ff.
[12] *Ibid.*, p. 201.

of expected further declines in profits. Correspondingly, the loan collateral of these firms melts away to the point where confidence turns to nervousness, and the action of some important creditor to liquidate part of his outstanding contracts and loans will tend to trigger a widespread liquidation in all major sectors of the economy. As the liquidation of claims ensues, forced sales, bankruptcies, and subsequent reorganizations become the normal course of affairs due to the highly complex "interstitial pecuniary relations" existing "between the several concerns or branches of industry that make up the comprehensive industrial system at large." [13]

Out of this calamitous sequence of events come two ruthless competitors, who deal the harshest blows to the old established firms that are at this point attempting to stave off the disaster of bankruptcy. The first is the arrival on the scene of a new enterprise, tooled with the most modern of technological equipment and capitalized at a rate which enables it to earn "reasonable profits at current prices." [14] The second new competitor is the recently reorganized firm that suffered liquidation early in the recession, had its capital structure written down and simplified, and can earn a reasonable rate of return now on its new capitalization.

The presence of this new competition forces the older struggling firms to make drastic alterations in their financial structures or fail. Beyond this, inasmuch as Veblen foresaw future prosperities as merely episodic, with chronic depression as the normal state of affairs, comprehensive coalitions of these business units appeared to serve as the most hopeful long-run solution. Still better, from Veblen's point of view, would be the eventual emergence of a "Soviet of Technicians," which would seek to maximize efficiency and output rather than profit.[15]

Looked at critically, this notion of the possible "revolutionary overturn" of the "Guardians of the Vested Interests" appears extreme, yet Veblen himself admitted that nothing in the existing situation should be considered a threat to, or should "flutter the sensibilities" of, the "Absentee Owners." [16] In calling for an "evolutionary" economics he is

[13] *Ibid.*, p. 188. [14] *Ibid.*, p. 224.
[15] T. Veblen, *The Engineers and the Price System* (New York: Viking, 1954), ch. vi.
[16] *Ibid.*, p. 169.

merely indicating changes which might eventually occur in the institutional milieu, and with which only a genetic approach could meaningfully cope.[17]

III

Turning now to the more familiar "Notes on the Trade Cycle"[18] of Keynes, we find him expressing the essence of his cycle views as follows:

[17] It is this insistence upon an evolutionary science of economics that has earned Veblen the title of "institutionalist"—this alone is an ironical classification when one recalls his aversion to "taxonomy" in any context. Veblen's former student, W. C. Mitchell, however, agrees with his approach, asserting: "The problems proper to economics . . . are problems of genesis and cumulative change in widely diffused habits of thought concerning ways and means. Such problems must be treated in terms of causation, not in terms of rational choice" ("Thorstein Veblen: 1857–1929," *Econ. Jour.*, XXXIX [Dec., 1929], 648–649).

Furthermore, "Among the most significant of customs are those investigated by economics, the working rules laid down by collective action for the conduct of the transactions among individuals belonging to going concerns" (W. C. Mitchell, "Commons on Institutional Economics," *Amer. Econ. Rev.*, XXV [Dec., 1935], 640).

With regard to Veblen's success in deriving solutions to the questions he raised, it has been observed that "Veblen's keenly probing mind raised, albeit not at all clearly or self-consciously, some exceedingly fundamental issues—the nature of science, methodology in economics, problems of modern capitalism, social evolution, social policy, sociological theory, etc. In his posing of challenging issues lies most of his claim to greatness, for his answers to those problems were often untenable" (A. K. Davis, "Sociological Elements in Veblen's Economic Theory," *Jour. Pol. Econ.*, LIII [June, 1945], 134, n. 9).

Finally, even the label "institutionalist" has been challenged by Homan: "I may as well bluntly state my opinion that an institutional economics, differentiated from other economics by discoverable criteria, is largely an intellectual fiction, substantially devoid of content" (P. T. Homan, "An Appraisal of Institutional Economics," *Amer. Econ. Rev.*, XXII [March, 1932], 15). While criticizing Professor Homan on other points, DR Scott agrees with him that the term "institutional economist" is "a misnomer when applied to . . . Veblen" ("Veblen Not an Institutional Economist," *Amer. Econ. Rev.*, XXIII [June, 1933], 274 ff.).

[18] Keynes, *op. cit.*, ch. xxii. Perhaps the most discerning review article of Keynes' *General Theory* is A. C. Pigou's "Mr. J. M. Keynes' General Theory of Employment, Interest and Money," *Economica*, III (May, 1936), 115–132. The review is critical, though good-natured. The last two sentences read: "We have watched an artist firing arrows at the moon. Whatever be thought of his marksmanship, we can all admire his virtuosity" (p. 132).

A complete set of evaluations of Keynes's contributions (there are differing opinions as to *the* most significant contribution), is provided by G. Haberler, A. H. Hansen, R. F. Harrod, and J. A. Schumpeter, "Keynes' Contributions to

Veblen and Keynes

The Trade Cycle is best regarded, I think, as being occasioned by a cyclical change in the marginal efficiency of capital, though complicated and often aggravated by associated changes in the other significant short-period variables of the economic system.[19]

After observing that most customary explanations of the upper turning point and "crisis" are couched in terms of rising interest rates, brought on by a scarcity of money for trade and speculative operations, Keynes admits that on occasion an initiating or aggravating role may be played by this factor but insists upon placing the emphasis elsewhere, saying:

I suggest that a more typical, and often the predominant, explanation of the crisis is, not primarily a rise in the rate of interest, but a sudden collapse in the marginal efficiency of capital.[20]

And in this regard Keynes again asserts that psychological factors and expectations are critical. At some point, as a boom progresses, doubts and disillusion arise concerning the "reliability of . . . prospective yield." Virtually all of the overly optimistic expectations of the preceding boom are now "replaced by a contrary 'error of pessimism.'"[21] Moreover, due to the refractory nature of these psychological variables, public policy must be so directed as to attack their pernicious tendencies indirectly to "overshoot." The damage is inflicted, as Keynes puts it, because "a boom is a situation in which overoptimism triumphs over a rate of interest which, in a cooler light, would be seen to be excessive."[22]

With markets organized as they are in free capitalistic economies, disastrous shifts in the estimated marginal efficiencies of capital are unavoidable.[23] It is not that there is over-investment "in the sense that an aggregate gross yield in excess of replacement cost could no longer

---

Economics: Four Views," *Rev. Econ. Stat.*, XXVIII (Nov., 1946), 178-196. These papers are much shorter, and, to me, appear to be more incisive than the essays in S. E. Harris, ed., *The New Economics* (New York: Knopf, 1947). Also, consult J. H. Williams, "An Appraisal of Keynesian Economics," *Amer. Econ. Rev.*, XXXVIII (May, 1948), 273–290. This article, plus the American Economic Association's symposium, "Keynesian Economics After Twenty Years," (*Amer. Econ. Rev.*, XLVII [May, 1957], pp. 67-95) should serve to indicate the nature of the "crystallized" opinion of the present.

[19] Keynes, *op. cit.*, p. 313.   [20] *Ibid.*, p. 315.   [21] *Ibid.*, p. 322.
[22] *Ibid.*, p. 322.   [23] *Ibid.*, p. 320.

be expected"[24] (in fact, Keynes cites the "great social advantages of increasing the stock of capital until it ceases to be scarce").[25] Rather, the case is one in which a "misguided state of expectation" operates in conjunction with a rate of interest which is unrealistically high (in terms of a "correct" state of expectation), especially in the long run, with the inevitable denouement being "a condition where there is a shortage of houses, but where nevertheless no one can afford to live in the houses that there are."[26]

IV

To draw parallels and points of contrast between two authors or their theories is generally a risky venture but often, as in our analysis of Veblen and Keynes, it would appear to be the most appropriate method of attack. Moreover, it should be noted that this form of eclecticism does not necessarily result in mere untheoretical description. For it can scarcely be denied that a variety of useful information may be obtained, policy decisions may be made more rationally, and even sophisticated models constructed as a result of the careful study of such "merely descriptive" cycle approaches as Lescure's and Mitchell's.

Similarly, not only Keynes's concern with underinvestment and underconsumption but also Veblen's emphasis upon overcapitalization are both, conceptually speaking, just as instructive today as ever they were. In certain areas their tenets overlap; in others they tend to diverge markedly, although in some instances the differences are largely terminological.

As an example of divergence, we might cite their respective concepts of profit and its role in the general neighborhood of the upper turning point. Keynes maintains that at this stage of the cycle "a sudden collapse in the marginal efficiency of capital"[27] occurs. He then uses the phrase "future yields of capital-goods"[28] as synonymous with "marginal efficiency of capital." To anyone unfamiliar with Keynes's special definition of the marginal efficiency of capital, this concept might appear to be the counterpart of Veblen's "pecuniary gain (the

[24] Ibid., p. 324.   [25] Ibid., p. 325.   [26] Ibid., p. 322.
[27] Ibid., p. 315.   [28] Ibid.

Veblen and Keynes

earnings),"[29] "rate of earnings,"[30] "current earning-capacity,"[31] "gains . . . as a percentage on . . . investment,"[32] and "prospective change in the earning-capacity of the firm."[33] But Keynes warns us that

> the marginal efficiency of capital is here defined in terms of the *expectation* of yield and of the *current* supply price of the capital-asset. It depends on the rate of return expected to be obtainable on money if it were invested in a *newly* produced asset; not on the historical result of what an investment has yielded on its original cost if we look back on its record after its life is over.[34]

Hence, prospective "yield" and replacement cost, in conjunction with the rate of interest, determine the volume of *new* investment for Keynes, while "prospective earning capacity," to Veblen, is critical for evaluating the appropriateness of the loan collateral base relative to which *existing* capitalizations have been structured. Veblen thus constantly stresses the continuity between the existing level of profits and the maintenance of *full* employment of already operating capital investment during the latter stages of prosperity. Expectation, in his model, is described in terms of "lively anticipation[s] of an advanced demand,"[35] and "habit[s] of buoyancy, or speculative recklessness."[36]

Keynes, on the other hand, emphasizes that the future level of investment, and hence the regulator of income and employment, is the derivative of prospective yield, especially after prolonged prosperity. It is at this stage of the cycle that expectations are described by Keynes as being properly expressed in such terms as "doubts and disillusion," "over-optimism," "error of pessimism," and "misguided state of expectation."

Expectations are thus accorded a central role by both Veblen and Keynes, but the Keynesian model demands a rate of investment

---

[29] Veblen, *Theory of Business Enterprise*, p. 186.   [30] *Ibid.*, p. 201.
[31] *Ibid.*, p. 237.   [32] *Ibid.*, p. 186.   [33] *Ibid.*, p. 187.
[34] *Ibid.*, p. 136. Keynes did believe, however, that his marginal efficiency of capital was "identical with" Irving Fisher's "rate of return over cost." This allegation has recently been demonstrated to be inaccurate. Cf. A. A. Alchian, "The Rate of Interest, Fisher's Rate of Return Over Costs, and Keynes' Internal Rate of Return," *Amer. Econ. Rev.*, XLV (Dec., 1955), 938–943; and comment by R. Robinson, *Amer. Econ. Rev.*, XLVI (Dec., 1956), 972–973.
[35] Veblen, *Theory of Business Enterprise*, p. 195.
[36] *Ibid.*, p. 196.

growth that is absent in the Veblenian scheme.[37] Whereas Keynes maintained that the viability of capitalism depended upon suitable adjustments in the "propensity to consume and the inducement to invest," [38] Veblen, the stagnationist, foresaw episodic prosperities with chronic depression as the more normal order of things.[39] Keynesian adjustments within the institutional framework of private capitalism would not have appeared efficacious to Veblen who insisted that comprehensive coalitions of heretofore competitive business units would eliminate most of the institutions of early twentieth century capitalism. In his words, "The higher development of the machine process makes competitive business impracticable, but it carries a remedy for its own evils in that it makes coalition practicable." [40] Later, of course, Veblen called for a "Soviet of Technicians"—an arrangement which would utterly destroy the sort of dual economy envisioned by Keynes.[41] In view of this distinction between the long-run prophecies

[37] Little evidence exists that Keynes was impressed by, or even familiar with, Veblen's cycle analysis. No reference to Veblen may be found in either the *General Theory* or *A Treatise on Money* (New York: Harcourt, Brace, 1930). Noting this, one commentator has remarked that "Keynes might have been better prepared for the higher levels of economic analysis had he made a thorough study of the work of Marx, Veblen, Hobson, and other exponents of economic heterodoxy." Cf. A. G. Gruchy, "J. M. Keynes' Concept of Economic Science," *South. Econ. Jour.*, XV (Jan., 1949), 255.

[38] Keynes, *General Theory*, pp. 380, 325.

[39] "Thorstein Veblen argued that the alternation of lively expansions and contractions is giving place to a chronic state of mild depression, from which business revives only when stimulated by favorable random factors" (A. F. Burns and W. C. Mitchell, *Measuring Business Cycles* [New York: National Bureau of Economic Research, 1946], p. 382. Mitchell has added: "We have no assurance that . . . cyclical movements tend to be uniform. Possibly they tend to grow progressively more violent, as Karl Marx predicted; possibly they tend to subside into brief and mild expansions followed by long and moderate contractions, as Thorstein Veblen surmised" (W. C. Mitchell, *What Happens During Business Cycles* [New York: National Bureau of Economic Research, 1951], p. 187).

Still another authority, M. A. Copeland, declares: "Veblen, it is true, propounded a secular stagnation hypothesis. But many of his followers did not go along with him in this respect. During the twenties and forties and even during the thirties they regarded such a view of the way our economy operates as a form of historical myopia" ("Institutional Economics and Model Analysis," *Amer. Econ. Rev.*, XLI [May, 1951], 60).

[40] Veblen, *Theory of Business Enterprise*, p. 263.

[41] Professor A. H. Harris adds something equally sinister: "Veblen thought that maximum industrial efficiency and welfare required drastic reorganization of the

Veblen and Keynes

of the two, it might be said that Keynes is primarily concerned with the warranted rate of *growth* of private capitalism, while Veblen would stress the *development* and ultimate demise of free enterprise capitalism under the impelling forces of evolutionary growth and change.[42]

The final comparison we wish to make between Veblen and Keynes pertains to the determination and the role of the rate of interest in their respective models. Veblen's rate of interest is a competitive price [43] (just as is the wage rate), but it is not derived by resorting to any of the rationalizations implicit in the baleful, hedonistic calculus. Instead of treating the emergence of interest as a corollary of the traditional supply and demand apparatus, he relates it to "Traffic in Vendible Capital" [44]—a term designating "the most important line of business enterprise." [45] The gains made in trafficking in vendible capital "are a tax on commonplace business enterprise, in much the same manner and with much the like effects as the gains of commonplace business (ordinary profits and *interest*) are a *tax on industry*." [46]

Keynes, of course, not only asserts that the "classical" theory "involves formal error" but also decries it as being a "nonsense theory." [47] With this Veblen would enthusiastically agree. But here Keynes departs by replacing the Marshallian supply and demand schedules for capital—which he correctly criticizes as offering an indeterminate solution—with his liquidity preference-quantity of money model,

---

economic system, and his proposals to this end have a strongly Marxian flavor" ("John R. Commons and the Welfare State," *South. Econ. Jour.* XIX [Oct., 1952], 222).

Despite these rather strong charges, some see Veblen as a sort of innocuous visionary, for example: "Apart from the absence of a systematic evolutionary methodology, the most important factor in Veblen's influence on American economics lay in his avoidance of policy proposals" (A. W. Coats, "The Influence of Veblen's Methodology," *Jour. Pol. Econ.*, LXII [Dec., 1954], 537).

[42] Writing in 1925, Veblen declared: "The question now before the body of economists is not how things stabilize themselves in a 'static state,' but how they endlessly grow and change" ("Economic Theory in the Calculable Future," *Amer. Econ. Rev.*, XV [March, 1925], Suppl., 51).

[43] Dorfman, *Thorstein Veblen and His America*, p. 282.

[44] T. Veblen, *The Place of Science in Modern Civilisation* (New York: Huebsch, 1919), pp. 380 ff.

[45] *Ibid.*, p. 381.   [46] *Ibid.*, p. 382 (italics mine).

[47] Keynes, *General Theory*, p. 179.

which, as both Hicks [48] and Hansen [49] have pointed out (again correctly), is equally indeterminate.[50]

But, however determined, Veblen and Keynes would nonetheless agree that the role of interest rates in the neighborhood of the upper turning point is not unimportant. The principal difference would be that Veblen accepts interest as an objective fact, a constant or "given," though perhaps embodied with some stochastic properties. As a tax on industry, interest arises out of the habitual matter-of-fact performance of trafficking in vendible capital—a further instance of capitalist "sabotage." He devotes no special attention to subtle changes in the structure of interest rates as the prosperity phase progresses.[51] Keynes, on the other hand, though maintaining that the "explanation of crisis is not primarily a rise in the rate of interest," [52] does contend that occasionally such a rise may play an "aggravating" or "initiating" part.[53] Furthermore, in the latter stages of a boom optimistic expectations probably include rising interest rates,[54] destined to soar still higher as the ensuing "collapse in the marginal efficiency of capital naturally precipitates a sharp increase in liquidity-preference—and hence a rise in the rate of interest." [55] "Later on, a decline in the rate of interest will be a great aid to recovery and probably a necessary condition of it." [56] Hence, shifts in the structure of interest rates are integral in the Keynesian schema; and although the shift may be inappropriate or perverse in the latter part of the boom, a contrary movement in the gloom of depression is felicitous.

[48] J. R. Hicks, "Mr. Keynes and the 'Classics'; A Suggested Interpretation," *Econometrica*, V (1937), 147–159.

[49] A. H. Hansen, *A Guide to Keynes* (New York: McGraw-Hill, 1953), pp. 140 ff.

[50] Professor Hansen, with characteristic lucidity, has demonstrated how the Keynesian interest theory can be reformulated so as to eliminate its objectionable features.

[51] Veblen does note that part of the difficulty in a downturn "is traceable to a discrepancy between the accepted capitalization, the interest charges, and the earning-capacity" (*Theory of Business Enterprise*, p. 225). But, in commenting on the vagaries of the cycle, he insists "that the rate of interest need not be notably low in time of depression, just as, on the other hand, a period of business exaltation is not uniformly accompanied by a notably high rate of interest" (*ibid.*, p. 221).

[52] Keynes, *General Theory*, p. 315.   [53] *Ibid.*
[54] *Ibid.*   [55] *Ibid.*, p. 316.   [56] *Ibid.*

Veblen and Keynes

V

As we have depicted them, the cycle views of Veblen and Keynes overlap in certain areas and diverge in others. The congruity is not unexpected in either case, inasmuch as both writers ranged broadly—though Keynes not to such an extent as Veblen. But the essentially macro character of Keynes's apparatus probably entitles him to first honors for presenting the more general explanation of cyclical economic disequilibrium.[57] For Keynes, by replacing Say's Law with the consumption function, has not only provided economists generally with an explanation of how economic expansions and contractions are ultimately damped, but for our current purpose of prognostication also has supplied us with an additional reason for short-run optimism: namely, current coefficients of average and marginal propensities to consume reveal that widespread underconsumption is not immediately indicated. Because Keynes's framework is broadly theoretical and comprehensive, Veblen's more constrained model properly becomes supplementary to Keynes's. Thus, in casting about for helpful constructs with which to analyze today's (October, 1957) internal economic situation in the United States, it seems evident that an explanation couched in terms of overcapitalization might well reinforce the insights gained from a purely conventional Keynesian method of attack.[58]

---

[57] This principle is illustrated by Hicks, who, while comparing the Keynesian formulation of the interest elasticity of saving and investment with that of the "classics," concludes: "It is true that when the two theories are properly understood, and fully worked out, they largely overlap; but they do not overlap all the way, and when they fail to do so, the Keynes theory has the wider coverage" (J. R. Hicks, "A Rehabilitation of 'Classical' Economics?" *Econ. Jour.*, LXVII [June, 1957], 289).

[58] Elsewhere, in a somewhat different context, it has been noted that exclusive reliance upon the aggregate approach of Keynes will result in serious lacunae if not rigorously elaborated; viz., "The 'classical' writers tended to pay too little attention to obstacles to effective demand; the Keynesians tend to slur over obstacles to supply" (D. M. Wright, "The Future of Keynesian Economics," *Amer. Econ. Rev.*, XXXV [June, 1945], 299). Nor should a distinction unreservedly be drawn between alleged Keynesian "realism" and the neoclassical conditional theoretical approach; e.g., "It is wrong to suggest that Keynes is more realistic than Marshall, in that, while the latter deals only with tendencies, the former deals with facts. Both alike deal only with tendencies" (A. C. Pigou, *Keynes's 'General Theory'* [London: Macmillan, 1951], p. 62). [Note continues on next page.]

Melvin D. Brockie

Taking their respective profit doctrines as the first point of departure, it is apparent that, although conceptually of divergent views, both men today would be scrutinizing carefully recent quarterly profit statements (current, as well as projected) which reveal that profit margins have been narrowing in the presence of intensified competition and a continuing rise in costs. To Keynes this leveling-off process would indicate, I believe, in the absence of overoptimism, that contemplated investment expenditure plans should be re-evaluated—not that the future status of existing capital structures should be deemed precarious. Contrarily, Veblen's possible position might be stated as follows: although prices are still rising, the fact that profit margins are narrowing, and may be presumed to continue to do so, constitutes sufficient reason for nervousness among strategically situated creditors. Accordingly, even though both theorists were to admit the importance of the psychological forces at work, Veblen would tend to be more apprehensive in the current complex of affairs than would Keynes.

At the core of these speculations lie the forecasts of expected investment and government spending. Keynes would focus special attention upon the recent leveling out or decline in investment on new plant and equipment and net foreign investment, as well as upon current attempts to reduce total Federal outlays for goods and services. And should interest rates change upward markedly (e.g., because of Federal Reserve activities), Keynes would be inclined to view such shifts with more concern than would Veblen, although Keynes admittedly believed that increases, at least, seldom are initiating factors in the neighborhood of the upper turning point. To the extent that prior increases in interest rates have already induced selective inventory reductions and capital expansion stretch-outs, they are, in Keynesian parlance, deflationary—in the absence of compensating factors. Veblen, accepting the structure of interest rates as an "objective fact," would still maintain that major attention should be focused elsewhere—namely, on current or immediately expected earnings on the business sector's "funded make-believe." Production in real terms may well increase in 1958, but Veblen would insist that

---

Furthermore, it is incorrect to imply, as some have recently, that Keynes' model is asymmetrical, that it is useful for analyzing deflation but not inflation. Cf. S. H. Slichter, "The Passing of Keynesian Economics," *Atlantic* (Nov., 1957), pp. 141–146.

Veblen and Keynes

the business community, reckoning as it does in terms of a different *numéraire* (i.e., money profits on an overinflated capitalization), will be disappointed with the economy's short-run performance; and in the process, of course, any optimistic long-term expectations inevitably will be transformed into feelings of pessimism and disillusion.

Finally, taking all the afore-mentioned variables into consideration, Keynes would probably be the more optimistically inclined with regard to both our projected short- and long-run levels of income and employment. With properly co-ordinated monetary-fiscal policy, with relatively high levels of gross private domestic investment, and with the built-in stabilizer of cold war, he might forecast no recession as severe as 1937–1938 either presently or in the foreseeable future. Beyond this, projected advances in technology (e.g., automation and atomic energy) and the persistent upsurge in population growth would appear to supply the conditions necessary for the sustained viability of capitalism.

Dissimilarly, Veblen, in analyzing current capitalizations and reduced profit margins, might be more inclined to draw parallels between the present situation and that existing in the nineteen-twenties. His argument presumably would be that, in the absence of increasing industrial efficiency, some strategic combination of business sabotage (which includes all devices for restricting production in order to enhance business profits, e.g., protective tariffs) and waste (by consumers, cold war, and so on) might enable the existing system to remain viable over the long period; but it is precisely this purposeful concern (on the part of some) with efficiency, coupled with a still highly unequal distribution of wealth and income, which will prove to be the overpowering forces working toward disequilibrium. Implicit in their resultant is the undoing of large portions of existing capital structures with concomitant pressures and demands for still more coalition, sabotage, and waste. He would remind us that this role played by business coalitions in his long-run schema has been increasingly in evidence as an objective fact in the American economy over the past few years. Mergers, both effectuated and proposed, in the automobile and railroad industries, as well as in the highly sensitive banking and financial community, may be readily cited.[59] As for

[59] A more comprehensive list would include, among others, coalitions among firms producing precision instruments, data-processing equipment, and electronics in its

Melvin D. Brockie

the present, a forthcoming recession and depression, possibly of the order of 1937–1938, would appear perhaps as a real possibility to him. And although he undoubtedly would not predict severe, uninterrupted depression, at least under present circumstances, the ineluctable forces of growth and change nevertheless imply rather immediate stagnation and ultimate capitalistic disintegration.

Although this latter Veblenian position seems untenable, at least his short-range analysis should be included in any evaluation of current cyclical economic affairs. Yet in few, if any, present-day forecasts is it evident that his short-run model has been employed—a most unfortunate oversight, since his cycle apparatus should be considered as an auxiliary to the broader Keynesian system. For Keynes's generality, implicit in an aggregate approach, still leaves ample room for Veblen's more specific interest in what income statements and balance sheets reveal about already existing capital structures.

---

broadest context. In many of these instances, the object of coalescing is to reap any possible advantages from integration, diversification or, in a wider frame of reference, increasing returns to scale.

[FOREST G. HILL]

8

Veblen and Marx

THE study of Thorstein Veblen can be intellectually stimulating, yet very frustrating. His writings abound in playful skepticism, bitter irony, and thinly veiled social criticism. He moralized even when he claimed to be ethically aloof or neutral. He dealt in large generalizations which were at various times sweeping ethical pronouncements, deductions from basic postulates, or broad descriptive statements based on wide observation and factual evidence which he neglected to cite. He did not try to distinguish between his ethical and analytical propositions or his deductive and inductive statements. His readers need not be reminded of his flamboyant, discursive, repetitious style of writing.

Seldom is Veblen's argument subject to precise, unambiguous interpretation. He defined his basic concepts in the most general terms. He resorted to the use of emotionally loaded terms or catchwords, which for him often had ulterior meanings at odds with customary usage. He borrowed concepts, principles, and evidence freely and sometimes indiscriminately from psychology, anthropology, sociology, economic history, and even biology. Using these varied materials, he advanced his argument slowly and cumbersomely, often proceeding on several levels of meaning. Consequently, his analysis is usually subject to misunderstanding and conflicting interpretations.

I

Veblen's work, however, poses many challenging problems for analysis in economics and related social sciences. These issues provide rich opportunities for fundamental inquiry, despite his often puzzling treatment of them. We may roughly group into four categories the major problems involved in evaluating Veblen or using his type of analysis. These classes of issues pertain to the general approach of economic theory, the analysis of economic development, the making of value judgments about economic institutions, and the charting of future institutional change.[1]

In Veblen's view economics has to be an evolutionary science devoted to the study of process and change in economic life.[2] He insisted that the chief task of economics is analysis of the evolution and performance of economic institutions. This analysis required the study of human nature and social behavior, in which Veblen employed such concepts as instincts, habits, cultural lag, and also institutions. Technological advance was the most dynamic force in institutional change, and he dichotomized between technology and institutions. For our own culture this dichotomy took the form of industry versus business, the machine process versus business enterprise. When we examine Veblen or attempt to work in his broad field of inquiry, we must assess the relevance and usefulness of his approach, postulates, and analytical concepts.

Veblen designed his general approach so as to analyze economic development and institutional change. We need to know whether he had an adequate theory of change. Issues of technological determinism are involved; and we must ask whether technological advance governs cultural change, whether institutions merely retard change, whether psychological and cultural factors play an important part in the process of change. Questions also arise as to the role of the state, national patriotism, religion, class conflict, and reason. In one way or another, Veblen exposes us to all these issues of a theory of economic change.

---

[1] Useful reviews of Veblen's theoretical position are found in Allan G. Gruchy, *Modern Economic Thought: The American Contribution* (New York: Prentice-Hall, 1947), pp. 31–132; John A. Hobson, *Veblen* (London: Chapman and Hall, 1936); and Paul T. Homan, *Contemporary Economic Thought* (New York: Harper, 1928), pp. 107–192.

[2] Veblen's leading theoretical essay is "Why Is Economics Not an Evolutionary Science?" (1898), reprinted in his *The Place of Science in Modern Civilisation and Other Essays* (New York: Huebsch, 1919), pp. 56–81. This volume contains most of his theoretical papers.

Veblen and Marx

These problems require, or else readily permit, value judgments about economic institutions and their functioning. Veblen often made veiled or barbed ethical judgments about the prevailing economic order. He apparently regarded all economic institutions—at least all those he chose to discuss—as inhibitory of progress, and therefore ethically objectionable. Much uncertainty prevails regarding his attitude toward socialism, democracy, and, in his terms, desirable institutional changes. He used maximum production or industrial efficiency as his normative yardstick and injected ethical norms into his instinct categories. As he used it, his analysis appears necessarily to involve ethical judgments; consequently, the issue arises whether this is inevitable with his type of analysis.

The charting of future economic change or social reconstruction involves a dual problem. There is the task of predicting what will likely happen, or what can realistically be achieved or expected through concerted action. If appropriate for this task, Veblen's evolutionary approach and theory of social change should permit answers to the analytical and factual questions of what can be predicted to be probable or workable. There is also the normative question of the desirability of these predicted developments. There are thus issues of how capitalism will change, and how it should be changed. Such questions also arise with respect to monopoly, state intervention, nationalism, imperialism, class conflict, and socialism.

The four groups or types of problems are directly or implicitly posed in all of Veblen's writings,[3] particularly in his evaluation of Karl Marx and later Marxian socialists. Veblen's analysis of Marx throws light on these problems and should help us to understand his own work. There is no question that he was greatly interested in Marx. We need to determine the extent to which he borrowed directly from Marx, the degree to which he was—as both Marxists and non-Marxists sometimes claim—a cleverly camouflaged Marxian theorist himself, and the degree to which he only pretended to adopt Marxian doctrines. To examine Veblen's ideas about Marxism should help provide a cross-sectional view of his whole intellectual position.

[3] Veblen's writings, activities, and interests are well described in Joseph Dorfman, *Thorstein Veblen and His America* (New York: Viking, 1935).

Forest G. Hill

II

The major reason for Veblen's interest in Marx is not far to seek. Veblen's main objective was the critical evaluation of American capitalism.[4] For this purpose he needed a theory of capitalism which would explain its evolution and functioning. In attempting to lay the basis for an evolutionary economics, he elaborated a critique of orthodox theory and also Marxian theory. He regarded Marx as an important original thinker who had asked essentially the right questions. Marx had studied the evolution of economic institutions, stressing the role of economic forces in their evolution. He had attempted to predict the future of capitalism and to pass ethical judgments on capitalism. Veblen was readily attracted by these elements in Marx's system, and he had a continuing interest in Marxian doctrines and socialist programs.

Efforts to compare Veblen and Marx have been many in number and strikingly varied in results.[5] Such comparison is apparently as treacherous as it is challenging. Veblen has been variously described as Marxist, utopian-socialist, agrarian-populist, and anarchist in his orientation. His social philosophy has been termed nihilistic, totalitarian, technocratic, and democratic. His basic ideas have been deemed

[4] Gruchy, *op. cit.*, p. 80.

[5] Veblen and Marx are compared in Arthur K. Davis, "Sociological Elements in Veblen's Economic Theory," *Jour. Pol. Econ.*, LIII (June, 1945), 132–149; Dorfman, *op. cit.*; Gruchy, *op. cit.*; Abram L. Harris, "Types of Institutionalism" and "Economic Evolution: Dialectical and Darwinian," *Jour. Pol. Econ.*, XL (Dec., 1932), 721–749 and XLII (Feb., 1934), 34–79; Hobson, *op. cit.*; Max Lerner, ed., *The Portable Veblen* (New York: Viking, 1948), "Editor's Introduction," pp. 1–49; R. M. MacIver, *Society: A Textbook of Sociology* (New York: Farrar & Rinehart, 1937), pp. 438–461; Wesley C. Mitchell, *Lecture Notes on Types of Economic Theory* (mimeo.; New York: Augustus M. Kelley, 1949), II, 218–221, 229–231, 246; Wesley C. Mitchell, ed., *What Veblen Taught* (New York: Viking, 1945), pp. xlvii–xlviii; *Monthly Review*, IX (July–Aug., 1957), series of articles on Veblen —see especially those by Solomon Adler, Paul A. Baran, Arthur K. Davis, and Paul M. Sweezy; David Riesman, *Thorstein Veblen, A Critical Interpretation* (New York: Scribner, 1953); Eric Roll, *A History of Economic Thought* (rev. ed.; New York: Prentice-Hall, 1942), pp. 483–500; Bernard Rosenberg, *The Values of Veblen* (Washington, D.C.: Public Affairs Press, 1956); and Paul M. Sweezy, "The Influence of Marxian Economics on American Thought and Practice," in Donald Drew Egbert and Stow Persons, eds., *Socialism and American Life* (Princeton: Princeton University Press, 1952), I, 473–477.

Veblen and Marx

both original and borrowed, largely from Marx. He has been depicted as an economic determinist of the Marxian variety, and his views on class conflict and the role of the state have been called essentially Marxian; he has been claimed, tolerated, amended, and rejected by writers of a Marxian outlook.[6] It would seem that Veblen is often believed to be turning to the left in his grave. Marxists who put Veblen in a favorable light typically seek for outward similarities in the writings of Veblen and Marx. They stress the similar descriptions and predictions made by Marx and Veblen but often ignore differences in approach and postulates. If they take notice of the latter, they distinguish between Veblen's dubious analysis and penetrating insights, which are then selectively correlated with those of Marx.[7]

In comparing these two theorists, however, it is essential to give precedence to their basic approaches and premises. Veblen's own theoretical position and his criticism of orthodox theory should be kept in mind when his evaluation of Marx's postulates and doctrines is examined. Furthermore, Veblen's explicit critique of Marx should obviously be given proper weight in any comparison of the two men.

Veblen urged that economics be made an evolutionary science of behavior.[8] It should explain the evolution and performance of economic institutions. He explicitly adopted Darwinian postulates of evolutionary change and tolerated no concepts of teleology, inevitability, normality, or natural law. But he was no social Darwinian in the accepted sense of this term, for he brooked no assumption of beneficent tendencies or inevitable improvement in social evolution. Instead he stressed cumulative change, brute causation, and blind drift, no doubt with a touch of dialectical polemic.

For Veblen the study of human nature was essential to economic theory. He envisaged institutions as changing slowly but incessantly by a process of habituation under the dual impact of material circumstances and human nature. To analyze the role of human nature,

---

[6] See the shading of opinion found in the series on Veblen in the *Monthly Review*, IX (July–Aug., 1957).

[7] Cf. the treatment of Veblen in Roll, *op. cit.*, pp. 483–500. Roll says that Veblen was concerned mainly with the ideological or psychological "superstructure" of the pecuniary culture, or the "epiphenomena of capitalism," that his analysis is weak and misguided, but that his historical insights are often valuable. See also the articles in the *Monthly Review* cited above.

[8] See Veblen's "Why Is Economics Not an Evolutionary Science?" in *Place of Science*, pp. 56–81.

he used the concepts of habits and instincts. He often spoke of the habits of thought and action which condition immediate behavior and coalesce into institutions controlling mass behavior. He may have oversimplified when he conceived of institutions merely as collective habits and of habituation as the process by which institutions evolve.

The concept of instincts has attracted more criticism than any other aspect of Veblen's work. He seemed to conceive of the instincts he employed—the parental bent, workmanship, emulation, and idle curiosity—as biological in essence and part of the "Darwinian" scheme of things. However, he distinguished instincts from tropisms or sheer physiological reflexes; and his instincts took on a surprisingly social and even rational character. He asserted that these instincts define the basic or generic ends of human behavior and that they involve a rational choice of means to satisfy these ends.[9] His instinct scheme permitted the clash of ends and the confusion of means and ends. For instance, the ends set by the parental bent or desire to promote community welfare could conflict with those defined by emulation or the self-regarding instinct. Further, since the instinct of workmanship served only proximate ends, the latter could take on the significance of ends in themselves at the expense of "generically human" ends. Of course, workmanship could also become the servant of emulation rather than of the parental bent.

Veblen clearly conceived that the instincts motivated behavior in an institutional context. Existing institutions regulated social behavior, often imposing ends divergent from the instinctive ends. Veblen used the term "imbecile institutions" to designate those social institutions, typically private property and nationalism, which thwarted generically human ends. In a sense, institutions ceased being means and became ends in themselves—and repressive, absurd ends at that.

The instincts used by Veblen constituted, together with the role of habits, his conception of human nature. He believed that basic human nature was unchanging or at least had been stable for centuries. Nevertheless, human nature was pliable in the context of shifting social conditions. Changing institutions and material circumstances could indefinitely deflect human nature, or the set of instinctive drives, without permanently altering it. Although institutions could thus

[9] For Veblen's analysis of instincts, see especially *The Instinct of Workmanship and the State of the Industrial Arts* (New York: Macmillan, 1914).

frustrate or overrule generically human ends for a time, this state of things might be unstable or temporary; man's basic nature might reassert itself, though not inevitably in any given period.

Sociologists in particular have asserted that Veblen used his instincts as ethical norms, or at least read social values into them.[10] This charge is no doubt warranted, for he used these "instincts" as the basis for criticizing institutions, even for terming them "imbecile." He often employed workmanship as a norm, judging the functioning of economic institutions by the criterion of industrial efficiency. At other times he used the parental bent and idle curiosity as norms. By idle curiosity he usually meant intellectual freedom, pure research, or unfettered experimentation and inventiveness—values he undoubtedly cherished.

Veblen's instincts seem to involve a compounded ambivalence. They make up a fixed or stable human nature, and yet they are flexible and are conditioned by institutions. They are apparently biological, but they also set the ends of human action and even serve as ethical norms. Despite their ostensibly physiological nature, they involve an intellectual element in the form of rational choice of means. Such instincts as the parental bent and emulation come into conflict with each other in an institutional context, and workmanship can become subservient to either of them. There is conflict not only among instincts but also between them and prevailing institutions. Veblen's analysis often ran primarily in terms of the institutions themselves, with the instincts left in the background as his formal conception of human nature and brought to the forefront only as criteria for evaluating institutions. All in all, his social psychology seems to be less akin to that of William McDougall than to that of William James or John Dewey.[11]

Veblen clearly needed a theory of human nature, or a set of as-

[10] Cf. Stanley M. Daugert, *The Philosophy of Thorstein Veblen* (New York: King's Crown, 1950), pp. 71–72; Davis, *op. cit.;* Homan, *op. cit.*, pp. 135–139; Talcott Parsons, "Sociological Elements in Economic Thought," *Quar. Jour. of Econ.*, XLIX (May, 1935), 414–453; Rosenberg, *op. cit.*, pp. 44–51; and Louis Schneider, *The Freudian Psychology and Veblen's Social Theory* (New York: King's Crown, 1948), pp. 65–89, 114–123, 131–138. With respect to the comparison of Veblen and Freud made by Schneider, see also John S. Gambs, *Beyond Supply and Demand: A Reappraisal of Institutional Economics* (New York: Columbia University Press, 1946).

[11] Cf. Homan, *op. cit.*, p. 189, and Mitchell, *What Veblen Taught*, p. xxxiv.

sumptions about it. However, he did not need, and probably did not have, a theory of instincts in the accepted sense of the term. Perhaps he seized upon a then-popular theory as a means of gaining attention —a not-uncommon practice of his—and redefined the theory for his own purpose. His "instincts" became more social, more rational, more normative in character than the usual instinct categories. By this pedagogical maneuver, he was able to attract notice, analyze institutional change, and even evaluate institutions. He could thus seemingly avoid the need to formulate his own ethical norms and make his value judgments explicit. Further, he could proceed without inquiring more deeply into human motives and the process of habituation. Although he by-passed these problems by manipulating the "instinct" concept, the value and clarity of his analysis thereby suffered.

These postulates of evolutionary change and human nature permitted Veblen to analyze the process of economic development. Central to his analysis was the evolution of economic institutions under the influence of human nature and material circumstances. The chief material force affecting economic change was technology, defined broadly to include accumulated scientific knowledge, industrial techniques, and acquired skills. With human nature assumed stable, the primary factors playing upon economic change were technology and institutions. These constituted Veblen's fundamental dichotomy, which he often phrased as the machine process and business enterprise, or industrial and pecuniary employments. Spurred on by workmanship and idle curiosity, technological advance was the dynamic factor in social change. Influenced by the emulative instinct, institutions played a permissive or restrictive role. Guided by the parental bent, technological advance could improve material welfare were it not for the change-resisting character of institutions.

Veblen adapted this basic dichotomy to the analysis of economic change by developing a theory of occupational disciplines. Here lay the significance of his contrast between pecuniary and industrial employments, or "business" and "industry." Although his theory of economic change is often interpreted as technological determinism, he strove for a psychological explanation. Instead of accepting a doctrine of economic determinism, he elaborated the psychological nexus which mediated between material forces and institutional change. He stressed the influence of occupation or type of employment upon

Veblen and Marx

the formation of habits of thought which crystallized into institutions. In an age of machine industry and giant corporations, most occupations were becoming predominantly industrial or pecuniary, with markedly different disciplining influences upon attitudes. Men in business pursuits habitually thought in terms of ownership and pecuniary gain; they readily accepted the institutional *status quo* and its value system. Men in industrial pursuits, however, were subjected to a radically different mental discipline. The thinking of industrial workers and technicians ran more in terms of mechanical sequence and material cause-and-effect terms. They gradually lost comprehension of pecuniary values; their loyalty to prevailing institutions declined as their conceptual scheme became indifferent or hostile to ownership and profit.[12]

The role of occupational disciplines in Veblen's theory of change becomes clearer when we examine his critique of Marx. It was a psychological theory conforming to Veblen's basic dichotomy and designed to explain institutional change. The theory illustrates his emphasis upon the essential place of psychological assumptions in economic theory. He ridiculed the "economic man" of orthodox theory with its outmoded or pre-Darwinian assumptions about human nature. He regarded men as active or dynamic by nature, with their wants and motives, or habits of thought and action, shaped by the changing material and psychological environment. He therefore rejected the assumptions of hedonism, that men passively seek pleasure and avoid pain, and of rational calculation, that men carefully measure utility and disutility in a rational effort to maximize satisfaction.

Veblen's criticisms of orthodox psychological assumptions demonstrate his method of evaluating economic theory. His technique was to attack a theory's basic postulates. He probed for its unstated preconceptions as well as its explicit premises. Although he sometimes selectively evaluated predictions derived from a theory, he was usually content to destroy its premises. His critique of orthodox theory should be noted, for it illustrates the method and even the substance of his criticism of Marx.

Veblen was content to lump together classical and neoclassical theorists in his sweeping attack on orthodox theory. Although this

[12] See his "Industrial and Pecuniary Employments," *Place of Science*, pp. 279–323, and *The Vested Interests and the Common Man* (New York: Huebsch, 1920).

procedure tended to blur individual differences among theorists, particularly some of the neoclassicists, Veblen deemed it sufficient for his purpose. His objective was of course to develop an evolutionary economics explaining institutional change. With this purpose in view, he rejected the preconceptions and postulates of traditional theory, especially its static approach and hedonistic assumptions. As noted above, he opposed all concepts of natural law and normality in economic theory, describing such theory as taxonomic and static. He likewise rejected its psychological assumptions of hedonism and rational calculation, charging that they were based on Benthamite utilitarianism and other pre-Darwinian psychological views.

III

When Veblen turned to an evaluation of Marxian theory, he followed the same method of attack.[13] He first criticized its basic postulates and then examined some of its specific doctrines. He expressed high regard for Marx as a theorist possessing an original, logical, powerful mind and a keen interest in change and institutions. He recognized that Marx was both theorist and propagandist, thereby contrasting Marx's logical grasp and polemics. He distinguished between Marx's theory of value and theory of development, rejecting the former much more completely than the latter. He concluded that Marx's conceptual system was pre-Darwinian and had to be revised along Darwinian lines.

In Veblen's view, Marx's preconceptions were derived from two chief sources, German Hegelian philosophy and English liberal-utilitarian thought. Marx's conception of social change was one of neo-Hegelianism or Hegelian materialism with romantic overtones that Veblen termed "sublimated materialism." The materialistic interpretation of history presupposed a dialectical process of development or progress—an unfolding process moving in terms of "inner necessity" toward a final goal. The class struggle constituted the dialectic, and the final term was socialism or the classless society. Veblen rejected the teleological concept of a final goal as pre-Darwinian.

Marx drew other major preconceptions from the Benthamite utili-

[13] "The Socialist Economics of Karl Marx and His Followers: I. The Theories of Karl Marx. II. The Later Marxism" (1906, 1907), *Place of Science*, pp. 409–456.

Veblen and Marx

tarians and classical economists, including Ricardo and the Ricardian socialists. In Veblen's opinion, Marx uncritically adopted natural rights and natural law preconceptions and a hedonistic psychology of rational self-interest. On these bases Marx elaborated his labor theory of value, with labor the source and measure of value, and the corollary doctrines of labor's right to its full product, of surplus value, and of exploitation of labor. He attributed rational self-interest not only to individuals but to entire classes, thereby explaining their asserted solidarity and motivation in the class struggle. Veblen rejected the concept of rational class interest and the labor theory of value, along with its corollaries and natural rights basis.

In sum, Veblen renounced Marx's basic preconceptions. Marx's Hegelian conception of social change and classical assumptions about human behavior had to be eliminated. Although Veblen rejected its foundations, he did not claim that he had demolished Marx's system. Instead, he sought to make it "Darwinian" by inserting new premises. He also wanted to retain something of Marx's approach, problems, and emphasis. He may have felt that Marx's theory of economic development could be salvaged if its foundations were adequately revised. Some students assert that he used Darwinism as a guise for his own implicit or attenuated Marxism. It may be, however, that he used an ostensibly revised Marxism as a vehicle for his "Darwinism," his own theory of economic development. He clearly asserted his own conceptual scheme in his "revision" of Marxian theory. This revision may have been a clever pedagogical device for presenting his own theoretical scheme and drawing attention to it as somehow smacking of Marxism. If Veblen had this design, it should be discernible in his treatment of individual Marxian doctrines and later Marxian socialists.

Veblen individually assessed a number of Marxian doctrines.[14] The labor theory of value Marx took from the liberal-utilitarian school. Marx treated it as implicit, or simply postulated it. Although it was merely tautological, he gave it a normative role in his larger theory. Veblen regarded the labor thory of value as irrelevant to Marx's main problems, the explanation of economic change and the creation of a functioning socialist order.

The doctrine of the right of labor to its full product was a corollary of the labor theory of value. It, too, was from the natural rights tra-

[14] *Ibid.*

dition and had a normative function. Veblen disputed the premise that labor had a natural right to its product. Instead, he suggested that the real issue was a distribution of income which would enable the industrial system to function.

The theories of surplus value and exploitation were further corollaries and likewise had a normative meaning for Marx. Veblen reasoned that these theories must be rejected in the form stated by Marx. The relevant problems could be analyzed in terms of surplus product instead of surplus value. Surplus product could be used as a tool to study exploitation, with emphasis centered on the relations between the serviceability, cost, and price of commodities. Serviceability typically exceeded cost but fell short of price. Veblen deemed this type of analysis adequate for the problem Marx had posed.

Marx's theory of accumulation was tied to the theories of surplus value and the reserve army of the unemployed, possessing the weaknesses of both. Marx related these theories in such a way that, as capital increased, wages and demand and employment fell. Veblen considered the theory of the reserve army quite vulnerable, since it implied continual population growth regardless of economic conditions, a view which was highly doubtful and certainly contrary to Darwinian principles.

Veblen asserted that the theory of increasing misery was not factually true. Over the decades, wages had not tended to fall below subsistence; absolute misery had not increased. The issue was one of relative instead of absolute misery, for dissatisfaction increased along with the growing inequality of wealth and income. He insisted that problems of labor's material welfare and unrest be analyzed in such terms as standards of living, pecuniary emulation, and "economic success."

The theory of the class struggle, Veblen argued, was a teleological Hegelian conception manifesting the drive of "inner necessity." It also had a strong hedonistic bias, since it presupposed rational calculation and equated self-interest and class interest. The class struggle would not inevitably result in socialism, nor could it be viewed as a rational process. It was more a "psychological" than a "materialist" process, for sentiment entered into it as well as reason and material circumstances. The chief "sentiments" that Veblen stressed were politics, nationalism, imperialism, and religion. He granted with Marx

Veblen and Marx

that the class struggle centered on private property. Even here, however, he questioned the line of class cleavage; potential conflict lay not between the "haves" and "have nots" but between the vested interests or absentee owners and the underlying population or "common man." In the latter category were the industrial workers, the technicians, and presumably the farmers, once they had suffered enough economic adversity. He thus replaced the Marxian class struggle with his theory of occupational disciplines, which he felt provided the necessary psychological link between changing material forces and shifting class attitudes.

Veblen did not explicitly assess other Marxian doctrines such as increasing concentration and monopoly, the tendency of profit rates to decline, crises and depression, the role of the state, and imperialism. His silence might suggest that he accepted them, at least in part. He certainly considered these phenomena important, for he gave enormous attention to them in his other writings. They actually constituted the core of his theoretical and historical analysis.[15] He perhaps felt that these doctrines were less trammeled by Marx's Hegelian and hedonistic preconceptions and were subject to empirical inquiry on their own merits. In his *Theory of Business Enterprise* Veblen dealt extensively with crises and depression along lines quite unlike Marxian theory. His theories of the state and imperialism showed outward resemblance to Marxian theory; in fact, he is often accused of taking them from Marxian sources. Although he was well acquainted with socialist literature on these subjects, he treated them in a somewhat different way. He gave as much or more stress to national sentiment than to purely economic factors—hardly the view of a confirmed economic determinist. As a result, Marxian writers have objected to his excessive concern with political and psychological factors in his analysis of imperialism and the state.[16]

The way Veblen evaluated Marxian doctrines would suggest that he "revised" Marxism for his own purpose. In his own words he made it "Darwinian," substituting cumulative causation for Hegelian dialectics in explaining economic change. He freed it from its classical,

---

[15] See especially *The Theory of Business Enterprise* (New York: Scribner, 1904); *Imperial Germany and the Industrial Revolution* (New York: Macmillan, 1915); *Vested Interests;* and *Absentee Ownership and Business Enterprise in Recent Times* (New York: Huebsch, 1923).

[16] This criticism is also made by Hobson, *op. cit.*, pp. 138–145.

hedonistic bias and abandoned the labor theory of value and related doctrines. In a real sense, Marxism became Veblenism; Marx's problems were given Veblen's solutions through use of Veblen's approach, postulates, and conclusions. Marxian insights no doubt lived on, but they took root in Veblenian ground and flowered in Veblenian splendor.

IV

Veblen maintained a large and apparently sympathetic interest in later Marxian socialist writers.[17] He indicated some approval of the revisionists, at least on the analytical side. He felt that they were getting away from the entangling, irrelevant labor theory of value, taking a more realistic view of the class struggle, and moderating their determinism. In Veblenian fashion, he suggested that environmental factors were impinging on Marxism. He grasped the paradox that changing material conditions were altering the deterministic Marxian theory of change along with the whole ideological superstructure of changing society. The environmental changes bearing most heavily on Marxist thought were the changing postulates of knowledge, the exigencies of Marxism as a political platform ensnarled in party politics, and major shifts in the industrial scene. He saw socialism becoming more Darwinian under these influences. He seemingly approved of this change; he was probably engaging in wishful thinking by injecting his own views into conjectures about the evolution of socialist thought.

Toward the German Social Democrats, however, Veblen showed definite hostility.[18] He described how they were caught up in a process of adaptation and compromise. They had compromised with the labor movement by embracing business unionism and ameliorative programs, with the agricultural population by accepting peasant ownership, and with nationalism by tolerating chauvinism, jingoism, and imperialist policy. As a party of reform, they had yielded to the exigencies of the industrial and political situation, and their socialist outlook had deteriorated. He pointedly asked whether this represented

[17] "The Socialist Economics of Karl Marx and His Followers: II. The Later Marxism," in *Place of Science*, pp. 431–456.
[18] *Ibid.*, pp. 447–456.

Veblen and Marx

a sterilization of socialist thought and how widespread it might be even outside Germany.

The question has been widely debated whether Veblen was at heart a socialist. Although he sometimes implied that he was, he never answered the question—perhaps in part for pedagogical reasons. He had some sympathy with new trends in socialist thought but remained suspicious of socialist movements. As for the pedagogical aspect of the question, he took delight in the "shock effect" of discussing socialism. This device effectively attracted attention, and Veblen was not above manipulating the issue of socialism so as to convey his own criticisms of capitalist institutions. He always expressed sympathy for the underdog, especially when the underdog stirred widespread interest which served as a springboard for launching his critical ideas about capitalism. He thus spoke up for the feminists, the farmers, Coxey's Army, and the Industrial Workers of the World; each of these topics served his purpose well. He also wrote with apparent sympathy about the Russian Revolution and Bolshevism.[19] Many writers have taken his seemingly favorable remarks about Bolshevism to signify his covert if not outright approval. Here was another ready opportunity to defend the unpopular underdog and thereby attract greater attention to his own views. His writings on such controversial topics as the I.W.W., the Russian Revolution, and Bolshevism dealt mainly with the problems and prospects of American capitalism. With more than his usual subterfuge and irony, Veblen used socialism as an opportune and effective attention-getter.

Those who insist that Veblen was really a socialist base their case primarily upon "A Memorandum on a Practicable Soviet of Technicians," an article he published in *The Dial* in 1919.[20] In it he seemed to predict, or even advocate, that a soviet of engineers backed by the industrial workers might take over the industrial system in this country. He used his theory of occupational disciplines to make this de-

---

[19] See various essays reprinted in Veblen's *Essays in Our Changing Order*, ed. by Leon Ardzrooni (New York: Viking, 1934), especially "The Barbarian Status of Women" (1899), pp. 50–64; "The Army of the Commonweal" (1894), pp. 97–103; "Farm Labor and the I.W.W." (1918), pp. 319–333; "Bolshevism Is a Menace —to Whom?" (1919), pp. 399–414; and "Between Bolshevism and War" (1921), pp. 437–449.

[20] Reprinted in *The Engineers and the Price System* (New York: Huebsch, 1921), pp. 138–169.

velopment seem plausible and worthy of contemplation. Virtually all students and critics of Veblen have taken this essay literally, although both groups have regarded it as an unrealistic, if not absurd, piece of analysis. There is no reason to suppose that he deemed this seemingly socialistic program to be practical. Indeed, he said, somewhat inconspicuously, that a soviet of technicians was most unlikely in this country in the foreseeable future. The engineers and workers were far too conservative and uncritically loyal to business principles for this development to be imminent. At no time did he either aid or disavow the early Technocracy movement.

Veblen's soviet or technicians idea may have been essentially a clever expository device for surveying the waste, conflicts, and frustrations of modern industrial capitalism. He used this device as a formal yardstick or null hypothesis for assessing and displaying these deficiencies, especially the waste caused by the restrictive practices of modern business enterprise and business unionism. This essay was a provocative way of summing up the implications of a series of essays collected together in *The Engineers and the Price System*.[21] By elaborating an ostensibly straightforward but controversial and probably outlandish "socialistic" scheme, Veblen effectively reiterated his critical appraisal of capitalistic institutions.

The nature of Veblen's value system is continually at issue in any examination of his writings. Although he was not an admitted reformer, he evinced some anxiety for reform in his wartime and postwar essays, written mainly between 1917 and 1920.[22] He was typically too pessimistic or cynical to avow specific reform proposals, and he eschewed the making of formal value judgments. He was temperamentally inclined to express judgments by indirection or suggestion, and he delighted in declaring that he intended no moral overtones when he employed such terms as "waste" and "sabotage." His ethical views have been described as either populist, utopian, or utopian socialist in nature. He used the term "industrial republic" to indicate an eco-

---

[21] The earlier essays in this collection are entitled: "On the Nature and Use of Sabotage," "The Industrial System and the Captains of Industry," "The Captains of Finance and the Engineers," "On the Nature of a Revolutionary Overturn," and "On the Circumstances Which Make for a Change."

[22] For these articles, see *Essays in Our Changing Order*. The essays collected in *The Engineers and the Price System* and *The Vested Interests* were also written in this period.

nomic order devoted to making goods instead of profits, to creating serviceability rather than pecuniary values. He never did make the nature of his "industrial republic" very clear. It has been interpreted as a socialist order, and he sometimes appeared to suggest this himself.

Veblen wrote most explicitly about his "industrial republic" in "Some Neglected Points in the Theory of Socialism,"[23] his first article in economics (which dates back to his year at Cornell University in 1891–1892). In this essay he contemplated extensive government ownership and control of industry. He spoke vaguely of the nationalization of industries under modern constitutional forms such as eminent domain and the power to tax. He apparently envisaged the merging of government and industry along constitutional lines of organization, so that the country's industry and political system would both be organized and regulated according to accepted principles of a constitutional republic. What he actually contemplated perhaps resembled outright socialism as then understood less than it resembles the current concept of the mixed economy or welfare state.

Little more can be said about Veblen's value system. As noted above, he used industrial efficiency and maximum production as norms, while his "instincts" no doubt served as ethical norms. He criticized the "imbecile institutions" which functioned at variance with these stated or implied norms. All the economic institutions he stressed apparently fell within this category. He characterized all institutions, at least all those he criticized, as regressive or only permissive of change. He has been criticized, even called an anarchist, for failing to see that institutions have a necessary regulatory function and are essential to society. He was far from clear on this issue and may have been misunderstood. He nowhere explicitly stated that institutions per se were unnecessary or undesirable, nor did he deny that his "industrial republic" constituted an institutional pattern. In any case, Veblen had little to say about the specific kind of institutional reorganization he regarded as feasible and desirable. It is significant that his close students and followers have been greatly interested in social control and reform along democratic lines. The question arises whether Veblen intended to have this influence. He must have been aware of it, but he did not bother to endorse or disavow it.

[23] Reprinted in *The Place of Science*, pp. 387–408.

Forest G. Hill

V

The frequent efforts to compare Marx and Veblen are clearly appropriate in view of the significance and influence of their theoretical systems. Such comparisons are challenging and instructive, even though they vary widely and are incapable of being made precise and definitive. This brief survey of Veblen's evaluation of Marx permits a few tentative comparisons of their strengths and weaknesses. It should be noted that the strengths indicated are relative and far from self-sufficient, while the weaknesses are often troublesome and debilitating. There are areas in which both men were strong, in which Marx was strong and Veblen weak, in which Veblen was strong but Marx weak, and in which both were weak.

On several points both Marx and Veblen showed strength. They chose as their central problem the analysis of capitalism and institutional change. They bravely originated comprehensive theories of economic development, with emphasis upon process, evolution, and the causal forces involved. They achieved a great breadth of analysis which included social change, economic history, analytical principles from other disciplines, and a huge body of factual materials. They had a strong theoretical interest in crises and depressions at a time when these subjects were neglected and little understood. In addition, they were quite willing, each in his own way, to criticize economic institutions and conditions. They felt, indeed, that it was their moral or intellectual duty to pass judgment upon the economic order.

Within the present context, there are certain areas in which Marx showed strength and Veblen weakness. Marx made his value judgments explicit, while Veblen typically did not. Marx was more forthright than Veblen, despite the fact that a careful examination of Veblen's writings substantially reveals his ethical norms. As already noted, Veblen produced confusion by implanting norms in his uncertain "instincts" and by characterizing institutions in such a way that all institutions seemed absurd and unnecessary. As with value judgments, Marx gave overt attention to policy, which Veblen almost never did. Marx used his theory and norms to formulate firm predictions and policies. Veblen made only highly qualified predictions, and on only a few brief occasions during and just after World War I

Veblen and Marx

did he discuss policy issues in terms of his own analysis and preferences. These broad differences between the two men largely reflected Marx's strong optimism and sense of mission and Veblen's pessimism.

Relatively speaking, Marx was weak and Veblen strong in certain significant respects. Veblen was much more willing and able than Marx to study the psychological processes involved in economic development. Veblen of course had the advantage of access to later psychological knowledge, while Marx had the disadvantage of his Hegelian and classical-utilitarian preconceptions. Marx assumed that individuals and classes were motivated by rational interest, whereas Veblen did not. While Marx was constrained by his economic determinism to stress the role of rationality and material forces in economic change, Veblen was able to devote attention to habits and sentiments. Marx oversimplified class divisions and motivation, while Veblen recognized the complexity of class phenomena.

Veblen's framework of occupational disciplines was more flexible than Marx's doctrine of class struggle based upon rational class interests. Veblen redrew the lines of class cleavage, which he saw as gradually shifting. He was more realistic in grasping the tendencies of modern trade unionism, the role of "sentiment," and the significance of special classes such as farmers, financiers, technicians, and craft unionists. In addition, Veblen's analysis was more open-minded and his predictions much more tentative and guarded than was possible in Marx's system of analysis, with its determinism and inevitability. Writing later with the benefit of greater knowledge, Veblen devoted more attention than Marx did to the changing structure and performance of industry, including monopoly tendencies, separation of ownership and control, and the role of credit and corporation finance.[24]

Both Marx and Veblen showed similar weaknesses in several areas of analysis. Each was addicted to the speculative method and the use of sweeping generalizations. They indulged in a good deal of speculative history, especially about the "stages" of economic development. Both were somewhat averse to the use of statistics and quantitative theorizing. A high degree of determinism is found in their theoretical analyses, especially in Marx. The choice here is between dialectical causation and "brute causation," between rational class

---

[24] Veblen's *Theory of Business Enterprise* is now a classic in this area, and his *Absentee Ownership* is written along the same lines.

interest and occupational disciplines, between economic determinism and technological determinism. Veblen overstressed the role of technology in social change, though not as much as is commonly supposed; and he compensated for this by analyzing the psychological processes involved. His theory of occupational disciplines, however, has never been considered very realistic. Although his critique of Marx's psychological premises was essentially valid, he raised doubts by his analysis of instincts and the habituation process by which institutions change. Both men built norms into their analytical postulates, Marx in his labor theory of value and Veblen in his "instincts" and in concepts such as industrial efficiency, serviceability, waste, and sabotage. Although Veblen was more indirect and cautious than Marx in making value judgments, neither, unfortunately, was willing or patient enough to distinguish properly between his positive and normative analyses.

As might be expected in the light of recent advances in the theory of employment and business cycles, both Marx and Veblen were deficient as regards the process of income determination implied in their theories of economic development. Their analyses of capital accumulation, underconsumption, and inequality of income were thus inadequate. This lack of a proper conception of income determination weakened their theories of development and especially their theories of crises and depression.[25] Their analyses contributed, however, to theoretical interest and progress in these fields. Veblen's writings influenced Wesley Mitchell's business cycle analysis, and they also contained elements which were later systematized in the Keynesian theory of income determination.[26]

Both Marx and Veblen developed one-sided theories of the state. Marx did not foresee, and Veblen barely acknowledged, the possibility that social legislation and social control of industry might greatly meliorate the defects of capitalism. They chose to view the state as the defender of the *status quo,* without granting that government intervention might perpetuate capitalism indefinitely by improving its performance. Neither of them foresaw, in other words, that the state could become a powerful instrument of reform within a still

[25] Concerning this problem in Marx, see Joan Robinson, An Essay on Marxian Economics (London: Macmillan, 1952).

[26] Cf. Rutledge Vining, "Suggestions of Keynes in the Writings of Veblen," Jour. of Pol. Econ., XLVII (Oct., 1939), 692–704.

Veblen and Marx

predominantly capitalist economy. As a consequence, they showed little concern for immediate policy of a meliorative nature. In a similar vein, Marx failed to see that trade unions would become a major force in improving wages and working conditions, while Veblen regarded trade unions as restrictive and of little consequence for economic progress. This negative and inadequate treatment of the state, reform, immediate policy, and labor unions shows that both men failed to design and apply their theories to meet the task of formulating needed changes within the institutional framework prevailing in their day.[27] This failure, which reflected their normative as well as their theoretical orientation, was undoubtedly their greatest weakness.

---

[27] C. E. Ayres, *The Theory of Economic Progress* (Chapel Hill: University of North Carolina Press, 1944), p. 278; Gruchy, *op. cit.*, pp. 103, 129–130; Hobson, *op. cit.*, pp. 134–136; Homan, *op. cit.*, pp. 167–168, 176, 178; Max Lerner, *Ideas Are Weapons: The History and Use of Ideas* (New York: Viking, 1939), pp. 136–138; and Leo Rogin, *The Meaning and Validity of Economic Theory* (New York: Harper, 1956), pp. 361–369, 400–410.

[ALLAN G. GRUCHY]

9

Veblen's Theory of Economic Growth

NO economic problem today commands more attention than the problem of how to achieve sustained and adequate economic growth. Advanced industrialized nations are confronted with the difficulty of maintaining a stable and adequate rate of economic growth, while industrially young or underdeveloped countries are grappling with the problem of how to rise from an economy of stagnation or very limited economic growth to one of rapid economic progress and advancement. These and other problems, such as the cold war and the ideological conflict between the East and the West, have turned both academic and professional economists to an investigation of the causes of both short-term and long-term economic growth. Such an investigation cannot ignore the scientific revolution through which we are now passing. The advances of recent decades in science and technology are leading us to a new industrial revolution which promises to alter the structure and functioning of our economy in many significant ways. In this situation the science of economics is undergoing a profound change. Economists who once limited themselves to what is called the "science of pecuniary advantage" are now pushing beyond the conventional boundaries of their science to study factors that escape the reach of the monetary standard. This situation is well described by Moses Abramovitz in his 1952 survey of the economics of growth, where he observes:

Economists have preferred to cultivate a science of pecuniary advantage. The study of economic growth will not permit them to indulge these proclivities. The insights which traditional theory can furnish will, of course, have to be worked to the limit. But we may expect that limit to be reached sooner in studies of secular change than elsewhere. If the economics of growth attains the rank it ought to have in our subject, we should expect to see history, geography, psychology, and sociology take a prominent place in the training of economists in the future. . . . More than ever, our problems seem to lie within their domains, and a closer federation is in order.[1]

I

Prior to 1929 academic economics paid little attention to the problem of economic growth. This was because economists had for the most part assumed that the nation's economy would continue to expand in a more or less automatic manner. Alfred Marshall's "moving equilibrium" was seldom disturbed by the consequences of irregular economic growth. In England and the United States Marshall and J. B. Clark had succeeded in establishing a kind of economics in both academic and business circles in which little doubt was ever cast upon the economy's ability to achieve automatically both full employment and sustained economic growth. Although Marshall and Clark had succeeded in winning over both the academic and business worlds between 1900 and 1929, there were other economists who questioned the validity of the growth assumptions which underlay the conventional economics of the first three decades of this century. Prominent among these heterodox economists was Thorstein Veblen, who criticized Marshallian economics on the ground that it largely ignored the fundamental trends in the economic life of the advanced western democracies. While these unconventional economists conceded that Marshall had done a dexterous job in dissecting his "stationary state," they pointed out that his economics was more concerned with "consistency" than with "evolution" or "growth." It was apparent that what Marshall and others of his generation lacked, *inter alia*, was an economics of growth.

After 1929 the advent of Keynes's economics did much to weaken the blind faith in automatic economic growth that had up till then permeated orthodox economics. Keynes's emphasis, however, is on equilibrium at less than full employment rather than on the process

[1] M. Abramovitz, "Economics of Growth," in *A Survey of Contemporary Economics*, ed. by Bernard F. Haley (Homewood, Ill.: Richard D. Irwin, 1952), II, 178.

Theory of Economic Growth

of long-term economic growth. While he has something to say about secular developments in the economic world, his main interest does not lie in this direction. Keynes's analysis is weakest when he turns to a view of the economy as an emergent process of growth and development. This deficiency stems from the fact that he fails to analyze fully the role of industrial technology in economic activities. We do not find in Keynes's economics any adequate investigation of the impact of technological change on the structure and functioning of the economic system. Whatever growth economics we do find in his work remains very much within the circumscribed area devoted to the immediate determinants of growth.

From its very beginning in the United States institutional economics has been largely a study of economic growth. In his first major study of the capitalistic system, *The Theory of Business Enterprise*, Veblen explains that his main concern is with the nature and "further drift of business enterprise." Contrary to what many critics of institutional economics have asserted, Veblen does not wish to dispense with neoclassical economics. What he is after is a "modernization" or "a revision . . . of more than one point in the current body of economic doctrines." [2] This revision of economic theory by Veblen takes the form of

[2] T. Veblen, *The Theory of Business Enterprise* (New York: Scribner, 1904), p. v. It is frequently alleged that Veblen wants to substitute his evolutionary type of economics for the inherited economics of his time. Such an argument can only arise from a failure to be sufficiently well acquainted with Veblen's writings, a weakness which is not uncommon among critics of institutionalism. What Veblen objects to is not neoclassical economics itself but the philosophical, psychological, and methodological assumptions which accompany this type of economics. What he wishes to do is to renovate these assumptions and in so doing to extend, modify, and round out the general body of neoclassical thought. He quite clearly points this out in his third essay on the preconceptions of economic science. "All this, of course, is intended to convey no dispraise of the work done, nor in any way to disparage the theories which the passing generation of economists have elaborated, or the really great and admirable body of knowledge which they have brought under the hand of the science; but only to indicate the direction in which the inquiry in its later phases—not always with full consciousness—is shifting as regards its categories and its point of view. . . . Foot-pounds, calories, geometrically progressive procreation, and doses of capital have not been supplanted by the equally uncouth denominations of habits, propensities, aptitudes, and conventions, nor does there seem to be any probability that they will be; but the discussion which continues to run in terms of the former class of concepts is in an increasing degree seeking support in concepts of the latter class." (See "The Preconceptions of Economic Science," in *The Place of Science in Modern Civilisation* [New York: Huebsch, 1919], pp. 178–179.)

Allan G. Gruchy

supplementing academic economics with a theory of economic growth, which seeks to explain the long-term forces fostering or hindering the expansion of the nation's total production of final goods and services. Veblen's theory of economic growth is important at the present time because the fundamentals of his theory became widely accepted by economists with an institutionalist slant. J. R. Commons, W. C. Mitchell, J. M. Clark, and others altered some of the major features of Veblenian economics, but they did not change the main features of Veblen's theory of economic growth. This theory continues to be the foundation of all that passes today as institutional economics. Veblen is therefore more than a milestone in the development of economic thought. Present-day institutionalists are directly or indirectly indebted to him for views about economic growth that promise to play an important role in shaping economic policy in this country for the next half-century.

Theories of economic growth may be divided into two basic types. In the first type of growth theory certain assumptions are made with respect to economic institutions and attributes of the population, and within the framework of these fixed assumptions the growth economist endeavors to work out the relationships between various growth factors or determinants of output that contribute to stable economic growth. In all theorizing about economic growth of this first type the major concern of the investigator is with "consistency" or "congruency." The aim is to reveal the relationships consistent or congruent with stable growth between capital stocks, labor supplies, natural resources, and total output.[3] In this area of analysis mathematical models may be usefully constructed to demonstrate the essential harmony or consistency among growth factors that conduces to the achievement of stable growth. Statistical studies are also useful to reveal the actual relationships among growth factors applicable to recent periods of growth in the United States and other countries. Growth theory of this first type does not usually cover a period of time long enough to bring about fundamental changes in underlying economic institutions and population attributes. For this reason the mathematical type of growth theory may be said to involve relatively short-term analysis. In this area of theorizing about economic growth,

[3] See for example B. S. Keirstead, *The Theory of Economic Change* (Toronto: Macmillan Co. of Canada, 1948).

Theory of Economic Growth

even where long-term growth analysis is attempted, few changes in the basic features of the nation's economy are permitted to influence or shape the investigation.

The second type of growth theory is primarily interested in "evolution" rather than in "consistency."[4] In this area of analysis the economist does not assume that, as growth of output takes place, the institutional framework of the economic system remains unchanged. Consequently the determinants of output operate within a changing economic framework. Not only do certain growth factors influence the size of the nation's total output, but they also affect the structure and functioning of the total economic system. For example, the accumulation of capital not only leads to an enlarged output. It also changes the size of business firms, the functioning of the market system, and the organizations and attitudes of both labor and agriculture. In this second type of analysis growth occurs over a period of time that is long enough to permit basic changes in both the structure and functioning of the nation's economy. The emphasis in this type of theorizing is not upon harmonious economic relationships among the immediate determinants of output that are consistent with stable growth but upon the interaction between the evolving framework of economic institutions and habits and the growth factors that function within this framework. Attention is drawn to those growth forces at work within the evolving economic system that foster or hinder the expansion of total output.

Veblen is not primarily interested in economic growth theory of the first type. He is aware of the immediate determinants of growth, such as the available supplies of labor, capital, and natural resources and the psychological propensities of the population, and he takes account of the factors affecting businessmen's investment decisions, such as the marginal efficiency of capital and the state of the loanable funds market. He is not satisfied, however, to define economic growth merely as a change in total output in a situation where the state of the industrial arts is taken to be unchanging. Veblen's theory of economic growth is a long-term interpretation that focuses attention upon the impact of scientific and technological progress and capital accumulation upon capitalist institutions and attitudes. Growth theory

[4] For a similar treatment of growth theory see W. Arthur Lewis, *The Theory of Economic Growth* (London: Allen and Unwin, 1955), pp. 10–18.

that emphasizes consistency rather than evolution tends to be merely a theory of expanding output. It defines growth in terms of a sustained increase in output. Growth theory of the second, Veblenian type emphasizes the point that growth is more than a matter of increased output. As capital accumulates and total output grows, the nature of the economic system itself changes in the long run. As Veblen would put it, in the long run there can be no economic growth without economic change or development. A theory of economic growth is more therefore than a theory of changing output; it is also a theory of economic development.[5] Veblen is interested in the process of economic growth, in what he describes as the "developmental process," or as "schemes of process, sequence, growth, and development." In emphasizing the developmental aspects of the growth problem Veblen goes beyond what is considered today by many investigators to be the proper boundaries of the economics of growth.

II

What Veblen means by economic growth is best explained in *The Vested Interests and the State of the Industrial Arts*. This volume, consisting of articles published in *The Dial* from October, 1918, to January, 1919, marks the high-water mark in the development of Veblen's theorizing about the capitalistic system. In this somewhat neglected collection of essays Veblen rounds out a quarter-century's theorizing about economic and cultural growth. In the *Theory of Business Enterprise* (1904) and later writings he had developed his thesis concerning the growing discrepancy between industry and business. But not until *The Vested Interests* did he attempt to quantify this discrepancy. This effort at quantification led Veblen into a consideration of economic growth from the point of view of the nation's total output or total income and its distribution between investment and consumption uses. He thus became a pioneer in the field of national income economics, but without the limitations that attach to much of the work now being done in this field. Judged by current statistical standards, Veblen's efforts in this direction were quite elementary. But it must be admitted that his scientific inquiries at this stage in the development of his

[5] *Place of Science,* pp. 59, 61, 71.

Theory of Economic Growth

economic thought were pointed in a direction that led to many highly significant generalizations concerning the growth process.

Like Kuznets and other specialists in the field of economic growth, Veblen would agree that economic growth has something to do with an increase in the nation's total output of goods and services. In its quantitative aspect economic growth is a matter of changes in real output or product. In order to explain economic growth it is necessary to set up a standard or measure by means of which this growth can be recorded. With Veblen as well as with other investigators the appropriate standard is an output or product standard. Such a standard, however, is really a double standard, since it has both quantitative and qualitative aspects. Economic growth is not only a matter of increased output. The character or nature of the output is also important, since continued growth depends upon the production of growth-stimulating types of products. It is obvious that continued growth calls for the production of such growth-fostering types of products as capital equipment, industrial plant, roads, schools, and other types of public assets, and also consumer goods that make the working population a more efficient labor force. When students of the growth problem define economic growth as a sustained increase in total output, they are making use of only the quantitative feature of the output standard.[6] Veblen is not satisfied with a merely quantitative approach to the problem of economic growth. He prefers to explain the problem in terms of both the quantitative and the qualitative changes in the nation's annual production. He follows a different path from that of the statistically-oriented students by inquiring into the make-up of the nation's annual total production and by centering his attention on the portion of that production which he considers to be of strategic importance. Not being a statistician and working before national income economics was established as a field of scientific inquiry, Veblen devotes much of his analysis to the qualitative aspects of the problem of economic growth.

In working out his theory of economic growth Veblen turns to

[6] This is the definition used by Simon Kuznets. It is obviously selected because it opens the door to a wide use of the quantitative method. An elaboration of this point is found in Kuznets' "Suggestions for an Inquiry into the Economic Growth of Nations," *Problems in the Study of Economic Growth* (New York: National Bureau of Economic Research, 1949), p. 6.

Allan G. Gruchy

aggregative analysis and makes use of the concept of a national economic account. In this account he strikes a balance between the total output of the nation on the one hand and the various uses on the other hand to which this output is put. He explains that total national output goes into either consumption or investment. By analyzing the actual total output and its various uses in any year the economist can observe the trends in total production, consumption, and investment, the interrelationships among those trends, and their significance for continued and adequate economic growth. Veblen's analysis of these product flows is extremely important because it leads him to consider what he takes to be the crucial factor in economic growth, namely, the national economic surplus or net industrial product. He derives this net product in the following manner. The actual "gross output of industry" or the "total output of product turned out by the industrial system" consists of a supply of final or finished goods and services. This total output is the nation's total annual production in the turning out of which certain costs are incurred. These actual costs include the subsistence of the working population and the replacement of the industrial plant and equipment that are annually used up in turning out the total product. The actual subsistence requirements of the workers are measured by the amount of goods and services they consume during the year. According to Veblen the actual subsistence of the working population by the end of World War I was at a "fairly tolerable" level in spite of the restrictive practices of the private business enterprise system.[7] By deducting the subsistence of the working population and the depreciation of the nation's capital stock from total national product, Veblen arrives at what he calls the net product of industry. He explains that "the net product is the amount by which this actual [total] production exceeds its own cost, as counted in terms of subsistence, and including the cost of the necessary mechanical equipment."[8] This net product is a "disposable excess of the yearly product over cost." Since it may be devoted to either consumption or investment uses, it comes to play a very crucial role in the expansion of the nation's total output of final goods and services. According to Veblen's analysis too much of this net product is devoted to con-

[7] T. Veblen, *The Engineers and the Price System* (New York: Viking, 1936), p. 30.

[8] T. Veblen, *The Vested Interests and the State of the Industrial Arts* (New York: Huebsch, 1919), p. 55.

spicuous or nonserviceable consumption. As he finds it, the net product of industry approximately coincides with the cost of maintaining the vested interests or "kept classes," who lay claim to a share of the nation's "annual dividend," or total output of final goods and services, while making no contribution to it. Although in actual practice some of the net industrial product is taken up by the limited net savings of the working population, Veblen holds that the bulk of this product goes to the vested interests with comparatively little going to private and public net investment.

Veblen goes on to refine further his analysis of gross and net product. Up to this point he has dealt only with actual gross output and the actual costs of securing this output. He now turns to a consideration of potential maximum total output and the minimum necessary costs of producing this output. He explains that actual total product includes many consumer superfluities such as "menial service, fashionable dress and equipage, pet animals, and mandatory social services." Productive work turns out only useful or serviceable goods and services. When the working population is engaged only in productive work, and the nation's man power and capital equipment are fully and efficiently utilized, the nation's maximum potential total output of serviceable goods and services is then realized. This maximum potential total product is much larger than actual total product, but Veblen does not find it possible to measure the difference between these two total products. In order to determine the maximum net serviceable product of industry Veblen deducts from the maximum potential total product of useful or serviceable goods only the necessary costs of man power and capital equipment, or what he calls the "necessary consumption of subsistence and industrial plant." [9] The necessary subsistence of the working population includes only those serviceable goods that are considered essential to sustain the flow of man power. The actual subsistence of the working population is larger than their necessary subsistence, since the former includes consumer superfluities that are not a part of necessary subsistence. Likewise, the necessary wear and tear of the nation's capital stock is the depreciation of only those plants and equipment that are allocated to the production of useful goods and services. The resulting "net return of output over cost," or potential net product of service-

[9] *Ibid.*, p. 63.

Allan G. Gruchy

able goods, would be the maximum surplus made possible by the full or unhindered use of the nation's technological knowledge. In this situation, as Veblen explains, "The disposable excess of production over cost [the maximum potential net product of industry] is a matter of the efficiency of the available state of technological knowledge and of the measure in which the working population is put in a position to make use of it." [10] Veblen agrees that there is no safe ground for an estimate of the size of this maximum potential "net aggregate product over cost," but he regards it as reasonable to say that the actual net product of goods "serviceable for human use" falls considerably short of maximum potential net product.

The net product of industry when maximized would, according to Veblen, greatly exceed the necessary cost of the maximum potential total output of serviceable goods. Veblen explains that any nation that is prepared to direct its material resources, man power, and capital stock into the unhindered or unrestricted production of seviceable goods will not only maximize its net industrial product but will also be in a position to allocate this net product to the production of growth-fostering capital goods. He cites industrial Japan and industrial Germany as illustrations of countries which in the second half of the nineteenth century devoted much of their resources to the expansion of their net industrial products, and which for a number of decades directed this product very largely into public and private investment rather than into the consumption of nonserviceable consumer goods. Were he alive today, Veblen would undoubtedly point to Russia and China as recent examples of the same kind of economic development.

Our analysis of Veblen's basic views concerning the nature of economic growth may be summarized in the following manner. According to Veblen economic growth or development occurs where a surplus of goods and services, a net product of industry, arises and is used to improve and enlarge the nation's capital stock and to maintain a vigorous and efficient working population. Economic growth is, in the final analysis, a matter of technological advance that can be measured by changes in the size of the nation's economic surplus. Veblen defines economic growth in a way that focuses attention on what he believes to be the crucial aspect of the growth process. This aspect he takes to be the creation of a surplus of goods and services

[10] *Ibid.*, p. 56.

that becomes available to the nation for investment and consumption purposes. The growth problem then becomes one of uncovering the factors that foster or hinder the growth of the nation's economic surplus. At this point in his analysis Veblen turns to an investigation of the consequences of technological progress and the accumulation of capital. When brought together in one body of generalizations, these consequences give us his theory of capitalist development.

III

Although economic growth is made possible by the combined use of labor, natural resources, and capital equipment, in Veblen's opinion capital equipment is the strategic productive factor. From his point of view capital equipment is essentially an embodiment of science or technology. Veblen explains that "the mechanical equipment and the standardised processes in which the mechanical equipment is engaged . . . embodies not the manual skill, dexterity, and judgment of an individual workman but rather the accumulated technological wisdom of the community." [11] In the handicraft era the individual workman was the creative productive factor in the sense that he dominated the economic process. Resources and capital equipment were subsidiary elements in a process where labor set the pace. After the Industrial Revolution the position of labor and capital were reversed, and in the new era of large-scale monopoly capitalism "mechanical equipment is the creative factor in industry . . . whereas the other factors engaged, as e.g., the workmen and materials, are counted in as auxiliary factors which are indispensable but subsidiary." By the term "creative" Veblen means strategic or decisive and not creative in any literal sense, since he states that all factors of production together create the total output of industry. This output is a joint or common product, a result of the co-operative efforts of all factors of production. No part of the nation's total product can be labeled the special contribution of any one factor of production. Nevertheless, in this joint or common production one productive factor may play a key role. Veblen states that in modern capitalism "capital equipment has a unique position since it embodies the community's joint stock of technological knowledge." Changes in technology alter the industrial process and

[11] *Ibid.*, p. 37.

the equipment associated with this process. Today it is technology, and hence capital, that sets the pace of economic activity, determines the extent to which resources become available for use, and fixes the limits within which labor may be utilized as a factor of production. The productive capacity of a community is largely determined by the amount and character of the available stock of capital equipment and industrial plant. This capital stock is the "decisive factor" in the growth of the nation's economic surplus.

The growth of the nation's net industrial product depends very largely upon improvement in technology and accumulation of capital. As Veblen sees it, technological change is a cumulative process which shows no sign of abatement. In a forward-looking essay on the technology of physics and chemistry he draws attention to the fact that "there has been a progressive mechanisation of the ways and means of living as well as of the ways and means of productive industry, and this mechanisation has in recent times been going forward at a constantly accelerated rate, and it is still in progress, with no promise of abatement or conclusion." [12] Veblen holds distinctly optimistic views about the future of technological development and the possibility of economic progress. Scientific and technological progress is incessant and unremitting and "by insensible degrees has run its creative tentacles through the technological system from the ground up." Although men originally conceive the ideas that flower in the form of scientific and technological progress, the technological system comes to have an existence of its own. This system is now passing through a period of unremitting growth, which inexorably piles discovery upon discovery and improvement upon improvement until no man can predict the course or final outcome of technological progress. The only certainty is that the course of technological change is uncertain. At times this change goes off in many different directions, which are seemingly unrelated. But technological changes, formerly isolated, are eventually united or blended in a manner that stimulates further change. We have then what Veblen calls the cross references or inosculations of technological growth.

Although man has much to do with the origination of technological

---

[12] T. Veblen, *Absentee Ownership and Business Enterprise in Recent Times* (New York: Viking, 1938), p. 251.

Theory of Economic Growth

growth or change, this change is a blind kind of development. Veblen describes it as an "unremitting proliferation," a blind process of budding forth or adding on. Since the process of technological change that underlies economic growth is a cumulative process not completely amenable to mankind's control, the course of economic evolution is not predictable in any precise way. As we shall see at a later point in our analysis, he remains thoroughly skeptical about the final outcome of capitalistic development. It is clear that technological progress and the accumulation of capital have a corrosive effect upon the structure and functioning of the capitalist system. Veblen is certain that technological change will continue to alter the American capitalistic system in many significant ways, but there is nothing teleological about his interpretation of the course of this change.

There is another aspect of Veblen's interpretation of the process of technological change of which account must be taken if we are to understand fully his theory of economic growth. Although according to Veblen's interpretation the process of technological change is in general a slow cumulative piling-up process, the impact of this process does not always take the form of a gradual change in the structure and functioning of the nation's economic system. On the contrary, there are many resistances to institutional change which shield the economy for a time from the full impact of technological progress. Consequently, economic growth is not a smooth, gradual process; instead, the transition from one economic system to another is frequently accompanied by much strain and dislocation. Accumulated technological changes come to a head at certain points in the movement of the historical continuum. They then burst through the resistances or barriers to economic growth to give us periods of rapid but sometimes socially costly transition. Each period of economic transition is followed by a period of cultural quiescence during which the consequences of accumulated technological change are digested. It was Veblen's interpretation that by the third decade of this century the accumulated pressures developed by technological progress were carrying us to a point where the barriers to economic change could no longer be easily maintained on a wide scale. The capitalist economy, as Veblen understood it, is passing through an era of transition. If by chance the transition should be to socialism rather than to military dictatorship, the full impact of technological progress would work out, he believed, in the form of an expanding economic surplus or net product of industry and the establishment of an era of abundance.

Veblen points out that technological progress and the accumulation of capital are accompanied by four important changes. The first relates to what he calls the "character" of capital. As capital accumulates a "mutation of character" takes place, and the nation's mechanical equipment and related industrial processes undergo significant alterations. Improved equipment and more specialized and more standardized processes raise the general efficiency of the industrial system. In the industrial process capital is increasingly substituted for labor as the mechanization of industry moves ahead under the spur of technological progress.

The second change relates to the size of the firm or its scale of operations. As capital accumulates in the key industries, a shift is made from "slight" to "large-scale" operations.[13] Technological progress shows up as a "continuous advance in the scale and articulation of the industrial process at large." As the size of the individual firm increases, the productivity of capital and labor also increases. Veblen's analysis runs in terms of combined units or inputs of man power and equipment. As the firm's scale of operations enlarges, the productivity of these inputs of man power and equipment rises. Over a period of time there is a change in both the qualitative nature of capital equipment and in the skill of workers. "During the era of the machine industry . . . the industrial system . . . all this time has continually been growing more efficient on the whole. Its productive capacity per unit of equipment and man power has continually grown larger." Thus technological progress and the accumulation of capital are accompanied by increasing returns in the long run. As the scale of operations increases and the industrial system becomes more complex, both the total and per capita output of goods and services rises. Even though population increases, capital changes both qualitatively and quantitatively in such a way as to enable the productivity of additional inputs of capital to rise. Veblen explains that in the long run the law of diminishing returns as a historical trend is inoperative. If it is assumed that no technological progress occurs in the short run, it is possible to make one's analysis in terms of a declining marginal pro-

[13] *Ibid.*, p. 209.

Theory of Economic Growth

ductivity of capital and hence in terms of the law of diminishing returns. But Veblen is not interested in the short run. His analysis of economic growth envisages a time span which is long enough to permit improvement in science and technology, and hence a rise in the marginal productivity of capital.

The third change wrought by technological progress and the accumulation of capital has been given little attention by many economists. This change in the structure and functioning of the total economy has occurred since 1850 as a result of the progress of science and technology. As capital has accumulated, not only has it altered the nature of the industrial process and enlarged the scale of operations of the individual firm in the key industries. It has also brought about many important changes in the institutional arrangements which together comprise the economic system. These changes can be summarized by saying that technological progress has tended to collectivize the economic system. Capital accumulation and the growth of collective action have been inextricably interwoven. During Veblen's lifetime not only business but also labor and agriculture turned increasingly to collective action in an effort to secure as large a share as possible of the nation's expanding total output. Veblen points out that after 1875 a new dual or hybrid economy made its appearance. As technology improved and the scale of industrial operations was enlarged, a cluster of "primary," "staple," or "key" industries developed in the industrial firmament. And around this central cluster or "tactical center" were the consumer goods industries and agriculture, in which technological progress and capital accumulation played less important roles. At the same time that capital accumulation fostered the growth of big business in the heartland of the nation's economy, it stimulated the development of large-scale organization among workers and farmers. The industrial union and the agricultural cooperative appeared after 1900 as a challenge to the supremacy of the large industrial corporation. In Veblen's time this challenge coming from labor and agriculture was not crowned with the success that it was to achieve after his death in 1929. If Veblen had foreseen how far organized labor and agriculture would go in successfully counterbalancing big business, he might have envisioned a different future for the capitalistic system than the one he sketched in *The Engineers and the Price System*.

Allan G. Gruchy

These major structural changes in the nation's economic system, which followed upon the accumulation of capital, were combined with significant changes in the system's functioning. Veblen's "revolution in corporate organization" brought with it a separation of corporate ownership from corporate management, a more centralized control of corporate activities, and a shift from "free" prices to what are today known as "administered" prices. The net effect of these divergences from the competitive norm of business enterprise was to introduce into economic life a large number of restrictionist tendencies. Furthermore, the restrictive practices of corporate enterprise soon became models to be followed by the industrial unions and agricultural cooperatives. Labor and agriculture adjusted to the new industrial order by turning to "collusive strategy and concerted action." Each advance in restrictionist collective action created additional barriers to the maximization of the nation's net industrial product.

The fourth change resulting from technological progress and the accumulation of capital occurs in the psychological attitudes of those who participate in the nation's economic activity. According to Veblen changes in the character of capital equipment, in the size of business enterprise, and in the structure and functioning of the total economic system have profound psychological consequences. Those who are close to the machine process develop habits of thought or economic attitudes that are appropriate to this process. They come to think in terms of mass production, tangible performance, and a scientific matter-of-fact approach. Classes remote from the machine process continue to have economic attitudes that are reminiscent of a past era in the development of the capitalistic system when labor rather than capital set the pace of industry. This uneven development of the psychological attitudes of various economic groups is the basis of Veblen's well-known dichotomy between the industrial and pecuniary employments. As we shall see, present-day institutionalists do not accept Veblen's simple clear-cut division between those who are remote from and those who are close to the machine process. They do, however, accept Veblen's view that technological progress and capital accumulation alter not only the structure and functioning of the economy but also the psychological attitudes of those who participate in its operations. In the economic analyses of the latter-day institutional economists these psychological changes do not work out

Theory of Economic Growth

so simply as they do in Veblen's theorizing, but nevertheless they do have extremely important consequences for economic growth.

What interests Veblen in relation to these four consequences of technological progress and the accumulation of capital is that some of these consequences favor the growth of the nation's net industrial product while other consequences impede this outcome. As he sees the matter, it should be a major concern of the economist to differentiate between the growth-fostering and the growth-hindering consequences of capital accumulation. This accumulation receives a much broader treatment in Veblen's analysis than it does in the hands of conventional growth economists, who analyze capital accumulation at a given level of the industrial arts and almost solely in terms of how this accumulation affects total output.

IV

The end toward which the logic of capital accumulation points in Veblen's economics is the enlargement of the nation's net industrial product, or economic surplus. But Veblen finds that there are many obstacles or hindrances to the achievement of the maximum economic surplus. It is clear to him that the cumulative progress of the industrial arts and the expansion of industrial capacity make an increasing national economic surplus a realizable goal. He is impatient to reveal the conditions and factors that interfere with the realization of this economic goal. Consequently, we find him turning his theory of economic growth down the avenues of a theory of economic organization, or more specifically, a theory of capitalism. Veblen's theory of capitalism is in essence an interpretation of the many hindrances to the realization of the economy's potential net product that Veblen observed over the half-century from 1875 to 1925.

In working out his theory of capitalism Veblen explains that the industrial system, as the result of continued technological progress, becomes increasingly complex and more delicately balanced. While this growing complexity and delicateness of balance indicate a rising level of efficiency, there is also a growing danger of interference by private business with the smooth working of the economic system that arises from the increasing monopolization of economic activity. The business interests are prone to interfere with the operations of the industrial system where the capacity to produce runs ahead of the capacity to consume. In the effort to maintain maximum profits, output is restricted and prices are raised. The potential maximum net product of industry is then not realized. Whereas the logic of our large-scale industrial technology looks in the direction of increasing returns and the maximization of output, the logic of private enterprise looks in the direction of a progressive decline in total output.

> Under these circumstances it seems reasonable to expect that the systematic retardation and derangement of productive industry which is entailed by the current businesslike management will work out in a progressive abatement of the margin of net output of the industrial system at large; that this progressive abatement of the net industrial output will presently reach and pass the critical point of no net return . . . and that in the calculable future the industrial system . . . will run on lines of a progressively "diminishing return," converging to an eventual limit of tolerance in the way of a reduced subsistence minimum.[14]

Veblen explains that the breakdown of the capitalistic system may be delayed by the expansion of wasteful expenditures in the form of military and public works expenditures. As technology progresses and capital accumulates, the tolerance of the industrial system continues to decline until the point is reached where interference with the industrial system by private business so drastically reduces the nation's total output that the capitalistic system can no longer function. The technicians and the underlying population will stand for a "diminishing return" only up to a certain point, beyond which the conflict between the business and industrial classes will no longer be tolerated. The outcome of this conflict is uncertain. It may take the form of a military dictatorship, if a successful coalition can be worked out by the military and property-owning classes; or it can lead instead to a socialistic regime of workmanship where all obstacles to the realization of the maximum net product of industry would be eliminated. The development of the economic system being essentially a matter of "drift," Veblen can only point out what he considers to be the possible directions that the course of future economic events may take. He was certain of only one thing, that the unregulated capi-

[14] *Ibid.*, pp. 421–422.

Theory of Economic Growth

talism of the last quarter of the nineteenth century and the first quarter of the twentieth century could not long endure.[15]

Although Veblen is not sure as to the outcome of capitalist development, he devotes considerable time to an analysis of what he hopes will be the economic system of the future, a system that will sustain economic growth and maximize the nation's net industrial output. Veblen's projected regime of workmanship is to be a system in which the nation's growth-stimulating and growth-facilitating forces are no longer hampered by the restrictionist practices and attitudes of private business enterprise. Instead, his socialist system is to follow a plan for maximizing the nation's economic surplus. Veblen explains that the incoming industrial order would be designed to correct the shortcomings of the capitalist system. His regime of workmanship would "converge on those points in the administration of industry where the old order has most signally fallen short; . . . on the due allocation of resources and a consequent full and reasonably proportioned employment of the available equipment and man power."[16]

The new industrial situation after the overturn of capitalism would call for three new institutional arrangements: the transfer of the means of production to public ownership, the setting up of a national economic planning council, and the construction of national economic budgets for the co-ordination and guidance of economic activities. The central economic planning council or, as Veblen calls it, the "central industrial directorate" would seek to maximize production by making a survey of the nation's productive capacities and then setting up "organization tables to cover the efficient use of the available resources and equipment."[17] In other words the central planning body would construct national economic budgets that would indicate the nation's expanding total production in some future planning period and also the desired distribution of this output among various groups of users. In Veblen's regime of workmanship the national economic budget would be used to supplement the price system as an allocator of economic resources. There is nothing in Veblen's inquiry into socialism to indicate that he would dispense with the price system,

[15] *Theory of Business Enterprise*, p. 400.
[16] *Engineers and the Price System*, p. 142.   [17] *Ibid.*, p. 153.

169

Allan G. Gruchy

operating within a democratic framework, as a means of guiding production. Presumably consumers would still be free to express their individual preferences for goods and services through the price system of the socialistic economy. But individual and collective economic preferences would have to be brought into harmony by the aid of the nation's economic budget and in accordance with a system of democratically approved national priorities. It is at this point in his treatment of the growth problem that Veblen introduces the related problem of economic welfare.

In Veblen's analysis economic welfare is a state of well-being or satisfaction that is dependent upon, or determined in part by, the availability of tangible goods. What primarily interests Veblen is the material aspect of economic welfare, or what he calls "material welfare." [18] This type of welfare has its roots in tangible commodities which are "serviceable" to both individuals and the community. According to Veblen a material product meets these two tests of economic welfare when it satisfies the needs of the individual and at the same time makes for race survival. The ultimate test of economic welfare insofar as it depends upon material goods is found in whether or not the material product "serves directly to enhance human life on the whole—whether it furthers the life process taken impersonally." [19] The decision as to whether or not a tangible commodity meets the test of "economic adequacy" or "social serviceability" must be made by technicians whose scientific knowledge enables them to determine whether or not a material product can bring a "net gain in comfort or the fullness of life." Material welfare, having a foundation in science and technology, is for Veblen fundamentally a matter of technological efficiency. Economic welfare as it relates to food, clothing, shelter, sanitation, educational facilities, and the like can be

---

[18] Although Veblen is well aware that there are other human needs beyond material needs, he has no special interest in the satisfaction of the nonmaterial needs of mankind. He adopts the position that once the nation is well supplied with useful material products, the satisfaction of nonmaterial needs would then be a relatively easy task. He sets up a system of priorities according to which urgent material needs come before less urgent nonmaterial needs. Wesley C. Mitchell follows a similar procedure in discussing economic welfare. See his essay on "The Prospects of Economics" in *The Trend of Economics,* ed. by R. G. Tugwell (New York: Knopf, 1924).

[19] T. Veblen, *The Theory of the Leisure Class* (New York: Macmillan, 1899), p. 99.

Theory of Economic Growth

readily objectified with the aid of modern science and technology.

Achieving sustained economic growth is an important problem for Veblen, because the extent of material welfare is determined in large part by the size of the nation's economic surplus. As this net product increases in size, a basis is laid for an increase in economic welfare. But Veblen does not confuse a rise in output with an increase in economic welfare. If the increase in output should happen to take the form of an enlargement of the supply of consumer superfluities, he would assert that economic welfare could actually decline rather than increase, since these superfluities may make race survival all the more difficult. Veblen is much interested in reducing the wastes and inefficiencies of the private enterprise system. He realizes that the first step in maximizing economic welfare is made when the nation's growing economic potential is more fully realized. But providing for a sustained rise in net industrial product is not enough to maximize economic welfare. In Veblen's regime of workmanship the national economic budget would project not only a rising net output but also increases in the kinds of products that would contribute most to the "material welfare of all the civilized peoples." In a democratic socialist system the public would turn to technicians for guidance concerning the "economic adequacy" or "social serviceability" of the nation's supply of tangible commodities. In these circumstances economic growth, as finally envisioned by Veblen, would be defined as a sustained increase in the type of tangible industrial product that would contribute most to the survival of the human race.

V

A comparison of the theory of economic growth of Veblen and of present-day institutionalists reveals significant similarities and dissimilarities. With respect to the consequences of capital accumulation, we find that present-day institutionalists are close to Veblen in many ways. They agree with him that the accumulation of capital is accompanied by changes in the character of capital, which over the long run raise its marginal productivity. They also find that technological progress and capital accumulation bring about fundamental changes in the very nature of the capitalistic system. Commons, Mitchell, Clark, and later institutionalists make much of the point that the

Allan G. Gruchy

growth of the nation's total production in the past half-century has been correlated with significant changes in the industrial system. They agree with Veblen that these changes have had the general effect of enlarging the area of collective action in control of individual action, until, as the economists of the first Council of Economic Advisers point out, we now live in "a day of large corporations, large labor unions, and comprehensive agricultural organizations, cooperatives and trade associations," as well as large government.[20] Although agreeing with Veblen that technological progress and capital accumulation have stimulated the movement of the economy toward more collective forms of economic activity than were to be found a century ago, present-day institutionalists do not accept Veblen's analysis of the direction of these collectivizing trends. This difference in the interpretation of the course of economic development stems largely from the fact that Veblen and later institutionalists observed different eras in the evolution of the capitalistic system. Veblen based his theory of capitalism on his analysis of the period running from 1875 to 1925, whereas the present-day institutionalists derive their interpretation of contemporary capitalism largely from a study of the period since 1929.

Veblen never tires of pointing out that the process of economic change is a matter of drift. It is not leading to any pre-determined outcome which can be revealed in advance by economic analysis. The collectivizing trends operating within the American economy must inevitably spell the doom of much small-scale business enterprise. But when the analysis turns to the shape of things to come, Veblen is much less certain. There is in his economics none of the Hegelianism that runs through much Marxist thinking and attaches a certain inevitability to the rise of socialism. Veblen is closer to Hume than to Hegel on this point. He always retains a healthy skepticism in his analysis of the future course of economic events. Veblen sees only two directions in which economic development may reasonably be expected to go, namely, fascism and full socialism, but present-day institutionalists see a number of possible lines of development such as welfare capitalism, laborism or democratic partial socialism, full socialism, fascism, and communism. Although a number of possible lines of economic development are open to the American economic

[20] Council of Economic Advisers, *First Annual Report to the President* (Washington, 1946), p. 17

Theory of Economic Growth

system in its future evolution, mid-century institutionalists, such as those associated with the first Council of Economic Advisers, the Joint Economic Committee, the Conference on Economic Progress, and the National Planning Association, regard controlled or welfare capitalism as the only type of economic system that is feasible at this point in the development of the American economy.

Present-day institutionalists, unlike Veblen, do not use a theory of economic exploitation. In Veblen's theorizing the exploitation of the working population by the vested interests hinders economic growth or the expansion of the nation's net industrial product. We find no similar theory of class exploitation in the writings of the mid-century institutionalists. According to their analysis the main obstacle to the achievement of sustained and adequate economic growth is the economy's inability to maintain growth-fostering balances between prices and costs and between total investment and total consumption. In the welfare capitalism of these institutionalists the main economic problem is how to secure a "collaborative guidance" of the nation's economy by the government and all major economic groups which will lead to sustained and adequate economic expansion. The problem is not, as Veblen would have it, one of eliminating the exploitation of the underlying population.

These differing interpretations of the course of capitalist development result in different economic policy goals. As has been explained earlier, Veblen uses the nation's economic accounts to reveal the net industrial product which in his opinion is being appropriated by the vested interests, but to which they make no contribution. He also uses the nation's economic budget to show how this net product could be utilized within a socialistic framework in order to achieve sustained and adequate economic growth. The present-day institutionalists likewise use the concepts of the nation's economic accounts and its economic budget, but within a different economic policy orientation. These latter-day institutionalists use the nation's economic accounts to show the impact on total output of imbalances between prices and costs and between total consumption and total investment. Their national economic budgets are designed to indicate the kinds of economic balances between these items that will contribute to sustained economic expansion.[21] Both Veblen and the mid-century

---

[21] For examples of this use of the "budgetary" concept by mid-century institutionalists see the National Planning Association's *National Budgets for Full*

institutionalists are seeking to uncover the relationships among total production, total consumption, and total investment which would foster sustained and adequate economic growth. Both Veblen's "central industrial directorate," or national planning board, and the mid-century institutionalists' national economic co-ordinating council, such as the first Council of Economic Advisers, have the same major task of securing the national goal of sustained and adequate economic growth. They also make the national economic budget the central device in their co-ordination of economic policies for achieving this goal. But Veblen's central industrial directorate would work within the limits of his socialistic regime of workmanship, whereas the present-day institutionalists' economic co-ordinating council operates within the confines of their controlled or welfare capitalism.

The institutionalists of today follow Veblen in keeping their analysis of economic growth close to considerations of economic welfare. They agree with Veblen that economic welfare is a matter of using scarce resources in order to maximize the satisfactions of individuals as members of society. Maximizing economic welfare requires a growing output of the types of goods and services that meet both individual and collective needs. The institutionalists' national economic budgets provide not only for growth but also for an expansion of economic welfare. Behind the list of priorities, which is embedded in their economic budgets, is an allocation of the nation's resources that reflects a vast array of individual and collective wants. In welfare capitalism these wants are provided for in large part through the operations of the private enterprise system, which, however, is supplemented by governmental guidance. This guidance is particularly important where collective economic welfare is the issue. This is the type of economic welfare that is shared by individuals as members of a community or larger political unit.

The mid-century institutionalists are not as critical as is Veblen of private enterprise as a method of providing for economic welfare. Since Veblen's time many of the distortions of the private market

---

Employment (Pamphlets Nos. 43 and 44; Washington, D.C.: April, 1945); G. Colm, *The American Economy in 1960* (Washington, D.C.: National Planning Association, 1952); G. W. Ensley, *Potential Economic Growth of the United States during the Next Decade* (Washington, D.C.: Joint Economic Committee, 1954); and L. H. Keyserling, *Toward Full Employment and Full Production* (Washington, D.C.: Conference on Economic Progress, 1954).

system have been reduced or eliminated. At present interest attaches more to public enterprise as a means of supplementing private enterprise in the effort to enlarge economic welfare. This means that the collective aspects of the welfare problem are now being stressed, since it is felt that efforts in this direction will be more rewarding than direct efforts to enlarge individual welfare. Consequently, the national economic budgets of the mid-century institutionalists direct more and more of the nation's resources into human and natural resource development, scientific research, public housing, public health, and other collective projects in order to enlarge collective welfare and at the same time provide a firmer foundation for the increase of individual economic welfare. In this work of enlarging collective economic welfare the technician or scientific expert comes to play a crucial role, just as he does in Veblen's analysis of economic welfare. Collective needs such as health, housing, education, and sanitation can now be objectified with the aid of scientific standards that are established by technical experts. These standards guide the government in its extra-market program of allocating scarce resources in order to expand the area of collective economic welfare.

The general aim of the present-day institutionalists is to strike a satisfactory balance between individual and collective economic welfare in order to maximize general economic welfare. While the main reliance for meeting the demands of economic welfare is still placed on the private price system under welfare capitalism, a recognition of the serious limitations of this system draws attention to the need for the kind of extra-market guidance that is provided under the national economic co-ordinating program of the mid-century institutionalists.

It is clear that Veblen would have repudiated these later exponents of institutionalism and their proposals for a controlled form of capitalism. As early as 1904 he asserted in *The Theory of Business Enterprise* that, from his point of view, nothing short of full socialism was the answer to the problem of how to remove the hindrances to securing sustained economic expansion. When discussing John A. Hobson's proposals to raise wage income, and hence consumption, at the expense of profits and saving, Veblen described Hobson's proposals as mere palliatives which were "manifestly chimerical in any community, such as the modern industrial communities, where public policy is with growing singleness of purpose guided by business in-

Allan G. Gruchy

terests with a naïve view to an increase of profits." [22] What would have been Veblen's position on this matter had he lived in the quarter century from 1930 to 1955? Would he have advocated the welfare capitalism of the mid-century institutionalists, or would he have advocated the pale "new socialism" of the British, Dutch, and Scandinavian labor parties? Or would he have continued to find the solution to the problem of how to maintain stable economic growth in the establishment of full socialism? These are questions that may be of broad speculative interest, but they are of little concern to the exponents of mid-century institutionalism in the United States, where socialism is today not a major issue, and will apparently not be so in the calculable future.

Although the policy recommendations of the mid-century institutionalists are quite different from Veblen's policy recommendations, it is clear that these institutionalists have much in common with Veblen. All institutionalists, including Veblen, are interested in a long-term theory of economic growth, which stresses evolution or change rather than the logical consistency of short-term growth analysis. Growth economics in the past two decades has become overspecialized. It is much too inclined to examine the immediate determinants of growth on the unrealistic assumption that the underlying economic framework does not change. Too much devotion to a narrowly defined growth economics causes the economist to ignore the many broader aspects of the growth problem. Far from being a simple, painless process of piling up automated factories and nuclear furnaces, economic growth, as Simon Kuznets points out, is "simultaneously a destroyer of no mean magnitude." As Veblen and later institutionalists have so frequently emphasized, economic growth is a painful, difficult process of altering the structure and functioning of the economic system to the end that the fruitfulness of our industrial technology may be realized in higher levels of output and welfare. It is clearly the task of institutionalism, as worked out by Veblen and later economists of a similar intellectual bent, to correct the nearsightedness of conventional growth economics, which arises from its failure to regard economic growth as an evolving process or sequence of change.

[22] *Theory of Business Enterprise*, p. 257.

[PAUL M. SWEEZY]

10

Veblen on American Capitalism

SINCE Veblen's writings, extending over more than thirty years, are almost all concerned, directly or indirectly, with American capitalism, a logical, and I think rewarding, study would be to trace the evolution of his thought on this increasingly important topic, from his first article on economics in 1891 through his last book, *Absentee Ownership and Business Enterprise in Recent Times*, published in 1923. Such a study would show both constancies and innovations, contrasts of emphasis and probably outright contradictions, different degrees of detachment or involvement, varying moods of hope and despair. By juxtaposing Veblen's thoughts with the historical reality, it would reveal the strengths and weaknesses of his diagnoses and prognoses; it would bring out the striking relevance of Veblen to our own time and problems; above all, it would leave no doubt about his towering genius as an insightful and creative social scientist. Needless to say, however, this is a more ambitious task than can be undertaken in a brief paper: the most I can attempt here is to sort out and arrange in order what I take to be the major aspects of Veblen's theoretical treatment of the dynamics of capitalism in general, and of American capitalism in particular.[1]

[1] For obvious reasons, Veblen treated the United States as the prototype of an advanced capitalist society, just as Marx, writing earlier, had assigned that role to Great Britain.

Paul M. Sweezy

VEBLEN'S INSTITUTIONALISM

First, let me state an opinion on a vexed and controversial subject, the nature of Veblen's "institutionalism." My purpose is to place Veblen among the theorists of modern capitalism and perhaps to help suggest standards by which to assess his achievement.

Veblen often spoke of institutions, but I do not recall that he ever called himself an institutionalist. The name was given to him by others, and in the first instance by those who regarded themselves as his disciples. The reason for this, I think, lies in Veblen's attitude toward the received economic theory of his day. Granted its premises, he had no particular fault to find with it. He simply regarded the premises as largely irrelevant to the elucidation of matters that really count. Perhaps as clear a statement as any to this effect occurs in his first postwar book:

> There are certain saving clauses in common use. . . . Among them are these: "Given the state of the industrial arts"; "Other things remaining the same"; "In the long run"; "In the absence of disturbing causes." . . . Now, as has already been remarked in an earlier passage, the state of the industrial arts has at no time continued unchanged during the modern era; consequently other things have never remained the same; and in the long run the outcome has always been shaped by the disturbing causes. All this reflects no discredit on the economists and publicists who so have sketched out the natural run of the present and future in the dry light of the eighteenth-century principles, since their reservations have not been observed. The arguments have been as good as the premises on which they proceed.[2]

To younger economists brought up on Marshall and Böhm-Bawerk and unfamiliar with any other school of economic thought, this sounded like an antitheoretical manifesto and was so interpreted: in brushing aside received theory, Veblen was assumed to be brushing aside theory in general. A natural corollary was to place him in the camp of the avowed enemies of theory, which meant, in the circumstances of the late nineteenth and early twentieth centuries, in the camp of Schmoller and the rest of the German historical school, who had fought the famous *Methodenstreit* with the Austrians in the closing decades of the nineteenth century. Those American economists

[2] *The Vested Interests and the Common Man* (New York, 1920), pp. 85–86.

On American Capitalism

who were themselves inclined to follow in the footsteps of the German historicists—for a variety of reasons, which do not concern us here, there were not a few of them—proclaimed Veblen their prophet and set out under the banner of institutionalism to dig out the facts of economic life without regard, as they thought, to the logic-chopping and obfuscation of the theorists.

In essentials, I think, the meaning of "institutionalism" is as simple as this and that all attempts to find something that can plausibly be called an institutionalist *doctrine* in Veblen's works are bound to fail for the simple reason that "there ain't no such animal."

Before World War II, this statement might have been greeted with skepticism, if not laughed right out of court, but today it may be found more congenial to the common sense of the economics profession. A host of factors have conspired to throw the spotlight of attention on problems of economic development, as distinct from problems of "normality" and "stationary states," and it is now generally recognized that an economist who falls outside the neoclassical schools does not necessarily land among the historicists. Marx has emerged from the underworld to which Keynes consigned him, and Schumpeter is no longer regarded as an "Austrian" with an eccentric business cycle theory. Veblen belongs to the same breed, and the time has come to treat him accordingly. I hope that what follows will make a contribution to this end.

THE MODERN POINT OF VIEW AND THE NEW ORDER

The general framework of Veblen's theory of capitalism is remarkably similar to Marx's and was doubtless largely derived from that source.[3] This could be documented by reference to any of Veblen's major works, but perhaps the most convenient for the purpose is *The Vested Interests and the Common Man*, which Arthur Davis has rightly called "in many ways . . . the best short introduction to Veb-

---

[3] There is no present need to go into the problem of how far this derivation was deliberate or unconscious. For some discussion of the influence of Marx on Veblen, see P. M. Sweezy, "The Influence of Marxian Economics on American Thought and Practice," in D. D. Egbert and Stow Persons, eds., *Socialism and American Life* (Princeton, N.J., 1952), I, esp. 473–477. [See also Article 8, by Forest G. Hill, in this volume.—EDITOR]

len's thought." [4] There Veblen argues in terms of what he calls the "Modern Point of View" and the "New Order," which are roughly equivalent to the relations of production and the forces of production in the Marxian scheme. The Modern Point of View is merely a shorthand expression for the principles proclaimed by the great bourgeois ideologues of the eighteenth century and given the institutional form of unrestricted private property, the sovereign nation state, and parliamentary democracy by the British, American, and French revolutions. The New Order is the mechanical system of production which, emerging from the Industrial Revolution, developed within its eighteenth-century shell and now threatens to burst it asunder. Or, to put the matter another way, the profound crisis of the twentieth century, come to an initial head in World War I, is at bottom the outcome of the tension between a social order that was stabilized in the eighteenth century and an industrial order that can function properly only if the restrictions of private ownership and national boundaries are done away with.

If this is an accurate distillation of Veblen's central thesis, there can be no doubt that it is essentially Marxian. This is not to deny important differences of detail and emphasis: for the moment, I am concerned only to clarify the main contours of Veblen's thought, and for this purpose he must be placed in the intellectual setting in which he belongs.

If the Veblenian framework is fundamentally Marxian, the same cannot be said of the way in which Veblen elucidates the inner dynamics of the capitalist mode of production. To this question we now turn.

THE INDUSTRIAL ARTS

In one sense, all theorists of economic development must accord a decisive role to the technological factor. This is, after all, the core of the productive system, and all the great economic changes of which we have knowledge have been associated with technological progress or regress. But of course all theorists do not treat the technological factor in the same way.

[4] A. K. Davis, "The Postwar Essays," in the special Veblen memorial issue of *Monthly Review*, July–August 1957, p. 92.

On American Capitalism

As is well known, in the Marxian theory of capitalism the prime mover is the accumulation of capital, an activity which capitalists are literally forced to engage in as a means to advancement and on pain of economic death. Technological development is motivated and controlled by the imperatives of the accumulation process, and the inventors and technicians who do the creative work are basically agents of the capitalists. Schumpeter's theory is quite different: in his view, capitalists are mere passive *rentiers,* and the active element is the entrepreneur working with borrowed funds, whose distinguishing characteristic is a genius for innovation in the realms of technology and economic organization. I cannot remember offhand that Schumpeter addressed himself specifically to the role of inventors and technicians, but there can be no doubt he thought of them as related to the entrepreneur much as Marx related them to the capitalist.

Veblen's view stands in contrast to both Marx's and Schumpeter's. Veblen's "absentee owners" are identical with Marx's capitalists, and when he speaks of "Captains of Industry" he is referring to pretty much the same group as Schumpeter's entrepreneurs. But that is about as far as the similarities go. The crucial difference is that Veblen, unlike the others, makes the sharpest kind of separation between business and industry—the realm of pecuniary values on the one hand and of material production on the other. In his view—and there was never any wavering or doubt on the point—*both* absentee owners and captains of industry operate exclusively in the sphere of business; their relation to industry is at best permissive and at worst destructive. From this it follows that in relation to the development of the industrial arts,[5] they play a negative rather than a positive role.

Nevertheless, in Veblen's view, the industrial arts do develop and progress, and at an ever accelerating pace. Moreover, it is precisely this process which underlies the whole of modern history and sets the alternatives before the human race. What did Veblen conceive to be the nature of this process? Since this is perhaps the most important question that can be asked about Veblen's theoretical system, I make no apologies for not having worked out a full answer. Nevertheless, as much of an answer as we need for this discussion is reasonably

---

[5] "The industrial arts" was a favorite term of Veblen's, but of course it was by no means original with him, having been in common use among economists of his day.

Paul M. Sweezy

clear. Veblen regarded technological knowledge as an attribute and possession of the community as a whole, and its increase as a social process. That its usufruct had come to be monopolized by a small segment of the community was due to the nature of the ideological and institutional stabilization which took place in the eighteenth century, not at all to any technological ability or creative urge of the monopolizers. Their role, if any, in developing the joint stock of technological knowledge, has been an obstructive one. To quote again from *The Vested Interests and the Common Man:*

> This body of technological knowledge, the state of the industrial arts, of course has always continued to be held as a joint stock. Indeed this joint stock of technology is the substance of the community's civilisation on the industrial side, and therefore it constitutes the substantial core of that civilisation. Like any other phase or element of the cultural heritage, it is a joint possession of the community, so far as concerns its custody, exercise, increase and transmission; but it has turned out, under the peculiar circumstances that condition the use of this technology among these civilised peoples, that its ownership or usufruct has come to be effectually vested in a relatively small number of persons.[6]

The real difficulty in interpreting Veblen concerns his conception of this social process of technological change, but fortunately there is no need to grapple with the problem here. For our present purpose it is enough to understand that he conceives of technological change as obeying its own logic and as essentially exogenous to the capitalist economy. The industrial arts, in other words, are the motor of the system, but the motor is fueled from outside, and the only controls that are applied from the inside are brakes of uncertain strength and holding power.

THE DYNAMICS OF DEVELOPMENT

The development of the industrial arts, and more specifically of what Veblen called the machine process, is, then, the key to modern economic history. Since this development takes place autonomously, it follows that the chief theoretical problem for Veblen is to analyze its impact on the economic process. His most comprehensive work on

[6] Page 57. Passages to the same effect could be cited from many of Veblen's works.

On American Capitalism

this subject is *The Theory of Business Enterprise,* on which I have drawn for much of what follows.

The machine process gives rise to large-scale production; large-scale production brings in its train the corporate form of organization; and along with corporations come the securities markets, promoters, underwriters, and the rest of the financial accouterments of modern big business. All this, in Veblen's view, marks a decisive change from the small-scale production and the individual owner-entrepreneur of classical economics. The center of attention of the larger type of businessman shifts progressively from the production of useful goods and services to the sale and manipulation of corporate securities, which in turn represent essentially the capitalized earning power of their respective underlying firms.

It is in this context that the consequences of continuous, and indeed accelerating, technological advance must be assessed. As Veblen saw it, the primary effect was a continuous lowering of production costs. With new machines and factories able to produce more cheaply than the old, the result could only be a steady undermining of existing capitalizations. And this, according to Veblen, must exercise an unremitting depressive effect on business in general. "It may, therefore, be said, on the basis of this view," he concluded, "that chronic depression, more or less pronounced, is normal to business under the fully developed regime of modern industry." [7] That Veblen regarded this as a major theoretical pronouncement may be gathered from his appending to it a footnote, saying, "With the above analysis may be contrasted Marx's discussion of the declining rate of profits and the manner in which he conceives overproduction, speculation, and crises to arise out of the tendency of profits to a minimum."

Veblen went much further than asserting the existence of a mere *tendency* to chronic depression. Writing in 1904, he thought he could say with assurance that the tendency had come to prevail in practice and that such relief from economic stagnation as had been experienced in the recent past was due to exogenous causes rather than to inherent recuperative powers of the system. This idea, of course, became familiar enough during the nineteen thirties, but in all the debate over the stagnation thesis which has taken place during the last two decades I do not recall having seen any references to Veblen, let alone recog-

[7] *The Theory of Business Enterprise* (New York, 1904), p. 234.

Paul M. Sweezy

nition of his pioneer role in this branch of economic theory. For this reason, it may be worthwhile to quote at some length:

> Since the seventies, as an approximate date and as applying particularly to America and in a less degree to Great Britain, the course of affairs in business has apparently taken a permanent change as regards crises and depression. During this recent period, and with increasing persistency, chronic depression has been the rule rather than the exception in business. Seasons of easy times, "ordinary prosperity," during this period are pretty uniformly traceable to specific causes extraneous to the process of industrial business proper. In one case, the early nineties, it seems to have been a peculiar crop situation, and in the most notable case of a speculative inflation, the one now (1904) apparently drawing to a close, it was the Spanish-American War, coupled with the expenditures for stores, munitions, and services incident to placing the country on a war footing, that lifted the depression and brought prosperity to the business community. If the outside stimulus from which the present prosperity takes its impulse be continued at an adequate pitch, the season of prosperity may be prolonged; otherwise there seems little reason to expect any other outcome than a more or less abrupt and searching liquidation.[8]

Veblen did not leave the matter there. The state of affairs depicted, he said, "calls for a remedy," and the "remedy may be sought in one or the other of two directions: (1) in an increased unproductive consumption of goods; or (2) in an elimination of that 'cutthroat' competition that keeps profits below the 'reasonable' level."[9] This, it will be seen, invites an analysis of two further basic aspects of economic development, namely, the changing pattern of private and public consumption, and the growth of monopolistic forms of organization and behavior.

Actually, Veblen never undertook a systematic inquiry into either of these subjects, in either *The Theory of Business Enterprise* or elsewhere, although a large part of what he wrote bears directly or indirectly on one or both of them. His general view in 1904 was that while something could be, and in fact was being, accomplished through an expansion of unproductive consumption, especially by governments, it was not enough: "So long as industry remains at its present level of efficiency, and especially so long as incomes continue to be distributed somewhat after the present scheme, waste cannot be expected to overtake production, and can therefore not check the un-

[8] *Ibid.*, pp. 250–251.   [9] *Ibid.*, p. 255.

toward tendency to depression." [10] The pressure to form ever larger and more comprehensive combinations was therefore irresistible and could be expected to continue until industry shall have been put "on the basis of so comprehensive and rigorous a coalition of business concerns as shall wholly exclude competition, even in the face of any conceivable amount of new capital seeking investment." [11]

It is not clear what effect Veblen expected this trend to monopoly to have on the tendency to chronic depression. He wrote *The Theory of Business Enterprise* in the midst of the first great wave of mergers, that is, before any pronouncement on the ultimate outcome could be ventured, and his purely theoretical statements are not altogether consistent or free of ambiguity. So far as individual combinations were concerned, he certainly thought they would fare better than their competing predecessors, and at times he seemed to transfer this conclusion from the firm to the whole economy. On the other hand, he was also of the view that combinations usually raised prices and reduced output, and he tended to transfer this conclusion, too, to the whole economy. If he had been confronted with these seemingly inconsistent lines of thought and asked to clarify them, I rather think he would have answered that both were right—that on the *business* level monopoly brought relief, while on the *industrial* level it produced a persistent underutilization of human and material resources. In Veblen's terminology, this would no longer be chronic depression—"depression" being for him a business rather than an industrial phenomenon—though its implications would be no less far-reaching.

On the whole, *Absentee Ownership,* Veblen's most important theoretical work on capitalism after *The Theory of Business Enterprise,* bears out this interpretation. Writing in 1923, he obviously anticipated neither the boom of the later twenties nor the depression that followed. Instead, he seems to have expected that a situation somewhat like the one then prevailing would continue more or less indefinitely; and in his view this situation comprised "reasonable" profits on the one hand and much unemployment and excess capacity on the other. His reason for imputing this kind of stability to the postwar economy was a belief that the process of monopolization had by then proceeded, not, to be sure, to its logical conclusion, but at any rate to the point where "One Big Union of the Interests" had matters securely in hand and would be able to eliminate any future "excesses" of inflation or

[10] *Ibid.,* pp. 257–258.   [11] *Ibid.,* p. 264.

Paul M. Sweezy

deflation. Under these circumstances, the center of conflict, and hence of change, in the American economy would shift increasingly to the field of labor relations.

Here again we may discern a basic similarity in the theories of Veblen and Marx: in the final analysis, both believed that the fate of capitalism would depend upon the course and outcome of a class struggle between capital and labor. But here again, Veblen's development of the idea is his own.

I speak of Veblen's development of the class struggle concept, but must add at once that this may be misleading. The truth is that there are in Veblen two quite distinct strands of thought bearing on this subject, and he never wove them together into a unified theory. The first, which is overwhelmingly predominant in *The Theory of Business Enterprise,* runs in terms of the discipline of different *occupations.* Business, according to Veblen, makes for a high regard for tradition, precedent, and things as they are. The machine process, on the other hand, inculcates in those who tend it a matter-of-fact attitude which is no respecter of authority or privilege in any form. These disciplines shape conflicting mental outlooks, the one conservative and the other essentially iconoclastic and radical. And the line of cleavage runs in the main between the owners and the workers, although even the former are not immune to the influence of the machine process, while among the latter the extent of the conditioning varies widely in the different occupational subgroups. Organizationally, "trade-unionism is . . . to be taken as a somewhat mitigated expression of what the mechanical standardization of industry inculcates,"[12] and as of 1904 there was no doubt in Veblen's mind that "the classes who move in trade unions are, however crudely and blindly, endeavoring, under the compulsion of the machine process, to construct an institutional scheme on the lines imposed by the new exigencies given by the machine process."[13] Read in context, this can only be interpreted to mean that the working class was both organizing and turning to socialism, which is pretty much what the Marxists were saying too. But this similarity in the conclusions of the two theories should not lead us to overlook their differences: Veblen's, as it appeared in *The Theory of Business Enterprise,* was one of occupational conditioning, Marx's of class interest.

The second strand in Veblen's thinking on the class struggle was

[12] *Ibid.,* p. 330.   [13] *Ibid.,* p. 336.

On American Capitalism

closer to Marx, and as the years went by it came increasingly to the fore until, by the time of *Absentee Ownership*, it had practically become the whole fabric of his thought on this matter. In this, his last book, one can find no more than traces of the old occupational discipline theory, while a class interest theory is repeatedly set forth in the most uncompromising terms. Speaking of "the new alignment of material interests," Veblen stated categorically: "The effectual division of interest and sentiment is beginning visibly to run on class lines, between the absentee owners and the underlying population." [14] It would be a mistake, however, to assume that this is a mere restatement in Veblenian language of familiar Marxian doctrine. Marx thought of the conflict of interest between capitalist and worker as turning largely around the *division* of the product between wages and surplus value. Veblen, while not neglecting this aspect of the problem, tended more than Marx to stress the *total size* of the product. "The material interest of the underlying population," he wrote, "is best served by a maximum output at a low cost, while the business interests of the industry's owners may best be served by a moderate output at an enhanced price." [15]

By stressing that there are two distinct strands in Veblen's thinking about class struggle, I do not mean to suggest that they are necessarily incompatible but only that he made no particular effort to bring them together within a single theoretical framework. It is quite possible, of course, for occupational discipline and class interest to reinforce each other, and there is one all-too-brief passage in which Veblen puts forward the suggestive thesis that it is the workers' "common necessities and common weakness"—merely another way of saying their class interests—"which compel the trade-unionists to take thought of their case in other terms than those afforded by existing legal institutions [and] are the means whereby the discipline of the machine industry is enforced and made effective for recasting the habits of thought of the workmen." And to this he adds:

The harsh discipline of these exigencies of livelihood drives home the new point of view and holds the workmen consistently to it. But that is not all that the mechanical standardization of industry does in the case; it also

---

[14] *Absentee Ownership and Business Enterprise in Recent Times* (New York, 1923), p. 6. It is noteworthy that this stress on the conflict of material interests is the central theme of the "Introductory" chapter.

[15] *Ibid.*, p. 10.

furnishes the new terms in which the revised scheme of economic life takes form. The revision of the scheme aimed at by trade-union action runs, not in terms of natural liberty, individual property rights, individual discretion, but in terms of standardized livelihood and mechanical necessity; it is formulated, not in terms of business expediency, but in terms of industrial, technological standard units and standard relations.[16]

Apart from the question whether this passage is right or not, which obviously cannot be made an issue here, it undoubtedly shows that Veblen had given thought to the relation between occupational discipline and class interest and moreover in his own mind had assigned to this relation a strategic role in the dynamics of capitalist development. That he never bothered to elaborate so important a point is an eloquent commentary on his unsystematic—and often highly frustrating—way of theorizing.

It might be thought that the logical outcome of Veblen's theory would be a prediction, as confident as Marx's, that capitalism must necessarily be replaced by socialism. After all, the machine process was extending its sway and its ulterior effects seemed all to point in the direction of a socialist consummation. If Veblen did not follow through to this conclusion, the reason is that the theory as sketched above was, from his point of view, only one side of the story. There was also the question of what the conservative classes could and would do to defend their interests, and only after this had been taken into account would a balanced assessment of future prospects be possible. To understand Veblen's views in this connection, we must first have a brief look at his theory of the state and of the relation between the economic and political aspects of capitalist society.

ECONOMICS AND POLITICS

For Veblen, as for Marx (but not for Schumpeter), the separation of economics from politics might be a necessary step in the analysis of this or that problem, but it could never be more than temporary and provisional and certainly could not be elevated to the status of a methodological principle. It is hence no cause for surprise that Veblen's theory of capitalism is, almost from the outset, as much political as economic. Thus we find, for example, that immediately after the "Intro-

[16] *Theory of Business Enterprise*, pp. 334–335.

On American Capitalism

ductory" chapter of *Absentee Ownership* there follows a chapter entitled "The Growth and Value of National Integrity," which is an essay in what orthodox social science would classify as pure political theory.

The Veblenian theory of the state under capitalism—leaving aside the question of the modern state's barbarian origin and dynastic descent—may be said to have two basic aspects: (1) On the one hand, Veblen takes it for granted as being too obvious to require argument that the state is the guarantor of the existing social order and that this means that its first and overriding duty is to safeguard property rights. It means further, and again as a matter of course, that the government is in the hands of the propertied classes and will be freely used by them to protect and promote their own interests. (2) Democracy of the Western European and American variety not only does not contradict this scheme of things but fits into it as an integral, and indeed even indispensable, working part. "A constitutional government is a business government. . . . Representative government means, chiefly, representation of business interests." [17] Or, more colorfully: "So the constituted authorities of this democratic commonwealth come, in effect, to constitute a Soviet of Business Men's Delegates, whose dutiful privilege it is to safeguard and enlarge the special advantages of the country's absentee owners." [18]

Now it is important to note that in putting forward this theory Veblen did not state or imply that democracy is a fraud in the sense that it excludes the underlying population from the governing process. His point is that the underlying population has been successfully conditioned to want only business leadership. The latter, for its part, would not be able to govern without "the advice and consent of the common run." [19] The question immediately arises, therefore, as to what would happen if and when the common run, spurred by its material interests and disciplined by the machine process, should stop wanting business leadership and should refuse its further consent. The whole logic of Veblen's theory points toward precisely such a crisis. Veblen, however, made no attempt to answer the question in this form—though of course any complete theory of democracy would have to do so—but instead concentrated on what the vested interests could,

[17] *Ibid.*, pp. 285, 286.   [18] *Absentee Ownership*, p. 37.
[19] *Vested Interests*, p. 16.

and could be expected to, do to prevent matters from reaching this pass.

Here his theory of "national integrity" (one of a number of expressions used to convey the same idea) enters the picture. To Veblen, the sense of national integrity, or plain nationalism, to use a shorter term, is one of the oldest and most deeply rooted of all human sentiments, being a direct lineal descendant of the solidarity of the savage tribe in the face of its enemies. Originally, and for literally millenia thereafter, this sentiment served the purpose of group survival, which explains how it happened to acquire something of the force and obduracy of an inherent trait of human nature.[20] In modern times, to be sure, nationalism has not only ceased to serve a useful purpose but has become a thoroughly harmful and disruptive force. As yet, however, there have been few, if any, signs of abatement of the intensity of nationalist feeling, and in most of his writings Veblen seems to imply that it would be utopian to expect any such development within a time period worth trying to take account of.

Nationalism fits into Veblen's over-all theory as the crucial instrument used by the vested interests to control the underlying population. The way this control works is twofold: (1) On the one hand, the interests of the owners are (successfully) identified with the interests of the nation. This enables the government to secure popular support for a program devoted in the main to the furtherance of class interests. In Veblen's words:

By stress of this all-pervading patriotic bias and that fantastic bigotry which enables civilised men to believe in a national solidarity of material interests,

---

[20] This is not the occasion for a discussion of Veblen's views on human nature, instincts, etc., but it is to the point to observe that his use of all such terms was quite consciously loose and variable, and it would be foolish to assign him to a particular school of thought or attribute to him a particular theory on the basis of his terminology. As a generalization, I think it is safe to say that he regarded human behavior patterns as being governed by a compound of habits acquired under the stress of environmental conditions. Old habits could be lost or changed, new habits acquired. But in the nature of things the process was bound to be slow, and in the case of deeply ingrained habits so slow that they must for most purposes be treated as data rather than variables. Ultimately, it was this belief in the stubbornness of deeply ingrained habits that accounts for Veblen's underlying pessimism. And it was this, too, which, more than any merely doctrinal differences, set him apart from the Marxian and other radical movements of his time.

On American Capitalism

it has come now to pass that the chief—virtually sole—concern of the constituted authorities in any democratic nation is a concern about the profitable business of the nation's substantial citizens.[21]

(2) More important in a dynamic sense, the vested interests are able, by adopting aggressive policies toward the outside world, to set in motion a process which exercises a disciplinary effect comparable in strength and opposite in direction to that of the machine industry. This process is the militarization of society which not only affects the economy through arms spending and the like but also impinges on the life of the people in a variety of direct and indirect ways. So important is this point to Veblen's total theory that a long quotation may not be out of order:

> The largest and most promising factor of cultural discipline—most promising as a corrective of iconoclastic vagaries—over which business principles rule is national politics. . . . Business interests urge an aggressive national policy and business men direct it. Such a policy is warlike as well as patriotic. The direct cultural value of a warlike business policy is unequivocal. It makes for a conservative animus on the part of the populace. During war time, and within the military organization at all times, civil rights are in abeyance; and the more war and armament the more abeyance. Military training is a training in ceremonial precedence, arbitrary command, and unquestioning obedience. . . . The more consistent and the more comprehensive this military training, the more effectually will the members of the community be trained into habits of subordination and away from that growing propensity to make light of personal authority which is the chief infirmity of democracy. This applies first and most decidedly, of course, to the soldiery, but it applies only in a less degree to the rest of the population. They learn to think in warlike terms of rank, authority, and subordination, and so grow progressively more patient of encroachments on their civil rights. . . . Habituation to a warlike, predatory scheme of life is the strongest disciplinary factor that can be brought to counteract the vulgarization of modern life wrought by peaceful industry and the machine process, and to rehabilitate the decaying sense of status and differential dignity. Warfare, with the stress on subordination and mastery and the insistence on gradations of dignity and honor incident to a militant organization, has always proved an effective school in barbarian methods of thought.
>
> In this direction, evidently, lies the hope of a corrective for "social unrest" and similar disorders of civilised life. There can, indeed, be no serious ques-

---

[21] *Absentee Ownership*, pp. 36–37.

tion but that a consistent return to the ancient virtues of allegiance, piety, servility, graded dignity, class prerogative, and prescriptive authority would greatly conduce to popular content and to facile management of affairs. Such is the promise held out by a strenuous national policy.[22]

To this should perhaps be added a much shorter passage from *Absentee Ownership*—where essentially the same theory appears in somewhat different form—showing that Veblen by no means thought in terms of a crude economic determination of political behavior such as is characteristic of vulgar Marxism (though not of the great Marxist thinkers):

Business-as-usual and the national integrity are joint and integral factors in that complex of habits of thought that makes up the official mentality; so that any irritation of the official sensibilities along either line will unavoidably bring a response along the two together and indiscriminately. In that parallelogram of forces in which business principles and the sense of national integrity combine jointly to move and direct the democratic officials there is no distinguishing the joint factors.[23]

THE FUTURE OF CAPITALISM

We are now in a position to assemble the various pieces of Veblen's theory into a coherent whole. We have seen that the machine process is the motor force of capitalist development, and that its progress is cumulative and independent of the will or actions of the businessmen. The machine process brings in its wake institutional changes leading at first to a state of chronic depression, then to a monopolized economy in which profits are protected but human and material resources are persistently underutilized. This condition of affairs in turn intensifies and sharpens a class struggle already implicit in the occupational division of society between business and industry. The logic of the struggle points to a progressive undermining of the eighteenth-century principles on which business enterprise rests, and ultimately to a socialist reconstruction of society. To this trend, however, the vested interests oppose a counterforce in the shape of aggressive national policies which, harnessing the people's fierce sense of nationalism, create the

[22] *Theory of Business Enterprise*, pp. 391–393.
[23] Page 430.

On American Capitalism

illusion of a solidarity of national interests and impose on society the retrogressive discipline of the barracks and the police state.

And the outcome?

Veblen felt sure only that, whichever trend got the upper hand, capitalism could not survive. The machine process pointed forward to socialism, national politics backward to barbarism. Neither would be compatible with business principles, and the reversionary trend would spell the end of modern science and technology. But which way the capitalist world would go, Veblen did not profess to know. In the measured words of the final paragraph of *The Theory of Business Enterprise*:

> It is difficult to believe that the machine technology and the pursuit of the material sciences will be definitively superseded, for the reason, among others, that any community that loses these elements of its culture thereby loses that brute material force that gives it strength against its rivals. And it is equally difficult to imagine how any of the communities of Christendom can avoid entering the funnel of business and dynastic politics, and so running through the process whereby the materialistic animus is eliminated. Which of the two antagonistic factors may prove the stronger in the long run is something of a blind guess; but the calculable future seems to belong to the one or the other. It seems possible to say this much, that the full dominion of business enterprise is necessarily a transitory dominion. It stands to lose in the end whether the one or the other of the two divergent cultural tendencies wins, because it is incompatible with the ascendancy of either.[24]

Twenty years later, at the end of his productive career and with only a few more years to live, Veblen returned to the same gnawing question. If I have understood the first and last chapters of *Absentee Ownership* correctly, he had not really changed his mind on any essential point of principle. But whatever hope he had once entertained for the "civilized" countries—there is no doubt that he had the United States chiefly in mind—had pretty well disappeared. The intervening period of imperialism, war, and chauvinism had done its dreary work. The relatively optimistic discussion of the socialist movement which occupies a prominent place in *The Theory of Business Enterprise* has no counterpart in *Absentee Ownership*. Unions now appear as narrow-minded interest groups animated by the business principle of the

[24] Page 400.

main chance. Diligent sabotage by employers and conscientious withdrawal of efficiency by workers had led to a stalemate of "mutual defeat," which was due to get worse and from which Veblen could see no escape. There is, to be sure, a faint echo of his former more hopeful outlook in the remark that "except for this mob-mind of national integrity it is conceivable that democratic institutions might have come to serve the common good; but because of this the rule of Live and Let Live has in effect gone into the moral discard."[25] But the total mood was now one of black despair:

> In the long run, of course, the pressure of changing material circumstances will have to shape the lines of human conduct, on pain of extinction. . . . But it does not follow that the pressure of material necessity, visibly enforced by the death penalty, will ensure such a change in the legal and moral punctilios as will save the nation from the death penalty.[26]

This passage occurs near the beginning of the book. It is nowhere countermanded in the four hundred-odd pages that follow, and it finds both sanction and emphasis in the gloomy ruminations that bring the book to a close. It can safely be taken as Veblen's last word on the outlook for American capitalism.

A FEW CONCLUDING REMARKS

With the knowledge of hindsight, it is of course easy to see that Veblen's theory was too narrow and confining to contain the tumultuous developments of the succeeding decades. The boom and bust of the twenties, the long depression of the thirties, and above all the unprecedented and virtually uninterrupted expansion after World War II —none of these fit into the Veblenian framework as it finally took shape in *Absentee Ownership*. And yet it seems obvious that we cannot on that account dismiss Veblen's theory as of no more than historical interest. On the contrary, anyone reading his major works on capitalism today must, I think, be struck by the fact that the vision which they embody—to use a favorite expression of Schumpeter's— remains astonishingly fresh and relevant. No one understood so clearly the growth of monopolistic (or, if you prefer, oligopolistic) big business with its ramifications and implications in such fields as advertising,

---

[25] *Absentee Ownership*, p. 38.   [26] *Ibid.*, p. 17.

distribution, and popular culture. No one grasped so thoroughly the unity of economics and politics. Above all, Veblen was, and remains, alone in assigning a decisive role in the development of capitalism to the reciprocating interaction of business principles and national politics. Others have described the economic impact of war, the psychological effects of militarism, the cultural incidence of nationalism; and none can deny that these forces have become increasingly important, if not actually dominant, in the world of the twentieth century. Yet only Veblen has built all these elements into a reasoned and coherent theory.[27] Finally, I imagine that I am not alone in thinking that Veblen's pessimism may be a good deal more meaningful and relevant than it is now fashionable to admit.

If these judgments are sound, as I believe they are, then the question may well be asked why so much that has happened in the last thirty years or so escapes the net of Veblen's theory. The answer, I believe, lies in certain serious, but remediable, weaknesses in his analytic apparatus. In closing, I would like to indicate, in desperate brevity, the nature of these weaknesses.

The root of the trouble was that Veblen, like most of his contemporaries, never gave any serious thought to working out a usable income-expenditure theory. He habitually and naïvely assumed the operation of Say's Law in the extreme form in which total income is automatically spent *and* remains constant over time. And he equally habitually wrote about phenomena—depression, inflation, deflation, and the like—which could not possibly happen if the assumption were valid. Much that he said about these matters was all right as far as it went, but this was invariably in spite of his analytic apparatus rather than because of it; and, not unnaturally, this apparatus time and again came to the surface, now to hide a problem, a few pages later to block off a promising line of inquiry, sometimes to throw a whole argument into a state of hopeless confusion. The result was, of course, that a number of very important questions were badly posed, wrongly answered, or allowed to drop just when they should have been most vigorously pursued.

---

[27] This generalization does not, of course, apply to the various Marxist schools of thought. It is only just to add, however, that their treatment of nationalism and its relation to business and governmental policies has never approached that of Veblen in point of depth or explanatory power.

Paul M. Sweezy

Veblen's theory of chronic depression, which, as we have seen, played an important role in *The Theory of Business Enterprise*, is the most significant case in point.[28] The causative factor, it will be recalled, is the progressive lowering of costs, and hence undermining of capital values, through technological advance. Veblen does not spell out the *modus operandi*, but the omission can be easily made good. Declining prices, bankruptcies, and the like, can exercise a dampening effect on new investment; and a low level of investment can, in turn, keep income and employment at depression levels. Moreover, Veblen's analysis seems on the whole to presuppose some such mechanism. The remedies for chronic depression that he discusses are (1) an expansion of consumption, particularly public consumption of an unproductive character, which obviously operates directly on the level of effective demand; and (2) the replacement of competition by monopoly, which may be assumed, at least initially, to have the effect of restoring the inducement to invest.

But as we read along in Chapter VII of *The Theory of Business Enterprise*, where these matters are dealt with, we make the rather surprising discovery that Veblen's interest is centered on the growth of monopoly and that in effect the theory of chronic depression is hardly more than a link in a longer chain designed to prove that "the tendency to consolidation is irresistible." [29] Having demonstrated this to his own satisfaction, Veblen went a step further, apparently taking it for granted that the phenomenon of chronic depression would disappear along with free competition. In any case, the problem drops out of sight before the end of Chapter VII and never turns up again in any of his later works.

It is hard to believe that this would have happened if Veblen had ever seriously thought in terms of the determinants of consumption and investment (hence of total income and demand). For in that case, he could hardly have believed that monopoly would permanently solve the problem of the inducement to invest, and it seems rather more likely that he would have come to precisely the opposite conclusion. And if chronic depression had remained in his mind, even only as a tendency, all of his subsequent theorizing about the stability and fate of capitalism might have been profoundly affected. The decade of the thirties would certainly have fitted nicely into such a

[28] See above, pp. 183–185.   [29] Page 266.

broadened Veblenian framework. Further, Veblen might have—I should think, almost certainly would have—been led to take up again and extend the theory of unproductive public consumption as a remedy for depression. This would have provided him with an additional link between economics and politics, between the needs of business and the results of a warlike national policy. And it would have left the door open for the elaboration of a distinctively Veblenian theory of the forties and fifties.

Veblen's work could be improved in other respects with the help of a clear income-expenditure theory. For example, the growth of selling and distribution costs, which Veblen analyzed in masterly fashion in Chapter XI of *Absentee Ownership*, takes on a new dimension and new significance in the light of such a theory. Just as in the case of expanding government activities, we see that what is involved is not only increased "costs" but also an ever swelling volume of unproductive consumption, which, in turn, has profound effects on the functioning of the capitalist economy.

My purpose, however, in these concluding remarks has not been to attempt to improve on Veblen, but rather the more modest one of showing that many of his most serious shortcomings can be remedied without giving up anything more weighty than his confusions. Of how many social scientists can this be said?

[JOEL B. DIRLAM]

11

The Place of Corporation Finance in Veblen's Economics

THE distinguishing feature of Veblen's general theory of the economic process is the importance he assigns to the financing of the modern corporation. His care in differentiating the age of the masterless man and the petty capitalist from that of the free-wheeling speculator and fabulous financier leads him to place corresponding emphasis on the economics of absentee ownership.

To single out the corporation as the characteristic institution of the modern economy is commonplace among economists. But Veblen's thought appears to be unique even today in tracing directly to the pattern of behavior of the corporate man, shaped by the conventions of corporation finance, the determination of the key economic variables of price and investment, the general level and direction of the business cycle, and the sharing of the product. He was, of course, far from limiting his analysis of the developing forces in society to those areas which are technically reserved for economists.[1]

Veblen did his best to exaggerate the differences between his views on the basic functions of corporation finance and those of the more orthodox school. For this reason, before attempting to appraise the validity of his analysis and its possible usefulness today, it is desirable

[1] The writer would like to acknowledge the helpful criticism of an earlier draft of this chapter by Myron W. Watkins, Irwin M. Stelzer, and Benjamin Caplan, and the research assistance of Christopher Green and Lois Hummel.

to pry apart his rather closely articulated system in an effort to restate the essential features of his model. Admittedly, the summary must retrace some familiar ground. But the review seems necessary if one is to determine whether a parallel approach today might not provide useful economic insights.

I

As Veblen sees it, the patterns of corporation finance are shaped in a society where investments are made for profit, industrial plants are capitalized on the basis of their profit-yielding capacity, accounts are kept in terms of a monetary unit, and there is a presumption of an orderly increase of the property invested.[2] According to the folklore of political economy, "savings will produce goods so soon as they are invested and capitalised."[3] But Veblen rejects the folklore. He denies that the financing of corporations through funds received from security issues adds to material equipment or industrial output.[4] Since this conclusion is so much at odds with current as well as the then-contemporary doctrine, a brief examination of his argument seems warranted.

In his earliest treatment Veblen insists at some length upon the sterility of "loan credit"—a term he uses to embrace common and preferred stock issue as well as securities more conventionally classified as corporate debts. "Borrowed funds do not increase the aggregate industrial equipment," first, because an expansion of bank loans to business represents not the transfer of liquid assets, but the mere expansion of bank deposits which are already far in excess of reserves.[5] Secondly, when individuals lend, they do so not out of liquid funds, but by turning collateral—real estate or securities—into "means of payment." This process cannot add anything "to the effective material apparatus of industry."[6] The final formulation is much the same. Savings are not material goods; they are merely "funds" which, transferred to the financier, may be invested in materials, equipment, and

[2] *The Theory of Business Enterprise* (New York: Scribner, 1904), pp. 84–87.
[3] *Absentee Ownership and Business Enterprise in Recent Times: The Case of America* (New York: Huebsch, 1923), p. 86.
[4] "Faith in the creative efficiency of capital funds and capitalized savings," he remarks, "is one of the axioms of the business community" (*ibid.*, p. 86).
[5] *Theory of Business Enterprise*, p. 101.   [6] *Ibid.*, p. 103.

wages. The only assured outcome of the mobilization of savings is a higher price for the goods transferred to the corporation financier.[7]

The "original capitalisation" of the equipment used in industry does not, however, constitute an extension of credit. If, somehow, the process of credit expansion and price inflation could be checked in midstream, then credit might merely shift the management of industrial materials from the owner to a more competent user.[8] Once the corporation is set up, the lure of promoters' gains inevitably seems to lead to security issue in excess of that which would just match the transfer of industrial assets (valued presumably at constant prices).

In spite of these statements, seeming to imply that all capitalization is inflationary, Veblen does, therefore, apply a kind of deflator to the corporate property to yield a solid and unfictitious value. In his discussion of mergers and combinations, he distinguishes between the "values" which are "of the nature of material goods" and the nominal capital that is merely good will equivalent to "presumptive earning capacity."[9] Hence, it seems reasonable to conclude that, where security issues correspond to material values, the corporation through "loan credit" (in Veblen's sense) may create industrial property. But Veblen is much more concerned with the prosperity phase of the business cycle where a swelling corporate demand for resources serves only to shift (already produced?) assets from one corporation to another and can do nothing to compress the output of consumers goods.[10]

In business depression, however, securities issued by firms at lower interest cost than that borne by the older firms will enable the newcomers to produce at lower costs (including debt charges) and to undercut the older firms.[11] Here, "loan credit" is by no means inflationary, since it makes possible net additions to industrial equipment and output by firms selling at lower prices.

[7] *Absentee Ownership*, pp. 86–87. [8] *Theory of Business Enterprise*, p. 98.
[9] *Ibid.*, pp. 126–127.
[10] In his discussion of the crisis following the "exaltation" phase of the cycle, he places primary emphasis on the consequences of the eventual discovery by the business community that the putative earning capacity on which the inflationary credit was based is inconsistent with actual earnings. Liquidation follows (*ibid.*, pp. 194, 207–208).
[11] *Ibid.*, p. 220. "Some new investment is going on with a well-advised expectation of reasonable profits on the basis of current costs."

Joel B. Dirlam

From Veblen's insistence that a large part of corporate security issuance is "inflationary" follows his conclusion that some portion of the security structure provides a "free" or "unearned" income. The relationship was suggested in 1904; it appears full-blown in *The Vested Interests and the Common Man*.[12] In a sense, it complements his doctrine that loan capital does not add to productive equipment. The income realized from this part of capitalization is "not a return for mechanically productive work done"; it is, however, drawn from the annual product of industry. It is the "conscientious withdrawal of efficiency" that by permitting a higher rate, creates the "free income." In the earlier book, on the other hand, he had placed much greater weight on the speculative element—on the insider's ability to manipulate the relation between putative and actual earning capacity.[13] The great modern fortunes were attributed to such manipulation.[14] But in the later book, it was the perpetuation of the charge on society that loomed uppermost—so much so that he concluded that half the net product of industry was drawn off by those who capitalized strategic curtailments of production.[15] The theme is repeated, but in no way altered, in *Absentee Ownership*.[16]

It would not be difficult to dispute this artificial separation of corporate earnings into the ethically justifiable and ethically unjustifiable. As Veblen himself concedes, with a nostalgic backward look at the old dispensation, the universal availability of no-par stock has merged assets into an undifferentiated whole, and made earning power the test of market value of the entire capitalization.[17] But his dif-

---

[12] In *The Theory of Business Enterprise*, he distinguishes between early practice, when corporate capitalization was based on "the cost of material equipment" and the then current method, which capitalized good-will—immaterial goods—by issues of common stock (pp. 137–146). The insiders can go on to manage the affairs of the corporation "for tactical ends" so as to maximize gains from vendible capital (pp. 160–167). But in the later book, the profits that convey value to the securities issued against good will are clearly segregated from earnings that are a "return for the productive use of the plant" (*The Vested Interests and the Common Man* [New York: Huebsch, 1920], p. 71).

[13] *Theory of Business Enterprise*, pp. 152–155.   [14] *Ibid.*, p. 167.

[15] *Vested Interests*, pp. 74, 76.

[16] In a well-known passage he refers to intangible assets as a "valid claim to get something for nothing" (*Absentee Ownership*, p. 348, n11).

[17] "It has come to be recognized that the only reasonable basis of capitalisation for any assets, tangible or intangible, is the earning-capacity which they represent" (*Vested Interests*, p. 66). "It is difficult, if not impossible, to draw a hard

Place of Corporation Finance

ferentiation is not intended to have immediate or practical application. It is rather subordinate to his analysis of the corporate practices that give rise to the free income. However, the causal link to financing is still important. The opportunity to issue securities against "putative earning power" forces the corporation to assure that earning power by methods that, as Veblen describes them, appear to be contrary to the public interest.[18]

II

Superficially considered, Veblen's analysis is part of the tradition of protest against watered stock and deceptive financial statements, which finally led to the Securities Act of 1933, the Securities Exchange Act of 1934, and other remedial financial legislation of the New Deal. These reforms might be regarded as a realization of his intellectual legacy. But there were others who, contemporaneously, were equally, or more, severe in condemning stock watering and manipulation by insiders. And more important, the conclusions Veblen drew from his analysis of such practices were not "on all fours" with those of the critics like William Z. Ripley, E. S. Mead, and Louis Brandeis. Ripley's testimony before the United States Industrial Commission in 1899 [19] attacked inflated capitalizations; the conservative *Commercial and Financial Chronicle* in the same year criticized promotions in terms

---

and fast line between that part of a concern's earning-capacity which is properly to be assigned to its plant and that which is due to its control of the market" (*ibid.*, p. 67). Nevertheless, he goes on to draw the line, and to try to pin down the source of the "free" income.

[18] In *The Theory of Business Enterprise,* he spoke of charging what the traffic would bear, of the primary criterion to the businessman of vendibility of output, rather than serviceability, and of the wastes of competitive selling (ch. iii), but he did not set forth the pricing consequences of the partial monopoly which he believed was enjoyed by almost every seller. The emphasis was rather on the waste of resources in advertising and selling. The relation of price policy to capitalisation was most fully developed in *Absentee Ownership,* and it will be discussed below. John R. Commons believed that Veblen's doctrine was weakened by his ignoring the limitations that courts had placed on the expansion of intangible values created by salesmanship and output restriction (*Institutional Economics* [New York: Macmillan, 1934], pp. 672–673). But Commons gave no examples of such limitations to what he called "reasonable value" other than utility decisions.

[19] Quoted in E. G. Campbell, *The Reorganization of the American Railroad System, 1893–1900* (New York: Columbia University Press, 1938), p. 320.

almost identical with Veblen's descripton of "inflationary" security issues.[20]

However, it is questionable whether Veblen was in any sense of the word a reformer—in the way that Adolph A. Berle and Gardner C. Means, Ripley, Brandeis, and Robert Healy [21] were reformers. When Veblen reviewed the familiar facts of the United States Steel Corporation promotion and pointed to the prevalence in mergers of the issue of intangibles, or when he predicted that without the baseline of par value stock business capital might move to a state of complete intangibility,[22] he nevertheless refrained from calling for the correlative reform.[23] Nor would he have felt constrained by the New Deal reforms substantially to modify his conclusions. After all, in *Absentee Ownership* he had pretty much abandoned his earlier insistence that manipulation contributed to, or was the primary source of, the great fortunes (though had he written at a later stage of the Big Bull Market, he might with justification have revived this part of his theory).

Veblen's assumption that the "abuses" of corporation finance were, in fact, its very essence, constituted the major difference between his point of view and that of the "reformers." In the testimony of James B. Dill [24] and Charles Claffin Allen—echoing the Report of the Chicago Conference on Trusts [25]—before the Industrial Commission and in Ripley's later summarization [26] the relation between overcapitalization (defined as security issue in excess of the "actual property value") and price policy is described in terms almost identical with Veblen's. The reformers, however, regarded the resultant prices as "exorbitant" —aberrations which could be eliminated by checking the overissue of securities.

[20] Quoted in G. W. Edwards, *The Evolution of Finance Capitalism* (New York: Longmans Green, 1938), pp. 186–187.

[21] It seems necessary, unfortunately, to recall that Healy was counsel to the Federal Trade Commission utility holding company investigation and a distinguished member of the Securities and Exchange Commission.

[22] *Theory of Business Enterprise*, p. 208, n1.

[23] See Alvin S. Johnson, "Veblen, Thorstein Bunde," in E. R. Seligman, ed., *Encyclopaedia of the Social Sciences* (New York: Macmillan, 1935), XV, 234–235.

[24] Industrial Commission, *Preliminary Report on Trusts and Industrial Combinations*, 1900, p. 1180.

[25] *Ibid.*, pp. 1194, 1197.

[26] *Trusts, Pools and Corporations* (Boston: Little, Brown, 1905), pp. xix–xxiii.

Place of Corporation Finance

But when the era of corporate finance succeeded the age of petty handicraft and small, independent capitalists, the businessman became a prisoner of the pecuniary calculus. "Money value is his habitual bench-mark." [27] The organization of society was such that men were disposed to ignore underlying realities of industry. In *Absentee Ownership* the same theme dominates the rather intricate fugue which at once embellishes and overloads the book: it is because businessmen regard the dollar *"sub specie aeternitas"* that the legerdemain of constantly inflated capitalization continues on the basis of anticipated earning capacity.[28]

Much of New Deal financial legislation extending through the Investment Company Act of 1940 was aimed at preventing deception, not in Veblen's sense, which would for its elimination require that men cease to think in terms of capitalized earning capacity, in other words, that they abandon what he regarded as *self*-deception, but rather in the sense of manipulation and fraud. To Veblen this would have been of minor significance. Thus, in administering the Securities Act of 1933, the Securities and Exchange Commission has enforced accounting standards that tend to limit asset-carrying values to cost, and hence check, to some extent, the issue of securities with book value in excess of cost of assets to the issuer.[29]

There are parts of the financial legislation of the 1930's however, which do more than strike at the dissemination of misleading information. The Public Utility Holding Company Act of 1935, in an anachronistic throwback to pre–World War I standards, expresses a preference for par as against no-par stock.[30] It prescribes in broad terms a balanced capital structure.[31] The amendments to the Bankruptcy Act [32] were intended to speed reshaping of security structures by substituting other types of issues for funded debt. Although the Holding Company Act sets "sums invested" as a standard for security issue, both the Securities and Exchange Commission and the Interstate Commerce Commission have in bankruptcy cases rejected this criterion as a primary determinant.

---

[27] *Theory of Business Enterprise*, p. 207.
[28] *Absentee Ownership*, ch. xii and *passim*.
[29] See Securities and Exchange Commission, *15th Annual Report, 1949*, p. 21, and Regulation S-X, *passim*.
[30] Sec. 7 (c). [31] Sec. 7 (d) (1). [32] Sec. 77 and ch. x.

Joel B. Dirlam

A preliminary question is whether a restriction of the book value of securities to asset cost will prevent the process of imposition of ever higher capital charges on the income of the community. It is not essential to the creation of Veblen's intangible property that values be incorrectly stated on the balance sheet. The restriction of asset-carrying values to their original cost does not, after all, prevent even utility stocks from selling in excess of their book value. The $9.00 dividend on American Telephone and Telegraph Company stock, which supports its market value, is an illustration of a charge which includes an element of "free income" levied against the community in excess of what would be justified by asset cost.

Thus Veblen, although underscoring the consequences of unlimited access to no-par stock in terms of "inflated" capitalizations, would have been less than sanguine about a legislative insistence on par. As he points out in *Absentee Ownership*, U. S. Steel Corporation stock and Standard Oil Company stock have "persistently" sold above par.[33] The "inflation of the capital-values of corporations and their assets has proved to be sound; in the sense that the inflated corporations have . . . reached such an earning capacity as to justify their inflated capitalisation."[34] Of course, this was written in 1923. Hence, a simple restatement of the balance sheet could not have eliminated the process which so concerned him, nor did he ever suggest that it would. As long as earning capacity was the principal test of value, and the "ordinary rate of profits" used for capitalization low enough, market values of securities would exceed the underlying cost of the industrial equipment used in the business. The difference would be intangible wealth, and the earnings that supported it a charge levied against the community.

From this standpoint, a large part of corporate earnings during periods of stock market booms would be consigned to the category of "subtraction from the body of income which would otherwise go to other, earlier claimants."[35] Veblen is applying to the corporate world in general the same standards that some prudent-investment advocates would apply to public utilities. An inflationary gap between market value and underlying book value would be the signal for a cut in the rate of return. But the behavior of utility securities shows that even

[33] *Absentee Ownership*, p. 346, n10.   [34] *Ibid.*, p. 348.
[35] *Ibid.*, p. 348, n11.

Place of Corporation Finance

the use of an original cost base in fixing prices will not prevent a bull market from inflating values. Changes in putative earning capacity will be sufficient to produce the expansion in values—or at least in stock quotations.

The New Deal financial legislation (even including the Public Utility Holding Company Act) cannot prevent swings in the capitalization rate, which in the form of ratios of earnings, dividends, or cash-flow to price are charted and forecast by thousands of security analysts. Although the knowledge of investors that tangible wealth (in Veblen's sense) may not be equal to what they are paying for their stock may well dampen their ardor on some occasions, this circumstance apparently has not been a potent factor in choking off bull markets. Nor can the reform legislation prevent the flotation of stock which might immediately upon issue be subject to inflationary valuation.[36] It is this ineffectuality that makes federal incorporation less of a threat (or reform) than it is sometimes supposed to be.[37] Even if all capital structures were regulated and security issues of all corporations now subject to the Securities Act of 1933 or the Securities Exchange Act of 1934 controlled to insure that their book value equaled cost, capitalized income would still determine value. Only if earnings were somehow controlled to move inversely to market capitalization rates would this form of inflation be eliminated. Certainly, the financial reform legislation of the thirties has not put an end to the cycles of pessimism and faith in "growth" that make the stock market

---

[36] The United Corporation was the apotheosis of promotions of the 1920's. The promoters financed the giant holding company by transactions that resulted in the public supplying the capital while they retained equity securities "out of proportion to the services rendered either to United or the national economy" (Sanford L. Schamus, *Studies in Finance* [New York: *Columbia Law Review*, 1937], p. 1137). A detailed study of how the promotion would have been affected by the New Deal reform legislation (other than the Holding Company Act) showed that The United Corporation would have had to issue a more informative prospectus, and might have been denied certain unlisted trading privileges, and that the most likely consequence would have been some checking of the speculative rise in United's common stock prior to the disclosure of its portfolio (*ibid.*, pp. 1196–1200).

[37] Schamus, who, in the perceptive inquiry referred to above, could only conclude that the Securities Act was incapable of coping with fundamental problems of corporation finance merely by disclosure, felt constrained to advocate control over the amount and constituents of the capitalization if federal incorporation was to be effective (*ibid.*, pp. 1199–1200).

what it is. In fact, the capitalization process is pervasive in our society; it is not confined to the stock market.

The regulation of corporation financial practices achieved by the New Deal nevertheless requires some revision in Veblen's generalizations. A new pattern of financing has emerged following 1933, with an increasing share of savings channeled through personal trust funds, insurance companies, investment companies, pension funds, and savings institutions such as mutual savings banks and savings and loan associations.[38] When economists inquire into the consequences of the swelling flow of savings, their primary interest has been the inferred effect of the institutionalization of savings on the flow of funds into investment and of the latter on the level of national income. These changes may be in part traceable to the higher standards of the accounting profession [39] and the lesser risk attached to reliance on prospectuses and annual reports of listed corporations.

Insofar as insurance companies, savings banks, and pension funds are required to confine their purchases to debt securities, the issue of these obligations will be a means whereby corporations can obtain capital by satisfying the conventions of the purchasers' regulatory statutes or indentures. The investment companies, on the other hand, direct that portion of savings that investors have determined can suffer possible temporary loss of value into the riskier, common stock segment of corporate security issues. In little of this institutionalization of savings is there to be found the inflationary influence that Veblen associated with the growth of capitalization; the securities are rarely used as collateral for loans by investment or insurance companies.

III

In two other respects it is necessary to distinguish between the implications of Veblen's analysis and behavior of the financial community as it has been reshaped since the reforms of the New Deal. In *The Theory of Business Enterprise,* Veblen had regarded as typical of

[38] Staff Report to the Senate Committee on Banking and Currency, *Factors Affecting the Stock Market,* 84th Cong., 1st sess., Committee Print (1955), pp. 94–96.

[39] See, e.g., Marquis G. Eaton, *Financial Reporting in a Changing Society* (New York: American Institute of Certified Public Accountants, 1957).

the system the exploitation of opportunities for their personal gain by corporate insiders, who were indifferent to whether this "disturbance" resulted in a rise or fall in the price of their company's securities. The requirements that corporate officers and directors disclose changes in their holdings, the detailed information now required in proxy statements, and the prohibition of pools and dissemination of intentionally false rumors have all combined to reduce in importance what Veblen regarded as the source of many of the great American fortunes.[40] Nevertheless, the availability of corporate officers' or promoters' profits from "disturbances" was not a key feature of his system. It was a by-product of the money illusion and the creation of "intangible wealth"; it depended upon taking advantage of the propensity of the financial community to think in terms of capitalized earnings rather than cost. It was the latter institution that Veblen regarded as characteristic of absentee ownership.

Some of the financial legislation of the New Deal which tries to insure that with control shall go investment and vice versa would seem to realize a Veblenian reform or at least to be inspired by his criticism. Yet, in actuality Veblen had little or no interest in divisions that might have occurred among groups of owners or creditors. In *The Theory of Business Enterprise* he contrasts with the position of the owners of the material equipment of industry—that is to say, the bondholders—that of the managers, who by virtue of their control of common stock were able to realize profits by infusing the immaterial assets with an increased value that would benefit their inflated share of total capitalization. But he does not go on to suggest how, in accounting or financial decisions, the conflict of interest between stockholders and creditors might harm the latter group. Hence, it is doubtful if he would have been disposed to attach much significance to the extensions of corporate democracy achieved by SEC proxy regulations, or the Holding Company Act prohibition of pyramiding. In general, as Veblen sees it, the interests of stockholders and creditors are antithetical because the inflation accompanying the expansion of capitalization will reduce the value of the interest and principal payments due the creditors; but more precise conflicts of interest are not mentioned. Even in his extensive discussion of the role of the holding company—the

[40] Insiders profits have not, of course, been eliminated; family "blinds" can be used, and profits on holdings for periods over six months can be realized.

instrument *par excellence* for permitting control without investment —he alludes only in passing to its usefulness for this purpose. In a holding company, "even more obviously than in the ordinary corporation, the owner delegates the powers of ownership, and retains only its rights and immunities"; he has a "slighter chance of personally influencing any action taken by the management."[41]

The consequences of delegation of power by the owners are that technical experts have assumed the oversight of the works, while the "employer-owner" shifted to a footing of accountancy.[42] Does this imply that the owners are in danger of exploitation by managers? Apparently not. In the first place, the division of function that seemed to him important was between the technical experts and the Captains of Solvency, who concerned themselves either with six-digit figures or the development of efficient techniques of effrontery, flattery, and illusion for expanding sales. According to Veblen, "the absentee owners large and *small* have come to control the ways and means of production and distribution."[43] Nowhere does he show any concern, even in his last book, for possible exploitation of the absentee owners by their hired hands. He assumes their interests are by and large the same. Hence, the insistence in the Holding Company Act on votes for common stockholders would have seemed unimportant to Veblen. Berle and Means and their disciples, among whom may be included the business schools and the self-conscious professional managers of the five hundred largest corporations, are not lineal intellectual descendants of Veblen.[44] Recent developments may have swung the pendulum toward his assumption. While the small and large stockholders may not have the same attitude toward payment of dividends, the common practice of giving top management stock options certainly helps to reduce the divergence of outlook between ownership and control.

Secondly, the technical experts, who became necessary as the absentee owners replaced the Captains of Industry, were engineers, not professional businessmen. It is doubtful that Veblen was impressed with Brandeis' conviction that professional ethics could be extended

[41] *Absentee Ownership*, p. 331. [42] *Ibid.*, p. 105.
[43] *Absentee Ownership*, p. 10 (italics mine).
[44] Nevertheless, it is curious that *The Modern Corporation and Private Property* (New York: Macmillan, 1933) nowhere mentions his name.

to business. On the contrary, he would see very little in the present systematic exploitation of the psychological and sociological disciplines, both for selling and in employee relations, that would require modification of his conclusion that "publicity engineers" are trained for "systematized illusions" "by all the reputable seminaries of learning." [45]

The shift to institutional investment has rendered obsolete Veblen's stress on the strategic role of the investment banker. In his later books he drew on the conclusions—though without mentioning their names—of Brandeis and the Pujo Committee. As a typical example of the power of the banker, he relied on Morgan's management of the U.S. Steel combination. The investment bankers had "come in for an effectual controlling interest in the corporations whose financial affairs they administer." [46] There is no question that the investment banker of today has shrunk in stature compared with his predecessors of the first two decades of the century. He sits on the board of some large corporations—but he controls the destinies of few.

What place is there for the banker on the "inside" boards of Standard Oil of New Jersey, Du Pont, or General Motors? The public utility holding companies and the railroads were the last strongholds of his undisputed power. With the railroad reorganizations of the 1940's and the introduction of competitive bidding for utility and railroad securities, the banker has in these areas become little more than a wholesaler of securities, forced to compete vigorously for a large part of his business and unable to trade upon established relationships.[47] Issuers have been largely emancipated from dependence upon organized markets.[48]

---

[45] *Absentee Ownership*, p. 306. Cf. Vance Packard, *The Hidden Persuaders* (New York: David McKay, 1957), with Wroe Alderson, *Marketing Behavior and Executive Action—A Functionalist Approach to Marketing Theory* (Homewood, Ill.: Richard D. Irwin, 1957).

[46] *Absentee Ownership*, p. 343.

[47] Even industrial companies not subject to competitive bidding requirements could, now that the mechanism has been evolved, use it if they chose—thus holding a threat over the heads of the bankers. See Paul L. Howell, "Competition in the Capital Markets," *Harvard Business Review*, XXI (May–June 1953), 83–93.

[48] Private placements, purchase and leaseback arrangements, as well as retained earnings have also contributed to the decline of the investment banker. See C. H. Schmidt and E. J. Stockwell, "The Changing Importance of Institutional Investors in the American Capital Market," *Law and Contemporary Problems*, XVII: *Institutional Investments* (Winter 1952). The phenomenal growth of in-

Joel B. Dirlam

IV

The factual validity of Veblen's thesis that the expansion of corporate capitalization is financed through inflationary bank credit should be tested. Veblen nowhere gives a precise measure of the amount of such inflation: he draws frequently upon the write-up in the original U. S. Steel capitalization to demonstrate the inevitability of wide discrepancies between real property values and security inflation. In furthering this inflation the credit extended by (or to) the investment banker was said to play an important role. Security inflation means to Veblen some form or other of deposit expansion. The inflationary security issues pump purchasing power into the economy and "bid up prices of whatever products are used in industry." [49] Veblen never seems to have modified this part of his analysis, although in *Absentee Ownership* the discussion of inflation of the capital structure merges with that of fractional reserve banking under the Federal Reserve System.

In the period before the establishment of the Federal Reserve System, the concentration of national bank reserves in New York did

---

stitutional holdings of debt (including pension funds), and of common stock by investment companies, has contributed to the change and raised other questions of shifts in control. In the years 1920–1925, total corporate debt rose $7.1 billion, institutional holdings $3.8 billion; from 1945–1950 corporate debt rose $19.9 billion, institutional holdings $15.3 billion (Schmidt and Stockwell, *op. cit.*, p. 16). Victor Perlo has attempted to revive the "banker domination" theory in his *The Empire of High Finance* (New York: International Publishers, 1957). He has to concede, however, the decline of the House of Morgan (ch. viii), and the idea of empire soon merges into something akin to a monopolized capitalism, where industrial power—such as that of the Du Ponts and Texas millionaires—confers financial power. In these circumstances—and when, in addition, it is necessary to assume that control is commensurate with stock ownership of insurance and investment companies (*ibid.*, pp. 79–87)—there is little left about the "empire" that is imperial.

[49] *Theory of Business Enterprise*, p. 108. Veblen goes on to say that the rise in market value of output does not keep pace with the inflation of business capital, because the expansion of purchasing power is dissipated throughout the economy: but the relation between the two variables does not seem important. If expanded credit permits a firm through a new security issue to acquire additional assets, it is not necessary that the price of output rise in proportion to the expansion in capitalization.

Place of Corporation Finance

lead to loans in large volume in the call money market. New issues not yet traded were also undoubtedly pledged as security for personal and corporate loans in the manner described by Veblen in 1904. What is not clear is the extent of the deposit expansion upon the basis of newly issued securities as collateral. The write-up of U.S. Steel's capitalization was not reflected inevitably or immediately in an expansion in demand deposits. As Eliot Jones points out, in the trust movement "the amount of cash required to buy out the manufacturers was comparatively small."[50] Promoters in the 1897–1901 merger movement took their profits in the form of securities, which they sold, or hoped to sell, like The United Corporation promoters three decades later, at favorable prices in the market. To the extent that these market prices were supported by call loans under the National Bank system, the trust capitalizations were partly supported by bank credit. But since the overwhelming proportion of the common stock issued was exchanged either for other securities or directly for other assets,[51] the support required from bank credit must have been slight.

There is little evidence that bank credit played a strategic role in the feverish expansion of capitalization of holding companies and investment trusts in the late 1920's. Only when corporations or speculators withdrew funds from the market was deposit expansion necessary. In 1928 and 1929, as is well known, corporations and individuals, not banks, supplied the funds for the last paroxysm of the market.[52]

It is difficult, on the basis of available information, to determine the extent to which the issue of securities, with par or stated values admittedly inflationary when tested by asset cost, actually triggered an increase in bank credit. We do have a measure, however, of the importance of new security issues as a source of corporate funds in the

---

[50] *The Trust Problem in the United States* (New York: Macmillan, 1928), pp. 283–284. R. W. Goldsmith's study shows, out of a total of $4.7 billion par or stated value of common stock issued during the years 1897–1903, that $198 million of new money was obtained (*Study of Saving in the U.S.* [Princeton: Princeton University Press, 1956], I, 505, Table V-24). Bond issues for cash of corporations other than railroads and utilities totaled $221 million during the years 1900–1903 (*ibid.*, p. 48, Table V-15).

[51] Goldsmith, *op. cit.*, p. 505, Table V-24.

[52] See W. J. Eiteman, "Brokers' Loans and the Absorption of Credit," in Twentieth Century Fund, *The Security Markets* (New York: Twentieth Century Fund, 1935), pp. 353–355; and *Factors Affecting the Stock Market*, pp. 56–57.

1920's. During this period, large industrial corporations placed little reliance on new flotations for expansion.[53] A study of the 1931–1955 period shows conclusively that three-fourths of corporate investment was financed by internally generated funds.[54] But Veblen's insistence that capitalization expansion is inflationary, and that the corporation does not mobilize funds, was, as pointed out earlier, subject to qualification. He conceded that savings may result from owners', promoters' —or even corporate—profits and that these seem to be in real form, even though these savings may be "involuntary or subconscious saving on the part of the community."[55]

Indeed, the post–World War II era, with its continuous injection of heady drafts of inflation and full employment, bears a remarkable similarity to Veblen's projection of the One Big Union of the Major Interests, which he saw extending into the future from 1923. Our "new order," where the price level progressively rises and the commercial and investment banking communities practice teamwork under the Federal Reserve Board's careful supervision and where no general liquidation of credit is to be apprehended, differs from his only in that the underpinning is provided by government spending.[56] The potential importance of this prop he overlooked. Only with this welfare state could the "science" of management have been carried to present lengths. Elaborate theories of capital budgeting, choice of investment opportunities, and machine retirement flourish and appeal to businessmen not only when there are the surplus funds to pay for research, but also when there is the comfortable assurance that markets will not disappear overnight.[57]

[53] A. R. Koch, *The Financing of Large Corporations, 1920–1939* (New York: National Bureau of Economic Research, 1943). Koch concludes that his sample of large manufacturing corporations had retained funds equal to 95 per cent of fixed capital expenditures during the years 1921–1939. See Table 13, p. 103. For 1921–1929, the proportion was 99 per cent.

[54] J. C. Dawson, "Trends in Corporate Investment and Finance: A Flow-of-Funds Analysis," University of Maryland Bureau of Business and Economic Research Studies in Business and Economics, X (Dec. 1956), 7.

[55] *Theory of Business Enterprise*, n2, pp. 168–170.

[56] The current "recession," for instance, could be at least partially checked as soon as the Administration reconciles itself to a tax cut.

[57] See, e.g., "Capital Budgeting," *Journal of Business*, XXVIII, no. 4 (1955), but cf. Richard B. Maffai, "Capital Budgeting: An Overview," *Engineering Economist*, I (Spring 1955), 9–20, and Arthur Lesser, Jr., "Engineering Economy—A Restatement of Objectives," *Proceedings*, Engineering Economy Committee of the

Place of Corporation Finance

We need exploration of the full implications of this revolution in solvency—which, finally, thirty years after he wrote, has come very close to approximating what Veblen anticipated in 1923 would be the consequence of the stabilization policy of the Federal Reserve. Almost universal adherence to gentlemanly competition, combined with the protection—through government contracts, if necessary—of the large corporation threatened by insolvency, seems to have been achieved. It will be interesting, however, to see how our corporate welfare state deals with the problem currently posed by the railroads.

V

Veblen's price theory, like his theory of corporation finance, is embodied in a model which synthesizes the practices of what he regards as the representative firm. There is no demonstration of its typicality: that has to be accepted on faith in Veblen's competence as an observer. He does not appeal to any recondite or subtle chains of reasoning to support his conclusions; the references, included as an almost obvious concession to conventional scholarship in *The Theory of Business Enterprise*, have become vestigial in *Absentee Ownership*. In the former book he sets forth the relation of price policy to capitalization in the course of his description of business behavior. The theory is altered little in the ensuing works as far as his analysis of individual determinants is concerned, although he reversed his conclusions about the movement of the general price level in *Absentee Ownership*.

Veblen made an ironic bow in the direction of conventional price theory in *The Theory of Business Enterprise:* competition may be the most important factor where an enterprise has little of the character of a monopoly.[58] But most businesses partake more or less of monopoly—through patents, location, control of natural resources, or good will created through advertising. In this respect, Veblen may be regarded as a precursor of E. H. Chamberlin. Firms with these monopoly elements determine the fortunes of modern society, and Veblen simply ignores the purely competitive firm.

American Society for Engineering Education, June 1954 (mimeographed), pp. 11–14. Research is not, however, infallible. See J. E. Judge, "Decisions Behind the Edsel," *Business Horizons,* I (Jan. 1958), 99–102.

[58] Page 54.

Joel B. Dirlam

Their common pricing principle (which would also apply to the competitive firm) is to charge what the traffic will bear. But at the same time the community has a standard, "more or less closely defined," of the ordinary rate of profits that any legitimate business should be able to earn.[59] This can no longer be the rate that would be enforced by competition. The modern business community according to Veblen has too much capacity to permit the competitive price to equate with a reasonable price. The constant reduction in the cost of production resulting from increased efficiency means ever-lower prices and chronic depression. The remedy is business coalition to neutralize the cheapening of goods resulting from industrial progress.[60] Such a coalition would fix prices at the level that would bring in the largest aggregate net earnings with due regard to demand elasticity and economies of scale.[61]

In *Absentee Ownership*, the "coalition" takes on a somewhat sinister form: it is the "Interests" who, to avoid unhappy consequences for capitalization and overhead charges, to remove the danger of cut-throat competition, and to permit competitive maneuvering to take place without hazard to the price level, have determined at one and the same time the level of credit and the character of competition.

The integration, in *Absentee Ownership*, of credit creation with price policy is the one area of price theory where Veblen changed his views significantly from the earlier treatment. Instead of being characterized by periodic swings from overoptimism to morning-after realism, with accompanying transfers of property from debtors to creditors, the economy had, in its own terms, proved itself. In the same vein he describes aptly and with remarkable terseness the peculiar characteristics of the holding company to which the Federal Trade Commission later devoted ninety-odd volumes of fact grubbing and analysis. But he concludes that the successive revaluations and recapitalizations which the holding company engendered, with accompanying extensions of credit, had been "justified by the event."[62] Of course, investment bankers and the holders of the newly created securities benefited at the expense of earlier claimants and workmen,

[59] *Theory of Business Enterprise*, p. 88. [60] *Ibid.*, p. 242.
[61] *Ibid.*, p. 258. Veblen avoids the conventional terms.
[62] *Absentee Ownership*, p. 345.

Place of Corporation Finance

but the intangible wealth, based on earning capacity, was nevertheless created.[63]

In *The Theory of Business Enterprise*, the possibility of "coalition" had been suggested. But competition was still keen, and the price level constantly declining. Chronic depression ensued—a malady of the affections of businessmen because they were stupid enough to be deceived by price relations, even though the volume of output remained unchanged or increased. This description, based on the state of business in the 1880's and 1890's, seems apt enough.

By 1923 he had evolved the concept of "business sabotage," [64] the reluctance of industry to produce at full capacity while employing the arts of salesmanship to make it possible to charge more for a restricted output.

To what extent is Veblen's price theory useful today? In its broad outlines it seems to reproduce the generalities of business thinking on what prices ought to be—but the pricing reality does not always match the goal. This exception may be important quantitatively—but Veblen is trying to confine himself, in his impatience to isolate the essential features of contemporary society, to those customs that he believes to be significant. Businessmen do think in terms of a "fair price"; they cannot always collect it, because competition sometimes prevents. Those industries where "coalition" is strong enough restrict output to avoid "cutthroat competition." This is, of course, accepted business mores. The president of Bethlehem Steel testifies before a Senate committee that, when demand slackens, price should rise in order to provide a "fair return" on the stockholders' investment.[65] The standard cost device is founded on a business assumption that a firm is entitled to a fair profit, to be earned by selling below-capacity output at a price related to the standard cost. When the capacity level

---

[63] *Ibid.*, p. 354.   [64] See *Vested Interests*, pp. 93–94.

[65] *Administered Prices*, Hearings before the Subcommittee on Antitrust and Monopoly of the Senate Committee on the Judiciary, 85th Cong., 1st sess. (1957), pt. 2, pp. 651–652, 658. The chairman of the board of General Electric Co., announced in November, 1956, that the company was going to restore the profit margins that prevailed before 1940 (*Wall Street Journal*, Nov. 29, 1956, p. 2). It is hard to accept Vice President Yntema's assertion that Ford has no pricing discretion, although it could sink hundreds of millions into the Edsel (*Wall Street Journal*, Feb. 5, 1958, p. 4).

Joel B. Dirlam

assumed in the standard cost yardstick is exceeded, profits in excess of the fair profit are earned. Unquestionably, pricing, in most of the key industries today (not Veblen's list)—automobiles, electrical machinery, chemicals, and appliances (with a differentiated product sold in a market where price changes are infrequent), or steel, cement, glucose, lead, gasoline, paper, and heavy chemicals (with an undifferentiated product sold by relatively few producers)—conforms to the Veblenian description. The modern economist may use somewhat different terminology, but it is surely the presence of "coalition" that distinguishes these industries from the ruck of textile manufacturing, retailing, food manufacturing, and the like—industries where price changes are frequent and profits are just left over at the end of the year, not planned.

VI

Are there further changes in the offing? What will be the consequences of continued pressure by accountants and businessmen for restatement of depreciation on the basis of replacement, rather than original cost? This proposal might indicate that the financial community is at last awakening to the insubstantiality of the dollar measure of profits. On the other hand, it could, as in the steel industry, be simply a device for justifying a price increase that might be even less palatable without the excuse.

What lies ahead for the corporate economy in an era when professionalization of management has accompanied domination of holdings of the different types of securities by different types of institutions? What effect will the new concentration of security holdings in institutions have on management policies? [66] Will the distinctions between

[66] In the perceptive article by Haughton Bell and Harold Fraine, "Legal Framework, Trends and Developments in Investment Practices of Life Insurance Companies," *Law and Contemporary Problems*, XVII: *Institutional Investments* (Winter 1952), 45–85, a serious attempt is made to meet the challenge posed by the insurance companies' holding, even in 1950, 54 per cent of net long-term private debt (p. 52). In the conclusion to their article, they speak of the recognition given to "responsible management" by insurance companies in judging the quality of securities (p. 85). For an authoritative study of the larger implications of the growth of mutual funds, see R. L. Weissman, *The Investment Company and the Investor* (New York: Harper, 1951).

Place of Corporation Finance

the security types come to have less importance?[67] Will funds for smaller and more venturesome business tend to dry up?

Even more important, what will be the influence of the professionalization of business management? The economists are at last being given a chance, through their influence on literate executives, to influence the pattern of business decisions in the image of their theories. Their constant insistence that businessmen should plan investment to maximize profits as measured by conventional economic calculus and program market development to key in with investment should clearly result in further increasing price rigidity. These tendencies are of course modified, fortunately, by unpredictable shifts in the level of business or in the demand for broad product classes, such as automobiles. Nevertheless, it seems likely that the contemporary economist who aims, like Veblen, at explaining corporate economic behavior will have to take increasing account of the interaction between accounting and business folklore and of the mythology of the schools of business administration.

[67] Bell and Fraine speak of the "almost universal recognition" in the twenties that earning power was at least as important as physical security in judging investment quality of a corporate obligation. The actual recognition must have been earlier than this, as *The Theory of Business Enterprise* demonstrates. Railroad securities, under Section 15 of the Bankruptcy Act, have a chameleon-like quality that, without formal bankruptcy proceedings, permits them to be turned from senior to junior securities, and vice versa.

[LESLIE FISHMAN]

12

Veblen, Hoxie, and American Labor

IT is never easy to understand the work of great economists during their own lifetimes; it is even more difficult both to understand and evaluate their theories after they have died. The late Professor Leo Rogin has suggested that we attempt this in two steps: first, that we try to grasp fully the meaning of the man's writings through the eyes of the theorist himself, that is, in terms of the problem as the theorist himself posed it; and second, that we examine, through our own eyes, so to speak, the validity of his theory. But how can an economic theory's validity be tested? We are not permitted controlled experiments. Human history is an ever changing pattern that appears to have no beginning and no end. What is important today may be insignificant tomorrow. What appears as a prime moving force to one person may appear as an insignificant and unusual disturbance to another. Does this mean that no firm estimate of a theory's validity is possible?

Not at all. With the benefit of hindsight, we can attempt to understand fully Veblen's economic theory—in terms of the problem he set for himself. Then we can take the next step. We can ask whether Veblen foresaw the major historical forces at work, so as to make the problems he posed both significant and operationally solvable; that is, were his problems defined in terms of historically significant variables, and were these variables changing in the way he described them?

In Veblen's case, these criteria of validity are easily affirmed—he was so right so many times. The problem of his generation, and of ours, remains that of adjusting pecuniary institutions to an industrial world which is astride a matter-of-fact science that is changing technology at an ever increasing pace. The twin horses of science and technology are galloping away with our chariot—even into the upper reaches of the ionosphere and space; but our socio-economic and political institutions remain earth-bound to the extreme. Moreover, growing disparity between scientific progress and social institutions is taking place, according to Veblen, against a backdrop of national dynastic states and empires, and inherited property relationships of use and wont. In what specific ills does this over-all and all-pervasive conflict result? A myriad of problems, the most important of which are war, poverty, depressions, and, most significant of all, the difficulties attending the rate of progress of science and technology, and side effects of that progress.

But even when a theorist's problem is valid, the big question still remains unanswered: Is the solution realizable? Will the institutions that the theorist believes to be abnormal actually undergo change in the manner predicted by the theory? Will these changes bring about the desired results—without important side effects?

This makes economic theory stand muster against the flow and pattern of history. This makes economics a science of history; a science of change, of development. It makes economics evolutionary, to use the term Veblen and Hoxie insisted upon.

What were the abnormal institutions for Veblen? The pecuniary institutions of natural rights and property. How were these going to be changed and made consistent with the industrial technology of science and the machine? By those whose outlook and psychology was molded by the industrial discipline—the workers, the engineers, the scientists. What was going to be the operative force at work? It is at this point that the chain of Veblen's theory broke. And it is here that Robert Franklin Hoxie was to step in. Veblen defined the problem. Veblen supplied the over-all framework. Veblen delineated the major historical forces. But Veblen was most uncertain about the key step—the operative force that would impel those under the industrial discipline to change the pecuniary institutions.

Interestingly enough, this is precisely Veblen's criticism of Marx's schema. As Veblen himself described it, "It is nowhere pointed out what is the operative force at work in the process." By process, Veblen

Veblen, Hoxie, and Labor

referred to the process of history. The Marxist deterministic class struggle was far too oversimplified for Veblen to accept. Moreover, the key motive force—impoverishment of the working class, whether absolute or relative—certainly did not apply, according to Veblen. In his very first publication Veblen underlined this basic weakness in the Marxian case:

> The system of industrial competition, based on private property, has brought about . . . the most rapid advance in average wealth and industrial efficiency that the world has seen. . . . The result . . . has been to increase greatly the creature comforts within the reach of the average human being.[1]

Veblen attempted to fill this crucial void in his own theory in several different ways. In his earliest work he stressed the role of emulation in goading those under the industrial discipline to action. The imitative consumption patterns of our society, with the enormous element of competition, can lead to increased dissatisfaction as living standards rise. Thus, as creature comforts are met, increased rivalry with one another can lead to increased displeasure and disaffection, particularly if the fruits of progress and production are inequitably distributed.

Dorfman believes that by the time Veblen wrote *The Theory of Business Enterprise* this emulation concept gave way to a more orthodox view—the social psychology engendered by the industrial discipline gives rise to attitudes, on the part primarily of industrial workers, that will impel them to challenge existing pecuniary institutions. And challenge them they will. Business unionism is only the outward surface expression of the trade-union movement. Veblen wrote that beneath the surface trade unions directly attack the pecuniary institutions: "The classes who move in trade-unions are, however crudely and blindly, endeavoring, under the compulsion of the machine process, to construct an institutional scheme on the lines imposed by the new exigencies given by the machine process."[2] Veblen described unions that held these views as the "maturest expressions" of trade unionism. An even more laudatory phrase was reserved for the individuals who took this position; Veblen called them "the more wide-awake body of unionist workmen."

[1] "Some Neglected Points in the Theory of Socialism," *Annals of the American Academy*, II (1891), p. 348.
[2] *Theory of Business Enterprise* (New York: Scribner, 1904), p. 336.

Leslie Fishman

Although Veblen did not spell out in specifics the exact manner in which those subject to the industrial discipline arrive at their beliefs, the general forces at work are clear. On the production line, in the scientific laboratory, in front of the engineering drafting boards, those employed in industry work with the materials of the real, matter-of-fact world and their outlook and opinions are shaped accordingly. In a mine thousands of feet below the surface, each man is evaluated by the way he handles his tools and the machinery, how he works with his fellow miners, how he gets the ore out. His "net worth," his credit rating, or the shrewdness with which he purchases real estate—all these count for very little in a mine shaft. Similarly, a scientist conditioned by the laboratory and perhaps interested in the state of the economy, is more likely to turn to an objective measure of total production than to the elusive profit and loss statements of business. Or take the case of an engineer planning a new suburban housing development. Would he be most concerned about the extent and placement of a new shopping center, to maximize the profit return of the project, or would he be more inclined to deal in terms of the needs of the new dwellers and the physical characteristics of the terrain? Eugene O'Neill in his play *The Hairy Ape* focused on this contrast—the life, the values, the outlook of a stoker in the hold of a ship compared with the values of the first-class passengers on deck. These represent the two employments Veblen refers to in the phrases, "the industrial discipline" and "the pecuniary discipline."

The first two decades of the twentieth century in America saw the machine revolutionizing production, transportation, and distribution and the corporate form of business triumphant across the land. Trade-union membership grew slowly and declined rapidly. The Socialist party reached its peak in membership and votes and then was torn to shreds by factionalism and the rising patriotic fervor attendant on World War I. Reform liberalism also reached its zenith, and under Wilson's leadership a series of basic reforms were passed in the varied fields of the tariff, the banking system, trade unions, trusts and trade, farming, suffrage, and the income tax. The industrial giant took shape, but Veblen's vision of those shaped under the industrial discipline became more blurred and somewhat obscure. He still held out the hope that "among workmen . . . uncritical habitual faith in this institutional scheme is beginning to crumble." [3] But he was forced to admit that with this crumbling "no constructive deviation from the received principles" is to be found.

By 1917 Veblen still anticipated the awakening of the common man —a realization that "these rights of ownership and investment uniformly work to his material detriment." Veblen predicted that, if ever this day comes, the common man will not trifle with details. Rather, it will be "something in the nature of the stand once taken by recalcitrant Englishmen in protest against the irresponsible rule of the Stuart sovereign." [4]

The post–World War I picture was apparently even more depressing. By 1923 Veblen wrote that the American workingmen "are still tangled in personalities, not realizing that their common adversary is a state of affairs rather than a conspiracy of sinners." [5]

In this brief recital of several passages of Veblen's views on American labor there is great danger of oversimplification and distortion. We should not think that this brilliant and incisive mind did not at any time appreciate the problems and difficulties that confronted American labor. He was only too well aware of them. His studies of the Industrial Workers of the World during World War I are classic, among the best work done on American labor. His generalizations about the nature of business unionism show how painfully aware he was of the limitations of American unions. His was a case of too much knowledge, rather than not enough. This caused him to retreat in later years to the engineers and scientists for hope of an operative force in American society along the lines of his earlier analysis.

Our primary concern, however, is with American labor as the potential operative force in Veblen's schema—operative force, not in the sense of blind historical necessity moving through an unreacting mass, but quite the reverse. Veblen's operative force results from human beings reacting with and through their environment—reacting at all levels of consciousness and concern. But they are reacting within the historical milieu dominated by an industrial society governed by pecuniary institutions. Just who is going to "disestablish" these pecu-

[3] *Instinct of Workmanship* (New York: Macmillan, 1914), p. 343.
[4] *The Nature of Peace* (New York: Macmillan, 1917), p. 364.
[5] *Absentee Ownership* (New York: Huebsch, 1923), p. 295.

niary institutions, as Veblen liked to refer to the process, remained an unanswered question. Robert Franklin Hoxie attempted to find the answer.

In many ways Hoxie was the least likely candidate for this important role. He came from a farm background. His early training in economics emphasized conventional theory. Economic theory, money and banking, government finance were the fields that attracted and challenged young Hoxie. His early articles in these branches of economics are significant works in their own right. Around the turn of the century it became clear that the Veblen outlook took possession of Hoxie, and he would never again be free of it. He could no longer view American society as a group of individuals, or the American economy as a group of homogeneous households and businesses. Everywhere he turned, Veblen's basic distinction between the industrial and pecuniary employments haunted him. A market place was no longer the arena where buyers and sellers meet and come to terms. Now it became another place where the basic cleavage in society emerged, where those subject to the discipline and values of prices, profits, and accumulation met to come to terms with each other and, even more important, with those who did the actual physical and scientific work of society—those subject to the industrial discipline. Those subject to the industrial discipline are, like all humans, molded and influenced by the conditions under which they work. The industrial conditions, however, are far different from those that surround the pecuniary markets. The industrial conditions arise from man grappling with machines, with raw materials, and with natural forces. The pecuniary conditions reflect a shrewd purchase, a hard sell, or a protective blocking patent. The one is oriented to the production of commodities and to the exploration of the mysteries of the universe; the other is oriented to the maximization of profits and the exploration of the mysteries of building and protecting corporate empires. Production and plenty guide the first; scarcity and profitability guide the second.

Where was Hoxie to focus this searching spotlight? Not on the pricing problem. In this realm Hoxie was willing to accept the theory of the neoclassical Marshallians, to whom he referred as the "modernized economists." With the tools of modern economics Hoxie was fully familiar. He could dissect a market in terms of supply and demand as

Veblen, Hoxie, and Labor

neatly as an experienced surgeon completes an appendectomy. Hoxie saw no contradiction between marginalism as a guide to price analysis and Veblenism as a guide to evolutionary economics. But in Veblenism a giant loophole remained to be plugged—the operative force.

Hoxie set to work with unlimited energy and zeal. The vast Veblenian framework was enlisted in an attempt to dissect and understand the labor movement. It soon became evident that his inquiry must extend far beyond the confines of trade unions. It would have to include the political expressions of the workers, the counterparts of the unions in the pecuniary sphere, the employer associations, also the courts and the law, and most certainly the ever changing technology that was forever weaving new patterns of custom, use, and organization. Hoxie applied a scientific matter-of-factness that was guided and directed by the Veblenian schema.

To achieve the crucial understanding of trade unions, Hoxie buried himself within the unlimited detail of union organization. Professor Hamilton recounts the story that proves how Hoxie penetrated even into the sacrosanct union field of membership figures. At the time when the I.W.W. was being publicized as the organization that threatened the stability of our basic institutions, Hoxie stormed into Vincent St. John's office in Chicago and claimed "to have the goods on him." Hoxie stated that the highly vaunted I.W.W. had a membership of only 14,300. "You're a liar," St. John cried back, "we have 14,310." [6]

Details did not overwhelm Hoxie. With the Veblenian framework as a guide, a beautifully conceived apparatus for the analysis emerged. Every phase and every aspect of the industrial discipline was subjected to minute inspection and finally fitted into its proper place. The elaborate latticework starts with an understanding of the aims of unions, proceeds to the policies and principles consistent with and necessary to fulfill those aims, and then to the methods and demands and attitudes which emerge in the day-to-day actions of officials and members. But even this intricate pattern of categories is much too simple to analyze the complex institution we term "unionism." Hoxie found that American unionism did not conform to a single type, as many of his academic colleagues maintained, but to four entirely different types— each with its own set of aims, principles, policies, methods, demands,

---

[6] Walton H. Hamilton, "The Development of Hoxie's Economics," *Jour. Pol. Econ.*, XXIV (1916), p. 875.

Leslie Fishman

and attitudes. Each type has its own remedial program, as Hoxie termed it, its own solution to the industrial-pecuniary conflict. And each type is a legitimate expression of the American worker and the American scene.

Some labor economists, particularly those of the view that there is only one legitimate son of the American economy to claim the title "American unionism," have hurled at Hoxie the epithet Veblen made famous: "taxonomist." Certainly Hoxie was a classifier, but he never aimed simply to classify. Hoxie's categories were the product of years of study, and they reveal the true nature of American labor in terms of the Veblenian outlook. Proof of the accuracy of these four basic categories is seen in their application to the present labor picture. None of the proponents of a unitary interpretation of the American labor movement would lump together the *Weltanschauung* of a George Meany, a Walter Reuther, a Harry Bridges, and a Dave Beck. These four examples offer present confirmation of Hoxie's four categories, conceived two generations ago: Meany the business unionist, Reuther the uplift unionist, Bridges the revolutionary unionist, Beck the predatory unionist.

Hoxie classified and categorized, not to make complex something which was simple, but rather to make the complex understandable and manageable. The only way he could do this was in terms of the Veblenian framework. To grasp the meaning and importance of the categories it is necessary to interpret each type of unionism in terms of the basic industrial and pecuniary conflict in the context of our machine age.

Business unionism accepts as inevitable the pecuniary institutions of capitalism. Its remedial program, arising out of the industrial environment, is directed entirely toward its own immediate economic ends. In pursuit of these limited ends it generally uses business methods of limiting supply. However, if it becomes obvious that other methods are needed to gain immediate economic improvements, these other methods will be adopted. Two important examples are political action and the support of the pecuniary institutions. If it is obvious that immediate gains are obtainable through political activity, or dependent upon such activity, the business union will enter politics. And if it is obvious that immediate economic gains are to be obtained only through change in the pecuniary institutions, then consideration of such change is likely, although the exact remedial program that would emerge cannot be predicted. Business unionism, then, is the unionism whose remedy is more here-and-now. Under "normal" conditions this leads to an autocratic and conservative union whose program will not deal directly with the larger issues posed by the basic pecuniary-industrial conflict in society.

Friendly or uplift unionism is "characteristically idealistic in viewpoint." Its remedies for the basic conflict in society run in terms of co-operative enterprises, profit sharing, or other idealistic plans. There is no serious questioning of the pecuniary mores of society or an attempt to change the basic institutions. Instead, there is often the claim that the union is acting in the interest of society as a whole. Thus, there is not a basic, irreconcilable conflict in society. Uplift unionism often claims to discover a middle ground that permits a just solution. Emphasis is on elevating the moral, intellectual, and social life of the worker, while accepting the pecuniary institutions. This reflects the idealistic view of the labor-capital conflict in society. It emphasizes immediate uplift reforms. Working with the assumption that personal security and dignity are obtainable for the worker under existing institutions, it is likely to accept programs that do not seriously jeopardize these institutions.

Revolutionary unionism, on the other hand, repudiates the existing pecuniary institutions. It completely embraces the industrial discipline and wishes to make dominant those institutions that reflect the industrial values. The socialist variant of revolutionary unionism pursues immediate economic and social reforms, but only as temporary expedients while man continues to live under existing institutions. Socialists emphasize the solidarity of the workingmen as a class and their productive orientation. Their ultimate answer is collective ownership of the means of production, an answer that would supposedly free man and the machine from the inhibiting forces of the profit mechanism. Other variants of revolutionary unionism are likely to eschew all short-run, immediate gains; the anarchist, for example, opposes all outside imposed discipline. His weapons are likely to be those most expressive of this revolt against industrial discipline—violence and sabotage.

Predatory unionism is the complete acceptance of pecuniary ends as applied to the labor movement. Gangsters or pecuniary-minded labor leaders might gain control of unions and use them to maximize their own personal gain. This unionism accepts the pecuniary institutions and attempts to capitalize upon control over the industrial discipline. From the point of view of the union, this involves an autocratic, boss rule which delivers enough "goods" to remain in complete control. From the point of view of the pecuniary environment, this involves application of sound business practices to a given market place, that is, monopoly control to maximize personal gain in return for the sale of a service. This would call for disciplining the workers and probably also disciplining competing producers. A corresponding case in business would be a corporate management group whose guiding principle was personal gain rather than the welfare of the stockholders.

In summary, Hoxie viewed trade unionism as an institution that has grown out of the matter-of-fact recognition by workers of the need for collective action to express their needs and aspirations for improvement of their standard of life. This movement is a response to an industrial environment in a society organized by pecuniary institutions. Since various workers and unions are differently circumstanced, they view the industrial-pecuniary conflict from different perspectives and have different programs. One must analyze and understand each of these four remedial programs for a true understanding of American unionism.

The brief recital of Hoxie's incisive categories of trade unionism illustrates how successful he was in establishing a classification that "was true to the modern economic situation." He had accomplished his immediate goal—a framework for evolutionary economics. But it still did not permit Hoxie to answer what he considered the ultimate question, "What, if anything, of a remedial nature can be accomplished?"

His quest for an answer proved futile. It proved futile because he was unable to resolve the schizophrenia he found in the American labor movement. The schizophrenia stemmed from the conflict between labor's short-run goals of business unionism and labor's long-run sympathies for basic institutional change. In some ways this split personality is similar to the split Veblen and Hoxie found in capitalism itself—between the pecuniary and the industrial employments. The trade union is brought into being to fulfill the immediate,

Veblen, Hoxie, and Labor

basic economic needs of the worker. Unless these needs are met by the union, the organization will fail. But to be successful in this endeavor, the union must play by the rules of the pecuniary game. It cannot be successful if it uses its own rules—rules that are a natural outgrowth of the industrial discipline. Thus, in the pursuit of essential short-run demands, unions often set forces in motion which will smother and even destroy effective expression of their long-run aims. This is, of course, another example of the dilemma Veblen used in his criticism of Marx. As immediate economic reforms are effectuated, the operative force for basic, institutional change is dulled or made nonoperative.

Hoxie encountered the same dilemma in his thorough and intensive study of the American Socialist party. Hoxie viewed the Socialists as the natural political arm for the remedial programs of the more mature wing of American unionism. However, the successes of the Socialists in 1910 to 1912 were based almost entirely upon their short-run reform programs. Hoxie warned that, if the revolutionary faction ever obtained control of the Socialist party and de-emphasized short-run reform, the socialist movement was doomed to become a small sect removed entirely from the main stream of American life. On the other hand, if the Socialists remained pure middle-class reformers, they would become indistinguishable from the other two parties and would lose the idealistic, class-conscious halo from which they derived their true strength and basic appeal. Either or both of the two political parties could outreform the Socialists on such issues as honest government, efficient administration, prison reform, factory legislation, and so on. The old-line parties had the experience, resources, and, above all, the respectability to effectuate short-run reform programs far more successfully than did the Socialists. What gave the Socialist party its unique character, its only hope for long-term growth and power, was its *socialist* character. But this was precisely the characteristic that was placed in jeopardy in the exact proportion to its success at the polls. To be successful, it had to emphasize short-run reforms. To the extent that it did, it created the very conditions which could potentially lead to its own destruction. In other words, how can either trade unions or their political parties operate successfully within the pecuniary institutions and at the same time preserve their integrity as organizations of the industrial employments? How can an operative force serve two masters?

Leslie Fishman

Hoxie posed this question in a most insistent and timeless fashion just a year before his death. In 1915 he was given a leave of absence from the University of Chicago to conduct an intensive inquiry into scientific management for the United States Industrial Commission. The investigation was a magnificent effort—the questionnaire itself comprised over five hundred detailed questions and reads even today as a complete, guided tour through our industrial establishment. Those interested in studying the implications of automation would do well to give Hoxie's inquiry a careful examination.

In the final report to the Commission, Hoxie spelled out two major forces that permeate scientific management, or automation, if you will. The first is man's perpetual desire to advance in science, knowledge, and efficiency. Unfortunately, often this advance is a "Frankenstein, temporarily destructive of human rights." But these human rights "are unquenchable, for in the long run they contain the very life of true efficiency itself." Conflict between these two forces, wrote Hoxie, is simply "marking time against the inevitable. It is inherent in the nature of things that they both live and fructify." [7]

Today, more than forty years later, it appears that we are still marking time against the inevitable. Despite enormous changes that have taken place in both the pecuniary and the industrial realms, the major problem, as defined by Veblen and Hoxie, remains unresolved. The instinct of workmanship, idle curiosity, scientific matter-of-factness—all manifestations of the industrial discipline—continue to be constrained and restrained by the pecuniary institutions. In 1957 this issue was raised in dramatic fashion by the successes of Russian science in the field of space satellites. In the re-examination of American science and education that has followed the first two sputniks, the Veblenian approach is everywhere in evidence. The market place, the pecuniary institutions are questioned as appropriate guides to stimulate and further science. For example, the popular magazine *Life*, in a recent editorial, analyzed the problem: "When they grew older, the Euphorians [Americans] gave up learning for earning. Earning was a sure path to happiness. . . . Most appalling of all were two major failings which the modern Euphorians atavistically called heresies—

[7] Robert F. Hoxie, *Scientific Management and Labor* (New York: Appleton, 1915), pp. 138–139.

Veblen, Hoxie, and Labor

discontent and curiosity." The editorial goes on to offer two alternatives, both of which contain striking Veblenian overtones.

The first [alternative was]—to do business as usual, but a little faster. . . . The second alternative was far less happy. . . . To train their children for the newer age involved a drastic remodeling of the happiness schools and a reinstatement of the heresies, discontent and curiosity, as honored virtues. . . . The second alternative demanded, further, that the teacher, the critic and the discoverer be permanently released from their imprisonment in Euphoria's moated ivy towers and allowed to sit down with the earners at dinner and given money enough to buy a new suit occasionally.[8]

Incidentally, lest anyone be under the illusion that similar problems, albeit in different forms, do not plague Russians living under different institutions, he should refer to the Russian novel *Not by Bread Alone*. The author, Vladimir Dudintsev, raises the same issue, in exactly the same form as did Veblen and Hoxie.[9] Under what kind of institutions can that strange individual, the discoverer, the critic, the idly curious, be permitted to develop and contribute to a standardized, bureaucratized, machine civilization?

But to return to Hoxie's original question, can American labor still be considered a potential operative force in the Veblenian sense of the term? Although the basic Veblenian framework is unquestionably applicable to the current scene, it is doubtful whether American labor will be an important operative force in bringing our institutions into greater congruence with scientific and industrial progress. What Hoxie has provided is the basic understanding of American labor which, when applied to the current setting, supplies the necessary and sufficient conditions under which labor would be an operative force. Unless these conditions are fulfilled, and it is not likely that they will be, labor in the United States will continue to justify Veblen's pessimism.

To explain this apparent contradiction (that the Veblen-Hoxie framework is applicable but that American labor is not a probable operative force) it is first necessary to characterize the present-day labor movement in Hoxian terms. American labor in 1957 is fundamentally different from the movement described by Hoxie fifty years

[8] *Life*, December 16, 1957, p. 39.
[9] Vladimir Dudintsev, *Not by Bread Alone*, translated from the Russian by Edith Bone (New York: Dutton, 1957).

ago in one basic respect—its size. Today over one-third of the actually employed working force is represented by a union. It is now easier to enumerate the unorganized areas than the organized. The nonunion industries are found primarily in white-collar fields (finance, insurance, sales, service, and the like), in those located in the South, and in those who have been sufficiently profitable and expansive to stay ahead of unionism (electronics, oil, instruments). Thus, unionism is a powerful force in almost all basic American industry. A qualification is in order. Even in those industries where unionism is considered strong (building trades, trucking, needle trades, and so on), there persists a sizable fringe of workers who are unorganized, and who are likely to remain so (workers in runaway shops or in substandard operations, the self-employed, union members on second jobs, and so on). These unorganized continue to exert a significant pull on the American industrial scene, particularly since a substantial segment of American management refuses to accept unionism as a permanent, legitimate American institution.

On the surface it appears that the new, powerful American labor movement can be characterized as entirely business unionist in nature. Almost a decade ago the national organizations of labor joined with governmental agencies to clean their respective houses of the most important present-day variety of revolutionary unionism, the Communists. In recent months this same kind of teamwork has turned on another of Hoxie's categories, predatory unionism. And there is growing agitation, particularly in business journals, to apply the same deft scalpel work against the outstanding practitioner of idealistic unionism, Walter Reuther. But, superficial appearances and governmental intervention notwithstanding, all categories of trade unionism are persisting in the United States, and some of the less popular categories are gaining strength. What is misleading and confusing is the failure to recognize that all types of unions have the same general immediate economic demands. The chapter in Hoxie's book entitled "The Economic Program of Trade Unionism" does not detail different economic programs for different types of unions because in general terms the immediate economic demands of business, predatory, idealistic, and revolutionary unions do not differ significantly. In large measure this accounts for the ability of these unions to want to work together, to affiliate to the same over-all body—as long as the national body ad-

Veblen, Hoxie, and Labor

heres to the common denominator of all unions, the basic economic program. However, if one goes behind the immediate economic veil of the unions to inquire, for example, into the methods used to obtain their demands, then the heterogeneity of the different union types is obvious. For example, Reuther will insist on large committee collective bargaining sessions. Beck always preferred the "sweetheart contract" approach. Bridges leans toward job-action and compulsory membership meetings. John L. Lewis, or any other business unionist, tends to favor top-man negotiation sessions. The disparities between the different types of unionism are equally evident in the vast other areas of unionism, from aims, policies, principles, and methods to attitudes and theories.

What are the conditions under which this diverse group of organizations could possibly become an operative force in the Veblenian sense? If to obtain immediate economic demands, or to survive, it became necessary to question the existing pecuniary institutions, then question them they would. The results of such objections are unpredictable, and each type of unionist would approach the problem in a different way. But the joint supremacy of union survival and union economic programs (which are certainly not unrelated) cannot be doubted. Some indication of union attitudes, if ever this quandary were to present itself, can be found in their response to the need for political activity.

When it became obvious that considerable political activity on the part of unions was required if they were to preserve and extend their economic program, almost all unions responded. Business unions traditionally are autocratic; they generally discourage membership participation except on a limited and carefully defined basis. Effective political organization requires a different approach, one that business unions are slowly and painfully learning. Similarly, our example of predatory unionism, the teamsters union, has become by necessity one of the most effective political organizations in America. Their campaigns against the so-called "right-to-work" bills and against proposed transportation legislation (e.g., the Weeks proposal) were exceptionally successful. In the case of both the automobile workers (Reuther) and the longshoremen (Bridges), political action has long been an integral part of their union activities.

The increased participation in our democratic procedures by unions has not been greeted in all quarters with enthusiastic praise. Major concern has been the response in business circles to the political organization of the one interest group whose members, families, and friends could control most national and many local elections. This concern does not arise because labor is hostile to the basic pecuniary institutions. The support of these institutions by labor has been unqualified. In fact, even on such issues that have contradicted their own self-interest, union leaders have sacrificed economic demands (only possible in a full-employment, prosperity economy) for what they considered the patriotic general good. An important case in point is union support of lower tariffs in the face of rising competition from low-wage areas, such as Japan. Moreover, union representatives in legislative bodies have shown remarkable restraint in pursuit of union economic demands—far more restraint than representatives from the business community or from farm areas.

Union leaders have repeatedly asked for minimum recognition at the council tables of the government. Recognition would imply that representatives of the business community are not the sole repositories of the important and essential attribute to a democracy—the ability to represent the interests of the entire community in an able, effective, and responsible manner. Management's insistence that labor not be granted that recognition can lead only to increased determination on the part of labor to become more effective in its political organization.

Capable political organization on the part of unions, if it were to become a reality, is still a far cry from Veblen's operative force. These organizations would seriously question the pecuniary institutions only under severe and unlikely conditions, where their very survival was at stake or where their minimum economic needs and demands were not met and could not be met. Under these incredible and hopeless circumstances the business and revolutionary unionist would certainly consider changing basic institutions. The idealistic and predatory unionist would probably be less willing to do so. However, it appears that impetus to change our institutions to make them more compatible with the scientific and industrial world of twentieth-century America is not likely to come from American labor in, as Veblen would say, the calculable future.

[PHILIP MORRISON]

13

The Ideology of the Engineers

THE most rigorous of tests for a social theorist is the verification of his pronouncements on the *subjective*. Here individuality and caprice disturb the most shrewdly plotted trend; here the complexity of men's minds and hearts and societies gives the lie, or the laugh, to the philosopher. How class-conscious is that able proletarian leader, Dave Beck, Sr.? How differentially sensitive to price and utility is the informed purchaser of the finny new Cadillac?

Veblen, too, entered a theory of the growth of a subjective frame of mind. He identified a revolutionary group in American society in the phrase: "The chances of anything like a Soviet in America, therefore, are the chances of a Soviet of technicians."[1] Just whom did Veblen have in mind? Herbert Hoover? Gano Dunn? Or do we see a newer prototype in the affable Dr. Wernher von Braun?

Of course Veblen was not fooled. His very next sentence ends ". . . it can be shown that anything like a Soviet of Technicians is at the most a remote contingency in America." That was the America of the Harding campaign. By the thirties these few essays of Veblen's had made him the unread prophet of many an economic sect and above all of that curious movement which made the word *technocracy* a useful noun. Today, in postsputnik America, the place of the technologist as a part of society is plainer than ever. He is present, for a novelty, in the round. He has to be paid, educated, invited (paramilitary) to the White House, and so on. It is not a bad time to inquire into what

[1] *The Engineers and the Price System* (New York: Viking, 1947), p. 134.

Philip Morrison

Veblen meant and into how far that meaning can be extended to apply to our increasingly technological times.

Since oblique approach is not uncongenial to readers of Veblen, I propose to epitomize his view of the engineer's ideology, not by a citation from Veblen himself, but by a phrase or two from a novel. The novel—not in itself a very good one—is by a brilliant and perceptive writer, who was as well a productive, hard-working radio engineer, and a student, disciple, and young Stanford neighbor of Veblen's. Hans Otto Storm shows us a cruise ship in 1938, run aground in the South Seas. She is overburdened doubly—with scrap iron for Japan and with a heavy mortgage. Her master, aging, fearful, incompetent, has sabotaged the radio—indeed this is a Veblenian novel—to preclude the call for help that would mean heavy salvage costs. A typhoon is feared, although the weather is still fine. The crew mutinies, and the ship is divided between two factions. The engine room belowdecks is still uninvolved. Down to see the wry old chief engineer goes the leader of the crew, now himself master of half a divided, impotent ship.

He did not ask Mr. Bents, are you with us. He was very practical. He just said, "Will you make steam? We've got to have lights and air and refrigeration, and if she floats off we've got to have the works. Somebody's going to do it, and I'm asking if it's going to be you."

Mr. Bents grinned a thin-lipped grin. . . . The situation was altogether to his liking. "Listen, big boy," he said, "we do our stuff. Sure I'll make steam. When that twiddle-diddle thing up there says push her frontwards why I'll push her frontwards, when it says push her back I'll push her back. I'll make steam for the boorgoosies [sic] or I'll make steam for the soviets. . . . But listen," Mr. Bents called after him. "You fellows keep out of the engine room. You might monkey with something or you might get hurt." [2]

---

[2] These citations are from the novel *Made in U.S.A.* (New York: Longmans, Green, 1939), by Hans Otto Storm, pp. 100–101. Storm is a novelist who expresses the view of the world as seen by a man, trained in science, and practicing engineering, better than any other I know. He was a Stanford student and family friend of Veblen during the old man's last decade. His works are very much Veblenian by citation and by deep idea. His jewel of a short novel *Pity the Tyrant*, touching the fascinating question of placing an advanced technology in a half-colonial land, his most ambitious work *Count Ten*, his earlier books, and his splendid essays, collected by David Greenhood in a volume called *Of Good Family*, are worth any reader's time. His premature death in 1941 has cost us an understanding of the ideology of the engineer which no other novelist has yet provided.

The Ideology of the Engineers

Here is the Veblen view of the role of the practitioners of the industrial arts. Society grows to depend upon their skills, taking them as a class, if not as individuals. "We've got to have lights and air and refrigeration." The technologists accept the role. They do their stuff, with that concern for skill and the particular which is Veblen's own. Moreover, they do it by use and wont, not much caring for the trappings of the state. One point only they must insist upon: the productive machinery which they build and tend cannot be allowed to suffer harm. Here was his explicit thesis of 1920: businesslike sabotage, by price rigging, salesmanship, and unemployment, had become a serious threat to the productive use of the great industrial machine. When the keepers of the industrial arts, the production engineers and their like, would draw together, overcome their disunity, outgrow the contamination of their leaders, and unite with trained workmen and the public at large, then they might end absentee ownership and place society on a reasonable basis. It is the impairment of the rational operation of industry that is the sin of business; the engineers, who find reasonable performance their way of life, cannot in the end brook this sabotage.

But whence comes this concern for reason by the engineer? Here is the heart of the matter; its working out is a keystone of all the Veblen edifice of ideas. It is interesting to trace at least in summary.[3]

The roots lie in the very biological endowment of those living organisms which respond to environmental stimuli more and more intricately as one ascends the phylogenetic scale. The Loeb model of the simplest of responses, that of the moth seeking the flame, is the beginning, but only the beginning. Such a response is all but automatic; in a sense it is without action. But more complex organisms seek goals in a far more subtle way. Within the organism is constructed in some sense a model of the situation, on which vicarious tests may be run, anticipating and predicting the future. Here is the rise of consciousness and the origin of thought. But such thought, such storage of information, as the current and useful jargon would put it, necessarily implies alternatives. And among alternatives, some must be rejected. Their modeling within the mind has been idle from the standpoint of the actual events. But it has nevertheless been indispensable.

[3] These topics have been treated in a similar way by the present author in a piece which appeared in the New York periodical *Monthly Review*, IX (1957), 99.

Philip Morrison

The existence of alternatives is the very essence of choice. So the conscious organism, finally man, comes to depend upon this ability to fashion inner more or less abstract models of the outer world or, better, of possible but not realized facets of the outer world. So one may describe the content of Veblen's notion of idle curiosity. In times when we can demonstrate that satisfying a chimp's curiosity will reinforce learning as well as will food rewards, this biological basis for the growth of human understanding is particularly satisfactory.

Equipped, or, if you will, ridden with this potential for idle curiosity, man can, and for his survival must, build theories. The oldest theories of the world are lost to us. But it seems plausible that the tone at least of those hunting and gathering cultures, which have been so well and frequently described, is not misleading, although it may not in detail reproduce the earliest forms. The "industrial arts" of the hunter and the food-gatherer are well known. They may be more or less rude or, as with the coastal Eskimo, reach a marvelous technological sophistication. But nearly everywhere the cosmology, the style of explanation, the nature of theorizing are the same. Animism rules. The hunter and the collector sees the great biological events of his own life and that of his prey as the typical explanatory metaphors of a cosmology. The shape of rocks or the wind's murmur or the seasons' round can be ordered in the categories of "procreation, birth, growth, and decay." The hunter knows hunger and repletion; he knows the coming of the caribou herd and the season of calving. And he builds a world picture of this material. There is a pithy enough phrase to sum up this view. We are familiar with it in our own heritage; it is nonetheless appropriate to a far different mode of life. When a formulated religion grows out of such a shaman's philosophy, it is natural for it to see the world as begotten, born, and its Godhead as Father.

Now there follows a later stage. Upon the base of agriculture, man makes himself into village dweller, then citizen, and even into imperial subject. Classes arise from the less-differentiated earlier groups, organized mainly around the biological family. Interdependence grows; the peasant farmer pays his rentals in grain. Military needs—for now a surplus forms in good seasons—may give rise to a feudal hierarchy, each in his place, and God above all. Thus the Schoolmen saw Europe, and thus they saw the order of the world, hierarchical by early decree.

The Ideology of the Engineers

Thus too the Chinese scholars saw the Mandate of Heaven run to the Emperor, even as his writ ran down to the foursquare and truly oriented governor's courtyard of the smallest town. Perhaps such an order arose at first from the nexus built among men by the requirements of irrigation. Whatever it was, it led here to a characteristic cosmology. The metaphor of the growth of the seed did not cease wholly to have meaning for a society of husbandmen, but their division into social groups had new meaning, and it became natural to picture the world as obeying articulated commands, not mere biological necessity. God was not simply Father, but rather now He was Lord and Suzerain.

Times change. The chronology we trace, with Veblen, is not so much a real one as it is an idealized sequence. It is meant less to encapsule history than to show the logical, rather than the temporal, sequence in the construction of the ideology of the engineers.

The changing times bring to the store of technique a new set of ways, those of the craftsman. Of course he was present in the earliest times. But the work of millwright and smith, of smelter, wheelwright, spinner, weaver, and dyer grew larger and larger in the total store. No longer was his craft a matter for kings or priests to own; more and more it entered into essential economic and even into everyday life. The complexity of the arts grew steadily. The gunsmith, the printer, even the compass-maker and the lens-grinder appeared; new skills, new needs, new powers for men. By the time of the rise of the engineer himself, by the days of Smeaton and Watt, the making of instruments —from sextants to clocks—was a well-established industry. It had even a history; in Augsburg and Nuremberg it had flourished through the sixteenth century, to decline in the Thirty Years' War; in London and Paris it was growing stronger as the Age of Steam dawned.

What is the style of work of the craftsman, on which idle curiosity now rests its theories of the world? He begins with a design, in mind or even on paper. He executes it with the experience and ease which mark his craft. The relation of the final product to his aim is exposed for all to see; it no longer shares the magical relationship of progenitor to offspring, nor that of lord to vassal. He has wrought it with his hands, by conscious design. On the other hand, he has not analyzed the work step by step. The marks of knife or lathe, the adventitious difficulties of tool or material, the little differences from part to part go all unnoticed. His skill has reduced them to second nature, almost to unconsciousness. The goal is the well-wrought object, and it has been reached by a complex and half-articulate human activity. Now the explanatory metaphor is clear. God is the Great Artificer. The world is his cunning design, operated by natural laws, a set of specifications the Master has worked out for his journeymen below. The causal relationship as a whole is direct and simple, informed by purpose throughout, like the work of the craftsman.

Now we come to the engineer, and to Newtonian science, with which his work is everywhere permeated. The categories of explanation, the nature of scientific theories, are so closely linked with the processes of machine production that it becomes impossible to separate them. For Veblen this is not mere chance; it is that "men have learned to think in the terms in which technological processes act."[4] Our theories are those of the machine.

What are these theories? What are these explanatory schemes, at once fundamental to our philosophy and yet well suited to production? The causal chain now runs step by imperceptible step, as through a machine, from the input of raw material to the finished commodity—standard, predictable, accountable.[5] A single causal chain, almost divisionless, works the material from moment to moment, from one position to the next. Every mark and feature of the outcome, however trivial or unintended, is a real part of the work, and must have some explicit cause; some jig or fixture, some tool, has made each one. All is orderly and sequential, but at the same time rather uniform, homogeneous. No longer is there a simple product and behind it somewhere the cunning hand of the knowing Maker. Now the machine and its maker do not much differ, for what made the machine was after all just another such machine! Nor is there a stopping place, in past or in future. The causal chain runs from effect back to cause, from there back to another cause, and so on, back and back. Nor does any effect fail to become the origin of a new causal chain, indefinitely into the future. Development is continuous, without distinction, flowing from moment to moment, from point to neighboring point, under various forces, stresses, and pressures. After Darwin, even the organic world evolves in such a way, "in a colorless impersonal sequence of cause and effect."

[4] *The Instinct of Workmanship* (New York: Macmillan, 1914), p. 328.
[5] The next paragraphs simply paraphrase the article cited in note 3 above.

The Ideology of the Engineers

So like the description of a factory proceeds this mode of explanation of the world. Trained in such a science, dimly aware of such a philosophy, practicing each day the careful matter-of-fact procedures of the method, the engineer of production himself comes to categorize the world in this way. He sees a kind of atomized analytical interdependence as the way of his machines and of the world. And when his machines work unevenly, when they are clogged with their own output, or lie rusting half the year, he will analyze this too, in his matter-of-fact way, and sooner or later determine that the paper-pushers of the front office stand against him. Salesmanship, contractual limitations, usages of every sort to maximize profit will appear to him as extraneous, for they cannot bear the step-by-step analysis of his method. He will in the end come to see all business as did Veblen himself, as mere sabotage of the productive set of machines and practices which are the modern industrial arts.

This is the sweeping outline of the growth of an ideology of the engineers. It is, above all, Veblen's prescience that he saw fifty years ago the growing importance of such an ideology. And in its breadth and unity it seems to me that this line of argument must be counted among the most persuasive of all Veblen's seminal accounts of the sociology of ideas.

But there is a flaw in the argument. Veblen writes: "The mechanical technology is dispassionate and impersonal, and its end is very simply to serve human needs." [6] Here is the rub. Veblen's humanity enriched the dispassionate, impersonal, "unbusinesslike" nature of the ideology with a human value. But in this impersonality, in this analytic rationality, there is really no guarantee of human value. Man is complex enough to build great machines, not only for the venal goal of profit, but for the mortal crime of murder in million-fold example. The differential analysis, the goal of effective use, does not necessarily imply a commitment to the constructive operation of the well-designed mechanism, however much the instincts of craftsman or philosopher suggest it.

Some years ago I was engaged in work with several highly talented chemists and chemical engineers, whose background was especially interesting for study of the ideology of the engineer. These men had worked as a group for a firm of modest size—some hundreds of mil-

[6] In *The Engineers*, p. 132.

Philip Morrison

lions of dollars of capital—but of international reputation. It is the M. W. Kellogg Corporation of New York. Kellogg is a leader in a singular and symbolic industry, chemical process design and construction. Its special forte is the custom design, construction, and testing of large and often novel chemical plants, say, a new oil refinery. If you, an oil producer, find oil in some out-of-the-way corner, from the Persian Gulf to the Arctic Circle, you will need to refine it with the sort of large and complex plant now in efficient use everywhere. Unless you are Jersey Standard or a main competitor, you can hardly afford to keep on hand the specialist staff necessary to build refineries, for your need for refineries is not constant. Kellogg's men will do it for you. They will come to your lands, sample the oil, decide how best to process it, develop if necessary novel means to do the job, draw up the complex plans, procure pipes, tanks, gauges, and columns in marvelous profusion, level a site in desert or tundra, find and supervise contractors, install the special gear, test it out, train your own employees as operating crew, and, when the plant is turning out high-octane gasoline or fuel oil to the tankers or the pipelines, leave you with a cheerful word and a fine high bill, and pass on to make other and better refineries for other clients somewhere else. They will scrupulously credit you with the profits of the few weeks' production they engaged in to test the plant, but otherwise they are not in the oil business. They sell capital equipment—or rather, industrial art. Most of the physical equipment—meters, piping, and forgings —they buy from suppliers. What they sell is a functioning organism, the plant.

My co-workers were proud of their Kellogg days. For, said they, Kellogg knew more about the way to build refineries than anyone else in the world. (Their competitors might feel the same; we waive that dispute.) What they pointed out was that such a design-construction firm had to have a deeper understanding of the rationale of its processes than did, say, the experts of Jersey Standard. For suppose that a Jersey team has designed and built a new refinery to produce for Standard, say, 20,000 barrels of product a day. Putting the plant on stream, they find that the design they chose was more than adequate; indeed, they can make 25,000 barrels a day. For no added cost of construction, they have secured increased capacity. This would be the normal means of ensuring design success; wherever uncertainty arose

The Ideology of the Engineers

in the design, a safe way would be sought by planning for a slightly increased capacity. There would be general lightheartedness and praise, for the extra capacity would some day come in handy! But not so for Kellogg. If they contract to supply a plant with 20,000 barrels capacity, it must of course fulfill that contract, or the customer will claim his due. But it cannot overfulfill by much, or the Kellogg management will frown. For any overcapacity acts to reduce the eventual market for Kellogg's services. So, said the Kellogg men, they were forced to the strictest of rational designs, neither too much nor too little, but right on the nose. They were the most matter-of-fact, the most scientific, the least speculative of designers. *And they limited output.* Thus can a severe scientific rationalism itself come to mean what Veblen must have held to be the most businesslike of sabotage.

The lesson is more general. Patient, step-by-step, scientific understanding is not in itself a basis for determined opposition to the restrictions imposed on the use of the industrial arts within the social framework. And this may go some way to explain why the engineers have not in historical fact formed as a group any important opposition either to the most wasteful or the most immoral of practices.

We can go even beyond, taking the lead from Veblen into our own times. There is throughout his writing in this topic a kind of half-ironic tone. He is committed to science, to the matter-of-fact, to the real, but he finds in the colorless, mechanistic scheme of science he has uncovered much that is unreal. The older metaphors have some validity: growth and law and craft seem to be present if we look beyond the commonplace world of the factory itself. The psychology of Jacques Loeb, the physics of the old Kelvin, the pregenetic evolutionary theory placed the world in too narrow, too mechanical a frame. Reality is far wider, and yet not wide enough to admit the myths and make-believe of the nonmaterial world. Veblen's science was nineteenth-century, or at best vintage 1910, and he says tantalizingly little about the revolution of Curie and Bateson and Einstein and the rest.

It is never quite clear just what sort of machine, or what sort of engineer, Veblen found typical of the scheme we have described. He writes of the typewriter and the telephone, and he frequently refers to the designers of the machine industry as "mechanical engineers." We may surmise that the rolling mill, the linotype, even the thermoelectric power plant, with dynamo and turbine, would stand for him as fair samples of the trends he had in mind. These are indeed representatives of classical physics at its peak: they operate by sequences of forces, part after part fitting, striking, moving on. We have only to add to direct contact forces between solids the evident extensions to electric and magnetic forces to which he refers at least a few times. Here the prototype of the "colorless impersonal sequence" is entirely plain. Craftsmanship has been shoved into the background, for the goal is not much different from the incidental. The marks on the product which come from accidental flaw or transient effect appear there just as inevitably and as naturally as the features for which the plant is built. The cunning skill which made the right result arise out of whatever the hands encountered, single-minded for the goal, is no longer seen. Nor, of course, do the signs of the life cycle or of the great decree appear. Nothing happens unless at the right place, at the right time, the cause of its occurrence is there.

But modern machine industry, modern science with it, no longer has solely that quality. For our times an automatic oil refinery or an electronic computer or an aircraft under automatic pilot will serve to symbolize the highest of machine forms no less than they imply the concepts of physical science. In such complex devices a quite different form of analysis enters. We do not surrender the view that there are matter-of-fact, point-by-point chains of causes and effects. But these chains are now highly multiple. They condition each other; not even the designer knows what the refinery will do next. The machine is capable of adjusting itself to accidental variations in raw materials or in external conditions. It no longer works by stereotype; now it appears to seek a goal. The metaphor of the craftsman has crept back in. Its tools work in different ways at different times, to produce a product always within acceptable limits, just as the sentient journeyman did. Everywhere are amplifiers; everywhere small causes can produce large and remote effects, as the acorn can grow into the oak, or the long-since whispered order can determine the tactics of the soldier. Thus the metaphors of life or of sovereign command no longer seem foreign to science either. The whole analysis, without once leaving the frame of mind of the Newtonian material world view, has become more subtle, more colorful, far more powerful. The machine no longer differs from the organism, nor even, it may be, from

The Ideology of the Engineers

the society; all the world at least becomes congenial with, if not yet comprehended by, the scientific explanation. In that explanation, probability plays its key part. The statistics of atoms or electrons or pulses or decisions or mutations or eddies of air all belong to the present explanatory framework of science and are one by one embodied in the great productive complexes of our time.

What follows for ideology? It appears to me that these matters imply one great feeling: the nature of scientific explanation no longer entails merely the rationally efficient. It implies much more the new, the novel, the innovative. It is not the careful planner of the assembly line—or his rational decision on the speed of the tool, the place of the man's hand, or the choice of material—who stands for modern industrial technique. He is still there, of course, more skilled than ever, more powerful. But there is beside him the planner of some brand-new device, which does quite automatically what was done before by men under that careful scrutiny. And also working there is the sophisticated synthesizer of a new material, a new process, a new path altogether to the much modified goal. It is the extraordinary creative power of the new technology, based on the fuller maturity of science, that captures the mind and molds the jobs of the generation here and ahead. One does not look for a simple continued rationalization of industry, but for a potent automation, a transformation great enough to render the present norms and standards and rational analyses not so much wrong—they are correct, for they flow from science—but rather irrelevant. Productivity waits not upon careful redesign and scientifically planned operations but upon similarly planned innovation many times more effective.

In this light is the ideology of the engineer of today to be seen. There are still the production men, the planners, the skilled, the careful. But the ruling spirit is no longer theirs, indispensable though they are. The ruling spirit is the rise of the new, the unforeseen, the *statistically* predictable. Not the rolling mill but the servo-controlled line making a new alloy plate, or the extrusion press spewing out parts made of an unguessed polymer, is what stands for the high industrial arts today. As the machines change, as the theory behind them evolves, so alter the minds of the men. Innovation is the key to the spirit of modern technique, and it is the touchstone of the most representative of its men. By that single standard will they test a social scheme.

Philip Morrison

While innovation prospers, while expansion continues, they will support any going social fabric, its unreason notwithstanding. Let it be an expanding corporate economy, or an expanding socialist system, each will command the full allegiance of its engineers. Stagnation, the end of growth, the antithesis of the new powers of novelty in scientific analysis, can alone raise doubts in such men. Then they will feel the need to ask why the novelty they know they can create has ceased to appear. It is not Mr. Bents, the operating engineer, who stands for the typical men of technology today; rather it is the quietly excited young fellow in Pittsburgh, London, or Leningrad who has begun to see how the atomic reactor can be made cheap and sure. It is such as he who must be made content or at least not openly frustrated.

It would be a pity to end without Veblen's closing mockery of 1920; it is better aimed today than it was then if my analysis above has any merit. He writes:

By way of conclusion it may be recalled again that, just yet, the production engineers are a scattering lot of fairly contented subalterns, working piecemeal under orders from the deputies of the absentee owners; the working force of the great mechanical industries, including transportation, are still nearly out of touch and out of sympathy with the technical men, and are bound in rival trade organizations whose sole and self-seeking interest converges on the full dinner-pail; while the underlying population are as nearly uninformed on the state of things as the Guardians of the Vested Interests, including the commercialized newspapers, can manage to keep them, and they are consequently still in a frame of mind to tolerate no substantial abatement of absentee ownership; and the constituted authorities are competently occupied with maintaining the status quo. There is nothing in the situation that should reasonably flutter the sensibilities of the Guardians or of that massive body of well-to-do citizens who make up the rank and file of absentee owners, just yet.[7]

[7] *The Engineers*, pp. 168–169.

[MYRON W. WATKINS]

14

Veblen's View of Cultural Evolution

FEW who are acquainted, even casually or at second hand, with Veblen's writings will challenge the premise that he was a cultural geneticist. As he himself might have put it: the point may well be taken for granted, on the basis not simply of explicit avowal but as well of an unmitigated propensity to view things in that light. One could even go further and state, in his own manner of understatement, that "as a matter of course" the inference is warranted from the circumstance that he belonged to the generation of a society undergoing concurrently habituation, in the sphere of action, to the discipline of the machine technology, and, in the sphere of thought, i.e., knowledge systematization, to the Darwinian hypothesis. For as Mitchell has noted, Veblen, like Hume, was and was not the child of his time. In his preoccupation with matters-of-fact he was more American than the Americans, yet neither did his contemporaries accept him nor did he accept the prevailing outlook and habit of mind.

Like Hume, too, Veblen was a skeptic, with no illusions regarding either the truth or the future. And that brings us directly to the point of the present inquiry. In most of his books, as well as in numerous essays, but perhaps pre-eminently in his 1906 Harvard lectures on "The Socialist Economics of Karl Marx,"[1] Veblen was at pains to distinguish sharply his conception of social process, or cultural change, from that of Marx and his followers. Marx was a Hegelian, even

---

[1] First published in the *Quarterly Journal of Economics*, XX (Aug. 1906); reprinted in the collection of essays, *The Place of Science in Modern Civilization* (New York, 1919). Citations below will be to the 1930 reprint.

though, as a neo-Hegelian, he inverted the role of fact and idea, of material forces and reason. Veblen was a Darwinian, in the sense of finding his model of *Weltanschauung* and the structure of reality—which to him, as a Kantian, meant conceptual apparatus for organizing experience—in the "scientific" construction, or hypothesis, if you prefer, of an unending, unguided, cumulative process of mechanistic cause and effect. In sum, Veblen's theory of reality was a theory of becoming, not a theory of being. The essence of things, in his view, was movement, change, action.

In one sense, and a rather basic sense, thus, Veblen and Marx, as well as Schmoller (whom Veblen likewise criticized, on other grounds),[2] were in agreement. Alike, they found the ultimate reality in a process of development. Alike, too, they posited conflict as the driving force of change. It was in the conception of how development proceeds and the nature of the conflict that they differed. For Marx, as for Hegel, it was a dialectical process, an unfolding of that which is implicit in one stage into that which becomes explicit in the next. For Marx, but not for Hegel, it is the materialistic conditions of life (production and exchange) that do unfold; they unfold under the impulsion of class conflict, and by their unfolding determine the course of history. Moreover, not only is the succession of stages predetermined by the logic of the process, it leads to a predestined end.[3]

Such an outcome could be projected only by renouncing (withal unavowedly) the presumed compulsion and ubiquitous primacy of raw, materialistic forces. This feat of bringing in by the back door the (orthodox) Hegelian spiritualism, or idealism, which Marx had kicked out the front door, at the outset, is neatly described as follows by Veblen:

The social order takes its form through the class struggle, and the character of the class struggle at any given phase of the unfolding development

---

[2] "Gustav Schmoller's Economics," first published in the *Quarterly Journal of Economics*, XVI (Nov. 1901); reprinted in *The Place of Science*, pp. 252–278.

[3] In this respect, Schmoller differed from Marx only in "cutting off" the development process at a point one might identify as the sublimated present, instead of at a utopian future. Parenthetically, in a most misleading interpretation of Veblen, John S. Gambs would bracket him, too, with the harbingers of utopia. In his booklet, quite appropriately entitled *Beyond Supply and Demand* (New York, 1946), he declares (p. 22), among other ludicrous distortions, "that a strong utopian bias was a dominant trait of his (Veblen's) make-up."

View of Cultural Evolution

of society is determined by "the prevailing mode of economic production and exchange."

The dialectic of the movement of social progress, therefore, moves on the spiritual plane of human desire and passion, not on the (literally) material plane of mechanical and physiological stress, on which the developmental process of brute creation unfolds itself. It is a sublimated materialism, sublimated by the dominating presence of the conscious human spirit; but it is conditioned by the material facts of the production of the means of life. . . . [T]he dialectic of the process—the class struggle—runs its course only among and in terms of the secondary (epigenetic) forces of human consciousness engaged in the valuation of the material products of industry.[4]

As Veblen pointed out, a consistently materialistic theory would have afforded no ground for an eventual salutary consummation (such as a classless society), or, indeed, for any final term whatsoever to the process. It could have led only to an aimless, cumulative sequence of "opaque cause and effect." In Veblen's view, as a critic of Marx, such was the implication to be drawn from the Darwinian theory of evolution, natural selection. It appeared to him that no teleological drift, much less meliorative trend, was compatible with the Darwinian hypothesis or, for that matter, with the postulates of modern science.

But did the rejection of any imputation of controlling design, of beneficent purpose, or of preordained goal in the historical process mean that Veblen himself entertained no theory of cultural development? Was there, for him, as for Heraclitus, nothing but eternal flux? Was no systematic pattern of social evolution discernible, or even possible?

One thing is certain. Veblen was not a system builder. If he did, in fact, either consciously or unconsciously, entertain a theory of historical process or social development, he left it for others to "assemble." So far as I am aware, although he never formulated such an hypothesis, he never denied that a valid one could be formulated.

With some hesitancy, therefore, and with no more than a minimum brace of confidence, I venture to "reconstruct" a theory of cultural change that Veblen may have held in a more or less amorphous form. The starting point of any such theory, granting exclusion of all vestiges of anthropomorphic, animistic, or theistic preconceptions, must be in some assumption regarding the constitution or lineaments of human

[4] "The Socialist Economics of Karl Marx," *op. cit.*, pp. 415–416.

nature. For it is only through men's behavior that a continuum, if any, in the process of historical change or social development can be traced. Whether the pattern of that behavior be determined wholly by reason, by sentiment, by passion, or by external conditions (stimuli), or by all these forces working together, and whether that pattern is traced by active, self-generated drives or by passive adaptation, in sum, whether it represents in any sense free choice, is the ultimate issue in framing a theory of cultural development. For if all men's actions always represent mere tropismatic reactions to external stimuli, the process of social development or cultural evolution can in no way be distinguished from that of brute creation; and the "theory" of what governs its course must be the same.

According to Veblen, drawing heavily on his contemporaries William James, John Dewey, Jacques Loeb, and William McDougall, the pattern of human behavior as we understand it is not fixed. It is governed neither by the hedonistic calculus derived from Bentham, as the classical economists explicitly, and Marx implicitly, assumed nor by tropismatic reactions, the outgrowth of centuries of biological adaptation. Nor is it otherwise predetermined. On the other hand, it does have a pattern, even though not a fixed pattern. The distinctive feature of the human animal is capacity for a certain range of premeditated, deliberative, purposeful conduct. Of course, this does not mean that all human conduct is spontaneous, self-generated, much less, rational. In part it is instinctive,[5] in part governed by conditioned reflexes.

[5] The term "instinct" has too many and diverse meanings, alike in popular and professional usage, to be very serviceable any longer in a discussion of psychological principles, even at second hand. Veblen was well aware of this terminological pitfall (as of others). See, for example, *The Instinct of Workmanship* (New York, 1914), pp. 1–15. Nevertheless, properly qualified and discriminatively applied, the term has its uses. With Veblen, instinct is not to be taken to refer to a physiological datum, although "the instincts are hereditary traits." They constitute an important element in man's native equipment, a feature that has helped the species to survive. But unlike another such element, the tropisms (which do have a physiological basis), they provide, or are conceived to provide, (a) spontaneous drives, not simply automatic patterns of response to external stimuli, and (b) a blunted, or not-very-specific, objective and a correspondingly indeterminate ready-to-hand pattern of action or response.

In accordance with their amorphous character, Veblen, unlike some of the contemporary professional psychologists, makes no attempt to enumerate the instincts. He is content to select some of the important psychological promptings of human behavior, as observed by him and as derived by him and other scholars from an-

View of Cultural Evolution

Insofar as human behavior is instinctive, its direction, vigor, and pattern are powerfully influenced, according to Veblen, by two sets of proclivities which work to cross-purposes. On the one hand are the group-regarding, or prudential, proclivities, and on the other, the self-regarding, or predatory, ones. Both are generically human traits; whether, for Veblen, one is more so than the other is an open question.[6]

The group-regarding proclivities that Veblen stresses, and finds most significant for his purposes, are the parental bent, the instinct of workmanship, and idle curiosity. The first is a disposition to take pains for the welfare of the community, to conserve its material and spiritual heritage, to avoid waste and to renounce profligacy. Among other things, it prompts charity, education of the young, and ministration to the old. In fact, it lies at the root, not only of many community good works, but also of many forms of amusement, recreation, and entertainment that cultivate the sense of unity and solidarity among fellow tribesmen, or countrymen. The second selected positive proclivity is the one upon which Veblen laid the most stress. It represents a disposition to "make things work," to contrive a neat and efficient performance of the work in hand, to avoid sloppiness, carelessness, slackness, and the outturn of shoddy products. The third element of what has been called Veblen's trinity is the penchant to find a satisfactory explanation of things, and particularly of the origin (near or remote, immediate or ultimate) of things. It is a prompting to the pursuit of knowledge *for its own sake*.

Veblen's ideas about the self-regarding proclivities and attendant sentiments are by no means so well crystallized as his selected specimens of the group-regarding traits. I would suppose that he would offer little objection, however, to the more potent of the former set

---

thropological and historical studies, and show how, in his estimation, they operate, directly and through continuous interplay upon one another, to set certain limits and give certain directions to the race's cultural use and wont. Conditioned by the environment, they play a prominent role in Veblen's account of how men have come to live and think as they do and how those modes of life and thought are changing.

My own personal view, to which I surmise Veblen, at the end, would have subscribed, is that his theory would have been clearer and his position less exposed to captious criticism if he had throughout substituted the term propensity for instinct. He frequently uses those terms, *inter alia*, as synonyms.

[6] And it is a crucial question, in my judgment, for determining what sort of cultural geneticist Veblen was, as will be discussed further in the concluding section.

being designated as the proclivities: to ostentatious consumption, i.e., a penchant for conspicuously wasteful expenditure and useless employment; to prowess, i.e., the demonstration of superior capacity in some sense compared with other persons or peoples; to dominion, or pugnacity, i.e., the assertion of the right and the might to rule or command others; and to prestige, or self-aggrandisement, i.e., the quest of adulation and honorific status or titles. It goes without saying that in the long-run perspective, which was Veblen's trade-mark, each of these self-regarding proclivities looks toward the establishment and recognition of an invidious distinction of one sort or another. It appears to me that the anthropomorphic bent, or, in a wider ambit, animism, was conceived by Veblen to provide, somehow, a background or substratum for these more specific drives; but I confess it is by no means clear to me just how the connection was supposed to run.

It should be understood, of course, that Veblen does not offer these selected proclivities, prudential and predatory, as an exhaustive catalogue of the varieties of animus which go to shape the pattern of human behavior, either at first hand or, through habituation, at second hand. It is simply that, in search of the forces which have played a major role in the process of cultural formation and transmission, he has fastened upon these seven (instinctive) proclivities as seemingly most helpful in contributing toward a plausible explanation of cultural development. Veblen would be the last person in the world to claim finality for his insights and inferences—and in ultimate analysis that is all his hypothesizing of these proclivities represents.

Inasmuch as the process of cultural change is nothing but a story of human achievement and human failure in adaptation to men's natural and social environment, it follows that these distinctive proclivities animating the race are the ultimate factors controlling the historical process. In other words, the process of social evolution is a function, basically, of the constitution of the human type. But the human type is more than the biological species. It is human nature plus human habits, which, as Veblen was fond of saying, constitute "second nature." Habituation is essentially a social phenomenon; habits are transmissible, not through the genes, but through inculcation and example from generation to generation. Nevertheless, they resist supersession hardly less than the instinctive proclivities resist frustration.

View of Cultural Evolution

These socially conditioned norms of behavior are the institutions that go to make up a culture.

The process of institutional origination, development, and decay is the process of cultural change. Since the elements of this process are human habits which spring from the distinctive human traits, which, in turn, are not "all of a piece" but rather look—and drive—in opposite directions, the process of cultural change is a process generated and dominated by conflict. For Veblen—again as for Heraclitus—it is the tension of opposites that "keeps things going." It is the thrust of the self-regarding proclivities (and the institutions embodying them) and the counterthrust of the group-regarding proclivities (and the institutions erected on their foundations) that, together, shape the course and set the pace of cultural evolution.

In one sense, thus, it will be observed, the outlines of a Veblenian theory of cultural change bear a certain resemblance to those of Marx. The central fact in each is the generative force of conflict. For Marx, however, the conflict is class conflict; for Veblen, institutional conflict. The Marxian class conflict is a conflict over the control and usufruct of the means of production and exchange. The Veblenian institutional conflict is a conflict over opportunities for the expression of fundamental human proclivities—which, as we have seen, are not all, by any means, concerned with material well-being. The social stratification in any given era is primarily a reflection of current institutional incompatibilities. But what sets apart the high and mighty from the "underlying population" is not invariably "control of the means of production and exchange." The conflict of interest inherent in social stratification is not always and solely traceable to outmoded, or anachronistic, *economic* institutions. In Veblen's view, the sway of a priesthood or an overlordship stemming from dynastic privileges of "the well born" may represent quite as trenchant and fateful an institutional conflict as domination resting on the ownership of, say, slaves, land, or "capital."

The relative opportunities which different institutional fabrics afford for a balanced development of men's native proclivities condition the survival of those institutional complexes. For while the resilience, patience, and endurance of human kind are quite great, they have limits. Too long or too severe a frustration or perversion of one or another of the abiding human traits rooted in millenia of prehistoric biological and social evolution can produce radical readjustments—rents in the institutional fabric.

At the same time, with Veblen there is no assurance of the outcome of this perennial institutional conflict, as there is, with Marx, of the eventual outcome of class conflict. All this is more clearly expressed by Veblen himself in a single paragraph.

The ways and means, material and immaterial, by which the native proclivities work out their ends, therefore, are forever in process of change, being conditioned by the changes cumulatively going forward in the institutional fabric of habitual elements that governs the scheme of life. But there is no warrant for assuming that each or any of these successive changes in the scheme of institutions affords successively readier, surer or more facile ways and means for the instinctive proclivities to work out their ends, or that the phase of habituation in force at any given point in this sequence of change is more suitable to the untroubled functioning of these instincts than any phase that has gone before.[7]

The self-regarding traits are not entirely negative in character, of course; they are a secondary source of innovation. Nor do the group-regarding proclivities always work out positively to promote the common welfare; they may, often do, obstruct one another. Nevertheless, so constant, ubiquitous, and unremitting are the obstructive forces generated by self-regarding traits and re-enforced by institutional lags that it appears to be only by chance or by infrequent, not-to-be-counted-on Herculean efforts that institutional inertia is occasionally overcome and the rigid crust of outworn, inhibitive, anachronistic habits of thought and modes of conduct "cracked open," or dissolved, thereby permitting the life-sustaining, forward-looking impulses a freer expression and a wider ambit.

Let Veblen speak for himself.

In the cases where it has happened that those instincts which make directly for the material welfare of the community, such as the parental bent and the sense of workmanship, have been present in such potent force, or where the institutional elements at variance with the continued life-interests of the community or the civilisation in question have been in a sufficiently

[7] *Instinct of Workmanship*, p. 19. To similar effect, see "The Evolution of the Scientific Point of View," a lecture before the Kosmos Club, University of California, May 4, 1908; first published in the *University of California Chronicle*, X, no. 4; reprinted in *Place of Science*, pp. 38–39.

View of Cultural Evolution

infirm state, there the bonds of custom, prescription, principles, precedent, have been broken—or loosened or shifted so as to let the current of life and cultural growth go on, with or without substantial retardation. But history records more frequent and more spectacular instances of the triumph of imbecile institutions over life and culture than of peoples who have by force of instinctive insight saved themselves alive out of a desperately precarious institutional situation, such, for instance, as now faces the peoples of Christendom.[8]

Veblen emphasizes two features of the process of cultural change as having a strong, and in certain conjunctures decisive, bearing on the outcome of this perennial institutional conflict. One, institutional borrowing, is a positive influence. The other, "contamination" of the native proclivities, *inter se*, is a negative influence. In many respects, these two influences, or factors, are correlative and complementary.

In a brief, schematic, illustrative outline they work out somewhat as follows, according to Veblen. A new way of doing things, a technological advance, is hit upon, perhaps by chance, perhaps by the practical, matter-of-fact insight of some exceptionally gifted and independent member of a group, spurred by the instinct of workmanship. But in Veblen's view it is fundamental that these technical innovations do not spring Minerva-like, full-blown from a Jovian inventor's head. Rather, early and late, they represent piecemeal accretions to, indeed essentially an outgrowth of, the community's slowly accumulated stock of technological capital. Likewise, a new way of looking at things is hit upon, in a similar fashion, by a "maverick" individual driven by the urge of idle curiosity. (Veblen inclines toward "transplanting" the Mendelian theory from biological genetics to cultural genetics, tracing all genuine mutations to "sports.")

If the new development is to be taken into, or absorbed in, the settled use and wont of the community, it must "make its peace" with these established habits. As a rule, this means that its application is restricted and hedged, if not by the "conservative" impulses springing from the parental bent then by the intervention of some animistic or similar disposition to subordinate matters-of-fact to matters of imputation. Like a Chinese lady in the days of the mandarins, its feet will be bound and, thus impeded, it will not go so far as it otherwise might. It will lose much of its inherent force by this "contamination" of, as

[8] *Instinct of Workmanship*, p. 25.

the case may be, the instinct of workmanship, the parental bent, the urge of idle curiosity, or whatever probing, pure, or provident impulse may have given it birth.

On the other hand, if and when, through contact or communication, be it peaceful or warlike, with a neighboring community, such an improvement comes into the latter's possession, it is apt to be taken over free of the ritual frills, taboos, and limitations that are matters of imputation. The borrower, more than the discoverer, is likely to look upon the device, or expedient, as sheer matter-of-fact and thus to be disposed to realize (develop) its full potentialities. Furthermore, it is not solely with respect to emancipation from this "spiritual" incubus that the borrower gets an advantage. On the purely practical level, the borrowing community can take over the improvement without the handicap of initial trial and error. For example, by standardizing the width and height of railway tunnels and bridges at the outset and constructing all of them in the optimum dimensions, it can avoid the enormous cost of virtually duplicated construction projects for many such specific facilities. This piling of Pelion on Ossa of capital outlays, while unavoidable to the innovator, would represent sheer waste to the borrower were he needlessly to indulge in such folly, by virtue of the availability of the device or expedient as a full-blown *fait accompli*, as is hardly likely.

The mediation of these two complementary features of the process of cultural change, conditioning as they do the mediation of the institutional and natural environment in the working out of the basic binary proclivities, prudential and predatory, in no wise alters the contingent character of the outcome. It only adds to the complexity of the process. The intervention of "borrowing" and "contamination" neither adds to nor detracts from the risks of cultural regression or the chances of cultural progress. In strict accordance with the postulates of modern scientific inquiry, the process of cultural change is conceived to be nought but a cumulative sequence of efficient, "opaque" cause and effect, unending, unteleological, and unconcerned with human fate or destiny.[9]

Yet for all his hard realism, his derision of idealism, his sardonic thrusts at human foibles, Veblen was not a cynic, as certain superficial critics who neither knew him nor understood him have alleged.

[9] Cf. "The Evolution of the Scientific Point of View," pp. 32–50.

View of Cultural Evolution

Much less was he a pessimist, a prophet of doom.[10] Finally, even less was he a propagandist, a polemicist, a would-be reformer—who "failed" to spark a revolution—as one of his most recent biographers has mistakenly assumed.[11] Surely, no one who knew Veblen personally will dispute that he was quite devoid of a pragmatic bias and, a fortiori, of a proselytizing animus.[12] He was the very archetype of a man *au-dessus de la mêlée*,[13] the embodiment of at least two of the traits in his "trinity," idle curiosity and workmanship, each for its own sake. But was there also a trace of the third member of the "trinity," the parental bent, notwithstanding all the popular misconceptions?

On this score, I doubt that anyone is entitled to lay down a presumptively definitive conclusion. It may be noted, in favor of an affirmative answer to the question, first, that the rigid exclusion of all preconceptions of preordination, a teleological process, or a melioristic trend,

---

[10] As his study *The Nature of Peace* (New York, 1917), clearly demonstrates.

[11] David Riesman, *Thorstein Veblen, A Critical Interpretation* (New York, 1953).

[12] I admit that some qualification on this estimate might be in order, based on the attitude evinced in what he wrote in his old age, say, after World War I. But surely the essentials for which a scholar stands are not to be drawn from what emanates from his study four decades after he reaches intellectual maturity, as, for example, in the case of Veblen, from such ebullitions as *The Engineers and the Price System* (New York, 1921).

[13] It appears difficult to reconcile with this view Professor Knight's interpretation of Veblen's posture. Knight finds implications not only of a normative tendency but of reformist zeal in Veblen's exposition of the role of alleged instinctive "drives" and institutional "habits" in shaping human behavior (Frank H. Knight, *The Ethics of Competition* [New York, 1935], pp. 21–22, 29, and 43).

While recognizing that a plausible case can be made out for such an interpretation, in my judgment it misses the mark. Veblen's use of savage satire and mordant wit to deflate current (conventional) "values" represented, I believe, essentially a device for establishing, beyond doubt or cavil, their impermanence, their source in institutions that invariably have a beginning and an end. In fact, at bottom Knight is following in Veblen's footsteps in contending, in the essay cited above ("Ethics and the Economic Interpretation"), that wants are not only ineluctably changeable but also indefeasibly subject to valuation by standards which are neither absolute nor, from the standpoint of the community as a whole, arbitrary. I would deny that Veblen, any more than Knight, was intent on promoting (securing acceptance of) *his* "values." His basic objective was to "unhinge" valuation from tradition and convention, to bring it "out in the open," to make it a deliberate, and so far as possible rational, process—both individually and collectively.

Alvin Johnson's biographical note in the *Encyclopedia of the Social Sciences* (XV, 234) gives an interpretation of Veblen's position in full accord with that advanced in the text above. Johnson, who knew Veblen well, states unequivocally that "he had no interest in programs of reform."

whether based on theistic design or on dialectical movement, by no means precludes a salutary drift as a fortuitous outcome of the operation of a chance concatenation of causal forces. It may be noted, secondly, that Veblen was given to referring to the earlier phases of cultural development as "lower" and the later, more recent, phases as "higher," or "more advanced." The instances of this usage throughout the entire body of his work are too numerous to need cataloguing. For present purposes, it will suffice to cite an incomplete series of such "professions" from one of his major works.[14]

It can hardly be disputed that a movement from a "lower" to a "higher" level connotes "progress," in some sense. If I were asked to specify in what sense Veblen presumably conceived this implicit progression, my answer would be, first of all, to quote a passage from Veblen himself which appears to me to bear on the issue. Speaking of the driving power of his trinity of group-regarding traits, he avers:

It is accordingly characteristic of this whole range of vaguer and less automatically determinate predispositions that they transiently yield somewhat easily to the pressure of circumstances. This is eminently true of the idle curiosity, as it is also true in a somewhat comparable degree of the sense of workmanship. But these instincts at the same time, and perhaps by the same fact, have also the other concomitant and characteristically human trait of a ubiquitous resiliency whenever and in so far as there is nothing to hinder. Their staying power is, in a way, very great, though their driving-force is neither massive nor intractable. So that even though the idle curiosity, like the sense of workmanship, may be momentarily thrust aside by more urgent interests, yet its long-term effects in human culture are very considerable. Men will commonly make easy terms with their curiosity when there is a call to action under the spur of a more elemental need, and even when circumstances appear to be favourable to its untroubled functioning a sustained and consistent response to its incitement is by no means an assured consequence.[15]

While the main thrust of this passage is to deny any *necessity* of progress, or improvement, in "the scheme of life," the clear implication is that the gist of progress if it occurs, and the criterion of whether it has occurred, is "the untroubled functioning" of men's instinctive proclivities. This might be translated, I would suppose, as opportuni-

[14] See *Instinct of Workmanship*, pp. 27, 36, 81, 104, 147, 182, 195, and 198.
[15] *Instinct of Workmanship*, pp. 86–87.

View of Cultural Evolution

ties for expression and development of basic human traits. But which human traits? In Veblen's binary system this issue is crucial. Is it the self-regarding traits or the group-regarding traits, the provision of opportunities for fuller and freer expression of which is the criterion of "progress" from "lower" to "higher" phases of cultural proliferation?

Let Veblen answer. In a continuation of the passage just quoted, he says:

The common man does not eagerly pursue the quest of the idle curiosity, and neither its guidance nor its award of fact is mandatory on him. Sporadic individuals who are endowed with this supererogatory gift largely in excess of the common run, or who yield to its enticements with very exceptional abandon, are accounted dreamers, or in extreme cases their more sensible neighbours may even rate them as of unsound mind. But the long-term consequences of the common run of curiosity, helped out by such sporadic individuals in whom the idle curiosity runs at a higher tension, counts up finally, because cumulatively, into the most substantial cultural achievement of the race,—its systematised knowledge and quasi-knowledge of things.[16]

Elsewhere Veblen states that the parental bent and the instinct of workmanship working in conjunction with one another,

have exercised the largest and most consistent control over that growth of custom and conventional principles that has . . . given rise to a system of institutions. This control bears selectively on the whole range of institutions created by habitual response to the call of the other instincts and has the effect of a "common sense" surveillance *which prevents the scheme of life from running into an insufferable tangle of grotesque extravagances.*[17]

Veblen adds that this surveillance has not always been decisive, of course, but that these two predispositions "have been the primary and persistent factors in (selectively) shaping" the pattern of human livelihood and community living. Thus, they have been the primary factors accounting for the millenia-long advance from "lower" to "higher" cultural levels—is not the inference warranted?

Complementing this implicit ascription of primacy, and ultimate "control," to these two members of the "trinity," Veblen has elsewhere ascribed at least a co-ordinate role, I would infer, to the third member.

[16] *Ibid.,* p. 87.   [17] *Ibid.,* p. 48 (italics mine).

Myron W. Watkins

In his essay "The Place of Science in Modern Civilisation,"[18] Veblen makes out the distinctive mark of the "modern," *ergo* the most "advanced" (on something more than a chronological scale), culture as the accumulation of matter-of-fact knowledge. It is in the pursuit of this objective, he finds, that a preponderant part of the attention and resources of contemporary society is focused. At the same time, he is at pains, however, to dissociate his observation in this respect from any implication that concentration on the advancement of practical knowledge is good and wholesome. "There is," he says, "room for much more than a vague doubt that this cult of science is not altogether a wholesome growth."[19]

And so we come to no definitive conclusion on the question of what sort of cultural geneticist Veblen was. The sharp contrast of the unmitigated addiction to the "scientific" point of view focused in cold objectivity on the impersonal sequence of opaque cause and effect and the inveterate, irrepressible predilection for the genial climate in which the parental bent, the instinct of workmanship, and idle curiosity hold sway remains unresolved. In my own view, Veblen would have had it so. His preference was to uncover problems, raise questions, incite inquiry, rather than to work out neat solutions.

The question of the significance and validity, in mid-century, of Veblen's theorizing on the process of cultural change goes beyond the review and recapitulation, which, as stated at the outset, was the primary objective of this essay. Nevertheless, the bearing on our present predicament of his distinctive approach to the questions of "how we got this way" and "whither we are going" has such timeliness that some brief reflections on the matter may be indulged.

Regarding the basic premise of the springs of human behavior, in giving a comparatively low rank to reason Veblen's theory certainly has not suffered obsolescence with the passage of time. Indeed, a confirmation of his viewpoint in this respect can be clearly discerned in current trends, both literary and scientific. On the other hand, the low rank Veblen's theory gave the sexual factor in shaping human behavior has been "left on a dry shoal upstream" by the Freudian tide.

[18] First published in the *American Journal of Sociology*, XI (March 1906); reprinted in the collection of essays to which this article gives the title, cited above, pp. 1–31.

[19] *Ibid.*, p. 4. The "not" is out of place, as the context makes clear.

View of Cultural Evolution

The virulence of institutional conflicts has underscored his insistence on their paramount role in determining the temper of the times and the pattern of cultural development. Internationally, the conflict between the Soviet system and the democratic system certainly confirms Veblen's analysis, in *Imperial Germany and the Industrial Revolution*, of the explosive consequences of borrowing a new technology and hitching it to a political vehicle designed for other than matter-of-fact industrial ends. Under the Soviets, ideological evangelism takes the place of dynastic aggrandizement; proletarian subservience takes the place of peasant docility. The machine technique has been taken over virtually intact and applied, as in agriculture, with a myopic regard for its stern dictates of mechanical efficiency, quite in accord with Veblen's prescient theory. Nor is that all, or perhaps most. Chemical synthesis appears to be likewise finding an exuberant reception, and responding with an exuberant growth, in its new home. An even more potent factor in the rapidly developing institutional conflict on the international plane is the borrowed technique of propaganda. Originally introduced, under capitalistic auspices, as a commercial expedient, the demonstration of its full potentialities for mass indoctrination awaited its transplanting and cultivation by uninhibited manipulators in an environment untrammeled by tribal taboos of fraud and such time-honored axioms as "honesty is the best policy."

In the domestic sphere, likewise, the conflict between the promptings of social mores, political tradition, legal precepts, and ethical norms, on the one hand, and the exigencies of corporation finance and of competitive business practice, on the other, may be obscured by the mummery of the organization men. But in spite of their steady recruitment and seductive stratagems there is little to indicate the conflict is being allayed. Similarly, assiduous advertising re-enforced by astute motivation research gives a superficial appearance of a smooth-running economic process. But as debt is piled on debt and opportunities for the spontaneous exercise of self-direction, alike in the sphere of production and of consumption, disappear, there are indications of ground for mistrusting that the common man can be counted on indefinitely to keep cheerfully heaving away at his institutionally imposed Sisyphean task.

Veblen was not a prophet, however, nor was he an agitator. His role was that of a catalyst in the process of cultural transformation. The inextinguishable individualism and congenital insubordination which marked his career I would rank high among the essential elements of his genius. Leon Ardzrooni, who along with Ellen Rolf, Wesley Clair Mitchell, and Herbert Joseph Davenport, knew him as intimately, in all probability, as it was possible to know him, was convinced that, at bottom, Veblen was a mystic. My own judgment would be that in the great tradition of Locke, Voltaire, and Goethe he was a humanist, devoted to, as Webster defines the type,

a system of thinking in which man, his interests and development are made central and dominant. Its tendency is to exalt the cultural and practical . . . and to encourage a spirit of revolt against existing opinions.

[CARTER GOODRICH]

15

The Case of the New Countries

THE part I venture to take in this co-operative enterprise deals with comparative economic history. I shall recall briefly Veblen's great contribution in this field, shall describe it as giving a lead that has been little followed by economists or economic historians, and then shall attempt to follow for a short distance one particular lead that concerns the comparative history of new countries.

I

The major and most obvious contribution of Veblen to comparative economic history is of course to be found in *Imperial Germany and the Industrial Revolution* and in the companion essay on "The Opportunity of Japan,"[1] both of which appeared in 1915. These works deal with the contrast between the economic histories of a nation, Great Britain, which developed the technology of industrialism slowly and to a large degree independently, and of nations which borrowed that technology and adopted it with great rapidity, imperial Germany and imperial Japan. In the book, a part of the argument moves on a strictly technological level. The borrowing area has the advantage of being able to take over the new technique at its developed best. It can buy or build machines of the newest model and put them to work in factories of up-to-date design within a network of transportation constructed to meet their needs. On the other hand, much of the industry of the first area is still carried on with older machinery which it cannot yet

[1] "The Opportunity of Japan," *Jour. of Race Development*, VI (1915), 23–38.

afford to scrap and with buildings and transport originally designed for an earlier stage of the technology. One of Veblen's familiar illustrations was "the silly little bobtailed carriages used in the British goods traffic."[2]

It may be said that this point perhaps more than others in Veblen's comparison has come into the common parlance and common thought of economists. Illustrations are frequently given of the penalty of taking the lead in technological innovation. A case I have had occasion to examine is that of the state works of Pennsylvania, which scored the engineering triumph of the first railroad crossing of the Appalachian Mountains and paid the penalty of its complete obsolescence in less than twenty-five years. Students of the movement of the textile and other industries from New England to the South have often pointed to the advantage of starting afresh in plants designed for the newest machinery. Another set of applications of the doctrine may be worth examining in these days when we appear to be as anxious to promote the welfare of the nonindustrial peoples by hastening their economic development as Veblen himself was to promote their welfare by protecting them *from* rapid development.[3] In current discussion the possibility of borrowing modern technology at its peak is commonly taken for granted as a great advantage for the developing countries, and might indeed be spectacularly illustrated if it should prove that some of them were able to apply atomic energy to industrial uses more rapidly than the developed countries.

Yet the same discussions have brought out two limitations in the application of the doctrine of borrower's advantage. In some cases, though by no means in all,[4] the newest techniques of the advanced countries,

---

[2] *Imperial Germany and the Industrial Revolution* (new ed.; New York: Viking, 1939), p. 130.

[3] "Outline of a Policy for the Control of the 'Economic Penetration' of Backward Countries and of Foreign Investments," in "Two Unpublished Papers of Thorstein Veblen on the Nature of Peace," ed. by Joseph Dorfman, *Political Science Quarterly*, XLVII (1932), 189–203. This memorandum, prepared for the House Inquiry of 1917, urged "a policy of retardation and continence" as opposed to the "urgent and unremitting pressure for the headlong 'Development,' that is to say for commercial exploitation, of all these outlying natural resources."

[4] See the thoughtful comments of John H. Dales in his *Hydroelectricity and Industrial Development—Quebec 1898–1940* (Cambridge, Mass.: Harvard University Press, 1957), esp. p. 263, n30. "A steel mill, an oil refinery, a pulp and paper plant, an automobile factory, a cotton-spinning factory or a radio works—

The Case of the New Countries

designed to meet situations in which capital is abundant and labor scarce, may where the opposite conditions prevail be less applicable than some earlier form of the machine technique. In the second place, much current discussion deals with the necessity of institutional changes in the less industrial countries—in habits of labor discipline, enterprise, and administration—before technology can be effectively borrowed. It would hardly be a distortion to say that much discussion of economic development and technical assistance today turns on methods of stimulating changes in habits of thought sufficient to bring the less developed countries to a degree of receptivity to new technology similar to that exhibited by imperial Germany and imperial Japan.

Veblen's emphasis, however, was on a precisely opposite point. What struck him was how little these countries had had to change their basic habits of thought to make effective use of the borrowed techniques. Germany and to an even greater extent Japan had taken over the machine technology without at the same time absorbing the complex of changed usages, habits, and manners of thought that in Great Britain had developed during the long process of industrial development. They were thus able, as he says of Japan, "anachronistically to combine the use of modern technical ways and means with the medieval spirit of servile solidarity." In England, on the other hand, the changes in industry had taken place slowly enough to work out their effect "upon the habits of thought of the community, and so to bring about a state of the institutional conventions answering to the altered state of the industrial arts."

What, then, were these institutional arrangements and habits of thought which, in Veblen's view, "answered" to the machine technology? In part, they were those which he summed up in a single sentence as "self-help" and "mechanistic logic." Through the years of handicraft and petty trade and early machine industry, the industrial population had developed habits of independence and of self-assertion against the older aristocracies; and the "matter-of-fact" attitude induced by habituation to the machine process was hostile to the type of personal loyalties represented by fealty to Prussian imperialism or by "the Spirit of Old Japan." On the other hand, the later stages of ma-

---

all are likely to be much the same the world over. The more elaborate the technology, it seems to me, the more rigid it is likely to be, and the more appropriate the assumption of fixed proportions becomes."

chine development had been typically—the article on Japan seems almost to say necessarily—controlled by large-scale business enterprise acting under pecuniary motivation. In Veblen's view such control is in conflict with the logic of a mechanistic technology—a conflict which is indeed a central theme of the general Veblenian body of thought. But this distinction is in part beside the point [5] in the discussion of the unique "Opportunity" of the imperial regimes to embark on dynastic enterprise while they could make use of the material power obtained from their newly borrowed technologies and before their control was weakened by the growth either of democratic or of pecuniary habits of thought.

Comparative economic history is thus based on institutional comparisons much broader than those on the purely technological level. Its example has been little followed, in part by reason of its sheer boldness and complexity. Again further application is at least tempting. Much of the argument can surely be applied to the case of Germany under Hitler. Indeed from this distance in time it would almost be possible to forget which of the German regimes was the subject of his essay. Joseph Dorfman made the application in 1939 in the following terms: "So well had Veblen caught the spirit of the Third Reich twenty years before its birth that its accredited spokesmen sound as if they were merely obeying Veblen's logic not only in broad outline but in specific detail." [6] Of greater current interest is the question of the applicability of the thesis to the new imperialism of Soviet Russia. In this case the origins and basis of loyalty to the regime are different from those of the cases Veblen studied, and its doctrines are stated at least formally in terms of mechanistic logic. Yet in one sufficiently frightening aspect, the Russian case conforms to the Veblenian description. It too presents an authoritarian regime wielding the newly borrowed and newly minted power of the most modern technology and operating without the checks that might be imposed by a population habituated by long experience to the practice of democratic insubordination.

The cases cited do not by any means exhaust Veblen's use of the

---

[5] But as a result of it Veblen regarded the difference between the Kaiser's Germany and the Businessman's America as somewhat less profound than it seemed to some of his enthusiastic World War-I readers.

[6] Introduction to 1939 ed., p. xii. See also p. xx.

The Case of the New Countries

device of the comparison of different economic orders in the development and presentation of his theories. A conspicuous part of his system is the ubiquitous use of the peaceful pagan economy of the early Baltic people and the occasional parallel use of pacific China as bench marks against which to measure and compare the characteristics of later economic orders. Perhaps these may be thought of as Veblen's variations on the *mens naturaliter Christiana* of religious history. Whatever their purpose and validity, they are essentially devices of static comparison and hardly fall within the definition of comparative economic history as the study of varying cases of cumulative economic change.

II

The comparisons I wish to explore are somewhat more modest in scope. They relate to the history of the so-called "new countries" that arose in the period of European expansion. Veblen's reference to them forms a brief passage at the beginning of the chapter "The Case of America" in *Absentee Ownership*. The differences to which he calls attention are two. The first, which he says is "not wide," is between the United States, considered as "the oldest and maturest of the colonies founded by the English-speaking peoples," and their "later enterprises in colonization," presumably Australia and New Zealand. The United States, he argues, took its "point of departure from the European situation" in the period in which "the principles of self-help, free contract, and net gain achieved their ascendancy" and at a time when "the system of Natural Liberty was still 'obvious and simple.'" For Australia and New Zealand, on the other hand, he says that "their institutional point of departure [was] blurred" by certain holdovers from "the return wave of reaction in Europe, as well as by those later-come stirrings of radical dissent that have questioned the eternal fitness of the system of Natural Liberty itself."

The second and wider difference is between the English-speaking peoples and "those other, South-European or 'Latin,' peoples who have had a share in the colonization of the new continents." When these peoples "were taking the lead in the winning of the New World, [they] were still living very busily in a more archaic and barbarian phase of the European culture, which belongs at a point in the sequence antedating the natural rights that make democracy." Thus, says Veblen, Spanish colonization "and in a degree the Portuguese, was an enterprise in pillage, inflamed and inflated by religious fanaticism and martial vanity." All this, he says, "has worked out in the creation of a class of colonial nations which have hitherto scarcely proved fit to survive under this newer order of things that has been imposed by the mechanical industry and the business enterprise which makes use of the mechanical industry." On the other hand, the new nations of British origin, in which the initial and "enduring preoccupaton of the people has been the exploitation of natural resources for private gain," have been much more receptive or as he says "addicted" to "democratic institutions, the mechanical industries, and business enterprise."[7]

If we pass over the harshness of the language—and some of it can later be rephrased in the gentler terms of a translation from the Spanish—these quotations may be taken as stating the questions, though by no means all the answers, for a venture in comparative economic history.

In comparing the United States with Australia and New Zealand, the contrast to be explained is in the degree to which economic individualism has been checked and modified by collective and state action. Australia put into power the world's first labor government, and in both Australia and New Zealand labor parties have for decades shared political power almost equally with their combined oppositions. Australia had the largest proportion of organized wage earners in the world at a time when trade unionism in the United States was a matter of a small minority. The labor movements of both the other countries have long professed the doctrines of socialism, while our own remains almost the only antisocialist labor movement that can be found. New Zealand in the eighteen-nineties led the world in labor and social legislation, and was followed more closely in Australia than in the United States. Government subsidy of developmental transportation took the form in both of these Commonwealth countries of government ownership and operation of the railways while in our case it took more often the form of government aid to private companies. We in the United States have been in the habit of thinking that the conditions

[7] *Absentee Ownership and Business Enterprise in Recent Times* (New York: Huebsch, 1923), pp. 120–122.

The Case of the New Countries

of new and frontier countries favor economic individualism, and it is therefore somewhat of a surprise to find that these still newer countries developed at so early a stage such a socialist and interventionist tradition.

The contrast to which Veblen pointed is a real one, and the explanation that he suggests is one for which much support can be found. Doubts of the system of Natural Liberty were characteristically expressed in the first issue of the *People's Advocate,* which appeared in Sydney in 1848. "In truth," said the editors, "we are sick of the everlasting babblement of the men who swear by Adam Smith." The explanation of the strength of the labor movement in terms of the importation of radical ideas is particularly favored by Australian writers. They like to point out that the six Dorchester Laborers, transported for trade unionism, and a number of Chartists were among the convicts sent to Australia, and that the Gold Rush of 1851, which brought to the country its first great accession of immigrants, attracted foot-loose rebels from the defeats of English Chartism and the continental revolutions of 1848. It may, to be sure, be objected that the unfortunate farm laborers from Dorsetshire spent only a short time in the penal colony, that no form of human activity could be less socialistic than participation in a gold rush, and that the United States also received thousands of Chartist immigrants and many more German forty-eighters than ever reached the South Pacific. Yet there is abundant evidence of a continuing close relationship between the labor movements of Australia and New Zealand and that of the mother country, as illustrated by the formation on shipboard of an Australian branch of the Amalgamated Society of Engineers, by discussions on an emigrant ship that gave rise to the eight-hour-day movement in New Zealand, and still later by the large contribution raised by Australian trade unions for the support of the London Dock Strike of 1888. In any case, the fact remains that immigrants to the United States in the nineteenth century came to a land whose habits of thought were already firmly established in an earlier individualistic tradition, while the countermovements of trade unionism and labor legislation and the early stirrings of modern socialism had already begun to be felt at the time when migrants were exerting a formative influence on the institutions of Australia and of still newer New Zealand.

Carter Goodrich

Before giving full acceptance, however, to this emphasis on differences in the importation and diffusion of ideas, I should like to urge consideration of another line of possible explanation based on differences in occupational distribution and geographic opportunities. It runs less in terms of the ideas the Diggers brought with them than in terms of what they found to do when the gold ran out. What they did *not* find to do, in any numbers either in Australia or in early New Zealand, was to take up land as small farmers. Instead they found the land "locked up," as the phrase went, in large sheep ranches. To their political leaders, as well as to a number of later writers, the explanation of the contrast with American "free land" seemed to lie in the field of political policy. For this there was certainly some color in early legislation. Yet nearly a century of legislative efforts to plant a "sturdy yeomanry" on the Australian land—in some cases by means much more drastic than our own Homestead Act—have effected so small an increase in the number of Australian small farmers as to suggest that the real difference lay elsewhere. In America a sturdy yeomanry could not be kept off the land. The greater difference lay not in legislation but in the fact that so much of America's well-watered frontier was hospitable to the family farmer growing wheat and corn while Australia's great stretches of drier land were better adapted to the large-scale operation of wool-raising.

The consequences for the distribution of population were obvious. Since sheep-raising required so little man power, people were early concentrated in the cities, and in the Australian case to an extraordinary extent in the two major ones. In 1890–1891 more than a quarter of the entire population lived in Sydney and Melbourne. By contrast, only 15 per cent of Americans lived in cities of more than 100,000 inhabitants. The differences in occupational distribution ran in the same direction. Although the small industrial undertakings in the newer countries were by no means comparable to the great manufacturing establishments of the United States, the proportion of the gainfully occupied that could be classified as in industrial pursuits was nevertheless higher. It stood at 31 per cent in Australia and 29 per cent in New Zealand, as against only 23 per cent in the United States. Mining employed 5 or 6 per cent in Australia and 7 per cent in New Zealand, as against only 2 per cent in the United States. Conversely, the pro-

The Case of the New Countries

portion engaged in "country" pursuits, primarily agriculture and grazing, was 38 per cent in the United States, but less than 30 per cent in New Zealand and 25 per cent in Australia.[8] The United States of Rockefeller and Carnegie and the Sherman Anti-Trust Act was in these terms the most rural of the three. Australia and New Zealand, for all their newness and the modest scale of their enterprises, were in this sense more industrial. Even on the land, moreover, the characteristic occupational division was that of employers and employees, as illustrated by the great importance of the Shearers' Union in the early days of the Australian and New Zealand labor movements. The effect was to give these two countries a notably smaller proportion of self-employed persons than the United States and a correspondingly greater predominance of employees. These factors might, therefore, appear to be a significant part of the explanation for their early and extensive resort to trade-union and governmental action on behalf of the wage earners.

This explanation receives at least a partial and suggestive confirmation in what has happened since 1890 in two of the countries concerned. In the case of New Zealand, the invention of refrigeration made it possible to sell butter in the London market twelve thousand miles away. This released the potentialities of areas, particularly in the North Island, which enjoyed abundant rainfall and extraordinary natural advantages for dairy industry. These opportunities were seized by small farmers, who obtained the land with the aid of favoring governmental measures. New Zealand became more rural at a time when the United States was rapidly becoming more urban and more industrial. As the farmers rose to a position of dominance in New Zealand economy, the political consequence, as John B. Condliffe has pointed out, was a cessation of the flow of new social and labor legislation and the return, at least for a considerable period, to a more conservative economic

[8] These are rough approximations, based on Census data collected in the three countries under somewhat different headings. The American classification of "manufacturing and mechanical pursuits" is brought into approximate conformity with the Australian and New Zealand category of "industrial" by subtracting "fishermen and oystermen" and the larger group engaged in the "extraction of minerals." The "country" category is obtained in the American case by adding "fishermen and oystermen" to the heading of "agricultural pursuits" and in the Australian and New Zealand cases by subtracting "mining" from the total of "primary producers."

policy.[9] A nation of small farmers was less inclined to advance a wage-earners' collectivism.

The other and more familiar change is that which has occurred in our own country. With the passing of the frontier, growing urbanization, and the rise of great industry and big business, we too became a "nation of employees." As a result of these underlying factors, and with the shock of the Great Depression reflected in the New Deal's legislative innovations, we have experienced what is by comparison with our own past an enormous increase in collective action and in governmental responsibility for the economy. Of this the adoption of a comprehensive system of social security and the growth of trade unionism in numbers and recognition are particularly relevant to the comparison with Australia and New Zealand. On these two points, the differences between them and the United States is clearly less wide than it was when Veblen described it, although there remains today —I believe—a significant difference in the extent to which the leadership of big business in economic life is confidently exerted and confidently accepted.[10]

The second comparison with which we are concerned is that between the Latin-origin and the British-origin new countries. Here what needs to be explained, at least if we disregard the political overtones of Veblen's statement, is the difference in economic levels and the fact that Latin America has not attained the extraordinarily high standards of living enjoyed by the new countries of British origin. Veblen's explanation of this, like most others that have been advanced, runs in terms of the contrast between the more industrial and businesslike heritage of the British as against the more medieval and military heritage of the Spanish and the Portuguese. In one case the ties lay with the part of Europe in which the combination of mechanical techniques and business enterprise was most in the ascendant, and in the other case with one of the parts of Europe in which these tendencies made only partial and belated progress. In the latter case, moreover, the settlements were launched a century before those of

[9] John B. Condliffe, *New Zealand in the Making* (Chicago: University of Chicago Press, 1930), chs. vii and viii.

[10] The argument of this and the preceding six paragraphs was stated more fully in 1928 in Carter Goodrich, "The Australian and American Labour Movements," *Economic Record* (Melbourne), IV (1928), 193–208.

The Case of the New Countries

the United States and two centuries before Australia's, at a time—around 1500—at which the economic transformation had not gone very far even in the technologically more advanced countries.[11] A Spanish-language writer, the Venezuelan historian Mariano Picón-Salas, explains the contrast in the following terms:

There is then in our origins, and in contrast with that other pragmatic and utilitarian current which was already beginning to form in the north of Europe and which was to reach its height in the industrialism and the mechanical civilization of the nineteenth century, a certain scorn of economic matters and an economic inferiority which would hold us back in the great technical and utilitarian adventure of the modern world. Perhaps the proud and at times conceited sense of his own manliness made the Spaniard so much the rebel against the mechanical. His medievalism made him prefer the warrior to the merchant, the soul to the body. Even today the Spanish peoples have not become fully acquainted with the usages of the capitalist economy.[12]

Picón-Salas' animus is very different from Veblen's, but I am sure that the latter would have accepted the antithesis between merchant-body and warrior-soul as expressing the contrast he had in mind.

Yet even this generally accepted and persuasive line of explanation will not cover all the facts without at least some recourse to more prosaic differences in geographic and demographic conditions. If the conquistadores in High Peru looked for gold, so did the first settlers of Virginia. The former found it; the latter did not; and it would be interesting to speculate on what the history of the thirteen colonies might have been if the Appalachian Mountains had contained the silver of Potosí or Mexico.

Moreover, the contrast between utilitarian and medieval traditions

[11] "The colonization of America by Spain was well under way by 1500; that by England was not begun until after 1600. The intervening years were marked by a transformation of European life and culture. This transformation was an integral part of the original heritage of the English colonies, but it was accorded a different reception in the older Spanish colonies" (Silvio Zavala, *New Viewpoints on the Spanish Colonization of America* [Philadelphia: University of Pennsylvania Press, 1943], p. 3).

[12] Mariano Picón-Salas, *De la Conquista a la Independencia* (Mexico: Fondo de Cultura Económica, 1944), p. 47. Perhaps the reader can find a better translation than I for the word "estilo" in the final sentence, which in the original is as follows: "Hasta hoy los pueblos hispánicos no han conocido plenamente el estilo de la economía capitalista."

will not explain the differences between different parts of the areas colonized by the two sets of peoples. Picón-Salas brings into the discussion a different type of British new country, Jamaica. After comparing it unfavorably with Spanish Cuba and Puerto Rico, he makes the following generalization:

If the British were good colonizers when, as in North America, in the South of Australia and in New Zealand, they found lands of temperate climate where it seemed easy to carry over the customs and manners of life of the mother country, they did not display equal cultural strength in the tropics.[13]

To this statement one other contrast should be added. The United States, Australia, and New Zealand were all founded in largely empty lands, in which the native inhabitants could be easily pushed aside; and the bulk of the population, for manual labor as well as for the directive roles, came from European settlement. In British Jamaica, on the other hand, as in Spanish Mexico and Peru or in Portuguese Brazil, the European newcomers came in only at the top, as conquerors, rulers, priests, proprietors, and the like, while the bulk of the manual labor was performed either by the native Indian population or, as in our South, by imported Negro slaves. The conventional terms describing these two types of organization are settlement and exploitation colonies. A recent author, considering the fate of the natives in the former cases, has suggested that they might be described as "extermination" colonies.[14] It is a term which Veblen would have enjoyed adding to his vocabulary.

Adam Smith, as you will recall, declared that "the colony of a civilized nation which takes possession, either of a waste country, or of one so thinly inhabited, that the natives easily give place to the new

[13] *Ibid.*, p. 42.

[14] "The English eliminated the indigenes; the Spanish preserved them as a reservoir of exploited labor. Thus the farm colonies were extermination colonies, whereas the exploitation colony could continue only as long as there were subject peoples left to exploit" (Harold Osborne, *Indians of the Andes* [London: Routledge and Kegan Paul, 1952], p. 165). The terms "farm colony" and "plantation colony" are from A. G. Keller, *Colonization: A Study of the Founding of New Societies* (New York: Ginn, 1908), p. 4. Still earlier, Paul Leroy-Beaulieu, *De la Colonisation chez les Peuples Modernes* (4th ed.; Paris: Guillaumin, 1891), pp. xii–xiii, distinguished between "colonies de peuplement" and "colonies d'exploitation." It should be added that the history of the Maori somewhat distinguishes the case of New Zealand from those of the United States and Australia and that the word "extermination" cannot be taken literally except in the case of Tasmania.

The Case of the New Countries

settlers, advances more rapidly to wealth and greatness than any other human society." [15] May not this, therefore, explain the differences in wealth between the three new nations of settlement origin and the nations of Latin America without the necessity of resort to *mystiques* of English bodies and Spanish souls? A partial test is provided within Latin America itself. Not all parts of it were established as exploitation colonies. Most of the southern part of South America, and smaller areas elsewhere, are regions of recent European settlement in what were almost empty lands. The Mexican historian Silvio Zavala has pointed out that there are more likenesses between the United States and distant Argentina than between the United States and nearby Mexico, and Charles H. Haring declares that "when the Spaniards settled in regions analagous to those of the English mainland communities, the type of colonization, in spite of great differences of political organizations, approximated more nearly that found in the latter." [16]

What, then, can be said of the economic attainment of Spanish regions of settlement origin? Is it like that of the English-speaking settlement countries or like that of the Spanish-speaking countries of exploitation origin? One set of attempted comparisons, Colin Clark's figures for a period before the Second World War, placed the per capita income figures of Argentina and Uruguay very close—I should say surprisingly close—to those of the new countries of British origin. His figures for 1950 still leave Argentina well above other Latin American countries but below most of the nations of Western Europe. The United Nations comparisons place Argentina and Uruguay a little above the next Latin American country but far below the United States, New Zealand, or Australia.[17] In the absence of more precise

---

[15] Adam Smith, *An Inquiry into the Nature and Causes of the Wealth of Nations*, ed. by James E. Thorold Rogers (2d ed.; Oxford: Clarendon Press, 1880), II, 144.

[16] Zavala, *Hispanoamérica Septentrional y Media: Período Colonial* (Programa de Historia de América, II, 3; Mexico: Instituto Panaméricano de Geografía e Historia, 1953), p. 25; Charles H. Haring, *The Spanish Empire in America* (New York: Oxford University Press, 1947), pp. 33–34.

[17] Colin Clark, *The Conditions of Economic Progress* (1st ed., London: Macmillan, 1940; 3d ed., London: Macmillan, 1957), Tables XI and XIX; United Nations, *National and Per Capita Incomes of Seventy Countries—1949* (New York, 1950). Most of Chile, Costa Rica, parts of Colombia, and the São Paulo region of Southern Brazil may also be thought of as "settlement" areas. If figures were isolated for the last of these, they might well prove to be higher than those for Argentina.

information, it appears safe to conclude that the Spanish settlement areas have attained standards of living somewhat higher than those of countries of exploitation origin but not as high as those of the areas of British settlement. If this is so, the settlement-exploitation contrast can account for only a part of the observed differences. Various other factors need to be explored, including the endowment of natural resources; but the analysis leaves ample room for reliance on Veblen's explanation in terms of the traditions and habits of thought derived from British and Spanish sources.

This is a partial answer, but it opens up more unsolved questions than it settles. If the comparisons seem to indicate that economic growth and business activity in the Spanish settlement countries have been inhibited by their heritage from the mother country, what are the means by which the influence has been exerted? Has the limitation been one of unfamiliarity with British industrial techniques and British business practices? This might be true of the earlier history but hardly after Argentina became a great field of British investment in the later decades of the nineteenth century. Does the explanation lie in a set of social valuations which gave greater recognition to achievements in other than economic fields? Or does it lie in the effects of Spanish customs on the class structure? If Argentina had a big man's frontier in the days when meat was the great product of the pampas, like that of sheep-raising in Australia and New Zealand and like our own western plains in the days of the cow country, why did it not develop a frontier of small farmer-owners, like those of the United States and Canada, when wheat took the place of meat as the major product? Can the difference be accounted for by geographical factors, or by social and political influence? How much weight is to be given to the relative helplessness, as compared to the established classes, of the Italian immigrants who became the tenant-cultivators? [18]

Again, the broad comparisons will not of themselves account for striking differences in the development of countries apparently subject to the same influences. Consider the two cases of Argentina and Uruguay, facing each other across the Plate estuary, with similar origins and class structure, with largely similar resources, and each with a large propertyless working class crowding the two cities of

[18] Isaiah Bowman, *The Pioneer Fringe* (New York: American Geographical Society, 1931), p. 303.

The Case of the New Countries

Buenos Aires and Montevideo, as that of Australia had crowded the cities of Sydney and Melbourne. Why should the political response to this situation have taken in one country the orderly form which turned Uruguay without political upheaval into what has been described as "South America's First Welfare State" [19] while in the other the political exploitation of the position of the *descamisados* took the form of the *justicialismo* of Juan and Evita Perón?

A similar set of questions arises when we examine the countries which began as exploitation colonies. At the beginning some of them rose quickly, in defiance of the dictum quoted from Adam Smith, to a level of wealth far surpassing that of any of the humbler settlement areas. An earlier namesake, Captain John Smith, had indeed grumbled at the Spaniards' good fortune and declared that they would have made as "small profit" as the Virginia colony if they had chanced upon a land "as Salvage, as barbarous, as ill-peopled." [20] This refers of course to the earliest days—the date is 1612—but at no time in their history could any of our thirteen colonies afford to construct buildings as magnificent as the Royal Mint of Potosí or the cathedrals of a dozen cities of Spanish America. Yet the wealthiest of these areas declined rapidly after the easily won gold and silver were exhausted, and the later history of the Spanish colonies of exploitation origin became in general one of economic torpor and stagnation, often accompanied by great political instability. How, then, can this be explained? How much of the answer is to be found in a less favorable ratio of population to resources than in the countries of settlement origin? Since the exploitation colonies were never empty areas, have we indeed any reason to expect them to possess economic advantages over populous regions in other parts of the world?

On the other hand, is it not possible to isolate certain institutional factors tending to inhibit the effective utilization of the resources that remained in these countries after their first riches were drawn off?

---

[19] George Pendle, *Uruguay: South America's First Welfare State* (London and New York: Royal Institute of International Affairs, 1952). Note also the titles of Simon G. Hanson, *Utopia in Uruguay* (New York: Oxford University Press, 1938), and Russell H. Fitzgibbon, *Uruguay: Portrait of a Democracy* (New Brunswick, N.J.; Rutgers University Press, 1954).

[20] John Smith, *Description of Virginia and Proceedings of the Colonie* (Oxford, 1612), in Lyon Gardiner Tyler, ed., *Narratives of Early Virginia* (New York: Scribner, 1907), p. 178.

Carter Goodrich

And may not these factors be related to the characteristics of the Spanish heritage as modified or even intensified by the structure of classes in an exploitation colony? One suggestion lies in the social valuations given to different types of distinction or achievement. Prestige and power and social position have come in all these countries from large land-holding and positions in government and in the law, in some of them through the church and in some through the army, and in many through wealth acquired in commerce and dealings in urban real estate. These last are typical areas of pecuniary activity which Veblen often described, and he would have found no difficulty in finding in these countries abundant examples of conspicuous consumption and absentee ownership. But if these are recognizably examples of business enterprise, they differ from the cases described by Veblen and they resemble the cases of many other less developed countries in the fact that it is business enterprise without a great industrial complex over which to preside. There has been little tradition of productive investment, and wealth has only rarely been sought or found in technology or modernized agriculture or manufacturing enterprise. In one extreme case, a small country wholly dependent on mineral exports for its foreign exchange was not long ago graduating lawyers annually from each of seven universities but producing only two or three mining engineers a year!

Since the favored occupations are so largely continuations of the roles performed by the Europeans in the early days of the conquest, may not these preferences in part be attributed to the colonial heritage? In certain areas the institutions of the early conquerors were perpetuated in the survival, as late as the middle of the twentieth century, of a system of land tenure under which the Indian rendered four or five days of unpaid labor to the landlord in return for the right to cultivate a little piece of land for the subsistence of his own family. It would be hard to devise a system providing less incentive to either side for innovation or for the economical use of the factors of production. Even short of such extreme cases, the heritage from colonial times appears to survive in something of a scorn of physical labor on the part of the upper classes and in sharp limitations on the economic opportunities and consequently on the incentives of the underlying population. In most of the nations that have grown from the former exploitation colonies, there remains a great gulf between the predom-

The Case of the New Countries

inantly white ruling classes and the underlying mass of the Indian—or in some countries Negro—population. May not these long and deep-seated cleavages within these nations represent one of the major barriers to economic progress? If so, there is reason for watching with special interest the development of two countries that have undergone revolutions having as one objective the incorporation of the Indian in the national life—Mexico, which did this so long ago that its revolutionary party has had time to change its name to the Party of Revolutionary Institutions, and Bolivia, in which the revolution is much younger and more precarious.[21]

III

The suggestions from which I have attempted to profit were thrown out by Veblen somewhat casually on his way toward the examination of "The Case of America." I have followed their lead only a short way, yet far enough—I hope—to suggest two conclusions. The first is that the economic development of new countries is a fruitful field for comparative study, that their stories show sufficient likenesses and sufficiently striking variations to make comparisons both possible and suggestive.[22] The second is that, in making such comparisons, the Veblenian insights into the transmission of institutional heritages should be supplemented and qualified by the analysis of differences in geography, in occupational distribution, and in other areas of matter-of-fact observation.

[21] Carter Goodrich, "The Economic Transformation of Bolivia," New York State School of Industrial and Labor Relations, Cornell University, Ithaca, New York, *Bulletin 34*, Oct., 1955. It should be noted that entrance into the "predominantly white ruling classes" of individuals with Indian or Negro ancestry is more common than is usually realized in the United States.

[22] This point is made very persuasively by Zavala in the passage on "The Comparative Method" in *Hispanoamérica*, pp. 32–35. Each of the countries, he points out, has had to "penetrar la tierra nueva, fundar los establecimientos, comerciar con la metropolí, independizarse." The specific reference is to the countries of the Americas, but in another passage (p. 24) he refers also to the British colonies in the Antipodes.

[DOUGLAS F. DOWD]

16

Technology and Social Change: Japan and the Soviet Union

VEBLEN was always primarily concerned with what he called "the main drift"—or, more elegantly, the process of social change. This was true even in his methodological attacks on conventional economics, where the brunt of his criticism was that such economics fell short of even beginning to explain where the economy—and thus, for Veblen, the society—was heading.[1]

I

For Veblen, society was in a process of continuous change. Such change has many and diverse origins, but the fundamental origin, as Veblen saw it, was the conflict between technology and social institutions. He saw technology as possessing an inner dynamic, stimulating ceaseless "social mutations," but social institutions as possessing an inner sluggishness, providing resistance to change. Technological change enables, requires, and may be encouraged by or retarded by institutional changes. To take a simple example, machine production enables and requires a specialized labor force and large-scale busi-

[1] In this respect, as in so many others, Veblen wrote in the tradition of Marx. But Veblen and Marx may be contrasted as often as they may be compared. See the essay in this volume by Forest G. Hill, Article 8.

ness organization; and the latter, in turn, may speed up or retard the application of the machine technique.[2]

If this were all that Veblen had to say on the matter, we would not be discussing him here. He was not concerned solely, or even most importantly, with the impact of technology upon economic institutions; he was always concerned with the social framework, with the quality and direction of society in the large. His position was that the working out of a given technology—and this was almost always the industrial technology—required and stimulated the creation of a complementary, suitable set of economic, social, and political institutions. To say "required" is not to say, for Veblen, that the "required" would necessarily or even probably come about, for he, of all social scientists, was impressed with the force of the traditional, the irrational, in social development. But he was also impressed with the intense and unremitting pressure put upon existing institutions by technological change. To block the development of those social institutions "required" by the industrial technology, Veblen thought, would in turn require an atavistic institutional turn, amounting to counterrevolution. The kind of thing he had in mind we have seen all too much of since 1915. Its most perfect expression was Nazi Germany.

It was not Veblen's habit to put things succinctly, or even unequivocally. He did not develop a "system of thought," a "theory" of economic or social development, or a "model." He was, however, a great generalizer, and there is, on any given question, a recurring pattern to his generalizations. That pattern, as it refers to the relationship between technology and social change, finds vivid and effective expression in his essay "The Opportunity of Japan,"[3] written

---

[2] For present purposes, technology may be defined as the field of relationships which stand between man and nature; social institutions as the field of relationships which stand between man and man. (There are, of course, those areas where technology and institutions mesh and combine in such manner as to make attempts to distinguish them from each other pedantic.) The former, for Veblen, may be thought of as arising mainly but not solely out of man's "providential instincts"; the latter as arising mainly but not solely out of man's "predatory instincts." See the essays in this volume by C. E. Ayres and Myron W. Watkins, Articles 3 and 14.

[3] First published in the *Journal of Race Development*, VI (July 1915); reprinted in Veblen's *Essays in Our Changing Order*, ed. by Leon Ardzrooni (New York: Viking, 1943), pp. 248–266. All quotations from Veblen in what follows are taken from this essay unless otherwise indicated.

Technology and Social Change

in 1915. In this essay Veblen comes as close as he ever did to compressing his thoughts on the determinants and direction of "the main drift."

Characteristically—and, I would add, desirably—the general principles of Veblen's thought are expressed with respect to a concrete case, rather than as a "general theory." It is nevertheless possible to use his analytical approach to Japan as the basis for an estimate of the "main drift" in other countries. The present essay will attempt this for the case of the Soviet Union. After examining the main outlines of "The Opportunity of Japan," we will use basically the same approach to guide an examination of the Soviet Union and will conclude with a consideration of certain relevant probabilities in the United States, which, as will be argued below, an estimate of the direction of affairs in Russia requires.

II

Although the conclusions Veblen draws from his study of Japan are startling, nothing of "fact" in the essay is in any sense novel or esoteric. Veblen is concerned to examine the nature of the "New Japan"—the Japan which existed after Meiji Restoration of 1868.[4] Before Veblen's argument is outlined, a few comments on the general meaning of the Restoration may be helpful.

Imperial Japan and imperial Germany had many things in common, among which one may count crude interpretations of their recent histories. Just as it has been too often assumed that Germany of a sudden "began" to industrialize in 1871, it has been assumed that Japan, with the Emperor restored, "began" its process of industrialization. In both countries, of course, there had been a long and slow process of gradual accumulation of skills, capital, "social overhead," and other ingredients of industrialism, *and* of political pressures pushing toward a new social resolution. These, taken together with external stimuli, combined to force a major political change, which in turn cleared the way for a speeding up of the "preparatory" social processes. In both countries industrialism grew rapidly during and

[4] The reader unfamiliar with the outlines of modern Japanese economic development will find a useful summary in G. C. Allen, *A Short Economic History of Modern Japan, 1867–1937* (London: Allen and Unwin, 1946).

Douglas F. Dowd

after the last quarter of the nineteenth century; in both countries under the auspices of a still dynastic, essentially medieval, guiding spirit.[5]

Specifically, for Japan, this meant changes conducive to commercialization and industrialization—comparable in many ways to those emerging from the revolutions in England and France in the seventeenth and eighteenth centuries: changes in land tenure and the formal abolition of feudalism; changes in tax policy; the lifting or modification of restrictions on communications, movement, and trade, on property, class mobility, and the like. But in addition, the Japanese state took an active role in aiding, encouraging, and subsidizing developments in transportation, agriculture, finance, education, foreign travel, and trade, and even in owning and developing (if only temporarily) certain strategic industries, to mention only the most important of its activities. Altogether, a deliberate movement to industrialize and to westernize—ending the long-standing policy of isolation and exclusion—was undertaken by the government, co-operating closely with private parties of power and substance. In Japan, even more than elsewhere, where public interest began and private ended, in time or in function, would have been difficult to say. As Veblen put it,

power vests in a self-appointed, self-authenticating aristocratic cabinet—under the mask of a piously nourished monarchical fiction—with the advice, but without the consent, of a "parliament" endowed with advisory power. This bureaucratic organ of control is still animated with the "Spirit of Old Japan," and it still rests on and draws its force from a population animated with the same feudalistic spirit.

It is in this unique combination of a high-wrought spirit of feudalistic fealty and chivalric honor with the material efficiency given by the modern technology that the strength of the Japanese nation lies.

All of this, as Veblen saw it, was the pouring of the new wine of modern industry into the old bottle of feudalism.

It is . . . only in respect of its material ways and means, its technological equipment and information, that the New Japan differs from the old. That superficial reorganization and amelioration of its civil and political insti-

[5] See Veblen's *Imperial Germany and the Industrial Revolution* (New York: Viking, 1946) for his analysis of Germany—an analysis basically similar to the one under consideration here.

Technology and Social Change

tutions that went into effect in the Restoration has not yet had time to remove the spiritual landmarks of feudalism or appreciably to weaken the servile-aristocratic bias that still guides the intrigues of the court circle, the policies of state, and the larger maneuvers of diplomacy.

The metaphor of wine and bottle will not hold for this relationship, however; for the technology and the institutions of a society may not be looked at as merely resting one within the other, as one ages. They are in a constant state of interaction; both wine and bottle change. The wine of modern industry ultimately requires its own, new bottle. Since social institutions are the ways in which men adapt their behavior (and their standards) to their environment and their means of existence, the institutional framework—in the absence of deliberate and comprehensive manipulation—is bound to "give" under the impact of a new technology.

The "Spirit of Old Japan" is an institutional matter; that is to say it is a matter of acquired habits of thought, of tradition and training, rather than of native endowment peculiar to the race. As such it is necessarily of a transitory, not to say transient, nature, depending for its maintenance on the continued maintenance of those workday habits of life out of which it has arisen and to which it owes it consistency.

In speaking of the "Spirit of Old Japan" Veblen refers to that "spirit" as it affects all segments of the population, those who constitute its "vested interests" *and* those who make up the "underlying [i.e., exploited] population." For society as a whole, the new technology offers its possibilities and makes its demands.

It should . . . confidently be presumed that, as Japan has with great facility and effect taken over the occidental state of the industrial arts, so should its population be due, presently and expeditiously, to fall in with the peculiar habits of thought that make the faults and qualities of the western culture—the spiritual outlook and the principles of conduct and ethical values that have been induced by the exacting discipline of this same state of the industrial arts among the technologically more advanced and mature of the western peoples. For good or ill, life under the conditions imposed by the modern industrial system, and by that economic system of price, business enterprise, and competitive earning and spending that always goes with it, is in the long run incompatible with the prepossessions of medievalism.

As for the militaristic component of the "old spirit," it would give way relatively quickly, as a new outlook, and more concretely, as new opportunities for the expenditure of energy and talent, would grow and multiply.

As soon as her people shall have digested the western state of science and technology and have assimilated its spiritual contents, the "Spirit of Old Japan" will, in effect, have been dissipated. Ravelings of its genial tradition will still trail at the skirts of the new era, but as an asset available for the enterprise in dynastic politics, the "Spirit of Old Japan" will have little more than the value of a tale that is told.

There will doubtless continue to float through the adolescent brains of Young Japan some yellow vapor of truculence, such as would under other skies be called *el valor espanol,* and such as may give rise to occasional exploits of abandon, but the joy of living in obscure privation and contumely for the sake of the Emperor's politics and posthumous fame will be lost to the common man.

In the realm of economic institutions, industrialism clearly sets forth a whole series of imperatives, if it is to thrive and grow. These "imperatives" make themselves felt most critically in the outlook, organization, and purposes of the business community, the size, quality, and outlook of the labor force, and in the changing interaction between the government and the economy. More specifically, in Veblen's words,

effectually to turn its usufruct of the western science and technology to account, it will be necessary for Japan, in all essential respects, to follow the lead given by the western peoples. [For,] the modern state of the industrial arts involves a certain kind and degree of popular education, and a certain impersonal, mechanistic organization and coordination of the material equipment (mechanical and human) and of the processes employed; . . . because nothing like the full advantage of the methods employed can be had except by entering into close relations of give and take, commercially and otherwise, with the other nations that have adopted the scope and method of mechanical industry. . . . But the unintended consequences of such a course must also follow. So, a competent system of communication, internal and external, is of the essence of the case, and in this matter the Japanese are already far on their way, with steamships, railway, telegraph, telephone, postal service, and newspapers, as well as an improved and extended system of highways.

With the breakdown of isolation, self-sufficiency, and localized cultures, there would also break down one of the necessary elements

Technology and Social Change

of "feudal fealty." Furthermore, in order for an industrial system to operate within reasonable bounds of efficiency, it is necessary for at least the rudiments of education to be imparted to the working force

This involves schooling . . . [and] the familiar use of printed matter. (It may be noted by the way that the percentage of illiteracy among the Japanese has fallen off since the Restoration at a rate that is fairly alarming for the stability of the established order.)

But more than simple literacy is involved. One of Veblen's favorite axioms was that life under the industrial system tends to promote "a matter-of-fact, and especially a materialistic, habit of mind,"

such as comports ill with those elusive putative verities of occult personal excellence in which the "Spirit of Old Japan" is grounded. . . . The spread of such matter-of-fact information and such mechanistic conceptions must unavoidably act to dissipate all substantial belief in that *opéra bouffe* mythology that makes up the state religion and supplies the foundation of the Japanese faith in the Emperor's divine pedigree and occult virtues; for these time-worn elements of Shinto are even less viable under the exacting mechanistic discipline of modern industry than are the frayed remnants of the faith that conventionally serve as articles of belief among the Christian peoples.

The business community itself, though (as in Japan) it may in general find itself in sympathy with, or even the promoter of, dynastic ambitions, will in its own activities, according to Veblen, come increasingly into conflict with the state at critical junctures. But the co-operation of the business community, both as producer and seller, is required if Japan's rulers are to be able to "turn to account" the modern technology for dynastic ends. "Incompetent, or even puerile, as this commercial enterprise may seem when seen in the large and taken as a means of the international co-ordination of industry," Veblen wrote, "it still affords the sole method available for the purpose" of achieving modern industry in the context of a commercialized world economy.

With the development of industry, and of a business community to run it, his individual welfare comes to be the dominant consideration of the businessman, and "so it throws pecuniary solvency into that position . . . that has once been occupied by pedigree and putative excellences of character." Business enterprise "does not directly contemplate or concern itself with serviceability to national, dynastic, or collective ends of any kind. It is a matter of individual enterprise, animated by motives of pecuniary gain."

This pecuniary enterprise that so comes necessarily to take the oversight of the industrial system has certain specific consequences, secondary but essential, which the Japanese community has not yet experienced in full, because the secondary effects of the industrial revolution in Japan have not yet had time to come to a head. The most obvious of these . . . is what might be called the "sabotage" of capitalism—the competitive working at cross purposes of rival business concerns and the control of industrial processes by considerations of net gain to the managers rather than of material serviceability.

The upshot of this development for Japan would be what it had been in other industrial countries, "equipment—rarely, if ever, worked to its capacity—often, over long intervals, at less than one half its capacity." Moreover, apart from the efficiency of the economic system, the goods chosen for production will be "turned out with a view, in respect of kind, time, place, and sophistication, to their profitable sale rather than to their serviceable consumption."

As business enterprise grows, its principles of behavior come to dominate the entire society, and with it the distribution of income and the composition of production, with debilitating consequences for dynastic means and ends:

with competitive gain as the legitimate end of endeavor comes also competitive spending as its legitimate counterfoil, leading to a ubiquitous system of "conspicuous waste." With this canon of right pecuniary living, reinforced by the new ethical principles of self-help and commercial solvency, comes in as a bench-mark in public life the well-worn principle of modern politics that "public office is a means of private gain." Hence the comprehensive system of "graft" that envelopes all civilized affairs of state. . . . So, again, through the competitive wage system, as well as by other channels of commercial indoctrination, the same principle of competitive consumption comes to permeate the industrial population and presently induces a higher standard of living, or more accurately of expenditure; which cuts into the disposable margin of production above cost, that might otherwise be drawn to the service of imperial politics.

If, as Veblen did, we may take the aims of the private and public rulers of the New Japan to be some combination of military strength,

Technology and Social Change

international prestige, geographical expansion, and private gain, the question then arises: for how long could the lingering social framework of the Old Japan be kept together under the effects of the powerful solvent of developing industrialism? Writing in 1915 Veblen thought that it was "still safe to say that hitherto the rate of gross gain in material efficiency due to the new scientific and technological knowledge is more than sufficient to offset [the] incipient spiritual deterioration." But,

if this new-found efficiency is to serve the turn for the dynastic aggrandisement of Japan, it must be turned to account before the cumulatively accelerating rate of institutional deterioration overtakes and neutralises the cumulatively declining rate of gain in material efficiency; which should, humanly speaking, mean that Japan must strike, if at all, within the effective lifetime of the generation that is now coming to maturity. . . . In order to an (imperialistically) successful issue, the imperial government must throw all its available force, without reservation, into one headlong rush; since in the nature of the case no second opportunity of the kind is to be looked for.

The Japanese did strike within the "effective lifetime of the generation [then] coming to maturity," and it is now clear that "no second opportunity of the kind is to be looked for." The lack of such a "second opportunity" may doubtless be attributed in part to the devastating defeat suffered by the Japanese in World War II; but well before that defeat Japanese society was coming to fulfill Veblen's prediction of "spiritual deterioration." By the mid-1930's, or even earlier, the business community (including the *zaibatsu*) was becoming ever more restive under the dynastic aegis; a labor and socialist movement was gaining significant strength; and the pressures for democratization had become widely evident.

To summarize, Veblen argued that the Japanese, bent on industrialization, could achieve that end relatively quickly. Among the many reasons for this were "the advantages of coming late," and the ability of the Japanese state to regard its people as "chattels, to be bred, fed, trained, and consumed as the shrewd economy of dynastic politics [might] best require." But the progress of the industrial technology carries as its price the adaptation of the society to a new institutional framework, one stimulating the development of commercialism and individualism, and emphasizing the cash nexus. The latter goals are incompatible with the "Spirit of Old Japan"—militaristic, nationalistic, honorific—and with its predatory aims. This "spirit" and its accompanying goals could be matched with the strength of modern technology only within a limited period of time—before the growth of modern industry had created new aspirations and new outlets for the economic, political, and social energies of the people. To wait longer would be for Japan to lose her advantage over the other industrial nations, or perhaps to lose her ability to make war at all, except upon extreme provocation.

The second stage of Veblen's ideas in this general area tends to confuse the issue as regards Japan. In "The Opportunity of Japan" he is concerned to show the development of a business society as ultimately inimical to dynastic ends. Occasionally in this essay, but quite generally in his other writings, he suggests or states flatly that in an even more advanced stage of capitalist development the business community will develop an active interest in the exacerbation of international animosities (and war), as a means of diverting the attention of the "underlying population" from the social costs—inefficiency, chronic tendencies toward depression, and the like—of absentee ownership. Within this stage business has come into full conflict with industry, and salesmanship with workmanship (to use Veblen's terminology); within this stage business will be inclined to manipulate the social framework atavistically—i.e., to return to the trappings of "feudalism" in order to stave off what Veblen called "the industrial republic."

III

How can the method of Veblen's analytical approach to Japan be applied to the Soviet Union? At the outset, it need hardly be said that the physical and institutional dissimilarities between Old Japan and Czarist Russia were many and profound, as are the major institutional and ideological differences between the New Japan and the Soviet Union.[6] But the similarities between the two nations, es-

[6] Clearly, since its economic institutions are socialist, not capitalist, the Soviet leaders have little to fear from the "debilitating influence" of business on the maintenance of the Soviet version of dynastic use and wont. But, as will be argued below, the rhetoric of communism and the impact of industrialism, taken together, may work toward the same end.

Technology and Social Change

pecially relating to the question at hand—what is the "main drift" in the Soviet Union?—are important and striking.

On the factual level, both countries deliberately industrialized at a rapid pace under centralized direction of varying degrees, both emerged late from a backward technological and institutional framework, both aimed at national industrial (and associated military) strength and international prestige. On the analytical level, this essay will assume one other basic similarity, the pressures toward a general reconciliation between the developing, modern industrial technology and the nations' social institutions.

The developments in no country in modern history have caused so much hope and fear, so much adulation and criticism, so much disappointment and shock, as have those in the Soviet Union. Sympathizers with the Revolution have tended persistently to overestimate the rate and degree of advance in standards of living and in "political morality"; hostile critics have persistently tended to underestimate the rate and degree of industrial and military achievements. Sympathizers appear to have been misguided by an implicit or explicit belief that a revolution could quickly and easily obliterate the force of accumulated tradition; critics seem, on the other hand, to have assumed that successful industrial development could be induced only within an institutional framework modeled on that of Great Britain or the United States (and often with the implied corollary that the developments of those countries were painless). Either set of beliefs requires a monumental indifference to what we know of the past.

It has been too easily forgotten that the outlook and behavior of the Russian Soviet leaders was initially determined more by their Russian background and environment than by their ideological commitments (even taking into account the substantial contribution to repressive techniques provided by Stalinism). The raw materials of economic development in the Russia of 1917—whether in terms of its people or its technology—were backward, except for a few islands of western influence and modern industry. Add to its economic limitations, and an autocratic and repressive political tradition, an illiterate population committed to a well-entrenched religion, and it becomes clear that much had to be overcome if industrialization and an institutionally modern society were to be achieved; so much needed to be overcome that no matter how the society were organized there

Douglas F. Dowd

would remain the necessity for sheer passage of time, to allow for the emergence of new generations of leaders and for the conditioning of the "underlying population" to modern ways and means.

A reasonably objective estimate of the shortcomings of the Soviet development requires that a large share of the responsibility be allotted to the economic, political, and social base in existence in 1917 —a base scarcely calculated to make the industrialization process easy or swift. If we remember, too, that prerevolutionary industrialization was financed in large part by foreign capital, which was entirely cut off after the Revolution, the problems facing the Soviet industrialization process are seen in their appropriate, difficult perspective. And even under the best "institutional" circumstances the quality and location of resources, considering Russia's vast distances, posed a knotty problem.

The first decade of the Soviet experiment can only be characterized as chaotic, fumbling, and hasty, as embodied in the periods of so-called War Communism and the New Economic Policy (1921–1927). The N.E.P. was apparently a recognition by the Soviet leaders—primarily Lenin—of the need to move slowly, if there was to be movement at all. It is equally probable that the initiation of the five-year plans in 1928 and all that went with them—particularly the collectivization of agriculture—was an outcome of the belief that not only the slow rate of development under N.E.P. but also its quality —of favoring the interests of the *petite bourgeoisie* and the kulak farmers—demanded that, if further errors were to be made, they be made by progressing too fast rather than too slowly.

After the Revolution, as before it, the small surplus available for the development of industry in Russia stemmed from primary production, particularly in cereals. The stimulus to productivity in agriculture provided by the commercialism of the N.E.P. yielded positive results, but the bulk of agriculture remained backward in its techniques, most of the increased production was absorbed in (to the Soviet leaders) undesirable ways, and the bulk of the peasantry remained backward in its outlook. If rapid industrialization were to be the goal, the Draconian steps embodied in the first five-year plan were probably necessary. It should be said, also, that the ruthlessness, the terror, and the oppression which accompanied the technological and institutional changes in collectivization and planning were at one

Technology and Social Change

with the traditions of Czarist Russia—although all this was doubtless carried out more efficiently by the Soviet leaders than by the Czars.

Industrial development, whether before or after the first five-year plan, was inefficient and messy, often approaching the level of low comedy. What else might have been expected of a nation attempting to run and to man modern factories with professional revolutionaries at the top and a mass of people at the bottom who may still have believed the earth to be flat, one can hardly say. Without pausing more than this for the well-known details of the first decade of planning in the Soviet Union, one may hazard the judgment that what was remarkable was not the numerous failures in economic affairs, but that there were any successes at all. And there were some successes, even if we look only at the considerable economic effort put forth by the Russians during World War II. Since that time, of course, there can be no doubt of the Soviet industrial achievement.

How are its achievements to be explained, given all the obstacles posed by the Russian physical and social environment? First, the Soviet Union possessed the kind of advantage Veblen made much of in his discussions of Japan and Germany, the advantage of coming late: the late-comer can borrow the newest, most advanced technology from the early industrial leaders and adopt it *de novo*, free from the resistance of vested interests, sunk costs, and the like. Secondly, by now it should be clear that the system of economic planning used by the Russians since 1928, although it contained, and still contains, many imperfections, was doubtless well-suited to the task of reorganizing and developing a geographically vast, backward economy —particularly through its ability to emphasize the rapid growth of heavy industry at the expense of consumption.

By the time of World War II the new technology, economic planning, and ideological and nationalistic exhortation combined somewhat successfully to provide the Soviet Union with a substantially developed industrial economy. But for the Russian people, as for the Japanese, the advantages of this achievement were largely potential, not realized. The emphasis on the development of heavy industry prior to 1938, combined with substantial military production since that time, kept consumer goods production, as is well known, to a level much below what it might have been. (But it may be argued that the long-run potential for consumer goods production is now considerably higher, for that reason.) Political control became tighter, rather than looser, during and after the late twenties, and the progress of industrialization made it easier, rather than more difficult, for such controls to become more rigid (as the international situation became more tense).

Having sketched the general background, we might ask, what of the present and the future? Several critical developments since World War II must be examined if such a question is to be answered. One can only speculate on the inner workings of the Soviet Union, of course, but the observations following appear to be consistent with what we do know of Soviet affairs in particular and of social affairs in general. They are also consistent with Veblen's approach to such questions.

Much has been made of the significance of Stalin's death in 1953 in terms of its having brought to power a new leadership—whether for better or for worse need not detain us at this point. But, to paraphrase an old saying, if Stalin had not died a natural death, an unnatural death would have been invented for him. For whatever changes have taken place in the Soviet Union since 1953 were under way before that time, and they have been brought about by strong, underlying, pervasive pressures within the Soviet Union, and by those bearing on the Soviet Union from outside.

There has been in the last few years a shift in the major power structure of Soviet society. In Stalin's time the three major sources of power were, in descending order of importance, the secret police, the Communist party, and the military. Since his death, the secret police has apparently been relegated to a functional, as distinct from a policymaking, role. At the present time, the army has been placed in a secondary position to the party, but it may be expected that the continuing power struggle in the Soviet Union will be between the now dominant party and the still powerful military group.

The secret police was an integral part of the Czarist structure of power, and it fitted easily into the conspiratorial, totalitarian nature of the Soviet regime. The most important reasons for its relative demise doubtless have to do with the politics associated with Stalin's death. That the new leadership group was not drawn from the secret police, which had earlier been most powerful, may be explained in part by the familiar ganging-up process of the two weaker parties to

Technology and Social Change

a tripartite grouping; but more importantly it points to (1) the tremendous importance of the military in the cold-war situation and (2) to the ability of the Communist party to hold power by means less and less dependent on terrorism. The latter is the key factor in assessing Soviet probabilities.

Not only does the Communist party have the ability to maintain (and extend) its power by virtue of the now powerful economy under its control, but also it is under various internal and external pressures to use that power in a manner which may be deemed beneficial. We may take the strength of the Soviet economy for granted, most observers would agree. But what are the "internal and external pressures" just mentioned? Here Veblen's approach becomes most helpful.

"Sheer time" has passed. The Revolution took place just over forty years ago. It may be assumed that the greater part of the present Soviet population was born after 1917. Moreover, for present purposes, that number would probably reach something like 75 per cent of the whole if we were to add those who entered adolescence after the Revolution. This percentage then includes most of the adults in the Soviet Union, which is to say, most or all of the future, and many of the present, leaders. All these people grew up under the rhetoric—i.e., the promises—of socialism, and they are largely attuned to the "workday habits" of industrial society. The slogans of the Soviet Communists—whatever their performance may have been—have promised and emphasized economic abundance, social welfare, cultural advance, and political freedoms. It is highly doubtful that these promises could have been fulfilled until just recently if the economy was to be industrialized as rapidly as it has been. It is highly probable that the promises could be fulfilled now or in the very near future without undue economic strain and without damaging the position of the Communist party (assuming the party were responsible for initiating such changes). It is even more probable that the Soviet people are increasingly aware of the possibilities inherent in the present Soviet economy, increasingly vexed by regimentation, and increasingly determined to see that promises, possibilities, and realities draw together.

It is not, of course, the promises which have changed in the past forty years; it is the objective situation. Immediately after 1917, and during the 1920's, military and persistent economic crises could be

Douglas F. Dowd

used as a justification for postponing Utopia—which could not have been realized in any case at that time. In the 1930's, the needs associated with basic industrialization, and the threat and actuality of war, again served the function of providing a rationale for shortages and repression. In the 1940's, war, reconstruction, and the cold war provided the sufficient basis for delay. But in the last few years these negative rationalizations have virtually disappeared (except the cold war), while simultaneously the Russian people have grown less willing to tolerate the gap between the promised and the real.

Economic difficulties remain in the Soviet Union, of course—as where do they not?—but they are now the kind that enable or require relaxation, rather than tightening, of institutions. Witness, for example, the recent moves to decentralize economic planning and the abolition of machine tractor stations. Whether or not these steps, or others of the same quality, will "work," the Soviet leaders now apparently feel able to take a more flexible attitude toward their institutions and able to risk a more reasonably organized economy. The weak cannot afford to take risks.

As for war, the cold war continues, but its economic demands upon the Soviet Union grow smaller rather than larger (as a percentage of its total output). More importantly, the Soviet Union is increasingly able, and appears to be increasingly inclined, to make its effort in the cold war more along economic than along military and conspiratorial lines. As its economic strength increases, there is less reason, at least, for it to rely on subversion and coercion and more promise of success vis-à-vis the "uncommitted" countries from a combination of economic and political achievements at home and economic aid abroad.

All these "pressures," of course, must be evaluated in terms of their impact upon a political oligarchy. How may the Soviet leaders be expected to react to these internal and external pressures? The two major alternatives should be clear: (1) a successful capture of power by the military (formally or otherwise), yielding a continuation, or even worsening, of the Soviet domestic scene in its totality and the heightened possibility of war; (2) the maintenance of control by the Communist party, substantively as well as formally—which is to say, for present purposes, attention by the Soviet leaders to the positive promises of the Communist ideology.

The emergence of the latter alternative would entail the gradual

Technology and Social Change

softening of political institutions and the improvement of living conditions within the Soviet Union and an increasingly peaceful competition for the loyalties of uncommitted nations. Internal pressures and the possibilities existent in the underdeveloped world are likely to push the Soviet Communist party in such a direction. We may assume that Khrushchev and those aligned with him are interested primarily in the maintenance of their own power; but it is necessary at the same time to recognize that the Communist leaders do subscribe to an ideology the explicit goal of which is human betterment. Where moves in that direction are both possible and expedient, such moves fall into the realm of probability. Most would agree that Khrushchev is an opportunist, that he would gladly hold power under varying circumstances; but in today's context he might well see that his best means of holding and solidifying power would be to improve domestic conditions and extend increased aid (already growing rapidly) to the underdeveloped countries.

But the first alternative of increasing militarism and nationalism would become the more probable to the degree that, as recently, the cold war becomes "warmer"—thereby giving the upper hand to those in the Soviet Union who are inclined toward the garrison state. If this is true, the role played by the United States in the cold war becomes critical in the determination of the "main drift" in the Soviet Union.[7]

The United States cannot, of course, directly affect the internal affairs of the Soviet Union; but the United States can affect the international environment with which the Soviet Union is intimately concerned, and it can significantly alter the terms upon which the cold war is fought.

IV

It may be argued on the one hand that a deliberate and straightforward effort to mitigate pressing social problems in the United States as well as serious American co-operation with other nations to solve their own economic problems would push the Soviet Union

[7] For a different view of the main drift in the Soviet Union, though still seen through a Veblenian approach, see the suggestions contained in the essays by Myron W. Watkins and Carter Goodrich in this volume, Articles 14 and 15.

Douglas F. Dowd

in the same direction, and on the other hand that an intensification of the military effort by the United States in the cold war would be likely to push the Soviet Union farther in that direction. Which path is the United States likely to take?

It should be clear to all that our enormous productive capacity enables us to move in either direction—or in both simultaneously—with little if any strain. We are constrained in what we do, or wish to do, not by production limitations, but by institutional (including attitudinal) considerations. Economically, we are easily able, for example, to take significant steps toward the improvement of living conditions in our own country, and we are able to contribute much to international economic health and to economic development abroad.

Although the United States is materially capable of moving along such lines, there are severe institutional obstacles to its doing so. The most important of these were foreseen by Veblen as early as 1904, in his *Theory of Business Enterprise*. Of all societies, he says, ours is the business society par excellence; our outlook is dominated by emulation and by an invidious, competitive materialism. Our basic optimism—provided with second thoughts only intermittently by economic crises—has led us to adopt a naïve individualism. Practical deviations from individualism (in the form, e.g., of social security) have come grudgingly, and late, and have been inadequate. We have built an almost unbelievably productive economy; but its health is now crucially dependent upon what Veblen termed unproductive consumption and unproductive public expenditures—upon what he might today have termed "inspired waste." The largest percentage of Americans have easy access to economic plenty, but our social outlook is ill suited to the problems presently confronting us and the rest of the world. We are enthralled, in a word, by what Veblen called "imbecile institutions." [8]

The paths we must take, if we are to induce the Soviet Union to move in directions desirable to us, are not in any sense impossible for us; but they are improbable for the predictable future. Persons besieged on all sides by threats of personal unhappiness if their con-

---

[8] Various of the essays in this volume make it unnecessary to spell out the present interpretation of probabilities (and problems) in the United States. See particularly those by Paul M. Sweezy and G. W. Zinke, Articles 10 and 17.

Technology and Social Change

sumption habits do not conform, and by national disaster if their nation falters in its military preparations, are unlikely to be sensitive to the higher demands of these times.

What makes this situation particularly tragic, if it is so, is that the American people have, as underlying attitudes, a strong sense of generosity, of decency, and of good will. The United States is probably the first nation in history to have achieved a stage of technological advancement that provides it with the ability—if not yet the will—to relax its concentration on questions of domestic economic scarcity. We are now objectively able to develop a systematic and effective policy toward issues requiring an ethical and co-operative outlook on national and international social problems.

Good reasons for such a turn in our outlook are abundant apart from any considerations having to do with the Soviet Union. But, if the preceding analysis of the "main drift" in the Soviet Union is correct, these "good reasons" take on compelling force.

For Veblen, of course, the existence of a compelling, "desperately precarious" institutional situation gave no guarantee that a people would rest on its "instinctive insight and save itself alive." On the contrary, cumulative causation and blind drift—not reason—is for Veblen the force behind social change. If this is correct, the outlook for the United States, and therefore for world peace, is a gloomy one. For the ideological emphasis and the institutional situation in the United States have been, and seem likely to remain, pointed in almost precisely the opposite direction from that which is most likely to support our, and the world's, life interests.

Perhaps Veblen will forgive us if, as we celebrate his hundredth birthday, we hope that he was wrong.

[G. W. ZINKE]

17

Veblen's Macroinstitutionalism

AN as yet largely unexplored aspect of Veblen's work is his conception of the meaning of technological change. He views it, not as a quantitative achievement, but in relation to the quality of institutionalized human behavior. A meaningful evolution of the industrial arts requires the quality of individual human performance—always group determined—to be for the common good in the sequence of new industrial situations. This is illustrated in the following summary quotation:

The state of the industrial arts requires that [all participants in the economic process] should cooperate intelligently and without reservation, with an eye single to the exigencies of [the] modern wide-sweeping technological system; but their habitual addiction to pecuniary rather than technological standards leaves them working at cross purposes.[1]

As a result of the pecuniary orientation, "workmanship comes to be confused with salesmanship, until tact, effrontery and prevarication have come to serve as a standard of efficiency, and unearned gain is accepted as a measure of productiveness." To salesmanship may be added the wastemanship of many lines of public expenditures designed to enhance the common glory rather than the common good. The effect is that wastemanship, public or private "intrudes into the most intimate and secret workings of the human spirit and contaminates the sense of workmanship in its initial move, and sets both the

[1] This and the two following passages are from *The Instinct of Workmanship* (New York: Huebsch, 1922), pp. 348, 349, 350.

proclivity to efficient work and the penchant for serviceability at cross purposes with the common good."

Veblen was always careful to remind his readers that the phenomenon of economic pressure groups working at cross purposes to the common good does not interdict the physical growth of output, income, and employment. The manner in which the common good is damaged by pecuniary and/or political emulation is qualitative. An example of this tendency in recent times was reported by George Gallup, Director of the American Institute of Public Opinion, in 1947:

> The chief complaint against employers is not what you might expect—low wages. More people named a broader, more inclusive fault. It is summed up in one reply from a white collar worker in a Pittsburgh steel company whose comment was typical of thousands in the survey: "Management hasn't got enough understanding of working people and their problems. Businessmen keep thinking of labor as a commodity instead of as human beings. The reason people join unions is because they feel that the boss won't pay any real attention to the welfare of the worker if left to himself. He's got to be forced to do things." [2]

What things? The quotation makes it clear that the great source of industrial tension is the conflict between the perception by the worker of his co-operative role in production and the scheme of industrial management, pecuniarily oriented. The worker is given only such information and allowed only such limited participation in the conduct of the enterprise as behooves an enlightened management to furnish in order to reduce absenteeism and turnover. For instance, in one large, "welfare-minded" enterprise the workers can obtain all the information they wish to ask for, but are discouraged from developing economic information on their own initiative. It is preferred that they should spend such funds as they have for the purpose of improving their recreational facilities, installing bowling alleys, having more outings, and the like. The reward for this all-and-none-questioning loyalty is a complex wage structure. This is internally so delicately "balanced" and revisable as to accommodate, in practically every respect, the petty pecuniary jealousies which a businesslike environment breeds in workers. Thus the common good is damaged even while production records are broken.

[2] New York *Times*, April 12, 1947.

Macroinstitutionalism

The qualitative corruption of man's natural bent for easygoing but informed co-operation is also manifested in the case of other participants in direct production and by consumers. World War II witnessed an extensive pooling of patents and sharing of strategic raw materials, but with the resumption of the normal scheme of life, production managers could be found who were gloating over supply shortages encountered by competitors. In later years consumers, subjected to the "hard sell," intensified their habitually wasteful consumption. They did this to the point of young mothers going to work in order to afford "obligatory social amenities" ill-designed to furnish an equal measure of genuine family satisfaction. Production rolled off the lines, but slums remained, as did juvenile delinquency and racial and international hatreds. The material basis of life was served quantitatively as never before, but as never before were the institutional elements so at variance with a viable utilization of technology and therefore at variance with the continued life interests of the community or civilization.

Veblen remains unique as an economic theorist who deals straightforwardly with the topic of the economic conditions of cultural decline. Marx had of course raised the issue, and by the turn of the century theories of cultural decline had appeared or were in the making. However, Marx's revolutionary activism, and the supporting reasoning of dialectics, kept him in the traditional concept of progress. Veblen does not abandon this traditional conception or continue in it. He simply considers it irrelevant.

Veblen deprives any economic institution whatsoever of the attribute of inherent stability. Instead, institutions are regarded as manifestations of adaptive variability or lack of it; in the latter case they are "imbecile institutions." In Veblen's view, any particular institution, and the complex of contemporary institutions, is the effect of antecedent social variations. These in turn are caused by earlier variations. There is no final cause which results in any given structure of economic organization, no essential reason for it. A given institutional structure is most likely to be the result of small-order deviations from some previous pattern of social behavior. The deviations, cumulatively reinforcing each other over historical time, may constitute a powerful social drift in the course of which economic production and consumption may become oriented in untoward directions. Thus, in Veblen, cumulative causation, with or without social purpose, takes the place of moving equilibrium or dialectic. The institution of private property is his prime case in point. All-pervasive in Veblen's time, it "appears to have cumulatively grown out of the self-regarding bias of men in their oversight of the community's material interests." [3]

The question always is whether a community can change its institutions in viable concomitance with environmental variations, natural or man-made. To argue that a given institution is well established because it has legal force may only be arguing for force to preserve maladapted behavior patterns. "What can be argued on the ground of cause and effect," says Veblen, "is the question as to what scheme of economic organization will help or hinder the survival of a given people or a given civilization." [4]

A scheme of economic organization rests on the logical relations of people's concepts of reality. Veblen follows Immanuel Kant in believing that such knowledge of reality as we have is subjective. That is to say, real objects exist and make direct impressions on the senses. Such logical relations as we presume to exist between real objects are, however, imputed by the human mind. In the process of imputing logical relations among real objects we tend to overlook the act of imputation and thus regard the imputed relations to the objects themselves, *as qualities of the objects.*[5]

Among external objects to the cognitive individual are of course other human beings. It may happen that an individual, or group of individuals, imputes qualities to another individual or group of beings. If these imputed qualities do not correspond to the matter-of-fact experiences of the persons to whom certain qualities are imputed, stresses arise in the community which may threaten it with elimination. This is illustrated by the current state of the world community.

Thus it follows that the economic problem of survival is pre-eminently a qualitative one. Quantitative accounts become meaningful only in terms of whether or not the quality of production, the direction of industry, is in viable correspondence with the matter-of-fact

[3] *Instinct of Workmanship,* p. 24n.
[4] *The Place of Science in Modern Civilisation* (New York: Viking, 1932), pp. 444–445.
[5] Veblen, *Essays in Our Changing Order* (New York: Viking, 1945); see the paper on "Kant's Critique of Judgment," pp. 175–193.

Macroinstitutionalism

survival requirements of any given social situation. For example, a $435 billion gross national product in 1957 may not have the same qualitative survival meaning as that same amount would have in a year during which there might be little or no "defense" production. Even in such a hypothetical year of unarmed peace we should have to distinguish between the production of goods which only intensify people's nervous anxieties and what John Ise calls "creative goods"—those which serve in building a richer and finer future. The 1928 gross national product, for example, would have to be diminished by many billions in an account of creative production.

Beyond this, allowance should be made for the quality of people's work experience—whether they understand and therefore can appreciate their role in the economy's "division of labor." This is an almost purely qualitative consideration, but a gross national product of $435 billion would be a hollow mockery in a slave state and does not have a true ring under the actual circumstances of production.

The economic problem, in qualitative terms, is capable of easy solution in a primitive society which produces only a bare minimum of subsistence, with all the members of the society working together. The qualities imputed by the members of such a society, to each other, closely correspond to the matter-of-fact relations between them. On the margin of subsistence an injury to one is quite apparently an injury to all. The scheme of economic organization is "naturally" co-operative.

Co-operative production and distribution can continue although a community develops a technology which permits it to produce an increasing surplus over creature needs by the division of labor. Only when the surplus is produced in a form capable of being privately hoarded and raided can a person's penchant for being community serviceable be overshadowed and/or confused by the motive of self-aggrandizement. Then it becomes possible for some people to seek differential advantage over others in the enjoyment of the usufruct of the community's technology. By differential advantage is meant a reward exceeding the measure of community-serviceable contribution. Obviously, all people cannot get ahead of each other. In the end production is co-operative.

Indeed, it is the nature of technology to become ever more based on productive co-operation, therefore more indivisible. This is the matter-of-fact reality. Growing surpluses of production, however, permit a sense of differential reality to develop in individuals and groups of individuals. A modern illustration is the official classification of dividends as income arising out of production. The recipient may consider this as a realistic description, but a reflective assembly-line worker is apt to have a different sense of reality in this connection. (The worker's matter-of-fact reflection may of course be blunted by exhaustion or be contaminated by a search to establish his own differential advantage, i.e., undue claim to income over and above the income received by maintenance workers.)

Differential reality conceptions set class against class, as Marx argued, and ultimately man against man, as Veblen delineated. Since man moves in a social environment, the anxiety to belong in a higher status category even sets man against himself—he becomes ashamed, e.g., of being "born on the wrong side of the billboard." The restless urge to "get ahead" of others and, in a manner of speaking, of oneself, undoubtedly contributes to the alarming increase of nervous breakdowns in our day.

Being institutionalized, differential reality quite obviously leads to a qualitative deterioration of community life. A pecuniary economic organization in which usufruct of the community's technology can be privately "capitalized," aids and abets people in rationalizing experience in terms of differential reality. Products are judged by their price, and men by their incomes. This means that the emphasis is on the division of the social product, differentially, rather than on its cooperative origin.

Countervailing tendencies may exist, as when the mere bulk of output surplus is such as to permit dispensing, e.g., with child labor. Young people are then encouraged to attend school. There they may find opportunities for creative self-expression and come to appreciate the matter-of-fact reality of the common good. This is provided, of course, that they are able to escape involvement in the many activities which sharpen their inherited sense of differential status. There is abundant evidence that quantitative growth of national output may add to the quality of individual and community life.

At best, however, a purely quantitative approach can only furnish the basis of a comparison of the rate at which community-serviceable production and consumption exceeds or lags behind the rate of waste

Macroinstitutionalism

in production and consumption. A qualitative judgment is required for drawing the distinction which lies at the heart of the quantitative comparisons necessarily involved in appraising the viability of the scheme of economic organization. From the standpoint of adaptive variability, no complex of institutions can escape this test.

Quality is directly correlative to quantity, positively so or negatively. To illustrate, it is common practice to identify an old-age pension in terms of a greater or lesser number of dollars at different times or in different places. Seen from a quantitative point of view, a pension of $100 per month may appear ample, as compared, e.g., to the earnings of people as yet at work, or to old-age allowances in the past or elsewhere, or as viewed in the context of projected tax revenues or regional or national income trends.

It is equally logical to identify the old-age pension in terms of its adequacy for meeting the particular survival needs of aged persons. Seen from this qualitative point of view, the pension of $100 per month might, however, leave unsolved actual problems of the aged person. One problem may be the lack of a specialized health service systematically organized to provide for categories of accidents and health deterioration peculiar to old people. In the absence of such specialized provision, an undRecoverable large part of the apparently ample $100-per-month pension may have to be dissipated in meeting medical bills. There may be a problem of an untoward scarcity of centrally located one-story housing, forcing the aged to pay unduly high rentals in order to enjoy housing which obviates the hazards of stairs or to live within reach of general community activities of a social nature.

It will be recognized that many contributions of modern institutionalism have been made precisely by establishing qualitative criteria for subsequent factual investigations of the economic feasibility of social legislation. Characteristically, the criteria have been raised and the investigations made in respect to particular institutions. Modern institutionalism is pre-eminently "microinstitutionalism." It is pragmatic and operates primarily on a case-by-case basis.

Veblen's institutionalism is by comparison characteristically "macroinstitutional." Like Karl Marx, Veblen addresses himself to the entire complex of economic institutions; he is concerned primarily with their interrelations. Thus he comes to grips with the entire "standard of living." The American standard of living, he points out, "is of a very elastic nature, capable of an indefinite extension." The driving force is emulation in expenditure. "In a general way, the need of expenditure in this direction grows as fast as the means of satisfying it, and, in the long run, a large expenditure comes no nearer satisfying the desire than a smaller one." So it eventuates that "the chief value in many articles of apparel, for instance, is not their efficiency for protecting the body, but for protecting the wearer's respectability; and that not only in the eyes of one's neighbors but even in one's own eyes. Indeed, it happens not very rarely that a person chooses to go ill-clad in order to be well-dressed." [6]

This qualitative demonstration of wastemanship in consumption is supplemented with impressive symmetry by a theory of wastemanship in production. From the supply side, price is determined not only by the technical coefficients of production but in addition by surcharges which only serve to allocate ownership claims on the usufruct of the community's technology—selling and finance costs, expense accounts, and so on. The technical coefficients of production are, in Paul A. Samuelson's words, only "shadow prices." Just so, on the demand side of price, a simple calculus of satisfaction is far in the background of the highstrung behavior of the emulative consumer buying goods or being persuaded to do so. As Herbert J. Davenport said, "price is just price"; it is remotely, and in some cases not at all, related to value when this is seen in the context of community survival. It is this imputation of community serviceability, a matter of the common good, which distinguishes value theory from price theory.

The classical concept of absolute value makes it appear as a quality of objects, regardless of the exchange relations of products.[7] The quality of objects, however, is a projection of the human mind, as has been shown. The capacity for reflective judgment operates, in economic matters, in terms of the state of the industrial arts. "This is a fact of group life, not individual or private initiative or innovation." [8] Hence a

[6] *Place of Science,* pp. 394–395.

[7] It is interesting to note that Alfred Marshall's discussion of value is confined to two pages of the *Principles,* in the course of which discussion he disposes of intrinsic value by stating: "Experience has shown that it is not well to use the word in (this) sense." Instead, "the price of anything will be taken as representative of its exchange value relatively to things in general, or in other words as representative of its general purchasing power." See, *Principles of Economics* (8th ed.; London: Macmillan, 1930), pp. 61–62.

[8] Veblen, *Instinct of Workmanship,* p. 103.

Macroinstitutionalism

projection of economic quality to goods and services, by individuals, must refer to conditions of social relations among the owners and exchangers of commodities and services. Marx made this clear in a humorous fantasy of coats yearning for buttons and tables for chairs. The fantastic nature of this illustrates the value-void of things *in esse suo*. However, if a theory of value reflects a preoccupation with the conditions of the common good, it may be implied without being doctrinally formulated. Marx pointed out to a correspondent that *Das Kapital* constitutes a theory of value even with the deletion of the chapters on the labor theory of value.

Veblen's writings constitute exactly this, a theory of value without specific doctrinal construction. One of the results is that what for Marx is surplus value appears simply as surplus product in Veblen. But it is the same idea. And both surplus value and surplus product are the essence of David Ricardo's concept of unearned rental income under competition and of Adam Smith's unearned monopoly income. The connecting link is the apperception of the quality of performance of economic institutions for or against the common good.

There follows a précis of the qualitative strand in classical economic thought. Veblen's macroinstitutionalism does not, of course, represent a substantive continuity with classical value theory; nor does it lay the foundation of a modern theory of value. However, if it is indeed essentially related to the classical tradition, Veblen's work is the point at which we can pick up the presently neglected qualitative strand of speculative economic thinking. The urgency to resume value theory is great, for both the classical economists and Veblen showed that value theory, which combines qualitative and quantitative analysis, brings to the fore the matter-of-fact reality of the economic world community—and points to the need for peace to sustain it.

There are few instances in the history of economic thought of a writer of great repute treating the work of another author of stature with the well-nigh loving care with which Veblen discussed Adam Smith. Leo Rogin has shown that Smith's grand theme of the natural advance of society lent reasoned support to a practical advocacy, to a program of policy and action. Smith recommended that British institutions be so reformed as to permit an increasing abundance of articles of staple mass consumption.[9] In several of his writings Veblen

---

[9] Leo Rogin, *The Meaning and Validity of Economic Theory* (New York: Harper, 1956), p. 106.

shows how Smith could believe, under the circumstances of his time, that an abundance of "wage-goods" might be secured by individual self-help, equality of opportunity, and free bargaining.

To Smith, production was essentially person-centered, not machine-paced; he conceived of industrial relations as highly personalized, because of both owner-management and the close contact of producers with their markets. The emphasis, in Smith, is on "the creative workman who makes things with his hands" or at least knows how to do it. To the workman "belongs an efficiency and merit of a peculiar substantial and definitive kind, he is the type and embodiment of efficiency and serviceability." [10] His bent for money-making is socially useful, for it is conceived as serving community-serviceable production. "And human relations outside of the workshop tend also by force and habit to be conceived in similar terms of self-sufficient individuals, each working out his own ends in severalty." [11]

Under conditions of creative person-centered production Smith could logically argue for policy to allow people free access to opportunities for profit-making. Observe that Smith in advocating this was not simply opposed to mercantilistic government intervention. In 1749, long before he wrote the *Wealth of Nations,* he had this to say: "Man is generally considered by statesmen and projectors as the materials of a sort of political mechanics. Projectors disturb nature in the course of her operations in human affairs." [12] Projector is an appellation of speculative promoters and manipulative financiers—persons who, in Veblen's terminology, operate on business principles without a motivating interest in production.

This was no simple cry for antimonopoly and antispeculation. Smith's approach is qualitative throughout. He made self-improvement the mainspring of healthy social evolution, by contrast with the Physiocrat's paternalistic approach. Smith did not originate a cult of individualism. He was aware of what Veblen later articulated: "The scheme of technological insight and proficiency current in any given culture is manifestly a product of group life—and manifestly the individual workman is helpless without access to it." [13] Adam Smith

---

[10] Veblen, *Instinct of Workmanship,* p. 243.   [11] *Ibid.,* p. 234.

[12] Stated in the course of a lecture series at Edinburgh. See Dugald Stewart, *Memoir of Adam Smith* (Edinburgh, 1811), p. 100.

[13] *Instinct of Workmanship,* p. 138.

believed that this access would be facilitated by offering people unhampered opportunities for profit-making. However, he never confused profit motivation, a means of economic organization, with the end of organization, namely, the advancing, enriched culture of the people. To object that Smith's profit motivation seems ill-designed to foster community-serviceable production and creative work experience is to ignore that his contemplated structure of production was person-centered and did not require heavy capital outlay, so that the technology was relatively accessible. That this conceptual quality of production was being superseded by the machine industry, which he observed in the making, renders Smith's organon relatively invalid even for his time, but nonetheless meaningful. One might well ask whether we are facing automation in Smith's qualitative perspective or the massive future quantities of gross national product.

David Ricardo struck out boldly in the Smithian tradition. His "labor-embodied theory of value" should have carried him to the heart of the relationship of technology and institutions. This is the qualitative meaning of his battle for the liberation of industry from neofeudalistic bondage to the land and its squirearchy. However, Ricardo's labor-embodied theory of value is profit-oriented in a technical sense. Piero Sraffa and M. H. Dobb explain:

The problem of value which interested Ricardo was how to find a measure of value which would be invariant to changes in the division of the social product; for, if a rise or fall of wages by itself brought about a change in the magnitude of the social product, it would be hard to determine accurately the effect on profits.[14]

The Ricardian analysis converges on the abolition of the corn laws as a means of elevating industrial profits. Elaborately he argues that wage pressures induced by a high cost of living (owing to grain import restriction) do not raise prices but diminish profits. However, as Rogin shows, the central predicament of Ricardo's England was the unregulated pursuit of private acquisition.

To this problem Ricardo did not dedicate his great talent for analysis. In Parliament he voted against a bill to secure minimum wages and labor standards for seamen; and, although he voted for

[14] *The Works and Correspondence of David Ricardo* (Cambridge, Eng.: University Press, 1951), I, xlviii.

Robert Owen's co-operation proposals, Ricardo allowed Owen to be humiliated before Parliament—instead of giving him the benefit of the Ricardian genius for speculative reasoning. The only noticeable exception in this regard is Ricardo's change of mind on the subject of the adverse impact of mechanization. Ricardo asserts that the trade unions are justified by the principles of political economy in their anticipation that technological displacement will, *ceteris paribus*, undermine wages. A qualitative note is struck when Ricardo predicts that technological displacement will doom many laborers to employment as menial servants. This insight notwithstanding, Ricardo does not proceed to a critique of the institutional arrangements under which such an eventuation is predictable.

Although Ricardo did not depart from an articulate qualitative appreciation of the contemporary problem of economic organization, the circumstances of the time invest his analysis and policy advocacy with strong qualitative implications. Under the circumstances he was arguing for the common good, for matter-of-fact reality against the oppressive differential status of decaying neofeudalism and residual mercantilism.

There is scarcely a need for elaborating on John Stuart Mill as the flower of the classical tradition, including for the purpose of this appraisal his articulate carrying forward of the qualitative strand of that tradition. His famed distinction between the technical nature of the laws of production and the human nature of the laws of distribution is well known. He argues for productive co-operation, for the reality of the common good. To illustrate, he envisions "the association of the labourers themselves on terms of equality, collectively owning the capital and working under managers elected and removable by themselves."[15] To government he assigns a creative role:

> Even in the best state which society has yet reached, it is lamentable to think how great a proportion of all the efforts and talents in the world are employed in merely neutralizing one another. It is the proper end of government to reduce this wretched waste to the smallest possible amount, by taking such measures as shall cause the energies now spent by mankind in injuring one another, or in protecting themselves against injury, to be turned to the legitimate employment of the human faculties, that of compelling the

[15] J. S. Mill, *Principles of Political Economy* (Ashley ed.; New York: Longmans, Green, 1923), pp. 772–773.

Macroinstitutionalism

powers of nature to be more and more subservient to physical and moral good.[16]

The question of Karl Marx's belonging to the ranks of economists has sometimes been held to be controversial. To this writer this is not a question concerning Marx, but rather a matter of defining economics. Because another study in this volume treats Marx and Veblen, it will suffice to point to the qualitative contribution of Marx.

Marx embodies economics as a central consideration in the philosophy of man and reality. Human mind and nature are represented as reciprocally determining, interpenetrating aspects of objective reality. This is conceived as a creative process. Human labor is the mediating agency in the productive relationship of man and nature. It is this relationship which constitutes objective reality; hence man cannot be conceived as having passively to accept the operation of external forces. There is no outside material basis of life which predetermines man's economic scheme of life. In none of its aspects does Marxist historical materialism constitute a theory of the psychological motivation of man passively responding under the one-way impact of natural forces.

The reciprocal interaction of man and nature implies that there is no natural necessity for men to be divisive in their efforts. There are no natural laws of economics to this effect, no blind natural forces whose divisiveness man must accept. The blindness is on the part of man, wrought by institutional arrangements which deny some men access to technology, to co-operation, fraternity, to conscious control of society based on scientific insight and learning. Historical materialism exposes the institutional roots of supposedly natural economic forces. Historical materialism attacks commodity fetishism, which imputes value to things in abstraction from the man-nature relationship they reflect—and eventuates in representing human labor in abstraction from the materials through which it must find expression.

Thus in Marx the qualitative strand of the classical tradition converges upon what J. W. Cohen calls the externalization of man. Marxism denies the sanction of natural necessity or realism to any

[16] J. S. Mill, *Principles of Political Economy* (1st American ed.; Boston: Charles C. Little & James Brown, 1848), II, pp. 559–560.

institutional scheme which blocks access to the productive man-labor relationship or which misrepresents individuals or groups as standing outside the history that their perceptions tell them they are helping to make. In Veblenian terms, externalization of man means imposing, by force or corruption, a scheme of differential reality not confirmed by matter-of-fact observation. Currently we know that this raises problems not only for capitalism but also in nations which are striving toward socialism.

Externalization of man is a phrase which summarizes the thesis of the present essay: the qualitative strand of the classical tradition, as delivered to us by Veblen, can and must enliven future research. This suggests procedure along three main lines:

1. Qualitative standards should be applied to the scientific investigation of community needs, as in the procedure used for studying community resources. Most economic studies of consequence, e.g., those of the National Resources Committee, have been preoccupied with the adequacy of resources to meet quantitatively described needs and have dealt with the qualities of the needs only inferentially. The present suggestion is for qualitative specification of needs on their own and on scientifically established merits. An example of this was the advocacy during the depression of handicraft-type industries and Danish-type folk schools to be established in agricultural areas using migratory labor. This advocacy proceeded from the consideration of the need of workers, old and young, to be identified with a settled, if varied, productive relationship. The proposal could not have been justified at the time in terms of location theory or immediate commercial-spending multiplier effects, yet analogous experience (in Norway, e.g.) shows qualitative departures to be economically feasible.

2. Macroinstitutional studies can be made for a local community, a region, or a nation, to serve as a basis for understanding the qualitative needs which arise for different segments of the population as the result of economic change. The problem of the blighted urban area furnishes an example. Qualitatively and comprehensively viewed in terms of the total economy inclusive of ex-urbanites, this presents difficulties and opportunities alike. Some of these are not directly perceptible in terms of financial and physical resources as ordinarily appraised; e.g., blighted areas at the core of a city, offer the opportunity of making centrally located, one-story, well-spaced housing

Macroinstitutionalism

available to meet the previously mentioned qualitative needs of aged people.

3. A most immediately valuable application of macroinstitutionalism can be made in giving guidance to foreign aid policies. Efforts to impose on underdeveloped areas such schemes of development as might be based on our customary perceptions of price relationships would be fantastic. It would result in foreign projects which never break ground; appropriations would be consumed largely in wasted administrative planning here and abroad. Only a value approach will do, i.e., one sensitive to those viable elements of community life in the foreign area that can be developed. Macroinstitutional analysis of the area sets the stage for fruitful policy and for its scientific and quantitative implementation.

[JOSEPH DORFMAN]

Bibliography of Veblen's Writings

1884. "Kant's Critique of Judgment," [1] *Journal of Speculative Philosophy,* July, pp. 260–274.
1891. "Some Neglected Points in the Theory of Socialism," [2] *Annals of the American Academy of Political and Social Science,* Nov., pp. 345–362.
1892. "Böhm-Bawerk's Definition of Capital and the Source of Wages," [1] *Quarterly Journal of Economics,* Jan., pp. 247–252.
"'The Overproduction Fallacy,'" [1] *Quarterly Journal of Economics,* July, pp. 484–492.
"The Price of Wheat Since 1867," *Journal of Political Economy,* Dec., pp. 68–103 and appendix pp. 156–161.
Review of Thomas Kirkup's *A History of Socialism,* in *Journal of Political Economy,* March, pp. 300–302.
Review of Otto Warschauer's *Geschichte des Socialismus und Communismus im 19. Jahrhundert,* in *Journal of Political Economy,* March, p. 302.
"The Food Supply and the Price of Wheat," *Journal of Political Economy,* June, pp. 365–379.
Review of B. H. Baden-Powell's *The Land-Systems of British India,* in *Journal of Political Economy,* Dec., pp. 112–115.

[1] Republished in T. Veblen, *Essays in Our Changing Order,* ed. by Leon Ardzrooni (New York: Viking, 1934).

[2] Republished in T. Veblen, *The Place of Science in Modern Civilisation and Other Essays* (New York: Huebsch, 1919).

Bibliography

1894. Review of Karl Kautsky's *Der Parlamentarismus und die Volksgesetzgebung und die Socialdemokratie*, in *Journal of Political Economy*, March, pp. 312–314.

Review of William E. Bear's *A Study of Small Holdings*, in *Journal of Political Economy*, March, pp. 325–326.

"The Army of the Commonweal,"[1] *Journal of Political Economy*, June, pp. 456–461.

Review of Joseph Stammhammer's *Bibliographie des Socialismus und Communismus*, in *Journal of Political Economy*, June, pp. 474–475.

Review of Russell M. Garnier's *History of the English Landed Interest (Modern Period)*, in *Journal of Political Economy*, June, pp. 475–477.

Review of Émile Levasseur's "L'Agriculture aux États-Unis," in *Journal of Political Economy*, Aug., pp. 592–596.

"The Economic Theory of Woman's Dress,"[1] *Popular Science Monthly*, Nov., pp. 198–205.

1895. Review of Robert Flint's *Socialism*, in *Journal of Political Economy*, March, pp. 247–252.

The Science of Finance, translation of Gustav Cohn's *System der Finanzwissenschaft* (Chicago: University of Chicago Press).

1896. Review of Karl Marx's *Misère de la philosophie*, in *Journal of Political Economy*, Dec., pp. 97–98.

Review of Enrico Ferri's *Socialisme et science positive*, in *Journal of Political Economy*, Dec., pp. 98–103.

1897. Review of Richard Calwer's *Einführung in den Socialismus*, in *Journal of Political Economy*, March, pp. 270–272.

Review of G. de Molinari's *La Viriculture—Ralentissement de la population—Dégénérescence—Causes et remèdes*, in *Journal of Political Economy*, March, pp. 273–275.

Review of Antonio Labriola's *Essais sur la conception matérialiste de l'histoire*, in *Journal of Political Economy*, June, pp. 390–391.

Review of Werner Sombart's *Sozialismus und soziale Bewegung im 19. Jahrhundert*, in *Journal of Political Economy*, June, pp. 391–392.

Review of N. Ch. Bunge's *Esquisses de littérature politico-économique*, in *Journal of Political Economy*, Dec., pp. 126–128.

Review of Max Lorenz' *Die Marxistische Socialdemokratie*, in *Journal of Political Economy*, Dec., pp. 136–137.

1898. Review of Gustav Schmoller's *Über einige Grundfragen der Socialpolitik und der Volkswirtschaftslehre*, in *Journal of Political Economy*, June, pp. 416–419.

[1] Republished in *Essays in Our Changing Order*.

Bibliography

Review of William H. Mallock's *Aristocracy and Evolution: A Study of the Rights, the Origin and the Social Functions of the Wealthier Classes,* in *Journal of Political Economy,* June, pp. 430–435.

"Why Is Economics Not an Evolutionary Science?" [2] *Quarterly Journal of Economics,* July, pp. 373–397.

"The Instinct of Workmanship and the Irksomeness of Labour," [1] *American Journal of Sociology,* Sept., pp. 187–201.

Review of Turgot, *Reflections on the Formation and the Distribution of Riches,* in *Journal of Political Economy,* Sept., pp. 575–576.

"The Beginnings of Ownership," [1] *American Journal of Sociology,* Nov., pp. 352–365.

"The Barbarian Status of Women," [1] *American Journal of Sociology,* Jan., pp. 503–514.

1899. *The Theory of the Leisure Class: An Economic Study of the Evolution of Institutions;* title changed in 1912 to *The Theory of the Leisure Class: An Economic Study of Institutions* (New York: Macmillan).

"The Preconceptions of Economic Science," [2] *Quarterly Journal of Economics,* Jan., pp. 121–150; July, pp. 396–426; Jan., 1900, pp. 240–269.

Review of Simon Patten's *Development of English Thought,* in *Annals of the American Academy of Political and Social Science,* July, pp. 125–131.

"Mr. Cummings's Strictures on *The Theory of the Leisure Class,*" [1] *Journal of Political Economy,* Dec., pp. 106–117.

1900. Review of Sir William Crooks's *The Wheat Problem, Revised, with an Answer to Various Critics,* in *Journal of Political Economy,* March, pp. 284–286.

Review of Arnold Fischer's *Die Entstehung des socialen Problems,* in *Journal of Political Economy,* March, pp. 286–287.

Review of Paul Lafargue's *Pamphlets socialistes: Le droit à la paresse; La religion du capital; L'appetit vendu; Pie IX au paradis,* in *Journal of Political Economy,* March, pp. 287–288.

Review of G. Tarde's *Social Laws; An Outline of Sociology,* in *Journal of Political Economy,* Sept., pp. 562–563.

Review of Basil A. Bauroff's *The Impending Crisis; Conditions Resulting from the Concentration of Wealth in the United States,* in *Journal of Political Economy,* Dec., pp. 159–160.

Science and the Workingmen (New York: International Library),

---

[1] Republished in *Essays in Our Changing Order.*
[2] Republished in *Place of Science in Modern Civilisation and Other Essays.*

Bibliography

a translation of *Die Wissenschaft und die Arbeiter* by Ferdinand Lassalle. Republished by German Publication Society in *The German Classics*, 1914, vol. 10.

1901. "Industrial and Pecuniary Employments," [2] *Publications of the American Economic Association*, Series 3, pp. 190–235.

"Gustav Schmoller's Economics," [2] *Quarterly Journal of Economics*, Nov., pp. 69–93.

1902. "Arts and Crafts," [1] *Journal of Political Economy*, Dec., pp. 108–111.

Review of Jules Gernaert and Vte. de Herbais de Thun's *Associations industrielles et commerciales: Fédérations—Ententes partielles—Syndicats—Cartels—Comptoirs—Affiliations—Trusts*, in *Journal of Political Economy*, Dec., pp. 130–131.

Review of G. Tarde's *Psychologie économique*, in *Journal of Political Economy*, Dec., pp. 146–148.

1903. "The Use of Loan Credit in Modern Business," *Decennial Publications of the University of Chicago*, Series 1, No. 4, pp. 31–50, republished without substantial change in *The Theory of Business Enterprise*.

Review of Werner Sombart's *Der moderne Kapitalismus*, in *Journal of Political Economy*, March, pp. 300–305.

Review of T. H. Aschehoug's *Værdi-og Prillærens Historie*, in *Journal of Political Economy*, March, p. 306.

Review of Maurice Lair's *L'Impérialisme allemand*, in *Journal of Political Economy*, March, p. 306.

Review of J. A. Hobson's *Imperialism: A Study*, in *Journal of Political Economy*, March, pp. 311–319.

Review of Brooks Adams' *The New Empire*, in *Journal of Political Economy*, March, pp. 314–315.

Review of Theodore E. Burton's *Financial Crises and Periods of Industrial and Commercial Depression*, in *Journal of Political Economy*, March, pp. 324–326.

Review of Lester F. Ward's *Pure Sociology: A Treatise concerning the Origin and Spontaneous Development of Society*, in *Journal of Political Economy*, Sept., pp. 655–656.

Review of Ludwig Pohle's *Bevölkerungsbewegung, Kapitalbildung und periodische Wirtschaftskrisen*, in *Journal of Political Economy*, Sept., pp. 656–657.

Review of S. Tschierschky's *Kartell und Trust: Vergleichende Unter-*

---

[1] Republished in *Essays in Our Changing Order*.
[2] Republished in *Place of Science in Modern Civilisation and Other Essays*.

Bibliography

suchungen über dem Wesen und Bedeutung, in *Journal of Political Economy*, Sept., pp. 657–658.

1904. "An Early Experiment in Trusts,"[2] *Journal of Political Economy*, March, pp. 270–279.

The Theory of Business Enterprise (New York: Scribner's).

Review of Adam Smith's *An Inquiry into the Nature and Causes of the Wealth of Nations*, in *Journal of Political Economy*, Dec., p. 136.

Review of Francis W. Hirst's *Adam Smith*, in *Journal of Political Economy*, Dec., pp. 136–137.

Review of Jacob Streider's *Zur Genesis des modernen Kapitalismus*, in *Journal of Political Economy*, Dec., pp. 120–122.

1905. Review of Robert Francis Harper's *The Code of Hammurabi, King of Babylon about 2250 B.C.*, in *Journal of Political Economy*, March, pp. 319–320.

"Credit and Prices,"[1] *Journal of Political Economy*, June, pp. 460–472.

1906. "The Place of Science in Modern Civilisation,"[2] *American Journal of Sociology*, March, pp. 585–609.

"Professor Clark's Economics,"[2] *Quarterly Journal of Economics*, Feb., pp. 147–195.

"Socialist Economics of Karl Marx and His Followers,"[2] *Quarterly Journal of Economics*, Aug., pp. 578–595; Feb., 1907, pp. 299–322.

1907. Review of Sidney A. Reeve's *The Cost of Competition, An Effort at the Understanding of Familiar Facts*, in *Yale Review*, May, pp. 92–95.

"Fisher's Capital and Income,"[1] *Political Science Quarterly*, March, pp. 112–128.

1908. "The Evolution of the Scientific Point of View,"[2] *University of California Chronicle*, May, pp. 396–416.

"On the Nature of Capital,"[2] *Quarterly Journal of Economics*, Aug., pp. 517–542; Nov., pp. 104–136.

1909. "Fisher's Rate of Interest,"[1] *Political Science Quarterly*, June, pp. 296–303.

Review of Albert Schatz's *L'Individualisme économique et sociale: Ses origines—son évolution—Ses formes contemporaires*, in *Journal of Political Economy*, June, pp. 378–379.

"The Limitations of Marginal Utility,"[2] *Journal of Political Economy*, Nov., pp. 620–636.

[1] Republished in *Essays in Our Changing Order*.
[2] Republished in *Place of Science in Modern Civilisation and Other Essays*.

Bibliography

1910. "Christian Morals and the Competitive System," [1] *International Journal of Ethics*, Jan., pp. 168–185.

"As to a Proposed Inquiry into Baltic and Cretan Antiquities," memorandum submitted to Carnegie Institution of Washington, published in *American Journal of Sociology*, Sept., 1933, pp. 237–241.

"The Mutation Theory, the Blond Race, and the Aryan Culture," paper submitted to Carnegie Institution of Washington and later elaborated into the two papers published in 1913.

1913. "The Mutation Theory and the Blond Race," [2] *Journal of Race Development*, April, pp. 491–507.

"The Blond Race and the Aryan Culture," [2] *University of Missouri Bulletin, Science Series*, Vol. 2, No. 3, April, pp. 39–57.

1914. *The Instinct of Workmanship and the State of the Industrial Arts* (New York: Macmillan).

1915. "The Opportunity of Japan," [1] *Journal of Race Development*, July, pp. 23–38. *Imperial Germany and the Industrial Revolution* (New York: Macmillan).

1917. "Another German Apologist," review of *England, Its Political Organisation and Development and the War against Germany*, by Eduard Meyer in *Dial*, April 19, pp. 344–345.

An Inquiry into the Nature of Peace and the Terms of Its Perpetuation (New York: Macmillan).

"The Japanese Lose Hope for Germany," [1] letter to *New Republic*, June 30, pp. 246–247.

"Suggestions Touching the Working Program of an Inquiry into the Prospective Terms of Peace," [1] memorandum submitted to a House inquiry, through Walter Lippmann, Dec., published in *Political Science Quarterly*, June, 1932, pp. 186–189.

"An outline of a Policy for the Control of the 'Economic Penetration' of Backward Countries and of Foreign Investments," [1] memorandum for a House inquiry published in *Political Science Quarterly*, June, 1932, pp. 189–203.

1918. "On the General Principles of a Policy of Reconstruction," *Journal of the National Institute of Social Sciences*, April, pp. 37–46; republished in part as

"A Policy of Reconstruction," [1] *New Republic*, April 13, pp. 318–320.

Report ad interim to Raymond Pearl on trip through prairie states in behalf of Statistical Division of Food Administration, published in *American Economic Review*, Sept., 1933, pp. 478–479.

---

[1] Republished in *Essays in Our Changing Order*.
[2] Republished in *Place of Science in Modern Civilisation and Other Essays*.

Bibliography

"Passing of National Frontiers,"[1] *Dial*, April 25, pp. 387–390.

"Using the I.W.W. to Harvest Grain,"[1] memorandum for Statistical Division of Food Administration, published in *Journal of Political Economy*, Dec., 1932, pp. 796–807.

"A Schedule of Prices for the Staple Foodstuffs,"[1] memorandum for Statistical Division of Food Administration, published in *Southwestern Social Science Quarterly*, March, 1933, pp. 372–377.

"Menial Servants during the Period of the War,"[1] *Public*, May 11, pp. 595–599.

"The War and Higher Learning,"[1] *Dial*, July 18, pp. 45–49.

The Higher Learning in America, A Memorandum on the Conduct of Universities by Business Men (New York: Huebsch).

"Farm Labour and the Country Towns," memorandum for the Statistical Division of the Food Administration, published in an elaborated form as:

"Farm Labour for the Period of the War,"[1] *Public*, July 13, pp. 882–885; July 20, pp. 918–922; July 27, pp. 947–952; Aug. 3, pp. 981–985.

"The Modern Point of View and the New Order," *Dial*, Oct. 19, pp. 289–293; Nov. 22, pp. 349–354; Nov. 16, pp. 409–414; Nov. 30, pp. 482–488; Dec. 14, pp. 543–549; Dec. 28, pp. 605–611; Jan. 11, 1919, pp. 19–24; Jan. 25, pp. 75–82. Republished as:

1919. *The Vested Interests and the State of the Industrial Arts*. Title changed in 1920 to *The Vested Interests and the Common Man* (New York: Huebsch).

"Bolshevism Is a Menace—to Whom?"[1] *Dial*, Feb. 22, pp. 174–179.

"The Intellectual Pre-eminence of Jews in Modern Europe,"[1] *Political Science Quarterly*, March, pp. 33–42.

"On the Nature and Uses of Sabotage,"[3] *Dial*, April 5, pp. 341–346.

"Bolshevism Is a Menace to the Vested Interests," editorial, *Dial*, April 5, pp. 360–361.

"Sabotage," editorial, *Dial*, April 5, p. 363.

"Congressional Sabotage," editorial, *Dial*, April 5, p. 363.

"Immanuel Kant on Perpetual Peace,"[1] editorial, *Dial*, May 3, p. 469.

"Peace,"[1] *Dial*, May 17, pp. 485–487.

"The Captains of Finance and the Engineers,"[3] *Dial*, June 14, pp. 599–606.

"Panem et Circenses,"[1] editorial, *Dial*, June 14, p. 609.

---

[1] Republished in *Essays in Our Changing Order*.

[3] Republished in *The Engineers and the Price System* (New York: Huebsch, 1921).

Bibliography

"The Industrial System and the Captains of Industry," [3] *Dial*, May 31, pp. 552–557.

" 'Open Covenants Openly Arrived At' and the Elder Statesmen," [1] editorial, *Dial*, July 12, pp. 25–26.

"A World Safe for the Vested Interests," [1] editorial, *Dial*, July 12, p. 26.

"The Red Terror—At Last It has Come to America," editorial, *Dial*, Sept. 6, p. 205.

"The Red Terror and the Vested Interests," editorial, *Dial*, Sept. 6, p. 206.

"Bolshevism and the Vested Interests in America," [3] *Dial*, Oct. 4, pp. 296–301; Oct. 18, 339–346; Nov. 1, 323–380.

"The Twilight Peace of the Armistice," [1] editorial, *Dial*, Nov. 15, p. 443. *The Place of Science in Modern Civilisation and Other Essays* (New York: Huebsch).

1920. Review of Keynes's Economic Consequences of the Peace,[1] in *Political Science Quarterly*, Sept., pp. 467–472.

1921. *The Engineers and the Price System* (New York: Huebsch).
"Between Bolshevism and War," [1] *Freeman*, May 25, pp. 248–251.

1922. "Dementia Praecox," [1] *Freeman*, June 21, pp. 344–347.

1923. "The Captain of Industry," [4] *Freeman*, April 18, pp. 127–132.
"The Timber Lands and Oil Fields," [4] *Freeman*, May 23, pp. 248–250; May 30, pp. 272–274.
"The Independent Farmer," [4] *Freeman*, June 13, pp. 321–324.
"The Country Town," [4] *Freeman*, July 11, pp. 417–420; July 18, pp. 440–443.
Absentee Ownership and Business Enterprise in Recent Times; the Case of America (New York: Huebsch).

1925. "Economic Theory in the Calculable Future," [1] *American Economic Review*, March, Supplement, pp. 48–55.
The Laxdæla Saga, translated from the Icelandic with an Introduction (New York: Huebsch).

1927. "An Experiment in Eugenics," published for the first time in *Essays in Our Changing Order*.

1934. *Essays in Our Changing Order*, ed. by Leon Ardzrooni (New York: Viking).

[1] Republished in *Essays in Our Changing Order*.
[3] Republished in *The Engineers and the Price System*.
[4] Republished in *Absentee Ownership and Business Enterprise in Recent Times; The Case of America* (New York: Huebsch, 1923).

Contributors

C. S. Ayres is with the Department of Economics, University of Texas, Austin, Texas.

Melvin D. Brockie is with the Department of Economics, California Institute of Technology, Pasadena, California.

Morris A. Copeland is with the Department of Economics, Cornell University, Ithaca, New York.

Joel B. Dirlam is with the Department of Economics, University of Rhode Island, Kingston, Rhode Island.

Joseph Dorfman is with the Department of Economics, Columbia University, New York City.

Douglas F. Dowd is with the Department of Economics, Cornell University, Ithaca, New York.

Leslie Fishman is with the Department of Economics, the University of Colorado, Boulder, Colorado.

Carter Goodrich is with the Department of History, University of Pittsburgh, Pittsburgh, Pennsylvania.

Allan G. Gruchy is with the Department of Economics, University of Maryland, College Park, Maryland.

Walton Hamilton (now deceased) was with the law firm of Arnold, Fortas and Porter, Washington, D.C.

Forest G. Hill is with the Department of Economics, University of Texas, Austin, Texas.

Norman Kaplan is with the Department of Sociology, University of Pennsylvania, Philadelphia, Pennsylvania.

Contributors

Philip Morrison is with the Department of Physics, Cornell University, Ithaca, New York.

Lawrence Nabers is with the Department of Economics, University of Utah, Salt Lake City, Utah.

Paul Sweezy is co-editor of *The Monthly Review*, New York City.

Myron W. Watkins is with the consulting firm of Boni, Watkins, Jason & Co., New York City.

G. W. Zinke is with the Department of Economics, the University of Colorado, Boulder, Colorado.

DATE DUE